GOING FOR BROKE: *The Chrysler Story*

GOING
FOR BROKE:
The Chrysler Story

MICHAEL MORITZ
AND
BARRETT SEAMAN

Doubleday & Co., Inc., Garden City, New York   1981

ISBN: 0-385-17180-3
Library of Congress Catalog Card Number 81-43044

"Few subjects of solemn inquiry have been more unproductive than study of a modern large corporation."

—JOHN KENNETH GALBRAITH,
The New Industrial State

ACKNOWLEDGMENTS

We would like to thank the staffs of the libraries of General Motors, the Motor Vehicle Manufacturers Association, the Detroit Public Library Automotive History Collection and the Detroit *Free Press*. Chapter Thirteen relies heavily on a series of meticulous articles by Gary Hector which appeared during the fall of 1980 in *The American Banker*. Other journalists in Detroit, especially the late Robert Irvin, generously shared their knowledge of Chrysler, while colleagues at *Time*, particularly S. Chang, Richard Hornik, Leon Jaroff and Edwin Reingold, willingly supplied additional material. Sarah Revels patiently typed most of the manuscript and others—including our editor, Adrian Zackheim, Laura Seaman, and Alfred Moritz—offered helpful observations. Finally, we would like to thank the many Chrysler executives and workers, union leaders, bankers, politicians and industry analysts who spared time to talk to us when they had far better things to do.

MICHAEL MORITZ AND BARRETT SEAMAN
Spring 1981

CONTENTS

GOING FOR BROKE: *The Chrysler Story*

CHAPTER ONE

Going Under Water

John Riccardo always maintained that Woodward Avenue was the best route between Bloomfield Hills and Detroit. The massive freeways that swept into the city from the north were too often bottled up with traffic between 7 and 7:30 A.M. Although its path was broken by traffic lights, Woodward was, like the myth of the men in the chauffeured automobiles who used it, uncomplicated and direct. Twice a day, five days a week, at dawn and after dusk, the long, polished cars shuttled between the secluded suburban estates and the merciless grind of the American automobile industry.

On Thursday morning, September 29, 1977, Riccardo sat on the passenger side of the front seat, reading sales and production figures from the previous day, while chauffeur Frank Romyka steered the dark-blue, four-door Chrysler New Yorker south along Woodward. The two men had already attended mass at Holy Name Church in Birmingham. It was, John Riccardo used to say, the only time of quiet he had all day: a fifteen-minute pause in the journey between his colonial home in Bloomfield Hills and Chrysler headquarters in Highland Park.

As chairman of the board of Chrysler Corporation, Riccardo headed the nation's third largest automobile company and tenth largest industrial company. He guided the affairs of the fourteenth largest industrial corporation in the world. In the realm of big business, few were bigger. On six continents, in thirteen different countries, a quarter of a million people filed into offices and factories decked with Chrysler's blue-and-white insignia. Chrysler was a parable of American industry. It had endured the economic slumps that viciously disposed of weaker companies and had grown to spread the lessons of American ingenuity, productivity and salesmanship around the world.

In an industry that left no time for reflection, the final week of September 1977 was especially hectic. At 9 A.M. that morning, Riccardo would preside over a meeting of Chrysler's nine-man Operations Committee, to decide whether to spend $72 million on a new luxury car for the French subsidiary. For men who spent $15 billion a year, the decision was almost routine: another pinprick in the tail of a dinosaur. The French plant, which sat on a languorous sweep of the River Seine outside Paris, was just one part of a corporation where every subsidiary, division, factory, manager and worker needed money. The car, code-numbered C-9, was an ordinary choice for a big business, but in the fall of 1977 even the ordinary decisions were getting tougher to make.

To outsiders, nothing seemed amiss. Chrysler and the U.S. automobile industry appeared robust. The four American auto companies were on their way to combined net profits of $5.2 billion in a year in which Americans bought 14.8 million cars and trucks. "Like a rocket entering its second stage," rhapsodized Ward's Automotive Yearbook, a trade handbook, "the United States auto industry in 1977 settled into the glow of 1976's stirring recovery from the severe 1974–75 business recession." At Chrysler, the comptroller's office was about to close the books on the eighth consecutive profitable quarter—the richest period in the company's entire history. Between the beginning of October 1975 and the end of September 1977, Chrysler had earned $668.5 million—and John Riccardo wasn't suffering. The previous year, he had taken home $700,066 in salary and bonuses. Riccardo knew that the spectacular financial performance was probably a fluke, though— and that was only one of many things he had to worry about.

His chief concern at the end of September was the reception that Chrysler's new 1978 models would receive. The Sales Department could normally project the likely annual sales from the public's response during the opening weeks of the new model year. Chrysler, Plymouth and Dodge cars and trucks had been rolling across the country on railcars for the past several weeks and were being prepared in more than 4,800 dealer lots for the official introduction that weekend. For 1978, Chrysler was covering slightly over half of the U.S. market with 42 models, compared to 138 for General Motors and 66 for Ford. This was an "off year" for Chrysler, a break in the remorseless cycle of entirely new models. Indeed, Chrysler had no genuinely fresh cars for

1978. Instead, the company was dropping two of its three full-size cars and keeping only the 4,800-pound V-8-powered New Yorker Brougham, the very car that Frank Romyka was easing down Woodward.

The launch of the restyled cars was going to be troublesome. Riccardo could scarcely remember when Chrysler had experienced a smooth launch. In 1969, the computers had fouled up the scheduling of production; in 1973, a new line of large cars had been launched into a market jolted by the oil embargo that followed the Yom Kippur War, and in 1974, the economy had taken a dive as Detroit had readied its advertising. Now Riccardo's salesmen had to sell off an unusually large inventory of leftover 1977 vehicles, which were clogging the showrooms. Chrysler had enough cars for 87 selling days when a 65-day stock was considered about normal. Part of Chrysler's inventory was composed of cars not built to any specific order from a dealer. Inside the company and around Detroit it was known as the "sales bank." When it ballooned out of control it brought all sorts of problems—and, to add to his worries, Riccardo had to live with a past promise. Just over a year before he had made the mistake of publicly announcing, "When the markets fall off again we won't have a big inventory around our necks to weigh us down."[1]

The 1978 models revealed Chrysler's and the rest of the industry's response to the Energy Policy and Conservation Act, passed by Congress in 1975. The Act gave the National Highway Traffic Safety Administration (NHTSA) the authority to start calculating the weighted average of each manufacturer's fuel economy, starting with the 1978 cars. Washington had never laid a firmer hand on Detroit, and by the end of 1978 each of the automakers was charged with producing cars with an average fuel consumption of 18 miles per gallon. For Chrysler, it meant maintaining a delicate balance between the 14-mpg, 400-cubic-inch New Yorkers and the 21-mpg compact Plymouth Volares. Congress called the balancing act Corporate Average Fuel Economy. It was known and reviled in Detroit by its acronym: CAFE.

It was clear that the Congressional legislation was going to change life in Detroit dramatically. Although the Act covered a range of energy matters, the clearest message was that American-made cars would be required to average 27.5 mpg by 1985. Incredibly, Congress had rejected suggestions by both the auto industry and the White House that the price of gasoline be allowed to increase gradually to help prod consumers into smaller, more efficient cars. That way, at least, Detroit would have an incentive to build them. Unfortunately, President Gerald Ford was not only unable to convince a Democratic Congress to deregulate fuel prices, he incited a rebellion that actually reduced the price of gas at the pump. On Woodward, Riccardo noticed gas station stickers advertising unleaded regular at 56.9 cents a gallon. A year before, those same signs had offered the same fuel for 60.9 cents a gallon.

In a topsy-turvy world, automobile engineers had to plan for a market that paid little attention to fuel consumption. The scare that had engulfed the country after the 1973–74 OPEC oil embargo had disappeared. Although the public had fled in a panic toward small cars, almost as soon as the oil started to flow again they had turned and streamed back toward larger cars, loudly painted vans and four-wheel-drive trucks. For consumers, the choice was just part of the American way of life; for the men in the laboratories and offices in Detroit, it was an unremitting nightmare. If Chrysler failed to make the fuel consumption targets specified under the 1975 law, it would be fined $6.5 million for every tenth of a mileage point it missed by. On the other hand, if it introduced small cars too soon, Chrysler risked the loss of customers. "You can prosper if you are a year or two behind," former treasurer Bill McGagh remarked. "You cannot if you're a year or two ahead." It was becoming clear to Riccardo that the market would go to the company that could build the biggest possible car with the lowest fuel consumption: something of a strain on the laws of thermodynamics.

To meet the demands of the law, Chrysler planned to have half of its 1978 production geared to small cars: compacts or smaller. The 1978 model line also included two subcompacts imported from Japan. Having decided that outside purchase was the only way the company could afford to sell small cars, since 1971 Chrysler had been purchasing Dodge Colts and Plymouth Arrows manufactured by Mitsubishi. Six years later, even with imported cars breaking all records by selling to one out of every six buyers, and with Americans buying nearly 2 million subcompact cars, Chrysler was still not big enough to expect a profitable share of that market. Even General Motors and Ford, with larger overall market shares and more dealers, could not make money from their own subcompacts. To be sure, analysts were predicting that small cars would take a larger and larger share of the market in future years, but none of them could tell Riccardo when that market would be large enough to allow Chrysler to turn some profits.

All the more reason to worry. Faced with the vague prospect of a burgeoning small-car market, a shaky energy supply and federal fuel-efficiency standards that all but required production of four-cylinder subcompacts, Riccardo himself had grabbed the ring in the spring of 1975 and approved a "mini-car," as many in Detroit still called them. With a group of his top American and European executives, Riccardo had spent two days in April 1975 at Chrysler Europe's design center near Coventry, England, looking at mock-ups of cars an age removed from the era of Detroit baroque. Part of the reason for Chrysler's slimmer profits in the third quarter of 1977 was the expense of final tooling for the car approved during that English spring. Riccardo was pumping over $40 million into Chrysler's Belvidere assembly plant outside Rockford, Illinois, where a turkey-farm of robots was being installed in preparation for the launch of the company's new cars: the Dodge Omni and the Plymouth Horizon.

Following a pattern established by General Motors (as most patterns were in Detroit), the automakers randomly assigned letters to each of their basic car sizes, known as platforms. The Omnis and the Horizons, long before they were given names, were simply called L-bodies. The L-body was to be the first small front-wheel-drive car built in the United States.[2] As long as fuel was cheap and plentiful so that cars could be big and inefficient without hurting the owner's pocketbook, front-wheel drive had been only an exercise for American engineers. The small-car market of the future (whenever it became a reality) was going to place a premium on space, though. A revolution in automobile engineering and production seemed almost inevitable.

General Motors was taking nearly seven years and $2.5 billion to build its front-wheel-drive X-cars from bumper to bumper. Chrysler was able to adopt front-wheel drive in less than four years and for half the investment, because its French subsidiary, the former Simca firm, had already mastered the design and production of the necessary parts. Chrysler was merely wrapping American engineering and styling around the Simca 1307. It was the first major advantage Chrysler had extracted from its painful nineteen-year bout with its international subsidiaries.

While the French connection allowed Chrysler to accelerate its plans for a small car, the company did not have the $400 million or the five years it would take to develop an engine for the L-body. Riccardo had no choice but to buy from elsewhere, knowing full well that Chrysler would have to settle for a higher price and a limited number of engines. Fortunately, in 1975, as Gene Cafiero, then head of Chrysler's North American operations, started to shop for engines, West Germany's Volkswagen was contributing to a worldwide surplus of four-cylinder engines. Chrysler agreed to buy 300,000 a year until it was ready to produce its own. The deal gave Chrysler a proven engine and Volkswagen an outlet for idle capacity. It was a precursor of the liaisons and alliances that would develop in an increasingly expensive and complicated automotive world.

The L-car was still a gamble—the biggest gamble Chrysler had taken in more than a decade. When the Omnis and Horizons arrived in January 1978, they would be sixteen months ahead of GM's front-wheel-drive cars and nearly three years ahead of Ford's "World Car," eventually sold as the Ford Escort and Mercury Lynx. The impending launch was a significant risk in a business that paid for mistakes in nine figures. *Motor Trend* magazine, one of the leading "buff books," paid tribute to Chrysler's gamble by naming the Omni/Horizon its "Car of the Year" and anointing John Riccardo its "Man of the Year" for 1978.

Now Riccardo had to decide whether to shovel out another $72 million on a European car at a time when the pressures to take more risks in the United States were just beginning to mount. The business was changing and the changes seemed to be accelerating too rapidly for Chrysler to keep up.

The only company that seemed to have a chance of keeping abreast of the changes was General Motors. Nothing that Chrysler or Ford attempted seemed to make much of a dent in GM. In September 1977, GM was selling between four and five of every ten cars sold in the United States. A Detroit investment analyst, Arvid Jouppi, who had once worked for Chrysler, was fond of comparing the U.S. automobile market to a river through which a variety of customers swam. GM, with its large number of models—from subcompacts to block-long limousines—was like a fisherman with nets in every part of the river. "Wherever the fish swim," Jouppi would explain, "GM has a net."

In the years since World War II, Ford had survived by jostling its nets in wherever it could find some room. Chrysler, during the Sixties, had attempted to fish across the entire river, but Riccardo had found that his more recent successes had come in places where GM and Ford had left some room: in light trucks, vans and compact cars. For safety's sake, he wanted to dangle more nets in other parts of the river, but it had become too expensive. American Motors Corporation, the industry's fledgling, at $2.2 billion in annual sales, had long ago decided to fish with small cars only. AMC had demonstrated one thing: building nothing but small cars in America might lead to a splendid CAFE, but it was no way to make a living. In 1977 AMC remained in business only through the sale of its popular, profitable and gas-guzzling Jeeps.

Federal mileage standards were about to narrow the banks of Jouppi's imaginary river. They would leave the company with the broadest range of cars, the greatest marketing clout and the most money dominating the stream. "The Energy Act of 1975," scoffed Wall Street analyst David Healy, "should have been called the General Motors Competitive Advantage Act."

It was a competitor's nightmare. Industry intelligence—less an elaborate system of spies than an informal network of gossipy suppliers who worked with more than one company and knew what each was planning—reported that GM was well on its way toward a complete turnover of its model line for the 1980s. The reports Riccardo gleaned from *Automotive News*, which was pushed into his mailbox hot off the presses every Sunday afternoon, bore similar news. He could only shake his head with a mixture of jealousy and grudging admiration when he thought of the executives on the fourteenth floor of GM's stone headquarters on West Grand Boulevard. It was difficult to understand that GM was intending to spend $5 billion a year on new cars for every year until 1985. Riccardo, with a mind that clicked like an abacus, knew that GM would be spending an average of $14.5 million every day (including Saturdays, Sundays and holidays) in every week in every month until the end of 1985—just for new plants and products.

Romyka turned the large New Yorker off Woodward, threaded through a narrow street lined either side with parked cars and headed toward a short causeway that skirted Chrysler's headquarters. The quarter-mile strip was named Lynn Townsend Drive, after the former chairman of Chrysler. Townsend had been a powerful, intimidating man whom Riccardo had followed, revered, feared and, on occasion, deeply resented. Townsend had retired as chairman in 1975 after fourteen years during which he had called most of the shots. Riccardo pondered something Townsend had said some time before he left: "Look out for 1980." It was a joke, of course—a reference to the curious fact that Chrysler always seemed in trouble at the turn of the decade. In 1950 it had been a devastating 100-day strike by the United Auto Workers, in 1960 there had been disastrous financial developments plus the great "conflict of interest" scandals surrounding Chrysler president William Newberg and in 1970 Townsend had jetted around the country to save Chrysler in the panic that hit Wall Street after the collapse of the Penn Central.

Townsend had long been aware of Chrysler's potential fragility. In 1960, his vision of the future shape of the industry had been made clear during discussions with the management of Studebaker. Then the smallest of the U.S. automakers, Studebaker had proposed a merger with Chrysler. Townsend cut short the secret meeting held in a motel near Chicago's O'Hare Airport by telling Studebaker chairman Sherwood Egbert, "I'm not sure that Chrysler will be around in 1980. Ford might not even be around."

In the late Seventies, it was almost impossible to know what lay in store at the turn of the decade. The task wasn't made any easier by the rumors coming from Ford's glass headquarters in Dearborn. There were stories of conflict at the highest levels of the company. Wags in the basement bowling alley of the Detroit Athletic Club, where Riccardo bowled a respectable 164, passed on rumors that Henry Ford II, board chairman and family dynast, had overruled his president, Lee Iacocca, on plans for a small front-wheel-drive car for the late Seventies. Riccardo knew that Ford, like GM, planned to down-size its full-size cars in 1979, but the prospect of a Ford range of compacts that wouldn't change offered some encouragement. It was one less headache for Riccardo.

Romyka guided the car past a gatehouse and Riccardo nodded at the guard. The dome of the styling studio gave the Chrysler headquarters the air of an austere campus. In front of the drab, five-story K. T. Keller Building (named after a tough engineer who had followed in Walter Chrysler's footsteps), the familiar Pentastar flapped on the aluminum flagpole. As the car rolled into the Keller Building's tiled garage, Riccardo snapped his briefcase shut. He swung his rounded shoulders out of the car and walked briskly to an elevator that carried him nonstop to the fifth floor and the teak-walled corridors of Chrysler's executive row.

For an hour, Riccardo sat behind his hexagonal wooden desk sipping coffee and preparing himself for the 9 A.M. meeting. A short briefing from two of his top managers was interrupted by a call from the head of Chrysler Europe. Riccardo took the call on a telephone that swung out below the top of the desk on a special platform. As he listened, his eyes rested on the autographed photo of Pope Paul VI that hung on the wall. Dismissing the two officials, he flicked through a summary of selected news clips and articles prepared by the public relations office. During the company's heyday, the chairman had been treated to four editions. Now it was down to two.

When Riccardo entered the fifth-floor conference room to chair the gathering of the Operations Committee, the assembly lines at all of Chrysler's Detroit plants had been running for more than two hours. There had been no special problems—no stoppages or shortages of parts. The wheels of the world's biggest industry, which once had attracted the most ambitious men in the United States, were turning smoothly and routinely. Most of the items on the agenda were settled with little discussion. Requests for extra funds to help with the new-model introduction and for several hundred thousand dollars for Chrysler's small outboard motor company were approved informally. Riccardo himself reviewed, as he would with increasing intensity in the coming months, the company's finances and listened to others report on production and cash forecasts. There were no surprises. Riccardo picked at some of the numbers with testy caution, a marked contrast to the smoother confidence of Chrysler's chief operating officer, Gene Cafiero.

Cafiero sat opposite Riccardo at meetings of the Operations Committee. Although the two were both of Italian descent, they were living antonyms, and had little respect for each other. "It would take the head of the Psychiatry Department at Columbia Presbyterian to figure those two out," Chrysler director Tom Killefer marveled. Riccardo was slight and gaunt. His four-hundred-dollar suit, bought from a Birmingham tailor, hung loosely, and his face was pasty from overwork. "John Riccardo," said a colleague, "walked in his sleep." Known to some as "The Flamethrower," Riccardo was more explosive than the truck he had driven along the Burma Road during the Second World War. Prone to violent outbursts, he was also a formidable corporate politician. "John Riccardo," they murmured behind the black doors that lined the dimly lit executive corridor, "gets mad and even."

Gene Cafiero was another matter. The son of a truckdriver, he brought to the boardroom a distinct Brooklyn accent and smatterings of the psychology courses he had taken at Dartmouth before graduating in 1946. In pockets of the corporation he gained the nickname "Plastic Man," partly because of the willing way he returned calls from the press and quoted managerial consultants, but partly because of his fascination with exotic materials. His wife, Nancy, had helped design his office with chrome and Lucite and had even flown to Sandusky, Ohio, home for part of Chrysler's small marine division, to help select fabrics for the fleet of motorboats. "Nancy is doing some design work," Cafiero told the Operations Committee once. "Does anyone mind?" No one objected, but the tittering had started quickly enough. Stocky and athletic, with strong, handsome features crowned by a thick sweep of dark hair, Cafiero toured plants like a movie star. With his sleeves rolled up, he preached a gospel of corporate community, exhorting his managers and workers to take risks and treat divisions like small, privately run companies. He once circulated a videotaped rendition of his philosophy through the corporation. Quality, he used to say, was everybody's responsibility. Cafiero was acquired by Chrysler along with Briggs Body in 1953 as an industrial engineer, a euphemism for a time-and-motion man; thereafter, he rarely bothered to correct the occasional assertion that he was an engineer. He pursued a relatively undistinguished career in the Stamping Group until Lynn Townsend plucked him from the obscurity of an Indiana machining plant to head Chrysler's oddly assorted collection of Latin American companies. Jetting from São Paulo, Brazil, to Buenos Aires, Argentina, and from Bogota, Colombia, to Caracas, Venezuela, and finally to a small, single-story factory guarded by reddish foothills near Lima, Peru, Cafiero ran a group—divided by language and the Andes—that was barely the size of one of Chrysler's North American assembly plants. Within a couple of years he had leapfrogged over scores of more senior executives to become head of Chrysler's North American operations: the third most important job in the company. When Town-

send retired in 1975 and Riccardo became chairman, Cafiero was promoted to the presidency.

John Riccardo and Gene Cafiero collided immediately. Their first
furious spat occurred over something completely arcane to outsiders,
but critically important to the men who run automobile companies:
the suspension for Chrysler's compacts, the Dodge Aspens and Plymouth Volares. The decision, made in the early Seventies, set the tone
for the relationship between the two men. Chrysler had long relied on
torsion bars (a beam that stretched beneath a car to weather the
bumps and shocks of the road). The heavily advertised torsion bar
was as much a part of Chrysler as the Pentastar. Cafiero, however, had decided there was plenty of reason to change. He had
driven some of the competition's cars and had been impressed by the
ride, the lighter weight and the lower cost of their coil springs. He
convinced his colleagues and disappeared on a business trip, content
that Chrysler would break with tradition and use coil springs on the
new compacts. He returned to find that his colleagues were endorsing
torsion bars with the same enthusiasm they had shown for the prospect of coil springs. John Riccardo had exercised his own powers of
persuasion. "There are two things this company stands for," Riccardo
had yelled at his associates: "unibody construction and torsion bars."
There was little room for reason, and even less when Riccardo implied that it would be torsion bars or their jobs. It was, needless to say,
torsion bars.

By 1977 the president and the chairman of Chrysler were barely on
speaking terms. Riccardo had become increasingly disturbed by what
he saw as the rapid deterioration of the company and had begun to
hover over Cafiero. He was convinced that Cafiero was letting the
organization run to seed. For his part, Cafiero complained that Riccardo would never sit still and plot long-term strategy. Riccardo,
thought Cafiero, was barely capable of concentrating on the succeeding week. He resented Riccardo's usurpation of the chairmanship of
the Operations Committee—a post that had traditionally belonged to
the company president.

Even their ideas about Chrysler's future were contradictory. Riccardo paid lip-service to the importance of finding niches in which
Chrysler could operate profitably, but he nevertheless exerted shades
of the same relentless pressure Lynn Townsend had used to boost volume during the Sixties. Cafiero, meanwhile, devised grand schemes to
boost Chrysler's image. He correctly perceived that Chrysler was
doomed if it kept selling cars to customers older and poorer than those
flocking into Ford and General Motors showrooms. He knew that
Chrysler buyers bought less frequently, relied more heavily on credit
and spent less on the highly profitable options.

Cafiero had outlined his plans to the company's top four hundred managers at a special meeting known derisively as "The Fireside Chat," held in an auditorium near the big Chrysler tank factory in Warren, Michigan. Inside the auditorium, Cafiero rolled back charts and talked the managers through a slide show. All Chrysler's cars, he said, pointing to the center of a dotted and circled matrix, overlapped. They were competing against each other as well as against the competition and were aimed at the same group of stodgy, cautious buyers, rather than at the range of people targeted by General Motors and, to a lesser extent, Ford. Chrysler had to appeal to younger, wealthier buyers if it wanted to survive. Some of the managers yawned and rolled their eyes as he talked grandly of transforming the Chrysler line into cars like Mercedes, Dodges into sporty cars like BMWs, and Plymouths into sturdy family cars like Volvos. They all knew he was fundamentally right—but it was a little like telling a seasoned football team that in order to win they had to block, tackle and execute plays without error. "Everybody's going to starboard; we'll take port," he announced. It was, by his own admission, a risky strategy, but Cafiero saw only one way out: by spending money on cars and, most of all, on advertising. Gene Cafiero wanted to spend Chrysler out of trouble.

Cafiero's blithe way with numbers made John Riccardo's hair gray even more rapidly. For all Cafiero's talk, Chrysler cars were still perceived as characterless and uninspiring; their buyers still old and poor. Relations with the workers who built them were still as tense as ever, and the quality of the cars that rolled out into the autumn morning was, if anything, getting worse—partly because of the relentless push for sales and partly because fewer people were assigned to make sure that the 161,800 employees in the North American plants were doing their part for Chrysler.

Barely eight weeks before, the tension had come to a head. Cafiero had marched into Riccardo's office in mid-July to announce that he had been offered the chief executive's job at another major company and was going to accept it. "You're not going to go," he told Riccardo, "so I am. Life's too short." Ordinarily it would have been a perfect opportunity to end a destructive partnership, but Riccardo feared that Cafiero's departure would rankle Chrysler's outside directors and perhaps prompt his own removal. A few days later, he went to Cafiero and mutedly asked him if he would first talk with the board of directors before making a final decision. Cafiero agreed. Four directors flew to Detroit and participated in a bizarre series of meetings—first in Cafiero's office, then in Riccardo's. Back and forth they trooped, playing shuttle diplomacy between the two top corporate officers. Eventually the pair made up over a handshake and the directors departed.

It was at best a cosmetic reconciliation—a truce between two school-yard toughs waiting to see who would slip in the next blow. Riccardo was only more frustrated by his inability to convince the board of what he perceived to be Cafiero's glib response to Chrysler's problems. As profit margins shrank across the industry, Chrysler simply could not afford internal strife. Cafiero, however, was fully aware of the disadvantages Chrysler faced, both at home and abroad. He well understood that his was a business that coldly punished its smaller members. Studies of GM and Ford, put into black loose-leaf folders by Chrysler staff at his behest, made for gloomy reading. Supplementing published reports with tidbits picked up from suppliers, the report showed that in 1977 Chrysler worked with an operating margin per vehicle of just under $700 in the United States and $600 abroad. Ford, by contrast, enjoyed a $967 operating margin in North America and, at $1,275, more than twice Chrysler's margin overseas. General Motors, Chrysler's staff calculated, operated with a $1,465 margin in the United States and $1,100 abroad. For companies that measured advantages in pennies and nickels, differences measured in dollars were serious, while differences measured in hundreds of dollars were lethal. "That's a monumental hurdle to get over," Cafiero kept telling his men. "In a downturn," he warned, "we're going to be underwater a lot faster than anybody else."

The penalties of size were built into every part of the business. Because they rolled out a richer, larger line of cars, GM and Ford made more money from the profitable full-size models. Many of the differences lay far from the showrooms, buried in the size of the company and its plants. At Jefferson Avenue, a Chrysler factory near downtown Detroit, the assembly line ran along an enclosed bridge over the street. Five separate gates required five different teams of blue-jacketed security guards. Twenty-foot bays, instead of the modern forty-foot bays, allowed fewer pieces of machinery to slide in and out. Barely two miles from Jefferson Avenue, puffs of steam blew from four brick stacks in the seventy-year-old Hamtramck plant. It cost Chrysler $15 million a year just to heat, and the company had to run the boilers in summer to keep the seals from drying and cracking. Inside, the multi-story assembly line was towed by a drive mechanism—nicknamed "elephant balls" by the workers—which caused costly losses of production because it kept breaking.

GM and Ford—GM more than Ford—used what the manufacturing men call "dedicated" or "captive" lines—assembly operations devoted to making a single part. Chrysler made an average of two and a half parts per line. Consequently, GM and Ford could use more automation; their plant managers didn't have to worry about changing and warming up presses or readjusting the equipment that nibbled and pecked along the line. In one assembly plant, Chrysler was forced to run two-door models, four-door sedans and station wagons along the same line, so that the men who fitted rear doors had nothing to do each time a two-door rolled by, giving plant managers distressing problems with "line balancing" and costing the company plenty in wages and benefits paid for no work.

All up and down the innumerable lines of the auto business, Chrysler lost money to its two big brothers. Suppliers were more likely to shave a few cents per unit off a 1.2-million-unit order from GM than to do so on a 500,000-unit order from Chrysler. Unable to justify building a part themselves, Chrysler's managers all too often had to go to an outside supplier to build the part, paying a premium for the help —and with plants concentrated around Detroit, rather than scattered around the country, Chrysler had to pay more in shipping costs. It was small consolation to Cafiero and Riccardo that Ford, too, paid a penalty to GM. "If Chrysler wasn't around," they hollowly reassured themselves, "Ford would be in a pot-load of trouble."[3]

The competition, moreover, was no longer just General Motors and Ford. Cheap gasoline in the United States and the subsequent disregard for fuel efficiency still preserved the two-tier world automobile market that had existed since World War II. Americans built and drove big cars while everybody else settled for little ones. But in the Seventies, when OPEC ruthlessly toyed with the price of oil, the old rules were under increasing pressure. The $72 million item on that morning's Operations Committee agenda was for a four-door luxury car to be built by Chrysler France. With a 109-inch wheelbase and options for either a 2.2- or 2.6-liter engine, it was still a small car by American standards. In Europe, though, the C-9 was bordering on the extravagant. It was supposed to improve Chrysler's dismal European performance the best way Americans knew: by building larger cars and selling them at higher prices. Chrysler Europe needed every bit of help. The large manufacturing plant near Paris, another at Villaverde —lying in the dusty clay countryside south of Madrid, Spain, and two in the United Kingdom (Linwood, just outside Glasgow, Scotland, and Ryton, in the English industrial Midlands) had produced one-fifth of Chrysler's worldwide output in 1977. Although the French and Spanish companies were profitable, the view from Chrysler's British headquarters in London's Bowater House, a stone's throw from the Carlton, was bleak. Chrysler U.K. was bleeding profusely and it was only thanks to a hastily arranged 1975 bailout by the British government that Chrysler was keeping its losses under $20 million.

Nothing illustrated the changing automobile world more clearly than the Japanese challenge. Riccardo was concerned about Toyota and Datsun which, together, were selling almost one million cars a year in the United States. Behind them, a gaggle of nine smaller producers, from Honda to Subaru, were keeping pace in what was beginning to strike Riccardo and other American executives as a well-orchestrated invasion. Two out of every three foreign cars sold in the United States in 1977 came on a boat from Japan. The models that poured onto the docks from the doors of the specially built auto transporters were, to Detroit's consternation, more and more closely attuned to American tastes. Toyota had sold its first car in the United States the year before John Riccardo had joined Chrysler. The 919 Toyotas sold in 1958 had been 4,000-pound monsters—little more than a roughly hewn car body sitting on a truck chassis—but in less than twenty years the Japanese had learned their lessons. The cars now had two sun visors, automatic transmissions, stereos, thick-piled carpets and velour seats. They were starting to be more American than Detroit's finest. To be sure, the Japanese, like the Europeans, stood in a better position to capture the growing population of small-car buyers, having long built fuel-efficient cars to sip $2.00 to $3.00 worth of gas and to dodge among traffic on narrower roads. The Japanese also seemed to have absorbed the many engineering, production and advertising tutorials given so freely in America.

For the moment, however, John Riccardo was far more concerned with money. The proposed French investment ran against the grain of his financial instincts. Beneath the surface of profitability, Chrysler was losing its market share. From a 16 percent share in 1976, the company was slipping under 14 percent—a desperately hard loss to swallow, considering that a single percentage point in a year when more than 10 million cars were made was worth nearly $500 million in revenues. Part of the loss might have been attributable to the growing strength of the Japanese and part to Chrysler's chronic disadvantages, but a large part could be traced back to the winter of 1974 and the spring of 1975. Toward the end of 1974, as Chrysler rattled toward a loss of $52 million, the Federal Reserve Board had begun closely monitoring the company's cash flow and Congress considered a billion-dollar tax credit to help Chrysler and two other troubled companies, Pan American and Lockheed. Fueled by chronic optimism, Riccardo and Lynn Townsend had built up an inventory of nearly 400,000 cars and trucks which had driven Chrysler deep into despair. For six months, the company had bled at a rate of $1.5 million a day, and the pair had reacted by embarking on one of the most draconian cost-cutting binges ever seen in Detroit. To keep the company afloat, Townsend and Riccardo had shut the gates around almost every Chrysler plant and furloughed hundreds of engineers. "For three months," remarked one of those men, with only slight exaggeration, "the only engineers around were working on government regulations." The clockwork timing that accompanies the birth of an automobile, as unalterable and sequential as gestation, had been rudely interrupted. Now, two years later, Chrysler was paying the price.

Bitterly critical of the 1975 cuts was Douglas Fraser, vice-president of the United Auto Workers union and head of its Chrysler Department at the time. The crusty Scotsman, who had four decades of experience with Chrysler—first as a worker and then as a labor leader—considered Townsend's handling of the company both inept and inhumane. The wholesale loss of jobs resulting from the '75 crisis had been a scurrilous prologue to the traditional bargaining for the three-year wage contract due for renewal in 1976. Relations with Chrysler's 100,000 UAW members had long been strained as it was, and the company had been lucky to escape a strike that year. Only at the last minute had Fraser withdrawn from the union's list of demands a proposal for worker representation on Chrysler's board of directors—an old vision of his, but anathema to Detroit's managers.

The package won by the union in '76 had raised the cost of Chrysler's production by a hundred dollars per car, though, and industry executives feared that the UAW was pricing them out of the world market. The union had always contended (with some justification) that productivity gains outpaced pay hikes—but Chrysler workers had some unusual problems. Around the inner-city plants, absenteeism was well above the industry average. Even after the main contract settlement, there had been wildcat strikes at some facilities, and a five-week walkout at the St. Louis truck-assembly plant in June of 1977 had cost Chrysler more than 20,000 units in production—more than $100 million in foregone sales.

From the workers' vantage point, Chrysler was hardly Valhalla. For those who showed up for work, the jobs were demeaning and lunch breaks still meant a sandwich wolfed astride a wooden bench alongside the line. Workers angrily denounced management's charges of shoddy quality. It was common knowledge among workers in the plants that friends and family of management could get free tune-ups, repairs, even new engines through the back door. If there was a discipline problem at Chrysler, the UAW argued, it cut both ways.

By the fall of 1977, it was as obvious to the people on the line as it was to John Riccardo that Chrysler was suffering from the programs delayed two and a half years earlier. "It takes nine months to make a baby," the engineers recited in Highland Park—but the top executives kept pushing them toward the delivery room, ignoring the risk of miscarriage.

They should have known better than to try to play catch-up with Mother Nature. One of the bloodiest births of all had occurred with the 1975 launch of the Aspen/Volare, and Chrysler had been desperately trying to correct the deformities for the past two years. "We pissed away a car," one executive acidly admitted. "We did the road-testing on the first hundred thousand." Complaints of an alarming tendency for the engine to stall when drivers stepped on the accelerator, of recurring brake failures and of hoods that flew open at high speeds were piling up in Highland Park and in Washington at the National Highway Traffic Safety Administration. The complaints were the last thing that Riccardo needed, and they dealt a round of stunning blows to Chrysler's reputation for solid engineering. More than 3.5 million Aspens and Volares were recalled to dealers for free repairs. The changes finally cost the company more than $200 million and the Center for Auto Safety ridiculed the cars as the 1977 "Lemons of the Year."

The stalling engines could be partly blamed on changing federal standards on emissions, which Chrysler engineers responded to by taking shortcuts in an effort to reduce pollutants. Part of the problem was caused by a sliver of metal inside the carburetor, specially chosen to save money. The brake and hood defects, however, were entirely due to poor coordination between engineers and manufacturing—a matter of bad management. Within months, an epidemic of fenders riddled with rust broke out. The reason: workers had failed to spray the underside of the fenders with protective zinc, and inspectors had failed to catch it.

The Aspens and Volares were just one of the lines that had been damaged by the cuts of 1974 and 1975. The Omnis and Horizons were going to miss the new model season by three months and were scheduled for introduction in January 1978, the worst possible time. At least their development period had been preserved—but General Motors' Alfred Sloan, Jr., had long ago devised the formula that made Americans, each October, turn into Pavlovian dogs yelping at the sight of sparkling chrome and sniffing in search of fresh Naugahide. To miss the annual change was costly, especially for a company that could barely afford to spend enough to make buyers even sniff in its direction.

After the launch of the Omni/Horizons, there would be a gap of ten months before a new, down-size large car, coded the R-body, would appear in the fall of 1978. There was great uneasiness about the cars that would eventually be called St. Regis and New Yorker—not so much because they were large, but because they were late. Management had vacillated on the design in 1975 and then tried to catch up. The car was, in the patois of the trade, "signed off." All the important decisions about its length and width, engine and appearance had been made. There were still some weeks left to make changes to the interior and to dicker around with baubles like hood ornaments and instrument panels, but the tooling had been ordered. Both Chrysler and independent machine shops were busy forging the presses and dies (some of which cost $20 million apiece) to bang out the car. By September 1977, the R-body program was a horrendous mess. Metal prototypes, which offer engineers and designers the first solid test of their blueprints, should have been tearing around Chrysler's Chelsea proving grounds outside Detroit for at least two months, but no R-body prototype existed. It would be six months before a car curled onto the test track and seven months before the engineers could start to make changes. If a decent car emerged, it would be a miracle.

Less expensive and certainly less risky were the cars planned for 1979 and 1980. As cars were crammed within shorter lengths and narrower widths, the need to vary themes grew more important. The L-24 program, a sporty three-door hatchback version of the Omni/ Horizon, was an attempt to do just that. Meanwhile, though actor Ricardo Montalban was busily rolling his Spanish "R's" in praise of the "genuine Corinthian leather" of the Cordoba, Chrysler was planning a new version for 1980.

However, there was no bigger nor more important car in the works that fall than the K-body. Detroit tradition held that a body style could be expected to last as long as ten years, suffering only occasional facelifts or "re-skins." In 1977, though, when the troubled Aspens and Volares were barely two years old, Riccardo and Cafiero were about to approve a replacement for those models, to be launched in the not-too-distant fall of 1981. The decision had been made and, by September 1977, was nearly a year old—but it was still miles and years from the market of 1981.

Many of Chrysler's top managers—including Gene Cafiero and Hal Sperlich, a product planner fired from Ford—had originally favored a conventional rear-wheel design for the K-car. Sperlich, who had left Ford shortly after completing work on the rear-wheel drive Fairmont, argued that the Chrysler K-car would have sufficient interior room and a good enough fuel-economy rating if it were built in the conventional (and cheaper) manner. Some others in the engineering department, heavily influenced by the Omni/Horizons and, as one explained, "bathed in the logic of European small cars," fought furiously for front-wheel drive. By summer, when the decision was made, the European school had won, Sperlich and top management had been converted and the Operations Committee had flashed a green light.

As Riccardo finished his early-morning briefings, modelers were busy peeling and scooping slices of clay from models to be presented for top-management review at the end of 1977. For all their concern about General Motors, Chrysler's designers were hardly aware that the compact they were shaping would be nearly identical to GM's X-cars. Although they had yet to trim the K-body from 176 inches to 175 inches (to allow eighteen rather than fifteen to fit on a railcar), its notched roof and flat hood offered a contrast with the X-cars that were being prepared at GM's Tech Center in Warren. But the K-car's weight, as well as its wheelbase, engine and passenger compartment, would be almost identical to the new GM line.

The K-car also represented the changes taking place in the world's largest automobile companies. One of the central features of the discussion of the French C-9 program that Thursday morning was the identification of parts suitable for both the large French luxury car and the compact American model. Both had front-wheel drive and both called for the use of a four- or a small six-cylinder engine. Chrysler at last had an opportunity to exploit the advantages of common production of major components. The new cars could fit both tiers of the world market and could be built from parts produced in different places. Despite the differences between the C-9 and the K-body, they roughly fit the definition of a new buzzword flashing around Detroit. The Chrysler cars promised to be "world cars."

Predicting the shape of future markets and developing such concepts to match them had always been a challenging game, though expensive. Now the stakes seemed too high and the chances for success too low. What if the C-9 turned out to be too big for the France of 1981, and what if Americans didn't want cars as small as the K-body? It was an unnerving choice in a business long unsuitable for the faint of heart. John Riccardo had never had much confidence in his own judgment about new cars. The growing uncertainty left him all the more disturbed that he was leaving major decisions in the hands of a chief operating officer whom he did not trust. He had no choice, though, but to live under the cool entente established in July, leaving the cars to others while he tried to figure out how in the world Chrysler could pay for all that needed to be done.

More comfortable with drawing up financial projections, Riccardo concluded that Chrysler's plans through 1982 would cost some $7.5 billion: more than double the investments made during the previous five years. Assuming a steady economy (as many were), Riccardo expected the market to supply some $3.6 billion in revenues plus another $2.6 billion in depreciation and amortization allowances. Like other executives, Riccardo moaned that the allowances were nowhere near generous enough to pay for the gutting of America's aging factories, but there was scant time for such thoughts. Somewhere, somehow, John Riccardo had to find another $1.3 billion.

One source of these funds, of course, would be the banks. The banking community had bailed Chrysler out in the wake of the Penn Central panic in 1970 and had agreed to provide fresh credit in the darkest days of 1974. The banks earned huge interest payments and scarcely bothered to question how the same company could lose $312 million in 1974 and 1975 and be massively profitable two years later. "Chrysler," the bankers told themselves, "was like a thin layer of water. When the wind blew it rose pretty fast and when the wind died down, it went down even faster." Big bankers and auto executives shared at least one truism—"Volume is the name of the game"— and Chrysler, wallowing in more debt than either Ford or General Motors, was the best customer in Detroit.

Riccardo also knew that Wall Street could be counted upon for at least $150 million in a well-timed preferred-stock offering. An employee stock plan—always good for morale—might be tapped for another $50 million a year. In the final analysis, though, Chrysler would have to average a net profit of $140 million for each of the next five years to pay for the cars it planned for the Eighties. Given that net profits during the previous ten years had only averaged $123 million, Riccardo knew there was not even the thinnest of safety nets.

Indeed, the nine Operations Committee executives couldn't afford to keep pumping money into Europe, into South America, into Australia, into real estate, outboards and chemicals, into anything except the cars and trucks it would take to stay alive in North America, where Walter Chrysler had carved himself a piece of a growing industry fifty years before. The baggage of the 1960s, collected with equal boldness by Lynn Townsend during the years when American managers and American dollars were supposed to be able to turn any factory into gold, could not be carried much farther.

John Riccardo was a worrier by nature, and that fall he had good reason to worry. The future was frustratingly obscure, but certain to be dangerous. The federal government was increasingly hostile and unsympathetic toward the problems of the industry. Workers seemed to grow more alienated by the day. Chrysler's internal controls were no longer in Riccardo's hands and perhaps were out of control altogether. Costs were rising; sales were falling. Resources had been cut too deep for comfort. In a business where numbers came in boxcars and the whims of any thousand customers meant a swing in profits or losses of millions of dollars, forecasting was a wild and often futile exercise. For what they were worth, the projections beyond 1977 were not healthy. Chrysler's fate, it seemed that September morning, was perhaps beyond any man's control.

The $72 million expenditure for the C-9 program was approved and the car itself was produced in France—not as a Chrysler, but as a Talbot "Tagora," a top-of-the-line model for a troubled division of the Peugeot Group—in 1981. In America, the K-car was born, too, but in a Chrysler and in an automobile industry worlds removed from the one in which it was conceived.

CHAPTER TWO

The Bang That Made Chrysler Corporation

Detroit's street names, unlike those in many other American cities, are steeped in memories. The major arteries, which meet in layered whirls of asphalt, are named after the founding fathers of the automobile industry. Edsel Ford, the only son of Henry Ford, is immortalized in I-94, a six-lane freeway studded with potholes and patches, which streaks across the city from east to west. The seven Fisher brothers, who supplied General Motors with car bodies, are memorialized in a stretch of I-75 that rises to seventy feet as it slices through the pall south of Ford's River Rouge plant. North of the gleaming 72-story Renaissance Center, I-75 becomes the Chrysler freeway, skirts the company's Highland Park headquarters and provides a thick seam for the town of Hamtramck. Detroit's city fathers, in a burst of liberal generosity, even named an unfinished freeway through the northern suburbs after Walter P. Reuther, the former president of the United Auto Workers.

Pat Monks, the WWJ-radio helicopter pilot who guides Detroiters through the daily rush hours, long ago dispensed with the official road numbers. In the chill mornings when exhausts form white, wintry wisps, Ford, Fisher and Chrysler become highways in their own right.

For Detroiters the names are as familiar as Kowalski, the local brand
of Polish sausage, Vernor's, the ginger ale bottled along Woodward
Avenue, or Stroh's, the gold-painted name that adorns the bright-red
beer trucks of the local brewery.

Near the Detroit River are streets that are barely noticeable on maps
of the city. The names record some of the car companies that expired
decades before their founders could be immortalized in concrete.
Around Chrysler's eight-story Jefferson Avenue plant, among a jumble
of rusting railway tracks, small tool-making shops and rudely boarded
shopfronts, the green-and-white street signs tell the tale of the early
automobile companies. The ventures commemorated by Alter Road
and Baldwin Avenue both splashed into premature bankruptcies. Mr.
Badger, now an avenue, chose to retire from the business in 1911. The
Essex Company, which lent its name to a broad road plying toward
the Grosse Pointe estates of the Fords, was acquired by the Hudson
Motor Company in 1922. Chandler Park, a charmless municipal golf
course splayed alongside the Ford Freeway, springs from a company
that bowed to a merger in 1926.

The streets whisper of the early 1900s, when the American automobile industry shook off the legacies of the bicycle- and carriage-makers
and grappled with uncharted problems. Never before had an industry
attracted such a disparate group. Farmboys mixed with aristocrats;
engineers conspired with sharp-eyed salesmen. Scattered in shops
around the Midwest and New England, the first manufacturers each
needed only a small plant and some ready credit. Beginning was easy
and failure even easier. Henry Ford, for example, rebounded from a
complete fiasco with the Detroit Automobile Company in 1899 to
found his own company in 1903.

The activity of the first two decades of the twentieth century unalterably shaped the course of the industry. In 1904, 4,195 cars were assembled by 60 companies. Within the next ten years, 531 companies
were formed and 346 perished. Companies found it easy enough to
sell cars; their problems were how to produce them. For the first generation of automakers, the attainment of respectable size became the
only guarantee of success. In 1908, the year of the appearance of
Henry Ford's Model T, 65,000 vehicles were manufactured. In 1917,
1,873,949 were produced. The need to produce in sufficient quantities
made the number of company owners shrink almost as fast as the industry expanded. By 1923, only 108 car makers remained, and this
number dwindled to 44 by 1927. One of the companies that survived
until the early 1920s was Maxwell, which, inevitably enough, left its
imprint on Detroit in yet another road name.

On the street signs of east Detroit are the traces of Chrysler's darker
past. The names of companies that eventually lost their identity to

Chrysler crisscross an area where poverty and faded affluence exist cheek by jowl. Chalmers, Gray and Brush are now avenues, but for the first couple of decades of the century they were small companies tangled in a confusing corporate quilt.

Of all the visible shades of Chrysler's past, Maxwell winds along the most extensive route. Today, appropriately enough, Maxwell borders Detroit's Indian Village, where the automobile magnates erected generous and gracious townhouses. Maxwell is the thread that binds the beginning of the twentieth century with the company Walter Chrysler was summoned to rescue in 1920. Jonathan D. Maxwell was an experienced man among inexperienced men. By 1902 he had been associated with three automobiles: the Haynes Apperson, the widely popular Oldsmobile and his own creation, the Silent Northern. During the next two years, he joined Benjamin Briscoe, a successful Detroit manufacturer of radiators and stampings, to organize the Maxwell-Briscoe Motor Company. Dogged by difficulties from the start, the pair encountered uncomfortable resistance when they tried to sell the company's shares, until the banker J. P. Morgan intervened and purchased $110,000 worth, which allowed ten of their two-cylinder cars to emerge in 1904 from a plant in Tarrytown, New York, formerly devoted to the manufacture of steam engines.

Briscoe, however, was driven by dreams. He had entered the sheet-metal business at age twenty with an inheritance of $452 and became the largest manufacturer of a new receptacle, the metal garbage can. Along with his brother Frank, who found France and music infinitely preferable to mechanical novelties, Briscoe had purchased and sold a 99-percent interest in Buick in 1903 for $10,000. Briscoe weathered the panic of 1907, which swamped many other auto manufacturers, and even briefly contemplated entering the taxi business until he discovered that his cars cost more to maintain than they could possibly earn. At the beginning of the 1908 selling season, when his company was respectably among the industry leaders, Briscoe approached William Crapo Durant with a bold scheme.

Briscoe's plan immediately tickled the effervescent Durant who, during the previous eight years, had transformed himself from the nation's leading wagon-and-carriage producer to the owner of Buick, the largest car company. Briscoe proposed to Durant ". . . a combination of the principal concerns in the industry. Not with the desire to sell all of the automobiles that were to be sold, but rather for the purpose of having one big concern of such dominating influence in the automobile industry as, for instance, the United States Steel Corporation exercises in the steel industry."[1] His plan to combine the fortunes of Maxwell-Briscoe, Buick, Ford and Oldsmobile ran aground twice. Henry Ford and R. E. Olds unexpectedly demanded cash for their companies and the wily Durant double-crossed Briscoe by quietly purchasing an option to buy 75 percent of Olds' outstanding stock. Briscoe's conspicuous failure became a hapless footnote to one of Durant's greatest coups: the September 16, 1908, formation of the General Motors Company from a combination of Buick and Olds.

Durant's heartless tactics provided Briscoe with a dubious recipe for survival: financial combination and the blanketing of the market with a variety of models. Henry Ford had chosen another tack: large production runs of a single car. Leaving the wreckage of his brightest vision, Briscoe pursued financial combination. He formed the United States Motor Company in February 1910. The new conglomerate was a collection of pronounced failures. The best-known member of the hastily assembled union was the Columbia Motor Company, guided by Col. Albert Pope, who had once been convinced that the combustion engine was doomed since "You cannot get people to sit over an explosion."[2] In happier times the company had sold the four-wheel-drive Electrobat, which had a range of about fifteen miles. Of late, noted a contemporary, Columbia had been "unsuccessful in making profits from the manufacture and sale of automobiles."[3] Lined up beside Pope's concern was the Alden-Sampson Manufacturing Company, headquartered in Pittsfield, Massachusetts. Very much the plaything of a millionaire owner, it managed to lose money on every five-ton truck it sold. Then there was the Dayton Motor Car Company, producer of the Stoddard-Dayton, which had graduated from farm implements to automobiles but was staggering beneath a thumping overhead. Its nearby competitor and new ally, the Courier Car Company, despite taking first prize in the 1909 Indianapolis race, simply failed to become popular. The freshly formed empire also embraced the Gray Motor Company, which tooled farm and marine engines in Detroit, while the final member of any substance was the Brush Runabout Company. Owned by Frank Briscoe and Alanson Brush, it made a one-cylinder, ten-horsepower car with a frame of hardwood and axles of hickory. It labored, however, beneath the ignominious slogan "Wooden frame, wooden axles and would'n' run."[4]

The quest for profits was doomed from the outset. Each company, even after consolidation into the United States Motor Company, continued to operate its own plants, which were scattered in several states. The parent attempted to issue $12.5 million of notes, but only succeeded in selling $6 million. Briscoe managed to survive only by stretching his credit to the limit, and one disgruntled employee pointedly noted that "there was more or less confusion in the sale of parts and in the collection of accounts."[5] The company duly tripped into bankruptcy in September 1912.

Within weeks of the bankruptcy, the carcass was revived. It first assumed the name Standard Motor Company, Inc., which was quickly changed to Maxwell Motor Company. The irrepressible Briscoe departed for France to establish Briscoe Frères at Billancourt while his first vice-president, Jonathan Maxwell, decided to flee altogether from the worrisome industry. The man behind the switch from Standard to Maxwell was Walter Flanders, who was credited with many of the production novelties at Ford. In partnership with Bernard Everitt, a bodymaker for Oldsmobile runabouts, and William Metzger, Detroit's first automobile dealer, Flanders had introduced the Everitt-Metzger-Flanders, known by the initials EMF. Flanders' company was merged with Maxwell, and the new president shed many of the widely spread and confusing subdivisions which had made 164 different chassis. On March 1, 1913, Maxwell started selling a four-cylinder Maxwell and Flanders' own six-cylinder. The latter shook off the initials EMF and was marketed as the Maxwell 6, but proved incapable of losing its nickname, "Every Mechanical Fault."[6]

The automobile industry's second decade was a paradise for speculators, and the Maxwell Motor Company was no exception. By 1916, Henry Ford alone was manufacturing over half a million cars, and the astonishing surge in production had been matched by a spectacular improvement in profits and stock prices. Between 1913 and 1918, Maxwell netted $17 million in profits, and the stock price sauntered from one end of the rainbow to the other: $1.75 in 1913 to $99 in 1916. Eugene Meyer, the banker who engineered the formation of Maxwell (and later publisher of the Washington *Post*) added a mint from Maxwell to the millions he won from his connections with the Fisher Body Company.

In 1917, Flanders, whose eye was more sharply focused on organization than on quality, negotiated a complicated lease with the Chalmers Motor Company. Hugh Chalmers had once been a salesman for the National Cash Register Company and had demonstrated a keener sense for advertising hyperbole than for automobile manufacturing. Various clauses allowed Maxwell to share the profits, property and assets of Chalmers for five years. Under the terms of the accord, Maxwell was permitted to assemble its own cars at Chalmers' Jefferson Avenue plant in Detroit. Thereafter, Chalmers proved a perpetual drag on Maxwell until Walter Chrysler finally consigned the company to oblivion in 1926.

The boom that followed the end of the First World War and the rapid rise in car prices provided Maxwell with a plump cushion. Indeed, the entire industry flourished and, in 1920, enjoyed a spring that broke all records. By the summer, however, the enthusiasm had curdled. Prices, which had risen 57 percent between 1917 and 1920, and a restriction of credit pummeled the industry. The Lelands, who manu-

factured the Lincoln, started 1920 with $8 million in cash and ended
the year with $11,000 in cash and $6.25 million in debt. Henry Ford
cut his prices by 30 percent and shut his factories in December.
Willys-Overland, Packard, Dodge and Studebaker followed suit. General Motors, embroiled in a private turmoil, was forced to issue common stock and halt production of all cars except Buicks and Cadillacs.

The collapse of the market had a devastating effect on the industry
and dealt a catastrophic blow to Maxwell. There were poignant similarities between Maxwell's plight in 1920 and Chrysler's in the spring
of 1979. A dismal selling atmosphere merely exacerbated chronic internal conditions. Maxwell had a bloated inventory, cars of poor quality and a clucking horde of nervous bankers. By the summer of 1920,
Maxwell's management had attempted to force the sale of cars to
dealers and distributors and the company was burdened with 26,000
unenticing cars, 16,000 of which were paying demurrage on railway
tracks because agents refused to accept them.

The agents had discerned features that the management of Maxwell
was either willing to ignore or had entirely neglected. The cars' rear
axles sagged to such an extent that the differential frequently slithered
onto the street, and the gas tank demonstrated similar tendencies.
With its inventory heaped up around the country, the last thing the
company needed was finicky bankers. Wall Street, which held $26 mil-
lion in Maxwell notes, had ample cause for concern. The banking
community in 1920 was confronted with exactly the same dilemma
faced by its successors sixty years later. Unable to justify further loans
to a corporation quite obviously heaving its last, the bankers (headed
by Chase Securities Company) were also reluctant to force a bankruptcy and thereby lose all the money already advanced. Someone,
somehow or other, had to salvage their money, and the bankers had
an obvious candidate for the task.

By the fall of 1920, Walter P. Chrysler had already endeared himself to the same group of financiers. They had previously lured him
from an early retirement in Flint, Michigan, to rescue the $50 million
advanced to another fading car company, Willys-Overland. Willys
was in dire straits. Chock-a-block with supplies ordered for a healthy
market, its owner, John Willys, had also embarked on an extravagant
expansion. The company had car plants in Toledo and Elmira and also
controlled the Curtiss Aeroplane Company and the Moline Plow Company of Moline, Illinois. The $10 million channeled into the con-
struction in Elizabeth, New Jersey, of a three-story plant only worsened matters. The factory even had a cafeteria large enough to feed
the twelve hundred workers who were supposed to build a new six-
cylinder car. "John Willys," Walter Chrysler later recalled, "sometimes seemed to feel that the company's problems could be met by a

couple of new gadgets and a coat of paint."[7] Chrysler, needless to say, did not. He installed himself in suitable splendor at the Biltmore and demanded $1 million a year for his troubles. He then proceeded to demonstrate a ruthlessness guaranteed to steady a banker's heart and even cut John Willys' salary from $150,000 to $75,000.

On taking control of Willys, Chrysler immediately ordered a halt to development work on the six-cylinder car. He cast around for engineers capable of designing a popular car and finally netted Frederick Zeder. The chief engineer of Studebaker, Zeder was at odds with his employers and joined Willys-Overland in July 1920. A graduate of the University of Michigan, he brought along his associates, Carl Breer, a Stanford graduate who had worked for Allis-Chalmers, and Owen Skelton, previously employed by Pope-Toledo and Packard. The trio were to have a profound and enduring influence on the shape and image of Chrysler Corporation and were, said Walter Chrysler, "parts of a single, extraordinary engineering intelligence."

No sooner had Chrysler begun to tangle with the thistles at Willys-Overland than he was approached with the bankers' latest problem: the $26 million advanced to Maxwell. Despite a reluctance to become enmeshed with another sorry company, Chrysler bowed to the personal entreaties of the bankers (one of whom had lent him the money to purchase his first car). He designed a sprightly arrangement with Willys, where he continued as executive vice-president, while assuming the chairmanship of the Reorganization and Management Committee of Maxwell, for $100,000 a year and a large pool of stock options. Under Chrysler's direction, the banks placed Maxwell in a friendly receivership, auctioned the company to the reorganization committee and furnished $15 million in additional loans.

Commuting between New York and Detroit, Walter Chrysler occupied a position guaranteed to trigger apoplexy among latter-day trust-busters. The bankers' savior was not above exploiting his privileged position, from which he could squint into the activities of two car companies. By day, Zeder, Skelton and Breer concentrated on designing a car for Willys-Overland. In their spare time, they worked on a car for Walter Chrysler. Yet all their moonlighting was wasted when Chrysler clumsily attempted a takeover of Willys-Overland. His guile was so transparent that the managers of the New Jersey company hurried it into receivership in December 1921.

Chrysler was not the only automobile magnate casting lascivious glances at Willys-Overland. Far more important than the spanking new factory were the blueprints and designs for the Zeder car. (By law, the designs fell under the hammer with the company.) Walter Chrysler dispatched an agent to the auction in June 1922, but met stiff opposition. Not only was General Motors represented, but William

Durant (recently ousted from GM) made a personal appearance to win the car he hoped would challenge Henry Ford's supremacy. Chrysler bailed out of the bidding at $3.125 million, General Motors faltered at $4.465 million and Durant triumphed with a $5.25 million bid.

After the auction, and with their designs lost to Durant, Zeder, Skelton and Breer were evicted from the Elizabeth factory. Setting themselves up in new quarters on Newark's aptly named Mechanic Street, the three started work on yet another car. Zeder furnished overall guidance; his brother-in-law, Breer, concentrated on the engine; Skelton devoted his attention to the body, springs and axles. Almost immediately pressed for funds, they turned to Durant. Quick to recognize an opportunity, Durant supplied $500,000 and allowed them access to their former test facilities.

While the engineering triumvirate hopped from Studebaker to Willys to partial independence, Walter Chrysler had been tussling with Maxwell. The first object of his attention was the 26,000-car inventory. He ordered the rear axles to be trussed, secured the wayward gas tanks and cut the price to $995. By the end of 1921 he had sold the cars at a profit of five dollars apiece.

The severity of Maxwell's predicament had been underlined by the company's new treasurer, B. E. Hutchinson. (Bernice Edwin Hutchinson remained with Chrysler until his retirement in 1953.) Something of a whippersnapper, he had left M.I.T. at the dean's invitation during his second year, worked as a reporter on the Boston *Globe* and shoveled cinders in his father's Chicago tack factory. He forsook the superintendency of an open-hearth furnace for a desk at the accounting firm of Ernst and Ernst and established his reputation by reorganizing company accounts. Soon after arriving at Maxwell, he wrote down the inventory by $11 million and coaxed a $12 million line of credit from the banks.

Not even Chrysler's success in 1922, when he dolled up the Maxwell, advertised it as "The Good Maxwell" and sold 48,250 (14,000 above 1920), could stanch the outflows which were largely caused by the continuing problems of the Chalmers Company. The way out of the mire was production of a new car, and the only prospective solution lay in New Jersey.

Chrysler renewed contact with Zeder in the fall of 1922, eyed the drawings for a new high-compression engine with enthusiasm, approved of the wooden model and niftily supplemented Durant's dwindling funds. Within a matter of months, the three engineers were installed in the former Chalmers factory in Detroit and were busily working on what was to be the first Chrysler car.

Ellis, Kansas, was an unlikely beginning for a name that was to be stamped on grilles and hubcaps around the world. In 1875, the year of Walter Chrysler's birth, the small town was caught between two worlds. Fending off the occasional rampage (of man and beast) from the short-grass prairie, it was also welcoming, in an oblique way, the mechanized intrusion of the railroad. Walter Chrysler was the third of four children. His father, a Canadian by birth, had spent his youth as a drummer boy in the Civil War before becoming a locomotive engineer for the Union Pacific Railroad. Chrysler's mother was a German-speaking Methodist who made her own soap and served buffalo meat at the family table.

As a schoolboy, Chrysler displayed all the requisite entrepreneurial traits. He hawked calling cards and silverware to neighboring housewives and fired off inquisitive letters to *Scientific American*. On one occasion he pestered the editors for more details of "the Harden hand grenade for extinguishing fires." Leaving school at age fourteen, he barely dallied in his first job as a delivery boy before beginning a four-year apprenticeship at five cents an hour in the local repair yards of the Union Pacific. Reveling in the grease and sparks of the railway yards, he fathomed the mysteries of connecting rods and valve settings and astonished his workmates by fashioning a set of tools. Yet neither his graduation to a world of beer, cigarettes and cards nor his position as second baseman for the town team could dampen Chrysler's desire for adventure.

Armed with his tools, a ready temper and cocky self-assurance, he shunted through the railway yards of the West, hopping boxcars from company to company and crawling into the thundering intestines of panting locomotives in Pocatello, Cheyenne and Laramie. Only marriage, at the age of twenty-six, to Della Forker, the daughter of an Ellis shopkeeper, forced Chrysler to settle down. Domesticity started in a rented apartment with $170 worth of furniture in Salt Lake City. He shed his overalls and became, in turn, a roundhouse foreman, shop superintendent and division master mechanic. But it was a new job with the Chicago Great Western, where Chrysler's expanded realm reached Minneapolis, Dubuque, Omaha and Kansas City, that allowed him to attend the 1908 Chicago Automobile Show. With a monthly income of $350 and savings of $700, Chrysler became infatuated with a $5,000 Locomobile painted ivory white with a khaki top and red upholstery. He plopped down his savings, wheedled $4,300 from the banker Ralph van Vechten, and spent the next three months delicately spreading every component over newspapers in a barn at the back of his house. "I did not simply want a car to ride in," Chrysler recorded thirty years later. "I wanted the machine so I could learn all about it. I was a machinist and these self-propelled vehicles were by all odds

the most astonishing machines that had ever been offered to men."[8]
Finally convinced that he understood the intricacies of his purchase,
Chrysler embarked on an outing that ended with the car being hauled
by a team of horses from the mud of a neighbor's garden.

Chrysler quit his job with the Chicago Great Western in a characteristic fit of pique and moved his family to Pittsburgh, where he
found work along the banks of the Ohio River building engines for the
American Locomotive Company. The clannish nature of American industry was demonstrated when James Storrow, a director at Chrysler's
new place of employment and a former president of General Motors,
arranged a meeting between the recent recruit and Charles Nash, the
president of Buick.

Nash, who had started by pounding iron in a blacksmith's shop for
William Durant in 1886, invited Chrysler to the Buick factory in Flint,
Michigan. Convinced that he could convert what was merely a refined
carriage-building company into a freshly oiled automobile factory,
Chrysler accepted the offer of a job, allowed his salary to be halved to
$6,000 and uprooted his family again.

Chrysler brought the lessons gleaned from the construction of locomotives to Flint. He chopped down a forest of roof supports and
insisted on piecework schedules. The varnish pots of carriage days
were banished from the paint shop and the painting period was shortened from four days to twelve hours. He ordered hundreds of machine tools and installed a moving production line. "Starting with the
assembly line," Chrysler remembered, "we worked backward through
the plant until everything was tied in. Every new thing was an invention." After three years, Chrysler, now Nash's replacement as president of Buick, demanded a $25,000 salary and coolly informed his su-
periors, "Next year I want fifty thousand."[9] Chrysler made Buick the
treasure chest of General Motors and brought in as much as half the
company's entire earnings. He became a vice-president and director
and watched his salary climb to $500,000.

Chrysler had to contend with Durant's sunny imperialism, however,
and his anger boiled over in 1920. Durant had previously sold a Buick
sales branch to a pal and had pinched a superintendent from a Buick
drop-forge plant without so much as consulting Chrysler. On both occasions, Chrysler had stormed to Durant's office in Detroit, was forced
to cool his heels while Durant answered the incessant telephone calls,
and eventually had bluntly told his boss to stop meddling—but a third
insult was too much for Chrysler. Attending a luncheon at the Flint
Chamber of Commerce, the president of Buick was astounded to hear
the contents of a telegram from Durant which announced that a new
$6 million plant for supplying frames to Buick would be built in Flint.
The toastmaster called on Chrysler (then engaged in tough bargain-

ing for frames from a supplier in Milwaukee) who furiously spluttered that "not so long as I stay here will General Motors have a frame plant in Flint."[10] The following day, at a board meeting, Chrysler fired angry questions at the GM president. Were there cost estimates for the new plant? Who had done the estimating? Where were the floor plans? On March 25, 1920, Chrysler, by then a forty-five-year-old multi-millionaire, resigned. Alfred Sloan, who occupied an office next door to Durant, later recalled, "I remember the day. He banged the door on the way out, and out of that bang came eventually the Chrysler Corporation."[11]

The announcement of the first Chrysler car at the national automobile show in January 1924 was largely an act of faith. Since the bankers' withdrawal in November 1923, the Maxwell Company did not possess the funds needed for large-scale production. Walter Chrysler admitted, "We had stretched our credit to the snapping point. . . . We were pretty close to ruin before we had made a start."[12] Chrysler staked his future on a public reception enthusiastic enough to persuade the bankers to change their minds. His sales manager secured the lobby of New York's Commodore Hotel and crowds swirled around the new cars, cleverly left unpriced. The bankers lurked in the background, narrowly eyeing the public's response.

The trade papers ecstatically greeted the Chrysler line. "The new Chrysler," gushed *Automobile Topics*, "is haunted by no family resemblance to other lines."[13] While the car's low-slung appearance was later given the credit for much of its success, the paper stolidly observed that "headroom is abundant and it is possible to enter without sacrifice of personal dignity or damage to millinery."[14] More important was the uncommonly quiet engine. Frederick Zeder had unbottled a corker. Until then, high-compression engines had been regarded as a peculiarly European folly which did, however, reduce noise and vibration. Chrysler's engine block was the first United States-produced high-compression six-cylinder engine; it gave the car a power and speed not normally associated with its class. The car featured other innovations. For the first time, a replaceable cartridge oil filter was added outside the engine, and four-wheel Lockheed hydraulic brakes were standard equipment. The car accelerated from 5 mph to 50 mph in a nippy thirteen seconds, had a top speed around 75 mph and got twenty miles to the gallon. The 1123/4-inch wheelbase was shorter than that of the Buick, yet the car was no less comfortable and the price, announced at $1,565, was exactly the same.

The bankers, including Ed Tinker of Chase Securities, were suitably impressed. Their equivocal behavior evaporated with the prospect of future profits, and bargaining over the terms of the new loan commenced. At one point, Chrysler and Tinker haggled in the back seat of one of the display cars, surrounded by a crowd of curious faces. At the end of the first day of the automobile show, Chrysler had managed to spark sufficient public interest to enable arrangement of the desperately needed $5 million loan.

With the financing assured, Chrysler busily set about breaking every available record. For the first time, a production schedule reached 100 a day within three months of the construction of the first car. By the beginning of June, production was running at 150 a day and in September the Chrysler outsold the Maxwell line. Within twelve months of its appearance, 32,000 Chrysler Sixes had been sold, a record for the first year's production of a new car.

Despite the distractions caused by the development of the Chrysler Six, Walter Chrysler was not too preoccupied to preside over a gradual shift of ownership and a consolidation of management. In the middle of 1923, he had assumed the presidency of Maxwell. He quickly began to exercise his stock options and, by August of 1923, Chalmers was a 90-percent-owned subsidiary. On the last day of 1923, Walter Chrysler announced the Michigan incorporation of Chrysler Motor Corporation with a capitalization of ten thousand shares at $10 par value. Chrysler was to be governed by the officers who previously had tended Maxwell's concerns.

The success of the Chrysler Six during 1924 paved the way for the inevitable. On April 9, 1925, a special directors' meeting of Maxwell Motors Company approved a takeover, through an exchange of securities, by Chrysler. "The change," warbled an industry house organ, "marks the successful termination of the biggest reclamation project the automobile industry has witnessed and practically the christening of a new business."[15] Chrysler Motors Corporation was incorporated in Delaware on June 6, 1925.

Hyperbole notwithstanding, Chrysler's achievement was remarkable. In August 1920, the Maxwell Company had been saddled with a total of $33 million of obligations and the unprofitable association with Chalmers. Chrysler had arrived on the scene, persuaded the bankers to part with another $15 million and, within another four months, had liquidated $11 million of debts. During the succeeding year, creditors received one-third of their claims in cash and notes for the balance of $13.5 million. In 1922, $8 million of the notes were redeemed. The second series was wiped out in 1923, and in January 1925, the remaining notes, due in 1934, were scrubbed from the balance sheet.

Within weeks of the official formation of the Chrysler Corporation, the company revealed its second car: the Four, which arrived in four body styles, with the cheapest priced at $895. The accompanying announcement proclaimed that the "purpose is to furnish in a four-cylinder car the same comparative merits embodied in the Chrysler Six." Yet the car also featured a major technical advance: for the first time, the engine was isolated from the frame, to dampen the jarring vibrations. In earlier cars, the motor had always been directly tethered to the metal frame. In the new Chrysler, the conventional bolting of the front end of the engine was replaced by floating platform springs, while at the rear the engine rested on rubber bushes.

At the 1926 automobile show, two years after the introduction of the Chrysler Six, the company unveiled a six-cylinder Chrysler Imperial 80 in seven styles. Dealers could now sprinkle their showrooms with nineteen models sitting on three basic frames. The Imperial was designed for the luxury market and boasted instruments with ivory dials, framed in a relief of oxidized silver.

During the summer of 1926, the fourth and final car was unwrapped. This was a four-cylinder Chrysler 50 with a top speed of 50 mph; it performed at 20 mpg. Above all, the car was cheap. It started at $750 and obeyed the precepts of what was already a guiding principle in the automobile trade. *Automobile Topics* was not tardy in observing that the latest Chrysler "means more owners in the light car field and consequently a greater number of potential buyers of higher priced cars in the course of time."[16] One measure of the company's health after the gradual introduction of its new fleet was the manner in which it sprouted around the nation. In Milwaukee, for example, during 1926, the local dealers took to patrolling the streets until three in the morning on the lookout for any Chrysler owners in distress. With a flexing of its corporate muscle, the company rented the largest electric sign west of New York, in downtown Chicago. There, in twenty-foot-high red letters, "Chrysler" appeared above six-foot-high numerals that flashed the model numbers: 60, 70 and 80. Chrysler cars were increasingly used to demonstrate prowess. In 1927, the Stover Signal Engineering Company organized a cross-country dash to illustrate the efficiency of its headlights. The drivers, in a Phaeton Chrysler, sent orders ahead by telegraph for ice cream and took one minute less than a week to travel from San Francisco to Los Angeles via New York. Chrysler had already provided a pace car for the Indianapolis race and, in 1928, five Chryslers were purchased by representatives of the Japanese government for the ceremonies surrounding the coronation of the new Mikado.

As buyers began to discover the merits of Chrysler cars, the factory began to add more expensive trimmings. In 1926 Chrysler provided the 70 and 80 Phaetons with the first adjustable front seats in the industry. A year later, Triplex glass, which supposedly neither shattered nor splintered, was offered as optional equipment. Meanwhile, the cars began to sport accessories fitting the company's new station. Wire wheels and cigar lighters were offered and, on occasion, car bodies were emblazoned with specially painted monograms.

Beyond the practical advances and the attendant frippery, Chrysler's profitability allowed an expansion of both manufacturing space and interests. The early success of the Chrysler Six allowed the purchase of the American Body Manufacturing Company, located directly across the street from the old Chalmers plant. In 1927, as a sop to Walter Chrysler's long-standing interest in speedboats, the company developed a separate Marine Division to manufacture the Chrysler Imperial marine engine. At the company's Highland Park headquarters, a new, four-story research building was erected. It included hydraulic lifts and dynamometers for the testing of cars, a 75-ton ice-making plant to simulate cold conditions and a passenger elevator replete with "super-selective push button control."[17]

Even marvelous elevators are no measure of success and, at the beginning of 1927, Chrysler, despite its perceptible growth, was still a minnow. Indeed, there was something faintly impudent about mentioning Chrysler's company in the same breath as Henry Ford or General Motors. During 1926, Chrysler produced 129,565 vehicles, a total that pales into insignificance alongside Ford's 1,137,181 or General Motors' 892,007. Chrysler's counterparts were smaller companies like Studebaker, the Hudson-Essex combine or William Durant's own organization.

Toward the end of the 1920s, the industry was beginning to concentrate on competition rather than on sheer growth. Nevertheless, in the years before the Great Crash, growth barely abated. In 1920, nearly 2,250,000 vehicles were produced, while in 1929 Americans purchased 5,333,687. In 1929, there was one automobile for every six persons living in the United States. The brutal advantage of size became more evident. Indeed, the virtual absence of new entrants into the business reflected the scale of the barriers. Snapping up a larger share of the existing market was becoming as crucial as grabbing a hunk of a larger market. Manufacturers were no longer vying merely to park the first car in a buyer's driveway. They were now aiming to persuade current owners to purchase a new, preferably more expensive, automobile. With the increasing heat of competition, company organization—planning, internal discipline and control of costs—became more important. For Walter Chrysler, pondering his next moves, Ford and General Motors offered a study in contrasts.

The new times, as Henry Ford was slowly learning, could not be met solely by increasing production of a simple, cheap car and distributing it through a far-flung, comprehensive sales network. His Model T, introduced in 1908, had garnered slightly over half the entire market in 1924, but its popularity fell precipitously during the succeeding two years as consumers opted for something newer and brighter than just another of the 15 million Tin Lizzies. By 1927, the nervous arguments of Edsel Ford and other subdued lieutenants finally convinced the innovator of the moving assembly line and the eight-hour day of the need for bold action. Ford did not flinch. For nine months, he closed down his mighty River Rouge plant, where sand and ore arrived at the dock and cars emerged into marshaling yards. Toward the end of 1927, he presented the American public with the new Model A.

Although the car beat Chevrolet in 1928, the Ford Motor Company never recovered from the obduracy of its owner. Ford had long seen positive virtues in his brand of autocratic management. In 1922, he described the features of a company that barely changed until his grandson's accession after the Second World War: "The Ford factories and enterprises," he remarked, "have no organization, no specific duties attaching to any position, no line of succession or of authority, very few titles and no conferences." What was anathema to Henry Ford had within a few years become the credo of the industry's new leader, General Motors.

In 1927, General Motors assumed the leadership of the industry. Apart from the years following the arrival of Ford's Model A, GM never relinquished it. The company's characteristics, like its leadership, have survived until the present. By 1927, Alfred P. Sloan had brought order to the unwieldy heap left by the impulsive Durant. After William Durant's final departure in 1920, General Motors was never again shaken by the whimsical folly of a single individual.

Durant possessed an eye that invariably fastened on opportunity rather than on detail. Within a year of forming General Motors in 1908, Durant had purchased the Oakland Company (later known as Pontiac) and Cadillac. Before his first period of enforced exile, which started in 1910, he had sucked in another eleven automobile manufacturers and fourteen suppliers. In 1916, his latest corporate creation, Chevrolet, virtually took over GM and forced the guardian bankers back into the eaves. Before the collapse of his paper empire in 1920, when the du Ponts took control, Durant had formed, in addition, the General Motors Truck Company, acquired a 60-percent interest in the Fisher brothers' body-making company, and guaranteed his supplies of electrical starters, lights and ignition equipment with the purchase of Delco. He even formed the General Motors Acceptance Corporation to cope with the spiraling demand for new-car financing.

Alfred Sloan became president of General Motors in 1923 and remained intimately connected with the company until his retirement as chairman in 1956. When he took over from Durant in 1921 "there was just about as much crisis, inside or outside, as you could wish for."[18]

A new plan for the organization of the corporation was drawn up by Sloan and adopted by the General Motors board in January 1921. Within five years of Durant's departure, Sloan imposed order. In the process, he provided a design for modern industry.

The structure imposed upon the company meant that its fate was guided by committee. Operating control was granted to the dozens of companies purchased by Durant, but their activities were closely monitored. "Certain central organization functions are absolutely essential to the logical development and proper control of the Corporation's activities," Sloan later wrote. Unlike Ford, who provided his salesmen with just one car, General Motors carefully began to provide a "car for every purse and purpose" and in so doing blanketed the market and established a presence in every social class. "We proposed," Sloan wrote, "that General Motors should place its cars at the top of each price range and make them of such quality that they would attract sales from below that price, selling to those customers who might be willing to pay a little more for the additional quality, and attract sales also from above that price, selling to those customers who would see the price advantage in a car of close to the quality of higher-priced competition."[19] By the mid-Twenties, Sloan's men were generating troughs of statistical reports, which governed the allocation of resources and provided a degree of financial control not seen before. The central staff brought GM's independent dealers to heel and started to base production on sales projections rather than to try and sell all the cars that were manufactured. The sales reports, which were churned out every ten days, gave the entire industry a rhythm and a yardstick, and the annual model change brought a regular jolt to the nation. "Many will wonder why the automobile industry brings out a new model every year," Sloan wrote. "The reason is simple. We want to make available to you, as rapidly as we can, the most advanced knowledge and practice in the building of motor cars. We want to make you dissatisfied with your current car so you will buy a new [one]—you who can afford it."[20]

To become a major presence, Walter Chrysler had to lock horns with Ford and General Motors. To grapple with Ford, he had to make a significant entry into the highly competitive low-priced market and, to challenge General Motors, he had to expand his line. In 1928, Walter Chrysler did both. In a remarkable triple play, he purchased Dodge Brothers, introduced the Plymouth and unveiled the DeSoto.

Chrysler's palpable lack of integration was penalizing profits and the Hamtramck plant owned by the Dodge Brothers offered many of the facilities Chrysler lacked. Dodge Main, for example, had a forge and a foundry, while in 1927 Chrysler still had to purchase forgings and castings.

John and Horace Dodge had been brought up in Niles, Michigan, the sons of a mechanic, Daniel Rug Dodge. Trained as machinists, the two redheads moved to Detroit, where they roamed around raucous saloons, developed a ball-bearing bicycle and opened a machine shop. In 1901, they achieved recognition with an order for three thousand transmissions for the curved Dash Oldsmobile Runabout. They later helped Henry Ford redesign his rear axle and engine. In 1903, Ford persuaded the brothers to supply engines for the new Ford in exchange for one hundred of the company's one thousand newly issued shares. (The Dodges paid for their one-tenth stake by providing $3,000 in cash and $7,000 in materials.) In 1914, following a furious disagreement, the pair sold their share back to Ford for $25 million. Using their accumulated wisdom, the brothers founded a company to manufacture a durable, rugged car priced about one hundred dollars above the Ford.

They built the first company test track, and the car gained a sterling reputation for dependability. General Pershing relied on it during his tangles with Pancho Villa on the Mexican border in 1915 and 1916. (It was during the Mexican fighting that a certain Lieut. George Patton, Jr., commanded fifteen men and three Dodges in the first U.S. mechanized cavalry charge.) As was fit, John and Horace, who refused to open any letters not addressed to the Dodge Brothers, died within eleven months of each other during the 1920 influenza epidemic. The company, then valued at $52 million, was left to their respective widows and, during five years of female stewardship, made a significant impact on the truck business with the purchase of Graham Brothers.

In 1925, the Dodge widows turned a handsome profit by selling their husbands' legacy to Dillon, Read and Company, the bankers, for $146 million. In a quest for quick profits, the new owners garnished the Dodge with trimmings, raised the price to such an extent that in 1928 it was priced at $1,500 (compared to $495 for the Model A Ford) and watched sales fall. Clarence Dillon was eager to rid himself of the fickle beast, which couldn't even pay dividends, while Walter Chrysler, whose head had been "full of visions of the splendid plants of the Dodge Brothers,"[21] was equally anxious to buy. The predictable feints, expressions of lack of interest and elaborate courting ended in a steamy five days in a suite at the Ritz-Carlton. Walter Chrysler emerged with a new company and Clarence Dillon with $170 million. The very night that the contract was settled, teams of men nailed large canvas signs announcing "Chrysler Corporation, Dodge Division" on the Hamtramck plant and Chrysler had multiplied sixfold.

This single purchase made Chrysler the third of the automobile companies. The combined market value of Dodge and Chrysler se-

curities amounted to $432 million, while their assets were a more-
than-respectable $258 million. The company now had eighteen plants,
a manufacturing capacity estimated at between 700,000 and 1,000,000
a year, and 12,000 dealers. If the Dodge purchase offered the prospect
of lower costs, greater production and a broader line of models, the
Plymouth marked the start of Chrysler's tussle with Ford and Chevrolet for dominance of the low-priced field.

"The Plymouth," a trade journal recorded in July 1928, "is offered
by Plymouth Motor Corporation, a division of the Chrysler Corporation with which the trade has not previously been familiar."[22] The introduction of the $670 Plymouth was surrounded with suitable hoopla
and the pilot Amelia Earhart accompanied the car at its first appearance in Madison Square Garden. The machine itself was supposed to
epitomize "the endurance, strength and rugged honesty of the American pilgrims."

The burst of activity in 1928 was capped with the arrival of the
DeSoto. Projected as a lighter six-cylinder with class, the DeSoto was
designed to fill the gulf between Chrysler and Plymouth. It started life
at the Hamtramck plant, and the similarity with the Dodge was quite
evident. It was shifted to its own plant in 1936.

Walter Chrysler's audacity provoked tittering on Wall Street and, in
a statement his successors might have been wise to ponder, Chrysler
sought to stifle the giggles. "We have no disposition or ambition to at-
tain mere size or volume," he proclaimed. "Sound business is not best
subserved by endeavouring to outdistance other great manufacturers. . . . The Chrysler business is being built step by step in relation to the capacities of the nation and of the industry as a whole. We
shall make no move which will even temporarily lessen the very
marked advantages which we enjoy in our capital structure. In other
words, if we grow, we will grow according to our financial, marketing
and manufacturing capacities—not beyond them, in a straining after
domination."[23]

The test of Chrysler's pronouncement was amply provided by the
Depression. The element of optimism in the company's expansion was
aptly symbolized by the New York skyscraper that Walter Chrysler
commissioned before the Great Crash. Like the seventy-seven-story
building, which for a short time was the tallest in the world, the company managed to penetrate the gloom of the darkest years. Indeed,
Chrysler emerged from the Depression stronger rather than weaker.

No small part of the company's resilience was attributable to the
way in which the chirpy Plymouth was marketed. In 1931, a four-
cylinder version capable of 20 mpg was squarely aimed at the $600
market. With a calculated display of one-upmanship, Walter Chrysler
took the third car produced across Detroit, picked up Henry and

Edsel Ford in Dearborn, took them for a demonstration drive, left the car for them to ruminate over and returned by taxi to the Plymouth plant. The Plymouth factory, built in 1928, was capable of producing 1,800 cars a day, and in 1935 was enlarged to trundle out 2,800 units—which, as the public relations men were later fond of boasting, was the greatest daily volume of cars assembled in a single automobile plant in the world. More critical than the size of the factory was the method chosen for distribution of the Plymouth. Chrysler's officers decided to offer the car through its existing dealers rather than create a new network. Despite its damaging long-term effects (see Chapter Three), the decision helped to preserve many of the dealers who were dependent on the more expensive Chryslers, Dodges and DeSotos. By 1932, Plymouth had inflicted a 14-percent dent in Chevrolet's and Ford's domination of the low-priced market.

Even more symbolic of the direction of the corporation than the marble pillars of the Chrysler Building or the spunkiness of the Plymouth was the decision, taken in 1930, to open the Chrysler Institute. Chartered by the state of Michigan, this company boot camp for engineers was the first institute of its kind licensed to grant degrees ranging up to doctorates. In later years, the institute supplied Chrysler and the rest of the industry with many of its most talented staff members.[24] It exemplified the commitment to research and development repeated time and again by Walter Chrysler. Even when the company was operating at 40 percent of capacity in the depths of the Depression, the management, said Chrysler, ". . . never cut one single penny from the budget of our research department. Any industrialist knows and understands that research work is what will keep any soundly managed industry alive and healthy."[25]

However, it was project "Q" that became the outstanding testament to Chrysler's commitment to research. Development started in the laboratories two years before the first deadening thump of the Depression and continued unhampered through years of unsurpassed misery. The final car came to serve as a cautionary tale for succeeding generations, and industry insiders still use it as a yardstick for failure. The strange machine, shaped like a bug, which had startled Michigan farmers during secret, nighttime test runs during the summer of 1933, was introduced in 1934 as the Airflow. Announcing the car, Walter Chrysler stated, "The public is always able to discriminate between what's merely radical and genuine improvement."[26] The public proved patently incapable of any such thing, and the popular rejection dealt incalculable harm to the prospects of making further bold improvements in safety, convenience and comfort. The Airflow was a flop unequaled by the later failures of the Edsel, the Corvair and the Pinto, none of which even pretended to make comparable advances.

The car drew together several strands of development, foremost of which was management's desire to sell the public improved comfort at a far richer price. Both comfort and convenience were improved. The designers heightened the roof and tilted the seats within a trussed steel-arch frame. (Unlike the conventional frame, the steel arch bore the brunt of the stress.) In a departure that influenced the entire industry, the engine was placed farther forward and rode above the front axle. This served to banish the rear axle from the passenger compartment and allowed the doors to be widened. The front seat was compared to a divan and the rear to a davenport. The more rigid body not only offered greater protection but also, when combined with improved springing, helped remove vibration and pitching. (The springs, for the first time, were specifically designed to match the rate of oscillation which the human frame could comfortably withstand.) All the changes, wrote a delighted reviewer, allowed the Airflow "to take a turn, even on loose shifting gravel, at 65 or 70 with the steadiness of a yacht coming into the wind."[27]

Many other benefits of the unimpeded research surfaced with the new car. The windshield on the Imperial Custom Airflow, for example, was made from one piece of curved glass—the first such use on a production vehicle. Even the hood, hinged at the rear, was in one section, rather than hinged down the center in the traditional way. The car was also the first to seriously conform to the principles of aerodynamics. Carl Breer, the engineer, noted that seven years of wind-tunnel tests had shown that "our cars were so poorly designed . . . they would actually run faster backward than forward." The Airflow incorporated in its mournful demeanor all the freshly learned lessons of ergonomics. The entire bulbous form was streamlined: headlights were sunk into the front fenders and flaps were placed over the rear wheels to let the air flow past the arches. The final version offered 40 percent less wind resistance than a conventional car of comparable size. One feature that was entirely overlooked in the unwelcome debate over aesthetics was an automatic overdrive transmission. While it was really a supplementary transmission fastened to the rear of an ordinary three-speed gear set, the new device reduced the ratio of engine speed to car speed above 40 mph without a manual shifting of gears.

If the public didn't exactly snap up the new Airflows, there were at least two satisfied customers: a New Castle, Indiana, mortician eagerly converted an Airflow to provide a new hearse, while the chairman of the Missouri, Kansas and Texas Railroad discarded his normal inspection carriage in favor of an Airflow equipped with steel wheels so as "to be closer to the rails."[28] Only 55,153 others purchased the car. Within a year, the front end of the car had been completely refashioned in a bid to spur public interest. In 1935, in a move indicative of the reception greeting the Airflow, Chrysler offered the newly shaped hoods to purchasers of the 1934 models. Despite these last-ditch efforts, the innovative Airflow was finally abandoned at the end of the 1937 model run.

Chrysler shrugged off the prolonged horror of the Depression years with surprising ease. In 1933, it was the only manufacturer to sell more cars and trucks than in the rip-roaring days of 1929. While Chrysler's average yearly wage dropped from $1,417 in 1930 to $1,047 in 1932, the work force more than doubled in the eight years after 1928. Although the stock price dropped from a peak of $140.75 in 1928 to a paltry $5 in 1932, Chrysler's finances were never seriously tested—a remarkable feat, since until 1936 the balance sheet was burdened by the $60 million of debt assumed with the Dodge acquisition.

The exigencies of the Depression made the control of costs even more critical than normal. Expenses associated with a high factory inventory were plainly something a company could well live without. In a highly significant development, given the problems of the 1960s and 1970s, when Highland Park was often swamped with unwanted cars, Chrysler instituted a rigorous ordering system for dealers. The increasing variety offered by manufacturers had made orderly production infinitely more complicated. In 1933, for example, Plymouths were offered in 258 combinations of color, upholstery and body. With no system to link dealer orders with production schedules, Chrysler quickly found itself unable to match five thousand cars sitting in a lot with five thousand frustrated customers.

To conquer the confusion, Chrysler instituted a program which, marveled *Fortune*, was "a technical triumph of some brilliance." The magazine explained that "the entire output of the plant is made only to order from the dealers. Orders coming in are sent daily to the control room where 35 copies are made and sent to the plants where all the necessary variable parts are dispatched to join the chassis. The timing is so perfect that the specific car ordered by the specific customer comes together as rapidly and as smoothly as though the 1,800 cars produced daily at the Plymouth plant were all identical instead of varied. . . . The whole thing takes only seven days from the time the order is received to shipment. . . . As a result delays are saved, larger shipments than before are possible and the cars on hand at any time are rarely more than one day's production. If a car remains in stock for as long as a week there is something wrong."[29]

Building strictly to dealer order, a policy which Lee Iacocca reverted to in 1979, was a brutal practice during the 1930s. With no guaranteed annual wage to pay, the cheapest and most efficient method of controlling a burgeoning inventory was to close the factory gates. Inventory control was something of a euphemism for forced un-

employment. Indeed, Chrysler's innovative scheme merely accentu-
ated the violent seasonal production swings that already existed. (The
industry, in an effort to relieve the high unemployment between the
spring selling season and the start of the calendar year, introduced the
1936 cars in the fall of 1935.) Walter Chrysler was unsympathetic to
complaints about the new inventory controls. In 1935, he reiterated to
his employees, through the company magazine, "It is out of the question to build finished cars in advance and store them, because no one
can predict models, equipment, furnishing, colors, etc."[30]

Like its competitors, Chrysler exerted a puritanical paternalism over
its employees. A male choir was started in late 1933, a company magazine in the following year and five hundred "especially deserving
sons"[31] were, every year, taken on a two-week educational tour.
Each boy contributed fifteen dollars, which he was supposed to earn,
while the company contributed the balance of the cost. The tour took
in cities and sights that reflected national virtue. The young pilgrims
tripped through Gettysburg and Washington, visited Mount Vernon
and paid calls at Annapolis and West Point before being shepherded
to the very monument of industry: the Chrysler Building.

At the same time, management remained implacably hostile to the
seeping threat of unionism, which began to intrude during the early
Thirties. At all of the automobile companies, managers were aghast.
Alfred Sloan believed that General Motors was providing its workers
with first-rate medical services, fine cafeterias, locker rooms, showers
and, of course, parking lots. The executives found it difficult to understand what the workers were even complaining about. In the early
Thirties, GM guaranteed workers with more than five years' seniority
that they would be paid for twenty-four hours' work a week when
they were temporarily laid off. When the worker had less than twenty-
four hours' work, the company advanced the difference and, when he
had more, he paid the company back without interest.[32]

Why on earth, the managers asked each other, would the workers
feel compelled to band together? The men were complaining about
capricious production schedules—but weren't the schedules based on
the health of automobile sales? They were complaining about harsh
dismissals and brutal justice—but weren't those prerogatives of management? And these men, these complaining hordes, were, dammit,
the best-paid in America. Their annual income was well above the national average, their hourly wage rate was 40 percent above that
which existed throughout the rest of the manufacturing industries.
Apart from a short strike of dingmen (the skilled workers who
knocked blemishes out of metal) in 1935, Chrysler escaped prolonged
trouble until 1937. The company's attitude was summed up by B. E.
Hutchinson's passionate appeal, at the 1935 annual meeting, for stock-

holders to petition Congress not to pass the Wagner Act, which threatened to allow workers to bargain collectively through a union chosen under federally supervised elections.

It was no coincidence that, in October 1935, scores of the Detroit Tigers-Chicago Cubs six-game World Series were posted on boards throughout the Chrysler plants. In 1936, there were three separate attempts to placate workers with the payment of bonuses and a simultaneous five-cent wage increase. Chrysler also resorted to less publicized methods of persuasion. Although its spying system was not as extensive as General Motors' "industrial cheka" (where foremen even inspected toilet stalls to see if a worker was producing), nor as brutal as Harry Bennett's three-thousand-strong Service Department at Ford, it still existed. When asked why the company hired spies, vice-president Herman Weckler, who was charged with responsibility for industrial relations, replied, "We must do it to obtain the information we need in dealing with our employees."[33] Chrysler escaped the first bout of sitdown strikes, which were directed against the industry leader, General Motors, rather than the toughest kernel, Ford, where the ex-boxer Bennett lay in wait with his gang of goons. Nevertheless, in 1936, when the UAW was busily organizing Chrysler, the management dismissed three thousand workers suspected of sympathizing with the union. (They were later reinstated.) When, in February 1937, the UAW gained exclusive representation at General Motors after discovering what could happen when a few men pulled some master switches and the rest sat down, Chrysler became the next target.

On March 7, 1937, 25,000 workers at Dodge Main, 8,500 at the Kercheval and Jefferson Avenue plants, 2,200 at DeSoto and 11,000 at Plymouth abruptly stopped work. The Detroit *Free Press* wailed that it was "the most dramatic wave of sit-down strikes that the auto industry has experienced in one day."[34] After four days of nervous negotiations, the company reaction was angry and immediate. "The demand that the UAW be given exclusive bargaining control over all our employes and all our plants is rejected,"[35] B. E. Hutchinson stormed. But on April 6, 1937, Chrysler finally recognized the UAW as a bargaining agent.

In the late fall of 1939, unrest again troubled the auto plants. At the Chrysler truck plant, workers merrily painted trucks different colors on either side and the entire industry ground to a halt. A walkout of 71,000 workers from Chrysler plants was held, protesting management's opposition to a closed shop and demanding that the union be given a say in setting production schedules. The Detroit *Free Press* was again horrified, editorializing that the strike was not merely inspired by communists but was "a serious sin against Detroit."[36] Michigan governor Frank Murphy prayed for divine intervention and, after

45 days, got intervention of another kind when the UAW was granted full recognition, time-and-a-half wages for work over forty hours a week and double time on Sundays.

If Walter Chrysler insisted on playing a personal role in the settlement with the union, he had been willing to leave the daily control of operations to trusted lieutenants. He preferred to worry about matters like the building of a swimming pool at his Great Neck, Long Island, retreat or the capacity of his ice-cube machine, or to indulge his passion for hamburgers. Company matters were left to the president he appointed on July 22, 1935—K. T. Keller.

Kaufman Thuma Keller became the guardian of Chrysler's legacy. "Keller and Chrysler between them," noted a prominent magazine, "have supplied the genes which have determined the corporate appearance."[37] From first to last, Keller was Chrysler's man. Like Chrysler and his immediate successors as president of the company, Keller was a small-town boy given to bursts of profanity and uncompromising ruggedness. Born in 1885 in the heart of Pennsylvania Dutch country, Keller was dissuaded from an early marriage and packed off to Europe by his father and grandfather. He met a traveling temperance orator aboard ship and for three years toured the British Isles as his $7.50-a-week secretary. On returning to the United States, Keller became an apprentice at Westinghouse, inspected axles for Chalmers and later was the chief inspector at Maxwell. Finally, as Buick's master mechanic, he came into regular contact with Walter Chrysler. After rising to a General Motors vice-presidency, Keller rejoined his former boss in 1926, was given the responsibility of absorbing Dodge Brothers and was made the president of Dodge in 1928. After Walter Chrysler's death from a cerebral hemorrhage in 1940, Keller became responsible for a corporate money spinner. A 1939 report on the automobile industry conducted by the Federal Trade Commission concluded that Chrysler made $66 in profit on every Plymouth compared to a $38 profit made on GM's Chevrolet and $5 on a standard Ford. Walter Chrysler and his cohorts had stolen a march on their competitors and capitalized on the profitable results of integration. Identical parts as important as front suspensions, rear axles and gear boxes had been cleverly bolted into cars built in each division. Even the engine for the Plymouth car was lowered into some Dodge light trucks. In forty years Chrysler had risen from the ruts of the carriage wheel to become second only to General Motors as the most profitable automobile company in the United States.

CHAPTER THREE

Asleep at the Wheel

As I have observed the industry, it has been impressed on me that in substantially every case where a company fell by the wayside, the controlling element was that the management worked its plants and machines right out of business.

—K. T. Keller, Chrysler president,
at the seventh Stanford Business Conference,
July 22, 1948

Chrysler marched into the Second World War and emerged decked with a five-star reputation for meeting, and beating, deadlines on all sorts of military paraphernalia. Converted Chrysler factories had been tooled to produce ambulances, troop carriers and swamp buggies. They machined delicate gyrocompasses and churned out wailing air-raid sirens. Factories accustomed to forging transmissions cranked out landing gear for aircraft and steel pontoon bridges for the invading Allied armies. Chrysler even fashioned ski runners for gliders and refrigerators for storing blood plasma. At the DeSoto plant, workers stamped wing-flaps for Martin Marauder bombers and plants which had produced the Chrysler car shoveled out 11,000 wings for

Navy hell-divers. The Second World War also started Chrysler's long association with the American battle tank. In Warren, then the rhubarb capital of Michigan, Chrysler erected a 113-acre factory (complete with marble-lined bathrooms) which was the birthplace for 25,029 medium and heavy tanks. The 7,500 Shermans were powered by "eggbeater engines" made from five V-6s designed for the 1942 Royals and Windsors. In Chicago, the automaker equipped and operated a 6.3-million-square-foot plant which sprawled over thirty city blocks and whose machine and assembly buildings alone were larger than the Pentagon. At the Dodge-Chicago plant, 18,000 eighteen-cylinder engines for the lumbering B-29 Superfortress were produced. Chrysler also engaged in far more surreptitious activities. Working behind a dowdy shopfront on Detroit's Woodward Avenue, a select team of engineers designed nickel diffusers to separate U-235 from uranium. The diffusers were carted off to Oak Ridge, Tennessee, where they speeded the Manhattan Project toward Hiroshima and Nagasaki.

But gold braid and tin hats are of little use at the end of a war. During the eight years that followed V-J Day, Chrysler squandered the advantages so painstakingly accumulated during the Thirties. The contrast between what took place at Dearborn and what failed to take place at Highland Park explains much of Chrysler's later troubles. While Henry Ford II did to Ford what Walter Chrysler, twenty years earlier, had done to Maxwell, Chrysler's management languished. K. T. Keller and his executives toyed with practical cars; demonstrated a laudable, if entirely misplaced, disdain for whimsical fashion; distributed generous dividends and maintained stubborn faith in the habits and outlook of an earlier generation. It was to Chrysler's everlasting misfortune that, at a time when Ford was reinvigorated by youth, Highland Park hardened with age.

Henry Ford II inherited a shambles. His eighty-two-year-old grandfather, who finally retired from the chairmanship in September 1945, left a management divided by fear, no cars of quality and an empty till. Ford, observed one contemporary, was "operating on a set of books that would put a country storekeeper to shame." Controls were so lackadaisical that a $50 million loss for the first seven months of 1946 was not discovered until months later. By then, however, Henry Ford II, a green twenty-eight-year-old, had lured Ernest R. Breech away from the presidency of Bendix and allowed him full rein over the domestic company. Notorious projects like the Brazilian rubber plantations, which had lost $20 million between 1927 and 1945, were unceremoniously dumped. The elder Ford's farm and mineral lands were quickly disposed of and the company's fleet of seven oceangoing ships was reduced to two ore barges. While 8,500 employees were skimmed from the payroll, Ford eagerly recruited ambitious college graduates. Management was strengthened with the appearance of the so-called "whiz kids," a group of Air Force officers who had become familiar with Ford's plight during the war. Among their ranks were Robert McNamara, later Defense Secretary during the Kennedy administration and head of the World Bank, Arjay Miller, later to become dean of the Stanford Business School, Charles Thornton, who later formed Litton Industries, and J. E. Lundy, who nursed Ford's financial affairs until his retirement in 1980. There was not a department in the company immune to the heat of change. Perhaps even more significant than all the other changes was the creation of a separate Lincoln-Mercury Division in 1946. Lincoln-Mercury dealers were split from the Ford dealers and each of the Ford divisions was given responsibility for everything but basic engineering. In 1950, Ford belatedly followed General Motors and established Ford Motor Credit to finance retail and wholesale purchase of Ford cars. Chrysler was the only member of the Big Three without a financial arm. A decision made in September 1946 started a crash program to develop the 1949 Ford, which was unveiled, none too early, in June 1948.

While Henry Ford II stirred up a tempest in Dearborn, Chrysler was becalmed. The habits of the prewar years died hard. Press previews were still rambunctious affairs held in the administrative building. Interior designers were still retained to carpet the executive garage and caterers still set up bars and dining tables in the fifth-floor executive suite. As ever, the previews lasted late into the night, with fights sometimes breaking out between reporters and company executives. More damaging than the drunken scuffles was the listlessness that spread across Chrysler, and the subsequent damage, from which Chrysler has never recovered.

After the war, Chrysler was run by an Operations Committee which met every two weeks and was composed of company president Keller and seven vice-presidents. The style of management had changed little from the early days of Walter Chrysler. One company official, in the early Fifties, likened the organization to the spokes of a rimless wooden wheel. At the hub was Keller, in direct communication with each department lying between the spokes, but for the departments, those spokes presented formidable barriers to communication. Only a man standing on the hub could see what was going on around the entire company. As the rigid separations became more deeply embedded, each department expanded into a miniature empire. There was nothing like General Motors' elaborate system of checks and balances. Chrysler had no teams of corporate officials scanning the separate divisions.

Division bosses, despite carrying the title of president, were little

more than glorified unit heads, and Dodge Division still did most of
the manufacturing for the entire company. (By contrast, the new
Lincoln-Mercury Division at Ford possessed its own manufacturing
plants.) The division heads had no tools for evaluating the performance of their operations and were simply instructed to sell as many
cars as possible. A vice-president still decided where officers should
leave their cars in the parking lot and requests for new machinery
were made on request slips, which were simply answered with "yes"
or "no."

The original engineering triumvirate of Zeder, Breer and Skelton did
little more after the war than buttress the imposing presence of the
six-story engineering and research building. At a time when mechanical triumphs were steadily outshone by styling changes, past triumphs
allowed the engineers to exercise their might over too many critical
decisions. Alan Loofbourrow, an engineer who joined Chrysler in 1937,
the day after he graduated from high school, later remembered, "The
engineering department had a completely free hand to do anything
they wanted." Engineering largely determined the size, styling and
content of cars, which would be presented for approval and only then
submitted to the careful gaze of accountants for detailed costing.
Unlike General Motors, which first determined a suitable rate of return and then worked backward from that, Chrysler's pricing policy
was virtually a postscript. "Good cost control," the engineers blithely
repeated, "lies within the draftsman's pencil." The influence of the engineers remained sturdy long after the departure of Breer in 1949 and
Zeder and Skelton in 1950.

Among the ledgers and the adding machines, B. E. Hutchinson
presided over a clean balance sheet until his retirement in 1953. He
stuck fast by his belief that Chrysler's guiding policy should be to
"engineer good products, provide good facilities with which to make
them, pay off your debts and divide what is left with your stockholders, giving them as much of it as you can." Even in 1950, after
suffering a hundred-day-long conflict with the United Auto Workers,
Hutchinson and the board still managed to pay out a juicy $2.34 divi-
dend, over a dollar more than at the end of the previous year. Hutchinson's attention was more closely absorbed by the evil of debt than
by the need for internal controls. There was no day-by-day control of
costs of current operations, little thought was given to a general strategy for investment in tools and machinery and scarcely any to projecting costs of future projects. Controls were so weak, complained a head
of Plymouth, that he was unable to find out how much it cost to build
one of his division's cars. At the company's Amplex plant, where ball
bearings were formed from powdered metal, the bookkeepers were

using a direct-labor method of assessment for operations that were in fact largely conducted by machine.

A similar contempt for newfangled ways was evident within the rudimentary sales organization. A. VanderZee, who headed the sales network, plainly stated, "What we know about retailing we have learned from the dealer and we encourage him to be self-sufficient in every respect." Not the slightest effort was made to curb the frisky dealers. Plymouths continued to be hawked by "bamboo curtain dealers"— men whose primary interest lay in the richer profits to be gleaned from Chryslers, Imperials, Dodges and DeSotos. (The imaginary "bamboo curtain" was used to hide the low-profit Plymouth, while the more expensive cars were energetically promoted.) The consolidation of Plymouth in 1928 with other lines was partly determined by the company's unwillingness to lose extra profits: the cheaper cost of distributing Plymouths allowed the marketing men to give dealers a smaller discount and consequently allowed the corporation more profit. Dealers resisted any attempt to wrest the Plymouths away, since they offered a comfortable safety net when the market softened.

A studied disdain for the need to adapt to the bolder order was displayed in Chrysler's handling of the United Auto Workers and in its dealing with the press. Both parties were considered interfering outsiders. Ever since Walter Chrysler had drained himself in the 1937 negotiations, Chrysler had retained an outside firm to cope with union demands. Labor relations were guided by Nicholas Kelley, a partner in a New York law firm who was made a Chrysler vice-president. (It didn't escape the union that a partner in Kelley's firm helped to draft the Taft-Hartley Act.) Chrysler had been the only company to refuse to comply with the umpire system for the settlement of grievances and, though the union won paid holidays from Chrysler in 1948, the company didn't even retain an actuary until late 1949.

The union had grown (to half a million members) and grown up during the days since the sit-down strikes. Bitter ideological and political fights within its upper reaches were quelled in 1946 when Walter Reuther was elected president. He quickly brought direction to the achievement of collective bargaining goals, establishing committees to study pension and health insurance programs. An extraordinary man (Murray Kempton described him as the only man he knew who could reminisce about the future), Reuther survived bloody fights with Ford stiffs and an almost fatal assassination attempt on a cool April evening in 1948, to light a progressive zeal that has never left the UAW. To the managers of the auto companies, Reuther was, at first, an oddity: a far cry from the union leaders who just wanted thicker butter on fresher bread. To the workers, who struck GM for 113 days during 1945–46 and who hurled water bags and firecrackers out of hotel windows at rowdy conventions, he was a symbol of upright ambition. As early as 1940, he landed on front pages with a plan to convert auto factories to allow production of five hundred planes a day. Before V-J Day, he suggested, with all his florid, bubbling rhetorical skill, that the government create a public corporation for building railroads and housing. He talked about "creative democracy" at a time when other unionists could scarcely spell it. He also told UAW members that "our job is to carve the fat off the companies."

The distance that existed between manager and worker was made abundantly clear in 1950 when Chrysler adamantly refused to come to terms with the UAW and agree to a pension plan that was already a *fait accompli* at GM and Ford, plus what was labeled as "the newest and most complicated gimmick in labor contracts"[1]—a 90-percent-company-paid insurance package offered by Ford. Chrysler practically refused to bargain whenever Reuther was present at the negotiating table, and the subsequent bitter 104-day strike wrought such havoc that the Detroit City Welfare Department employed Chrysler workers to trim hedges and paint fences. Upon settlement, Reuther refused to attend the customary photograph session with Chrysler officials, saying, "The attitude of the corporation has sunk to a new low. We would not dignify the company by posing with them."

By the end of 1950, with Chrysler anxious to avoid another costly stoppage, management granted the UAW a cost-of-living adjustment and an annual improvement factor (granted two years previously by General Motors and Ford) along with a $100-a-month pension for workers over sixty-five. Although the union, and Reuther particularly, liked to imply that the cost-of-living clauses were skillfully extracted from the companies, the opposite was true. In 1946, General Motors president Charles E. (Engine Charlie) Wilson aimed to bring stability to labor relations and win an accord with the increasingly powerful union by lengthening the annual contract. He proposed a two-pronged plan to ease the transition. First, prompted by the 17-percent inflation in 1946 after emergency price controls were lifted, Wilson favored a Cost-of-Living Adjustment (COLA) to tie increases in the average annual wage rate to inflation. Second, he designed an Annual Improvement Factor (AIF) to give workers a share in the increased profits resulting from rises in productivity.

Defending his proposal, in words that would make his successors squirm, Wilson argued that "present high wages are more the result of inflationary money pressures than of unreasonable wage pressures by the union. . . . It is not primarily wages that push up prices, it is primarily prices that push up wages."[2] As for the AIF, the union and the companies have, from almost the very first contract (an uncluttered single-page document) agreed on a fundamental principle: tech-

nological progress—the productive partnership of men and machines—
is the one intelligent approach to increased employment and higher
wages. As a matter of ritual, a clause in every contract ponderously re-
iterates that "to produce more with the same amount of human effort
is a sound economic and social objective."

Willing as the union was to clutch the AIF to its chest, the formula was better suited for an age of expansion, when all could share
in the gain, than to slumps when, theoretically, all should make equal
sacrifices. The basis for the annual increase has never been productivity changes in the automobile industry, but rather the average
change throughout the rest of the economy. The reason, according to
Alfred Sloan, was to avoid the "intolerable discrepancies between the
wages paid in industries where technological progress is rapidly increasing and the wages paid where technological progress must be
limited—as in the so-called 'service industries.'"[3] The AIF was a
clear refutation of all the principles of free enterprise that Sloan and
his colleagues so fervently admired. Although the auto magnates were
prepared to admit that cars had to compete against other attractive
durables, they refused to extend their logic to labor contracts. Although all of them tried to squeeze every last penny from suppliers,
they argued that different labor contracts were out of the question,
since they would offer competitive advantages. Similarly, the companies obliged themselves to abide by the rules of the new AIF, irre-
spective of whether productivity rose as predicted at the start of each
new contract. After 1955 the AIF, in the definition worked out by
the companies, made no distinction between the most efficient manufacturer and the most slovenly.

If Chrysler was not about to sully its floors with a labor department,
it had no intention of lying prostrate before the demands of the press.
All communications were fed through T. J. Ross and Associates, Inc., a
New York public relations agency. A touchy relationship sank to an
all-time low in 1947 with a small fire in Dodge Main. The Chief of
Plant Security, suitably named Ben Gunner, was convinced that the
press had no business with the fire. He met newsmen, waved them
into a guard shack and slammed and locked the door. One photog-
rapher who had the temerity to complain after being released was
pitched over a fence for his troubles.

Above and beyond all the local difficulties, it was the corporation's
president who forged Chrysler's fate. K. T. Keller bustled in and out
of the company's small styling studios with very rigid ideas about the
appearance of cars. Plucking a stubby pencil from his suit pocket, he
would scribble sketches, plans and ideas on the backs of envelopes.
Sometimes he would insist on personally supervising the layout of new
machines on a factory floor. Unlike Alfred Sloan who, at the end of

the war, concluded that the consumer would rank styling first, automatic transmissions second and high compression engines third, Keller thought that practicality should outweigh any other considerations. In 1949 he created the industry's first all-steel station wagon and established a standard measurement by ruling that the rear floor should accommodate a 4-foot-by-8-foot piece of plywood. Far more damaging were his ideas about the shape of the family car. In 1949, when the industry introduced its first line of new cars since 1941, long, sleek automobiles were lavishly unveiled by Ford and General Motors. At Chrysler, hints about the cost of retooling had led observers to expect dramatic novelty. Instead, Chrysler delivered dumpy Plymouths that bore the hand of Keller, who had personally ordered an extra one and a half inches of height. The reasons for the emphasis on height, he explained, was "that there are many parts of the country containing millions of people, where both the men and ladies are in the habit of getting behind the wheel, or on the back seat, wearing hats."[4] He was cruder before a skeptical Detroit press corps. "Chrysler," he insisted, "builds cars to sit in, not to piss over." The 1949 cars rolled out to a slogan made popular by General Motors X-cars thirty years later: "Bigger on the inside, smaller on the outside," read the ads as Chrysler contrived to fly in the face of fashion. Yet the mistake was temporarily obscured by consumers ready to buy anything that rolled. (Even the 1949 Ford, which one observer reckoned had eight thousand defects, was snapped up.)

Just months after the preview for the 1949 models, Keller became chairman of the company, a position left vacant since Walter Chrysler's death. Chrysler's glittering war record prompted President Truman to request that the new chairman head the Pentagon's guided missile program. Although Keller's attention was thereafter divided between the heavens and the highways, his influence was felt at Highland Park until his retirement in 1956. His last significant act as president was to lay an uninspiring hand on the 1953 cars.

At a time when the public was fast becoming convinced that there was little else but style to separate the labels that rolled off the end of the Detroit lines, Keller held fast. General Motors and Ford lengthened hoods and puffed up fenders while Chrysler actually shortened their 1953 cars. A mere eight weeks after introduction, dealers began to bootleg the cars to secondhand merchants. The first of Chrysler's many years of reckoning was 1953. Although sales increased, earnings were down by 5 percent and the stock price slumped from 96¼ to 56¼ as Chrysler forever lost its hold on second place. Ford, having skillfully weathered its own private agony, edged toward a quarter of the market while Chrysler slithered to little more than a fifth.

The end of fighting in Korea coincided with a recession which, as the bootlegged cars showed, strengthened the buyer's hand. The independent automakers, which had garnered an 18.6-percent share of the market in 1946, rapidly lost their blush. Crosley foundered in 1952. A year later, Kaiser-Frazer merged with Willys-Overland, and in 1954 American Motors Corporation was forged from two unprofitable companies, Hudson Motor Car Company and Nash-Kelvinator Corporation. By 1955, when Kaiser-Frazer abandoned the manufacture of small cars, only five producers, including Studebaker, remained.

While Ford and General Motors adapted to changing perceptions, Chrysler clung to the belief that superior engineering would permit premium pricing. In the past, Chrysler's mechanical triumphs had permitted such a strategy. Messrs. Zeder, Skelton and Breer had, after all, knitted together a solid string of firsts: the high-compression engine, fully automatic spark control, roller-bearing universal joints and automatic overdrive. After World War II, apart from the advent of fully automatic transmission, innovations in Detroit were about as rare as a Ford in a General Motors parking lot. Although Chrysler still supplied more than its share of novelties, no technological breakthroughs comparable to earlier advances were achieved. In 1949, for example, Chrysler's primary achievement was a key-operated combination ignition and starter switch; a year later, the roll-down window in the tailgate of a station wagon was magnified into a considerable marvel. As the industry entered its somnolent years and drivers became accustomed to cars that would start at the turn of a key, and change gears automatically, Chrysler's belief in the extra value of engineering was a sad delusion. As the Fifties progressed, the price difference between Chrysler and the competition disappeared. Traditionally, Fords had been sold at between $20 and $30 above the Chevrolet, while the Plymouth sold at $100 above the Chevrolet. Come 1953, the difference was trimmed to between $60 and $70. By 1956, it had fallen to between $40 and $45, and within another year it had vanished. Some Plymouth models even carried sticker prices lower than the equivalent Chevrolet.

Clobbered by the disappearance of its pricing advantage, Chrysler also had to cope with the cost of more frequent styling changes. Ever since Henry Ford acknowledged the need for freshness with his 1927 Model A, major changes had occurred every four or five years with "facelifting" alterations in between. After the Korean War, the cycle began to shorten. Greater affluence, the freeways that were being built from coast to coast and stronger faith in the reliability of automobiles combined to fill suburban driveways with second and third cars. The changes heightened Detroit's eagerness to tempt (and prod) buyers into more expensive cars. The newest style, provided that it avoided the outlandish and was supplied in a sufficiently imposing manner, inevitably held an advantage. With the more rapid changes came spiraling costs. Even in the mid-Fifties, a new silhouette, which usually offered nothing more than a change in form, could cost a manufacturer $100 million. Retooling costs rose, depreciation periods were shortened and profitability, especially for the smaller companies, was reduced.

Beyond the extra costs, which were amply reflected in financial statements, the new practices imposed extra burdens on almost every department. Chrysler, not equipped to deal with a revolution in frippery, was hard pressed to cope with the new market forces.

The man given the task of responding to the changes was a burly Texan, Lester Lum Colbert. In 1954, at the first preview over which he presided, Colbert informed the assembled press of Chrysler's new goal. It was something that previously always had been taken for granted: a 20-percent share of the United States car and truck market. Like his predecessors, Colbert hailed from a small town: Oakwood in the East Texas pine country. He was a successful cotton trader at an age when most boys are still tossing marbles. Arriving at Harvard Law School with five thousand dollars in accumulated trading profits, he hijacked a fire engine during an otherwise undistinguished career and left in 1929 without a recommendation from the dean. Colbert rapped on Wall Street doors until Nicholas Kelley, a partner in Chrysler's law firm, impressed by Colbert's dress and confidence, offered him a job.

His first task was to help reorganize a small facial tissue company in Pennsylvania owned by Walter Chrysler's son-in-law. Pleased by Colbert's work, Walter Chrysler summoned him to his office atop the Chrysler Building, where he sat surrounded by a collection of penny clocks. Chrysler invited Colbert to start a legal department within the company and, several days later, the pair was sipping contraband whiskey in a plush suite aboard *The Detroiter,* the overnight train which ran from New York to Detroit. Convinced that he had the stuff of an automobile man, Keller dispatched Colbert to night school to learn the details of blueprints and machine tools. Colbert handled part of the 1937 labor negotiations, but made his mark during World War II as manager of the massive Dodge airplane plant. With work bogged down in the mud of a Chicago spring, Colbert hired twenty-five horses from a local riding academy so that he and his supervisors could spur construction. The plant contributed much to the war effort and a little more to the career of Tex Colbert. By the end of the war, he was president of the Dodge Division. Colbert was offered a job by Henry Ford II in 1948, but he stayed on to become the president of Chrysler in November 1950. Until Keller retired from the chairmanship in 1956, though, Colbert labored under the uncompromising influence of men rooted in the Thirties. Indeed, he had to transform a company cradled in the comfort of the late Thirties to one capable of entering the Sixties. Throughout the second half of the 1950s, Chrysler was perpetually in the throes of reorganization. When one policy was discredited, another would be tried in a continual effort to make up the ground surrendered in the postwar years.

Almost immediately, Colbert, despite Keller's objections, retained the management consultants McKinsey & Company to provide suggestions for a comprehensive overhaul of Chrysler. Buried in the six-foot-high report were recommendations that Chrysler should become an international company, decentralize its domestic management and curb the influence of the engineering department.

Colbert attempted to decentralize almost everything he could lay his hands on. A flock of vice-presidents was created to take control of separate operations. However, the centralization of the earlier regime, coupled with its amateurish approach to college recruitment, forced Colbert to a desperate ploy. In the middle of an industry that prides itself on promotion from within, he was forced to place newspaper advertisements for new managers. Everywhere Colbert turned, he encountered imposing pockets of resistance. He attempted, for example, to convert the Central Engineering Department into a policy and service organization which would reach into every division, but by 1956, with his policies foundering on indifference and outright hostility, Colbert made an about-face. All engine production was consolidated in a central manufacturing division. The sales representatives were snatched from the divisions and put into a central staff. Although the Dodge Division virtually ignored all attempts at integration, by 1958 Chrysler was as fully centralized as it ever had been under Walter Chrysler or K. T. Keller. The only important tasks left for the division heads were cost control and purchasing—and the purchasing system, which suffered several upheavals, was in itself adequate testament to Colbert's failure. Even the formation of a Purchase Analysis Group in 1956 to supervise annual orders was not sufficient to placate the General Accounting Office, which monitored Chrysler's military contracts. The GAO witheringly reported in 1958 that Chrysler's "apparent acceptance of a lack of cost control under time and materials subcontracting indicates . . . a need for close supervision." As a result, the Army Ordnance Corps withdrew Chrysler's authority to sign time and material subcontracts without prior approval.

Colbert quickly discovered that land and plants were more tractable than junior managers. In a massive expansion of Chrysler's plants, he built three new assembly plants, a couple of transmission factories and a sizable stamping plant, plus boosting Chrysler's glass-making ability. VIP's were whirled by helicopter around the 3,800 acres of the company's new proving ground and, with the $75 million purchase

of Briggs Body, Chrysler was assured of a constant and captive supply
of car bodies. In the thirteen years after V-J Day, Chrysler invested
$1.3 billion in new plants, of which $936 million was spent, after
Keller's departure, between 1953 and 1958. Yet growth did not come
from within, and in 1954 the balance sheet was blotted with a
hundred-year, $250 million loan agreement with the Prudential Insur-
ance Company.

The uncertainty in the executive suite seemed to extend to the cars.
At the 1955 preview, Colbert, along with his chief stylist, Virgil Exner,
attempted to curb Chrysler's accelerating weakness with an elaborate
show of "new fashions in motion." Inspired by a McCann-Erickson
campaign dubbed "The Forward Look," the new platoon out-
measured the opposition in practically every way. The Plymouth was
stretched 10½ inches to 204 inches (compared with 198 for Ford and
196 for Chevrolet) while the Dodge lined 212 inches of curb. The cars,
which rolled out in 173 two-tone and even some three-tone combinations, sported automatic transmissions on the dashboard and temporarily boosted Chrysler's market share to 16.8 percent (from 12.9 percent in 1954).

Whatever else might have been lacking, Chrysler was not short of
marketing tricks. At twenty separate displays staged for dealers in
1956, the sky was dappled with fireworks and the features of each car
were explained on a forty-foot-high movie screen. That year, all
Chrysler cars were available with 16⅔-rpm record players. It was an
option that purchasers chose to ignore, despite earnest promises that
not even the boldest bounce could spoil a tune. Other customers were
besieged with the jingle "It's de-lightful, it's de-lovely, it's De-Soto."
Management clearly thought otherwise: the car was permanently dis-
continued with the next model change.

Chrysler's predicament was presented in bold relief with the 1957
cars. Despite an early flurry of approvals, the cars helped push the
corporation close to disaster a year later. Convinced that Chrysler
could regain a larger market share, Colbert cut twelve months from
the thirty-six-month cycle for developing new cars, substantially increased production costs and imposed added burdens on the engineering and manufacturing departments. The 1957 cars bore the scars of
the forced pace. When production started, only 44 percent of the dies
were complete. The doors and windows leaked, the body panels
rusted and several series of engines were poorly designed and scrap-
pily built. Dealers took to drying out mats and cross-over wires in the
showroom. Not only did the 1957 cars offer appalling quality, they
also offered fins. Although Cadillac had given the world fins in 1948,
Chrysler's 1957 versions outshone earlier efforts. The "flight-sweep"
cars were larger, lower and wider than any on the road. In a dramatic

counterpoint to Keller's chair-high seats, passengers now found themselves reclining directly above the suspension.

Almost as spectacular as the flaring fins was Colbert's failure to drum order into the chaotic dealer network. There had never been close supervision of the dealers from Detroit and there was little concern about showroom standards, the accumulation of inventory or any of the other problems that habitually plague car dealers. Chrysler continued to be concerned only with the money paid by independent distributors or wholesalers, who then sold the cars to dealers. Early in Colbert's tenure, the dealers made plain both their strength and their spirit when on Good Friday, 1954, they presented what was described as an "extraordinary pair of demands which would have shocked even the U.A.W.'s Walter Reuther."[5] They demanded that the factory immediately cut the price of Dodges and allow a dealer to attend the next board meeting. The company complied with the first request, but recoiled before the second.

In an effort that extended for almost a decade, Colbert endeavored to create a separate Plymouth dealer network. Plymouth's overall market share, which had occupied a spacious niche in the Thirties, dropped by almost half after 1946 to 6.46 percent in 1949. Freshly recruited Plymouth dealers were franchised by the newly formed Chrysler Motors Corporation, but Colbert paid dearly for his coup: he was forced to offer the Dodge dealers a substitute for the Plymouth. Thus, unlike General Motors, which had always gone to extreme lengths to prevent internal cannibalism, the new Plymouth Division was competing against Ford, Chevrolet and Dodge.

The dealers were not the only obstreperous bunch. The bitterness of the 1950 strike set the tone for much of the labor unrest that bedeviled Chrysler thereafter. Although Colbert took pains to call on Walter Reuther and even gave UAW officials an early peek at 1955 models, the union dismissed what some heralded as a revolutionary approach to labor relations for what it was—a hearty sales pitch.

If some of the union's demands in 1955 were a surprise, the manner of their presentation turned into a ritual. In previous years, union representatives would visit GM's headquarters on West Grand Boulevard, Ford's in Dearborn and Chrysler's in Highland Park. The companies would then denounce the union demands as preposterous while Reuther and his colleagues would lambaste the management for intransigence. More important than the posturing, though, was the gentlemen's agreement arrived at by the Big Three. The companies that escaped a strike henceforth automatically matched the "pattern agreement" signed by the target company. For the twenty-five years after the end of World War II, the target company was always Ford or

Chrysler, where the union felt it could obtain the greatest gain with the least amount of pain.

As important as the rhythm of the three-year contract established in 1955 were the supplemental unemployment benefits won from Ford, the target that year. A forerunner of the guaranteed annual wage, the so-called "SUB benefits," a supplement to State Unemployment Compensation, required that the companies contribute to a fund to provide workers with 65 percent of their normal pay for the first four weeks of any layoff and 60 percent for the succeeding twenty-two weeks. When the Ford negotiators first heard details of the scheme, they were horrified. John Bugas, Ford's Vice-President of Labor Relations, told Reuther, "This is something that we will never, never do." Reuther admonished, "Never say never, John."[6] Even after Bugas had been made to eat his words, the company insisted that the guaranteed semi-annual wage was not guaranteed, semi-annual or a wage—but it was a momentous change. For the first time, the automakers had to pay their workers whenever the factories closed.

Chrysler was more seriously upset by labor unrest than either General Motors or Ford. In the mid-Fifties, in an attempt to improve productivity, the work force was severely pruned—a move that made those who remained more militant. Unlike its competitors, who had understood the advantages of widely scattered assembly plants, Chrysler's factories sat on the doorstep of the union. More significant still was the traditional autonomy of the Chrysler locals, which was heightened after the company purchased the Briggs Body Company in 1953. Under Emil Mazey, later secretary-treasurer of the union, the Briggs workers (known as "The Dead-end Kids") earned a reputation for untrammeled militancy. Quick tempers and a tendency to down tools at the slightest provocation were beyond the scope of the UAW's Chrysler Department, which was split between the ebullience of Mazey and the more moderate inclinations of its joint leader, Norman Matthews. Tensions between union headquarters and the suspicious locals were heightened when a Chrysler executive leaked the knowledge of the former's sympathy for Chrysler's growing labor problems. If the union hierarchy privately blanched at the behavior of its Chrysler members, much of the trouble was also due to Chrysler's unwillingness to allow factory foremen to settle disputes. By the time isolated incidents had been referred to the relevant authority, the unrest had inevitably spread. Art Hughes, the UAW's Chrysler Department administrative assistant, recalled that "the prime reason for the existence of Chrysler foremen was to get production out." Thousands of wildcat strikes sprang from the bewildering confusion. Fumes in the paint shop would send the painters out. An argument over whether smocks or overalls should be worn would make the assemblers quit, and metal finishers often refused to tolerate their dusty surroundings. One typical wildcat, deplored by management and union officials alike, occurred in the summer of 1954. When a few Dodge Main assemblers struck in a dispute over the number of screws needed in the molding that secured windshields, 45,000 workers were made idle. Violent swings in production, caused by deteriorating sales performance, did not contribute to the stability of the work force and inevitably affected quality. Pat Quinn, president of the Dodge Main local, observed at the time that "We have a war over standards in the bad years. In the good years they [Chrysler management] just don't care."

Labor unrest was positively the last thing Chrysler needed in 1958. The year was an unmitigated disaster and the results of the first quarter prompted commentators to wonder aloud how much longer Chrysler could survive. During the first three months, Chrysler shipped less than half the cars and trucks delivered during the comparable period in 1957. Although the other companies were affected, with GM's sales dropping by 17 percent and Ford's by 36 percent, only Chrysler reported a loss. The loss of $29.6 million (after tax credits) on the year was the first spurt of red ink to blot the income statement since the worst years of the Depression. Proof of Chrysler's troubles came when the financial officers scurried to one hundred banks to arrange an emergency $150 million line of credit.

No small part of the extra burden was caused by the need to accommodate the public's demand for compact cars. The industry had willingly forgotten some of the lessons of the early years. Henry Ford had sold the Model T as "a good car at a low price" while Charles Kettering, the innovator who lay behind the self-starter, Duco paint, ethyl gasoline and much of GM's early success, had warned in 1924 that "the wanton consumption of horsepower in propelling heavy motor vehicles portends disaster."[7] Streets, he noticed, "are absurdly congested with these great empty vehicles," and he hastened to alert the automakers of the "signs that point the way to a smaller, less expensive car." During World War II, Walter and Victor Reuther had urged the construction of a victory car: a small car that all the companies would pool their resources to build and sell at the same price.

Immediately after World War II and during the recession at the end of the Fifties, Americans had conducted fleeting love affairs with small cars. Even before the end of 1945, General Motors and Ford announced plans to build small, lightweight cars that would provide another generation with its very own version of the Model T, but by the fall of 1946, the manufacturers changed their minds. GM's car eventually emerged as the Holden in Australia and Ford's as the Vedette in France. Only Chrysler, which announced plans for a small car in 1946, stuck by its decision. In 1949, alongside the full-size Plymouths and

Dodges, Chrysler wheeled out shorter, two-door versions—priced between $30 and $50 below their larger counterparts—which were dropped within three years.

At the beginning of the Fifties, the independents, though hampered by poor quality and flimsy dealer networks, showed the large companies the danger of bringing out small cars carrying anything other than low sticker prices. The Nash Rambler, Kaiser's Henry J., the Hudson Jet and the Willys Aero were all priced below the standard Chevrolet and failed to sell in anything like the volumes needed to turn a profit.

Anxious to believe any signal that showed Americans were unwilling to tool around in noisy little tin cans, Detroit primped their cars, adding flounces, gaudy ornaments, lashings of chrome, tricolor combinations and slick, wraparound windshields. The automakers believed that a used American car would quite comfortably satisfy America's incomprehensible demands for cheap transportation. No matter how many arguments Detroit leveled against small, economical cars, consumers would not be swayed. High-ranking automobile executives constantly told audiences that no compact car priced under $2,000 with less than a 300,000-unit run made economic sense. The public failed to heed their advice. In the mid-Fifties, they began to demand more V-6s, better fuel consumption and, most painful of all, cheaper purchase prices. With the onset of the 1958 recession, the demand grew.

The only cars that seemed to fit the bill were the small Ramblers of George Romney's newly formed American Motors and the curious little imports. From a paltry 58,000 units in 1955, imports rose to 379,000 (or 8.1 percent of the market) in 1958. Rambler sales more than doubled between 1957 and 1958, reaching 186,000. The combination of the cheap Rambler and the cheaper imports became something more than a local irritation. It demanded attention. Within another twelve months, the imports were selling 609,000 (10.1 percent). Rambler sales had blossomed to 363,000, and even Studebaker sold 133,000 of its 108½-inch-wheelbase Lark. The public's lust for smallness was more than embarrassing. In 1959, the combination of the imports, the Rambler and the Lark took almost one-fifth of the entire market, threatening to take a large chunk out of profits—for, by the end of the Fifties, Detroit had carefully deserted the low-priced market. The major automakers now found themselves stranded on a plateau where the pickings had appeared to be much richer. In 1959, only 39 percent of all U.S. production was priced at or below $2,400. The proportion had risen to slightly more than half by 1960. In 1961, it approached 60 percent.

Not only did compacts make nasty inroads into corporate profits, they also forced Chrysler in particular to abandon its drive for interchangeability of parts between models. Management would have preferred to delay its compact entry until it could have made a simultaneous launch with its standard-size cars, but the new Valiants, Ford Falcons and Chevrolet Corvairs were part of a larger change. Within five years the Big Three were aiming to introduce over thirty new cars. As was to become pathetically predictable during the succeeding twenty years, Chrysler was caught at the worst possible time. If it wished to remain competitive, it had no alternative but to match its rivals step for step. So, in the middle of the worst business slowdown since the end of World War II, Chrysler embarked upon a massive model change and at the same time had to endure more personnel troubles as well. Colbert deftly fashioned his own noose on April 28, 1960, when he chose William Newberg to become the next president of Chrysler. During the months that followed, the expression "conflict of interest" became a common phrase in the American vocabulary. By the time the tawdry dealings had been thoroughly examined, various questions had arisen about the quality of Chrysler's management. At the end of the public battle, most of the old guard had either resigned or retired. The company mounted a public relations campaign that would have an uncanny similarity to the one that followed the 1979 loan guarantees.

William Newberg was a brusque engineer who had joined Chrysler as a test driver in 1933. He hopscotched his way up the corporation in Colbert's footprints, working for his mentor at the Dodge-Chicago plant during the Second World War and later being appointed head of Dodge. By 1960, he was complaining to fellow executives that Colbert was taking an unseemly amount of time promoting him to the presidency of the corporation.

Chrysler's stock dropped as Newberg rose. The company's miserable fortunes fueled the ire of a bushy-browed Detroit lawyer who owned five thousand shares. In Sol Dann, Chrysler could not have met a more determined foe. A former supporter of the Irish freedom fighters and the Irgun, Dann had sued General Motors, heckled American Motors' George Romney and charged Studebaker-Packard with misrepresentation. In 1958, he began to send waves rushing toward Chrysler, aiming to wash Colbert from the bridge. While Dann was never able to prove that a number of improbable business connections had resulted in Chrysler paying higher prices or suffering lower profits, his carefully orchestrated histrionics had the desired effects. For four years, he was a fixture at Chrysler stockholder meetings that attracted overflow crowds. Dragging laundry bags full of evidence and setting up card tables stacked with books and papers, he charged the company with "nepotism, payola, bribery and misconduct." In 1961, when he was nominated as a director, Dann pleaded incompetence and informed the chairman, Tex Colbert, "I don't feel I know anymore about building automobiles or running a corporation than *you* do, Mr. Chairman."

The first victim was Newberg who, sixty-four days after his appointment to the presidency, was summoned to a special board meeting in New York. He was abruptly asked to resign, and returned to Detroit on a separate plane from the other directors. Back in his office, he was forced to clear his desk under the eyes of a company official. The reasons behind Newberg's departure were successfully concealed for several weeks, with the press vainly speculating that Colbert had not granted the degree of latitude Newberg expected. Meanwhile, Colbert's resumption of the presidency prompted a renewed burst of activity from Dann. In a further series of suits, he charged that Chrysler was forced to purchase welding gas, headlamps and trim from companies with which its executives enjoyed incestuous relationships.

Meanwhile, the real reasons for Newberg's dismissal were revealed when Chrysler sued him for $450,000, the alleged profits resulting from his interest in companies which manufactured hinges and door-trim panels solely for Chrysler. Within a year of his enforced retirement, Newberg turned on Colbert. Through a statement read at the 1961 annual meeting, he charged, "We can never again have a strong Chrysler under the czarist rule of Mr. Colbert."

The personal feud culminated in a fight between the two men in the locker room of the Bloomfield Hills Country Club. Finally, the battle was resolved in an out-of-court settlement in 1970 when Newberg received $85,000 from Colbert and Chrysler.

In Highland Park, introspection suddenly became fashionable. Under the supervision of four outside directors, Chrysler's own lawyers and auditors embarked on an investigation that resulted in the dismissal of Jack Minor, a marketing director, for allegedly receiving commissions from advertisements placed with companies in which he had interests. The New York law firm of 1948 presidential candidate Tom Dewey, which was specially retained to set a seal of approval upon Chrysler's internal investigations, duly seconded the in-house report, which had concluded that some officials did indeed hold stock in supplier companies, but "in all instances the size of the holding and the circumstances surrounding it are such as to satisfy us that the interest did not involve any reasonable likelihood of affecting the executive's judgement in acting for Chrysler."

Newberg's resignation and Colbert's return to the presidency had not pacified Dann. Finally Colbert resigned from the chairmanship and presidency on July 27, 1961. Too young to qualify for the company's pension program, Colbert assumed the chairmanship of

Chrysler Canada to tide himself over until he reached retirement age.

For slightly less than two months after Colbert's resignation, Chrysler labored on without a chairman of the board. Finally, on September 21, 1961, George Love, then chairman of the Executive Committee, assumed the post. Born in 1900 and educated at Andover, Princeton and the Harvard Business School, Love added a competent and polished presence to Chrysler's severely tarnished image. He had originally joined the board, on Colbert's invitation, in 1958. After details of the scandal began to rain down on the company, it was Love who took charge of the internal inquisition. He assumed his duties at Chrysler while continuing as chairman of the Pittsburgh-based Consolidation Coal Company. Dann was, at last, pacified, despite the fact that Consolidation Coal gradually increased its stake in Chrysler until it owned more than 7 percent of the common stock. "Where there is Love," Dann told the stockholders at his next annual appearance, "there is hope."

Love, however, played down his role at Chrysler. "I don't know what a carburetor is," he said, "and I'm too old to learn." Heading a search for a new president, Love authorized approaches to Edward Cole, then general manager of Chevrolet (and later president of General Motors), and Semon E. Knudsen, general manager of Pontiac (who later became president of Ford). Snubbed by Cole, Knudsen and others, and worried lest the directors be sued for dereliction of duty, Love agreed to become father confessor to the man who had been administrative vice-president of Chrysler for under a year, Lynn Townsend. At the age of forty-two, Townsend had sufficient time to control the fuel and air that gushed into the corporate carburetor. As the Detroit *News* wistfully observed, he had "enough years left to become as firmly and affectionately identified with Chrysler as Alfred P. Sloan, Jr., was with General Motors."

CHAPTER FOUR

"The Big Thing Was Volume"

This country is filled with developing industries. And there are lots of chances. You simply want to make yourself smart enough to recognize them before the other fellow does. If I were you, I'd qualify myself for accountancy. Young accountants are sent around by their firms to audit the books of companies everywhere. They have a skill that makes them mighty valuable in business; indispensable. They often get chances to go to work for companies whose books they have audited.

—Advice offered by Walter Chrysler to a young man in 1937

It is easy to see why Lynn Townsend's conception of the future was a lot brighter, bigger and bolder than the reality he found in 1960. At home, it seemed that every self-respecting American would live in the suburbs and have a couple of cars parked in the driveway. Prices were steady, the country was emerging from a recession and each year a million more youngsters were due to turn sixteen than a decade ear-

lier. For the first time, auto executives talked openly about the possibility of selling 10 million cars and trucks in one year. At Chrysler the
internal forecasts predicted an 11.8-million-unit market by 1970 and
more than 15 million annual sales by the middle of the Seventies.
Overseas markets promised to rival the North American market in importance, and U.S. companies were starting to ship their technology
and managerial talent to Europe and South America with increasing
enthusiasm. It was fast becoming obvious that any American manager
who planned substantial corporate growth would have to turn his
company into a multinational. Surveying the history of mergers and
bankruptcies that had occurred within the automobile industry during
the previous forty years, it was clear that any company wishing to be
a true member of Detroit's Big Three in 1980 would have to be rolling
cars out of factories scattered around the world. Most important,
Americans were the unchallenged masters of business, and the
greatest industry of all was the automobile industry. GM's Charlie Wilson had been President Eisenhower's Secretary of Defense and John
Kennedy turned to Ford's Robert McNamara for his. Detroit was
where the tigers worked. And for Lynn Townsend, as for the bosses of
General Motors and Ford, the hunting looked good.

At Chrysler, the game looked ever juicier. If the previous generation
had failed from a lack of imagination and a shortage of ambition,
nobody was going to accuse Lynn Townsend and his recruits of lacking flair. These men weren't the innovators of old; they were of a generation that had attended the business schools endowed with the
riches of the founding fathers of American enterprise. They were
bushy-tailed MBAs who had long been drilled that what was good for
American business was certainly good for them.

In the fall of 1961, Chrysler bought full-page newspaper advertisements in cities across the country and told all who cared to read
them "What's ahead for Chrysler." The new generation of Chrysler
men, said the ads, intend to "Fix what's wrong, keep what's right and
move ahead." There was plenty to fix, little to keep and far to go.
Chrysler's market share had toppled to 10.7 percent in 1961. The company's reputation for quality had fallen by the wayside with the 1957
cars, while the corporate image had been sullied by the scandal in the
corporate suite; there were only skeletal foreign subsidiaries and
even non-automotive parts of the company had been neglected; yet
everywhere, there was a chance to make a sweet killing. If he played
his cards right, Townsend did indeed have a chance to make his name
part of the folklore of Detroit.

In later years, Lynn Townsend was all too frequently and all too
glibly dismissed as an accountant who ran an automobile company by
the numbers. Townsend, they came to murmur in increasingly gleeful

whispers around the bar of the Detroit Press Club and anywhere else the full-time observers of the automobile industry gathered, knew nothing about cars and too much about Generally Accepted Accounting Principles. He was, said the press corps, worthy of Detroit's most fulsome insult: Lynn Townsend was "a beancounter."

In his better years, Lynn Townsend was more alive to the main chance than many a Detroit executive with twenty years more experience. He had none of the sizzle and razzmatazz always associated with another young whiz, Ford's Lee Iacocca, but in his own insistent way, Townsend was a poker player who dealt a hand of marketing aces. For half a dozen years, his efforts seemed wildly successful. There was scarcely anything he could do wrong. The directors began to dote on him, and the stockholders readily applauded his every move.

Lynn Townsend was determined to sell Chrysler cars anywhere he could, and he did. "I've never seen a car that wasn't sold," he was fond of saying. For Townsend, volume was the beginning and the end of the automobile industry and one of his primary aims was to return Chrysler to the role of a full-line manufacturer. For a time it all seemed to work. The once half-empty order books began to fill; the plants began to hum; the freight trains rolling from the railheads were stacked full of gaily painted cars and Chrysler sold more cars and trucks than ever seemed possible during the gloom at the end of the Fifties. "The big thing," said Townsend, "was volume."

Lynn Townsend was never a bashful man and, for the first fifty years of his life, he had no need for modesty. He was born in 1919 in Flint, Michigan, where Walter Chrysler was still head of Buick. Lynn Townsend, Sr., was a farmboy from Hadley, Michigan, who after high school found work at the Chevrolet Motor Company and became a skilled mechanic. He had a knack for accumulating and understanding money and, with his savings, began to invest in rental properties in Flint. In 1923, mainly to alleviate the asthmatic attacks of his wife, Georgia, the senior Townsend packed his brood into a large Dort touring car for a muddy trip to their new home: Los Angeles. Young Lynn was lucky ever to see the promised land. Just outside Los Angeles, during a pause for water, he slipped into a fast-flowing irrigation ditch and almost drowned.

With his family installed in a Beverly Hills home (complete with a backyard aviary), Townsend, Sr., opened United Motors, an "orphan" repair shop to service cars made by companies that had fallen by the wayside. Tutored at home by an ambitious mother who dispatched him to learn the violin at the Hollywood Conservatory of Music and Arts, Lynn Townsend bowed into public life by hopping straight into the second half of second grade. His flair for numbers was acquired during weekends spent at the garage watching his father do the book-keeping. Within four years, though, the good life evaporated. Georgia Townsend died in 1929, the Depression dented the repair shop's business and Townsend, Sr., died of a heart attack while driving down a Flint street in 1933.

An orphan at fourteen, Townsend went to live with his uncle, a company controller in Evansville, Illinois, where he graduated from high school within weeks of turning sixteen. Too young for college, he spent the next fifteen months working for a local bank. He ran bounced checks back to clients, collecting from them on the spot, and ferreted into every department of the bank. Convinced that he was cut out for banking, Lynn Townsend proceeded to the University of Michigan. Although he had a small monthly income from his parents' estate, it scarcely covered half his expenses, so he landed a job at a local accounting firm and peeled potatoes at a fraternity to make ends meet. One former roommate reckons that "Lynn not only put himself through school, but when he graduated, he had more money than when he started." Townsend soon married (the daughter of an accounting professor) and quickly acquired a 1937 Dodge and a bachelor's degree in 1940.

Although he scarcely dazzled the undergraduate school, Townsend's performance at the graduate business school was a different matter. Accounting professor William Paton, among whose twenty thousand students was former General Motors chairman Frederic Donner, remembered that he had "never taught a student who had a greater flair for accounting and financial analysis than Lynn Townsend." In 1941, Townsend finished second in his class, but had to skip graduation ceremonies to attend the birth of his first child. One day later, he rolled up for work at the Detroit offices of accountants Ernst and Ernst. Shortly after flying through his CPA examinations, Townsend joined the Navy Supply Corps, went through boot camp at the Great Lakes base and a supply course at the Harvard Business School, then was assigned to the aircraft carrier U.S.S. *Hornet* off Okinawa. Within a year of V-J Day, George Bailey, a managing partner of Ernst and Ernst, invited the young accountant to join his newly formed firm— Touche, Ross, Bailey and Smart. Townsend quickly accepted and almost as quickly came into contact with Chrysler Corporation. He helped conduct the yearly audit in 1947 and thereafter began to peer behind the lines of the financial statements, but it wasn't until 1954 that Townsend and Chrysler began to get on intimate terms. With K. T. Keller distracted by his Washington business, Colbert summoned the company's auditors to try to straighten out the antiquated financial management system. Outside help turned out to be unsatisfactory, so Townsend was hired in 1957 as comptroller and given full rein to provide discipline. Once installed, he hired financial experts from Ford and introduced three cost-control programs: a current-profit plan which allowed daily control of costs and operations; a capital-investment program to control expenditures on tools and a forward-cost-control program to control costs on new cars. All Townsend really did was to provide the shape and form of financial programs that had become articles of faith at General Motors and Ford. Nevertheless, the achievement was considerable and, as keeper of the purse, Townsend's influence seeped into every department. He wasn't blind to his privileged position and predicted to contemporaries that, within two years, he would be president. He wasn't far wrong. Astonished at the Young Turk's success, the board gave Townsend responsibility for purchases of overseas companies and, in 1959, invited him to join their circle. In 1960, in the wake of the Newberg scandals, Townsend, as the freshly appointed Administrative Vice-President, virtually controlled the daily workings of the company. At the time, Robert Anderson (later chairman of Rockwell International) then Chrysler's Chief Product Planner, considered his boss "One of the most intelligent men I have ever met. His grasp of things is phenomenal."

Townsend's appearance at the breach was similar to Lee Iacocca's two decades later. Nothing escaped his scrutiny. He roamed the styling studios, purchased computers and wielded a well-balanced paring knife. Heeding the lessons of the late Fifties, when Chrysler introduced a precise electronic push-button transmission that flopped because most people were used to conventional levers, Townsend strove for less radical innovations. He sought to keep Chrysler's cars within the styling boundaries prescribed by General Motors. Too late to influence anything earlier than the 1963 models, Townsend managed to save Chrysler from launching an asymmetrical Plymouth. The designs for the car called for a raised headrest on the driver's side only, three sets of taillights and a third crease running off-center along the top of the hood. That, coming on top of a Plymouth with a rear like a duck's butt and a Dodge ending in a conch shell, would have taken Chrysler beyond the bounds of decency.

Unable to alter the 1962 cars, Townsend spent $125 million making late changes to the 1963s. He eliminated the low-volume Lancer and replaced it with a super-compact Dart and managed to change every piece of sheet metal within fourteen months. He tore up plans for the 1963 Plymouth less than a year before introduction and managed to move up the 1964 Dodge by a year. The results were indisputable. Ronald Esserman, a Chicago dealer, reminisced, "It used to be that when the cars came in here from Detroit, the doors didn't fit, the moldings didn't jibe, and the upholstery wasn't straight. This year everything fits perfectly." The public thought so, too. A market share that had reached an all-time low of 8.3 percent in February 1962 rose to 12.4 percent by December 1963, ten weeks after the introduction of the new Townsend line.

Unlike Colbert, Townsend was not intimidated by subordinates arguing that cuts should not be made. "If you cannot do this without disrupting your operations," he informed his underlings, "I'm sure there is someone else who can." Within months of becoming Administrative Vice-President, Townsend had reduced the white-collar payroll by seven thousand (25 percent of the entire force). The company's comptroller found himself with two assistants rather than three, and seven hundred clerks were replaced by a single IBM 790 computer. The merger of the Chrysler-Imperial and Plymouth divisions—for Townsend thought any division should produce at least 500,000 units a year—cut staffs ranging from public relations to product planning. (DeSoto had crumpled in 1960 as a result of the trend toward compacts and the dwindling demand for higher-priced cars.) Townsend ordered the doors closed at the Chrysler-Imperial plant in Detroit and a foundry in Indianapolis. He combined the work of two transmission plants, reduced the number of courtesy drivers, sold the fleet of private airplanes and fired the pilots. The result, said Townsend, was a reduction in the break-even level to 600,000 units, without doing anything, he said, to reduce the company's potential. Noting that Chrysler's distribution system remained the single greatest problem, Townsend moved nimbly. Chrysler's distribution headaches had worsened when DeSoto folded; DeSoto dealerships had become new Plymouth outlets, sometimes barely blocks away from existing Plymouth showrooms. To help bolster the distribution network, Townsend lured Virgil Boyd away from American Motors. The son of an Iowa dirt farmer who lost his spread during the Depression, Boyd had operated Nash and Buick dealerships before being hired in 1954 to spruce up American Motors' sales operation. To assist Boyd, who became a vice-president and General Sales Manager, Townsend scooped Stewart Venn, an expert in dealer relocation, from Ford. Another defector from Ford was Elwood Engel, hired to temper Chrysler's flamboyant styling. Most thought Lynn Townsend had performed a magnificent job. The New York Financial Writers dined off Supreme of Shrimp and broiled swordfish as they entertained him as their man of the year. At the end of 1962, *Time* called Chrysler "the comeback story of U.S. business" and from a cover which bore the banner "Toward a World Market" there beamed the ruddy face of the new Chrysler chief.

Townsend wasted no time before ordering blueprints to cash in on the predicted bonanza. At the end of 1963, a massive expansion program was announced, and soon the new factories began to sprout from the ground. There is no more poignant example of a forsaken future than Chrysler's Belvidere car assembly plant, which started to throb in 1965. Built about seventy-five miles northwest of Chicago, the plant's water tower, ringed with Chrysler's blue-and-white corporate colors, cast its pop-eyed gaze over the surrounding cornfields. Inside the 2.1-million-square-foot factory, Chrysler installed all the latest electronic marvels. Townsend took pleasure in recounting that the site itself was chosen from eight possible choices in six minutes by a computer fed with fifteen thousand pieces of information; the public relations staff settled for more mundane comparisons. The construction of Belvidere, journalists were informed, soaked up 85,000 cubic yards of concrete, enough to build a sidewalk from Chicago to Madison, Wisconsin. The Belvidere assembly plant was on a par with any plant that existed; even the famous General Motors Lordstown plant, opened in 1966, was scarcely more sophisticated. The annual capacity of 220,000 units was, said the time-and-motion experts, the most efficient size for a modern automobile plant.

Fifteen miles west of St. Louis, Missouri, a 942,100-square-foot truck-assembly plant was built to trundle out 98,000 trucks a year. To feed the new plants, Chrysler made dramatic changes and additions at its manufacturing plants—the factories that feed parts and supplies into the thunderous maw of assembly plants. While the vehicle assembly plants expanded by a quarter during the Sixties, the manufacturing plants more than doubled in size. The proudest piece was the Sterling stamping plant, an immaculate flat building which rose close to the General Motors Technical Center on the fringes of Detroit. In 1965, the plant began munching deck lids, hoods and quarter panels out of 2,000 tons of steel a day. With 400 presses and 32 lines, it was, for a time, the largest plant of its kind in the world. In Kokomo, Indiana, one of the world's largest aluminum ore-casting plants roared into business in late 1965 and within another year a new foundry in Detroit began melting 110 tons of ore into engine blocks, crankshafts and flywheels every hour.

While Chrysler placed its imprint on entire states, it also made smaller purchases that changed the shape and tone of small communities. In 1968, for example, Chrysler bought a couple of factories in Ann Arbor and Scio Township, Michigan, which began to send speedometers and other gauges to the manufacturing plants. The people of Lyons, Michigan (population 800), a sleepy town lying along the banks of the Grand River, surrounded by fields sown with soybean and corn, soon started shipping vinyl roofs and interior trim for Lynn Townsend's new stable. At corporate headquarters, the architect Minoru Yamasaki was retained to design a new product planning and styling center opposite the stodgy K. T. Keller Building.

While Chrysler poured concrete across fields, the most visible demonstration of the revived spirit was the Pentastar, a thin, bristling white star emblazoned on a bright-blue pentagon. It was Townsend's own idea. After spending months traveling around the country visiting Chrysler dealers, Townsend returned to Detroit convinced that there were more Howard Johnson's bright orange roofs than Chrysler outlets. On inquiry he was staggered to discover that the opposite was true. Chrysler, he decided, could create similar illusions. So the New York firm of Lippincott and Margulies was commissioned to create a symbol of unity.

Soon the Pentastar was popping up everywhere, replacing the old "Forward Look" emblem of two superimposed boomerangs known contemptuously within the company as "The Dingbat." Before the end of 1965, more than five thousand large blue-and-white signs were installed at dealerships. A squad of fifty vigilantes was charged with rigorously enforcing its use and dealers were issued with minute instructions about the proper display. Chrysler was now eminently visible on Main Street, U.S.A.; Ford and General Motors later scurried to mimic the new signs. Naturally, Chrysler's exhibit at the 1964 World's Fair was dominated by a building constructed in the shape of a Pentastar. (The carefully contrived effect was spoiled by an NAACP protest against a twenty-minute animated stage show that depicted car parts merrily assembling themselves to a refrain of "Dem bolts, dem bolts, dem car bolts.") Chrysler engineers at Cape Canaveral had small Pentastars fastened to their hard hats and at televised launches sat with the symbol emblazoned on their shirts for the world to see. Before long, executives strolled around the corporate headquarters with special pin-size Pentastars in their lapels.

The dashes of blue and white in every Chrysler advertisement and on every Chrysler building were the most obvious signs of the effort placed behind aggressive marketing. A large part of Townsend's early success was attributable to brash and expensive promotion that wasn't based on the gimmicks associated with car salesmen possessed of an easy lip and a firm slap across the back. Townsend's promotions extended much further. He was determined to sell Chrysler cars anywhere he could, and to do that he needed a financial organization that could provide reliable financing to dealers and customers; a leasing organization to cope with the burgeoning rental and fleet markets; and a realty company to help with the sales outlets.

Almost immediately, there was one special program that seemed ideally suited to bolster Chrysler's reputation for high-quality engineering: the gas-turbine car. With Townsend's approval, the gas-turbine engine was transformed from an engineering experiment into splashy, breathless prose. There was nothing new about Chrysler's tinkering. The history of the "cyclone in a box" stretched back to before World War II, although the development of the first turbine capable of powering an automobile was not announced until 1954. In 1956 a production Plymouth sedan, powered by a gas turbine, ran from coast to coast.

Under the stewardship of George Huebner, a Chrysler engineer who devoted his life to perfecting the turbine, a new generation appeared with much hoopla in the fall of 1963. The omens were not propitious. At the press preview held at Roosevelt Raceway on Long Island, two of the cars conked out. One was repaired and driven to Manhattan, where it broke down in the rush hour on the corner of 40th Street and Third Avenue, leaving hapless Chrysler officials to hail a cab. Nevertheless, two turbines were driven across the country in an effort to reinstill confidence in the quality of Chrysler's engineering. Fifty $250,000 cars, specially designed in Italy by Ghia, were handed over to consumers (selected from twenty thousand applications) for road tests. The company muttered about production within three years, although George Huebner, viewed as something of a radical by his fellow engineers, warned that the turbine would "have to compete with eighty years of piston engine progress." One million miles and 203 drivers later, it became obvious that people weren't prepared to pay more for a turbine than for a conventional engine, and Chrysler never reached the point of committing money for even a limited production run. However, the engine, which, it was boasted, could run on fuel oil, white gasoline, moonshine and even Chanel No. 5, brought a windfall of favorable publicity.

During his early days as chairman, Townsend fired another arrow that was greeted with much tut-tutting from GM and Ford. Having carefully studied the warranties offered by other consumer industries, particularly companies making electrical appliances, Townsend decided almost overnight that Chrysler should do something similar. Confident that the Chrysler components could stand the test (and knowing from information on the competitors that they would be hard pressed to follow) Townsend rode roughshod over stiff internal opposition and, in 1962, introduced the first warranty to cover the engine, transmission and rear axle for five years or 50,000 miles. (Before October 1960, when Ford lengthened the terms of the standard warranty to cover 12 months or twelve thousand miles, the industry had only stood by its major components for three months or 4,000 miles.) After Chrysler's fierce attack, Ford and GM preferred to stick to a less expensive version: two years or 24,000 miles. But by 1966, with Chrysler gaining a larger market share, their patience evaporated and battle was joined, with all companies offering "5 and 50s." Chrysler quickly responded with yet another scheme by enlarging its warranty to embrace steering, suspension and road wheels on all 1967 models, but even the new terms couldn't counter the competition's blasts. Barely a year later, Chrysler stiffened its terms to cover just the first two owners (rather than all owners) and by 1971 the 5-50 was a thing of the past. Nevertheless, there were still other ways to gain temporary advantages, and in the fall of 1967, Chrysler latched onto yet another opportunity. While the other manufacturers installed shoulder harnesses and seat belts in their 1968 cars at the start of production, Chrysler waited. Federal standards only required that seat belts be installed in cars built after January 1, 1968. Thus, for several months, Chrysler saved about fifty dollars a car.

By far Lynn Townsend's proudest creation was Chrysler Financial. Housed later in a fifteen-story, white-fronted cube that overlooks a spacious, landscaped cemetery in a belt of land between Detroit's northern suburbs and the grimy town of Pontiac, it had been established in 1964 as Chrysler Credit Corporation, a subsidiary designed to provide funds for both the dealers and the retail customers. Chrysler Financial arrived later than either General Motors Acceptance Corporation (GMAC) or Ford Motor Credit, the in-house bankers for the other two automakers. But this was hardly due to negligence on Walter Chrysler's part. As ever, General Motors had been a step ahead of the opposition. GMAC was started in 1919, the natural outcome of a decade during which the infant industry had struggled to provide its new dependents, dealers and retail customers, with funds. Because banks viewed automobiles as something of a needless luxury, they had been unwilling to provide either the continuous flow or the quantity of funds required to provide stability. Ford, meanwhile, took an equity participation in the Universal Credit Company in 1928. Chrysler took its first steps into direct consumer and wholesale financing in 1934 with the purchase of a minority stake in the Commercial Credit firm, to offer customers "new and advantageous rates."

In 1938, the government, suspecting that the automakers were fixing the price of financing, began criminal proceedings against GMAC, which ended ambiguously. However, the equivocal verdict resulted in civil proceedings aimed at forcing the automakers to divest themselves of their financing interests. Ford and Chrysler rapidly obliged, but General Motors stood firm until the consent decrees were finally amended to permit retention of GMAC. Ford then established Ford Motor Credit in 1950, but Chrysler remained dependent upon the banks and independent finance companies, who were fair-weather friends at best. Meanwhile, the demand for credit had blossomed as families footed the bills for two cars and dealers demanded loans to finance the expanded lines that now filled showrooms. With the establishment of Chrysler Financial, the company began to enjoy the benefits long taken for granted elsewhere. The subsidiary, for example, accommodated the pronounced seasonal fluctuations in inventory caused by the spring selling season and the model changeover. On both new- and used-car deals, the captive financial arm ensured that the size of the down payments conformed to competitive rates. In earlier times, Chrysler had been forced to either ask customers to supply a larger down payment or lose a chunk of the profit margin. Dealers not only were assured now of borrowing rates in keeping with the national average, they also were protected from cyclical credit crunches when banks were quick to withdraw loans. Most importantly, Chrysler Financial was, for many customers (in a business largely dependent on repeat purchasing) the most familiar and enduring link with the parent company. The link was reinforced by the arrival of the monthly bill. Scarcely had the finance company opened its doors than it began to offer life and automobile insurance. Even Chrysler's dourest critics admit that the finance company was a considerable triumph. Under the guidance of its president, Gordon Areen, a soft-spoken accountant hired by Townsend, it expanded throughout the Sixties. In May 1967 it purchased the outstanding capital stock of Redisco, American Motors' financing subsidiary, and in 1968 it shelled out $15.7 million for the Los Angeles-based Allied Concord Financial Corporation. The increased borrowing capacity helped Chrysler Financial multiply tenfold while earnings rose from $5,000 in 1965 to nearly $21.5 million in 1970.

Wads of available financing made the leasing market all the more accessible. Chrysler had always been rudely beaten in the highly profitable leasing arrangements with car rental agencies and with government and factory pools, and Townsend knew it. In 1962, when the leasing subsidiary was formed, Chrysler's share of the passenger-car fleet market was a sorry 11.3 percent. During the next four years, the market more than doubled in size while Chrysler, in turn, practically doubled its share. The new subsidiary had two functions: one was to establish a network of companies to lease and service vehicles to local and regional firms and to individuals. (For the most part, existing Chrysler dealers were granted licenses to take on the new business.) The second purpose was to lease directly to major rental, corporate and government fleets. The battle to succeed in the leasing market illustrates the competition Chrysler faced. In 1964, Ford, irritated by Chrysler's uppityness, cut leasing prices, and in 1965 General Motors did the same. Finally, pressured by dealers incensed by Chrysler's encroachment on what had been more than just a profitable sideline, General Motors embarked on a fierce price war.[1] Eventually, General Motors and Ford dropped their prices to such an extent that Chrysler couldn't compete and still make a profit on its leasing business.

As part of the effort to spiff up the image, bring some order to the dealerships and, of course, bolster volume, Chrysler Realty was formed in 1967. The realty company turned out to be an awkward stepdaughter for Chrysler—removed from the auto industry yet an important part of the company's distribution system. The formation of Chrysler Realty was the work of a man who knew how to play the angles. With profits slumping during the first quarter of 1967 and the factories working well under capacity, Chrysler badly needed an injection of working capital. At a special meeting of the board, the directors approved a plan that allowed Chrysler to sell 250 new-car dealerships to a subsidiary—Chrysler Realty—which would pay with the proceeds of a $150 million note. The debt issue improved the balance sheet of the parent company, but it also catapulted Chrysler into the diversified real estate business. Much of the impetus behind the formation of the realty arm came from a shock Lynn Townsend had suffered while heading Chrysler's Canadian operation during the late 1950s. Within a week, both of Chrysler's dealers in Ottawa had drawn their shutters; it didn't take too long to discover that General Motors had bought the buildings. Chrysler had immediately bought a couple of new sites for outlets in Ottawa and, at the turn of the Sixties, the company began to get seriously involved with a dealership program in both Canada and the United States.

Mainly because the profit margins of Chrysler dealerships were too low to attract outside capital, Chrysler, in 1961, started the Marketing Investment Division, which erected the buildings and provided capital to dealers too strapped to start on their own. Once the showroom was bustling with business, the manager was, theoretically, meant to buy Chrysler's share of the investment. At the end of 1961 there were 66 Chrysler-financed dealerships, which sold 2.9 percent of all the cars and trucks sold by Chrysler in the United States. By 1972 Chrysler had poured almost $100 million into the MID program and there were 267 "company shops," which accounted for 13.9 percent of all U.S. sales. The program allowed no dilution of risk and never lived up to expectations—largely because the sort of manager attracted by Chrysler's offer to provide a share of the equity was not likely to rustle up the money needed to buy the business. Chrysler found itself setting up salaried dealership managers across the country, rather than enterprising local entrepreneurs.

Other Chrysler dealers saw the "company stores" as a blatant intrusion by the corporation. Many of the old-timers furiously charged that the MID dealers received preferential treatment, the choicest cars and all the wholesale and retail financing they needed. But where the old hands saw a frightening departure, Chrysler's bosses found an invitation to prosper from diversified real estate speculation. Inevitably, despite management's protests to the contrary, it was never clear where the automobile business ended and the real estate operations began. Townsend, at the start of his tenure, had been very aware of the importance of planting new dealerships on streets or corners where the traffic patterns and neighborhood income were suitable. "Chrysler Realty," Townsend explained, "took real estate operations out of the hands of automobile people who didn't know much about them and put them in the hands of real estate people who didn't have to worry about the automobile business." With the start of the realty operation, though, much of the discipline exerted from headquarters was lost. Although the Chrysler sales department was allowed to exercise a vote, the choice was limited to plots selected by real estate men who knew next to nothing about running automobile dealerships.

Along with Westinghouse, ITT, Gulf & Western and the Norfolk and Western Railroad, Chrysler rushed into real estate. In 1967 Chrysler Real Estate president Ed Homer, the former head of a shopping center company, announced plans for a $100 million planned community for twenty thousand people on land north of Detroit which had been purchased during the 1950s to house a new corporate headquarters. Chrysler also bought 774 acres two miles west of Bloomfield Hills for a luxury housing development and built townhouses around a couple of artificial lakes in Ann Arbor. Soon Chrysler was leasing an office building in Mobile, Alabama, buying property on Chicago's Loop and purchasing shopping centers in Nevada, California and Kansas. Apartments sprang up in Mission Viejo and ocean-front condominiums in Fort Lauderdale and Boca Raton. The smallest member of the Big Three even developed student dormitories at the state universities of Arizona and California.

The most spectacular purchase came in 1970. Newscaster Chet Huntley, who had previously filmed a flattering documentary on the turbine engine cars, charmed one of Chrysler's New York public relations staff, who dutifully arranged a meeting with Lynn Townsend. Chrysler, along with some other companies, subjected to the same Huntley charms, bought 10,000 acres in the Gallintin River Canyon, fifteen miles northwest of Yellowstone in Montana. The resort, which was originally designed to accommodate two villages, a convention center and the inevitable sprinkling of condos, was dogged with bad luck from the start. On occasion Chet Huntley himself swept out the dining room as bulldozers rolled past unfinished cabins. Chrysler eventually sold out of Big Sky, as it was called, in 1978.

Chrysler Realty was by far the largest foray the parent corporation made outside the automobile business. Although Ford and General Motors have extended their business into all sorts of transportation—GM is the largest manufacturer of railway diesel engines in the world,

while Ford is surpassed only by International Harvester in farm trac-
tors—neither had wandered far from what they understood. In the
mid-Sixties, largely in an effort to cushion the cyclical shocks, Chrysler
looked farther afield, but, burdened with massive plants, the company
was not easily turned into an ITT of the automobile business.

In the end, the non-automotive interests never accounted for more
than 5 percent of company sales, though they attracted—particularly
during the race to the moon—a disproportionate amount of public attention. The auxiliary interests fall into two categories: what Chrysler
calls "diversified operations" and the "defense-space" group. The former were made up of Chrysler's Amplex, Chemical, Marine and Airtemp divisions. Of the four, Amplex changed least under Townsend,
though it still managed to grow by more than a quarter before 1970.
Originally formed in 1928, the division made delicate machine parts
from compressed metal powder, a technique that saved the machining
required with conventional metals. Besides supplying Chrysler's own
needs, Amplex supplied makers of snowmobiles and home appliances
with its metal-powder components, ceramic magnets and cold ex-
trusions. In the late Sixties, the Chemical Division, which comprised a
Friction Products Group (makers of exotic lubricants, rustproofing
and pickling oils for the steel industry), and a Chemical Products
Group (makers of adhesives and sealants), rode into uncharted waters
and doubled its sales in 1968 when Townsend approved the purchase
of two plants. One, in Sandusky, Ohio, started to produce upholstery,
door panels, headliners and vinyl roofs. Another, in New Jersey,
started to supply vinyl and other fabrics for footwear, sporting goods
and luggage makers.

Airtemp originally had been little more than a plaything for Walter
Chrysler, Jr., when it was started in 1934. It wasn't until the late Sixties, when demand for air conditioning bloomed, that the division
started to grow. Between 1965 and 1969, new plants—in Bowling
Green, Kentucky; Dayton, Ohio; and Toronto, Ontario—tripled its size.
Satellite plants were built near Chrysler's expanding overseas operations in Spain, Australia and South Africa. Along with the domestic
and commercial air conditioners and gas, oil and electric furnaces, Airtemp also dabbled in military optical range finders, ballistic components, ammunition racks and air cleaners. As befitted the emerging
multinational, Airtemp air conditioners appeared in the most unlikely
places: in Frankfurt's underground system; in a Hilton Hotel in Ku-
wait; in a textile factory in Taiwan; and in museums in Bogota and
Brunei.

The shopping spree also extended into another of Walter Chrysler's
special interests. Chrysler had manufactured marine engines since
1927 and, by the early Sixties, the company supplied one-third of the

market for inboard engines. In 1965, after the purchase of the West Bend Company, located in Hartford, Wisconsin, and the Lone Star Boat Company, in Plano, Texas, Chrysler started to sell outboards, sailboats, large powerboats and boat trailers. Within a year boats were being sold like cars. The latest models commanded a national press preview, a freshly organized dealer network, reams of glossy sales material, retail financing and even a five-year warranty on hulls. Chrysler bought stretches of water in Florida and Michigan to test their cabin cruisers and aluminum and fiber-glass boats. All the boats bore suitably sonorous names: there were Buccaneers and Bass Runners, Mariners and Conquerors.

Chrysler's connections with the military endured less strain than its relationships with many of its automotive customers. With $3.4 billion in military supplies delivered during the Second World War and another $1.3 billion of medium tanks, fighter-aircraft parts and jet-engine components delivered for the Korean conflict, Chrysler continued to churn out the M-60 battle tank throughout the Sixties.

The Townsend years witnessed the glory of the Space Division, which, as a tribute to its importance, was spun off from the company's Defense Division. The experimental rocketry of the Fifties gave Chrysler an invitation into outer space. Since October 1952, when twenty-six Chrysler engineers were assigned to the Redstone Missile Program in Huntsville, Alabama, and the care of Dr. Wernher von Braun, Chrysler had caressed the fringes of space. Chrysler's missile connections allowed the first troop launching of a ballistic missile, eased the first high-altitude nuclear detonations, shoved the early, ponderous satellites into orbit and rocketed a couple of apes around the world. From the Redstones it was but half a step to the Mercury program, in which astronauts Alan Shepard and Virgil Grissom sat atop Chrysler rockets on their suborbital flights. With the company's selection as prime contractor for the Saturn booster program, Chrysler started its own space division in 1962 to design, engineer, produce and test the Saturn 1 and Saturn 1B launch vehicles. While NASA built the early launch vehicles, Chrysler built the rest in a sprawling plant in Michoud, Louisiana, and provided the engineers for all the Saturn 1B Apollo missions, including the first Apollo lunar module and manned Apollo flights. Chrysler's publicists ran a hot and cold affair with the space program, despite having a remarkable perfect record for launches. Outside the gates to Cape Canaveral there was a "job shop" carrying the familiar blue-and-white Pentastar, and Lynn Townsend often scooted south to hand over formally yet another of the boosters or attend a launch. On occasion the intrusion of the automobile men horrified the men and families closely connected with the launch. In 1968, during the Detroit–St. Louis Cardinals World Series,

Townsend left his dinner guests at the Cape Canaveral Hilton frozen
when he began a toast on the eve of the launch by fliply mentioning
that his wife, Ruth, had inspired the trip. "Wouldn't it be fun to go
see a launch?" Ruth had asked her husband. The engineers had seen
plenty and didn't think they were very amusing.

Even the fury of the Vietnam War did not raise the combined sales
of the defense-space operations to anything more than 4 percent of
total company sales—yet Townsend made more trips to Louisiana and
Cape Canaveral than he did across Detroit to the headquarters of the
United Auto Workers. The expansion of the factories and the need to
keep them operating close to capacity made Chrysler extremely vulnerable when it came to dealing with any group—dealers or auto
workers—that had the power to close them down or slow the line. At
the beginning of the Sixties, the UAW was at the peak of its strength.
While some others in the labor movement had decided that corruption
brought greater rewards than virtue, the UAW had remained true to
its ideals. Secretary-treasurer Emil Mazey even bounced one of
Walter Reuther's expense accounts because it contained a $1.50 dry-
cleaning chit. The UAW leaders had ventured far beyond Hamtramck
and Dearborn. They advocated National Health Insurance, marched
in civil rights protests in the South, preached against nuclear war, supported Cesar Chavez and his farmworkers in California and funneled
funds from the CIA to labor unions in Europe.

The union leadership worked out of Solidarity House, a five-story
glass-and-aluminum office building overlooking the mallard ducks
paddling on the Detroit River and built on land once owned by Edsel
Ford and Chrysler Corporation. Sprinkled among the offices was a
corps of professionals recruited from universities and research organizations; they were more familiar with legal tracts and actuarial
tables than a factory punch-clock. These non-card-carrying staff members armed Reuther with some of the punches for the toe-to-toe
bargaining with the companies. From 1962, the head of the union's
Chrysler Department was Douglas Fraser. Just as Reuther was known
to union members and management alike as "Walter," so Fraser
became known as "Doug." His career paralleled the history of the
union. He was born December 18, 1916, in Glasgow, Scotland, where
his father used to return from work at a local distillery with pil-
fered whiskey to light the fire. He arrived in Detroit, with his parents, at the age of six. Leaving Chadsey High School in the eleventh
grade, he was fired from his first job—packing cork insulation around
water heaters—for trying to organize a labor union. He found a
new job at Chrysler's DeSoto Division, where he became a metal fin-
isher, a welder and president of Local 227 in 1943. Fraser first caught
Reuther's attention when he ran against a candidate supported by

the leadership in an internal election. "I'd prefer to have him on my side," Reuther is supposed to have remarked. In 1947 Fraser joined the Chrysler Department; in 1951 he began an eight-year stint as one of Reuther's assistants. One contemporary remembers, "With Walter there was one star and a lot of satellites. But Doug was never a satellite; he was always his own man."[2]

Fraser and Reuther were not men to toy with. Chrysler had escaped a strike during the bargaining rounds of 1958 (when the industry was buried in a recession) and in 1961 (when it was judged too weak to endure a prolonged stoppage). In 1964, the prospect of a strike threatened to wreck Townsend's work and the Chrysler president made the mistake of letting the union know it. At a meeting in his office he told the union leaders, "Give us one more year and we'll be back on our feet." As the Chrysler delegation trooped out of the door, Reuther whispered to Fraser, "Chrysler's the target. Let's give 'em the squeeze."

Anxious to keep the plants open, Chrysler relented after a week, and the UAW made more progress than at any time in its history. Workers became eligible for an early-retirement program which allowed them to leave at the age of sixty with a $400-a-month pension after thirty years of service. Widows were granted automatic benefits; the companies were required to pay the full cost of hospital and medical services, as well as group life, health and disability insurance; they had to grant bereavement leave of three days, give a worker a holiday on his birthday, provide two extra paid holidays a year and forty hours of paid absence allowance (or an extra vacation week) and even to supply, at no charge, prescription safety glasses. GM and Ford negotiators were staggered and Louis G. Seaton, GM's labor relations vice-president, later told Reuther he would never have gotten $400 a month from GM—at least not without "a hell of a fight."[3]

The UAW could file grievances, complain about line speed and threaten a strike, but only in the United States and Canada. Outside North America, Chrysler fast discovered other perils. At the start of the decade, much of the future for the American automobile manufacturers seemed to lie overseas, and Lynn Townsend wasn't the only Detroiter to have a globe in his eye. At home, General Motors was projecting an annual growth rate of only 3 percent, while Ford's estimate, at 2.8 percent, was even bleaker. The auto giants were hard pressed to see where higher profit margins would come from. In the United States, they were coming to rely increasingly on the replacement market. At the time when Townsend was taking charge at Chrysler, the American consumer not only was buying European cars, but was also demanding smaller, lighter and, above all, cheaper cars from Detroit (see Chapter Three). Lewis D. Crusoe, a General Motors executive, glumly observed, "People no longer think it's wonderful to go someplace sitting down."[4]

Europe, by contrast, looked like the promised land. Sales in the United Kingdom and the Common Market had increased on average by 15.5 percent a year since the early 1950s and, in many ways, the European market resembled the U.S. market before World War II. There was no annual model changeover and, though the number of people per car had fallen in Italy from 90 in 1952 to 21 at the end of 1961, and in the United Kingdom from 27 to 8 during the same period, the continent still looked distinctly underdeveloped compared to the United States where, in 1961, there was one car for every three people. There were plenty of Europeans who had never driven a car; they seemed to be ideal game for American executives long used to tempting buyers into plusher and more expensive machines. Sonorous warnings about an offensive on the second front thundered forth from Ford and General Motors. General Motors chairman Frederic Donner estimated that the overseas market would reach 8 million cars within the decade, while Ford's economists believed it would pull ahead of the United States before 1970. Donner told the press that General Motors' overseas assets would be increased by more than a third before the end of 1961, while Henry Ford declared that his company's spending abroad would total $220 million in 1961, not counting the $363 million paid to the shareholders who owned 45 percent of Ford of England. In the month of John Kennedy's inauguration, *Fortune* projected that "a manufacturer like Ford will one day become a truly international company, its international division achieving parity in profits and sales with the domestic operation."

In 1960, Ford profits from operations abroad topped $100 million for the first time, while General Motors sold some $1.8 billion worth of vehicles abroad. Both companies had long been engaged in manufacturing overseas, and of the two, Ford, thanks largely to the continuity of purpose that existed between Henry Ford and his son and grandson, was the most experienced. At the very first Ford stockholders' meeting, held on October 15, 1903, the stockholders had urged the company director to "take necessary steps to obtain foreign business." By 1907, Fords were being sold in at least sixteen foreign countries and advertisements for the Model T were even printed in Japanese and Chinese. Fords were driven across the Alps and traversed the Gobi Desert, while at the 1911 coronation of George V as emperor of India in Delhi, the local Ford agent dutifully informed his American superiors that "the procession was magnificent, there were elephants, camels, Ford cars and everything else all mingled together."[5]

By far the proudest of Ford's overseas operations was the sprawling manufacturing plant in Dagenham, England. Henry Ford wanted his

British company to be "the Detroit of Europe" and, with a capacity of 200,000 cars a year, it was the largest auto plant outside the United States when it started production in 1931. Elsewhere, agents had followed Henry Ford's instructions and snapped up large chunks of land close to water to receive parts and ship cars in Denmark and Belgium. In 1929, wooed by tax breaks offered by the then Mayor of Cologne, Konrad Adenauer, Henry Ford acquired 52 acres on the banks of the Rhine. Ford also established a beachhead in Australia and Latin America. Although Dearborn still exerted a stiff control over the foreign operations, Ford mainly hired local nationals to staff its foreign subsidiaries and, more importantly, developed cars and trucks suited to local conditions. The overseas companies gradually acquired the trappings of the parent: credit companies and dealer networks.

Ford had also grappled with the frustrations of conducting business abroad. In France, Ford had entered into its only major joint venture with a foreign producer, but the pre- and postwar experience with Ford SAF turned into a financial drain; in 1952, Ford dispatched a manager to spruce up the company and make it fit for a sale. Ford sold the French plant's staff and dealer organization to Simca in 1954 and, in return, obtained a 15.2-percent share of Simca equity.

By 1960, Ford was one of the companies most experienced in foreign business and held a 29-percent share of the United Kingdom market and a 10-percent share in West Germany. By comparison, General Motors had displayed far less enthusiasm and still conducted all its foreign operations through an isolated office in New York.

Ironically, Walter Chrysler had been among the first group of GM executives to explore the opportunities in Europe in the Twenties. Walter Chrysler and his colleagues had faced the same sort of questions Chrysler Corporation was facing forty years later: whether to buy abroad; which companies to buy; whether to purchase minority or majority stakes; whether to continue the export of cars and trucks from the United States; how to cope with European nationalism and how to deal with tariffs, duties and local content requirements. Rebuffed in their first attempts to buy European companies—Citröen in France and Austin in the United Kingdom—GM finally settled on Britain's Vauxhall Motors which, in 1925, had an annual volume of only 1,500 units and, according to Alfred Sloan, was "a kind of experiment in overseas manufacturing." Four years later, GM plunged deeper with the acquisition of Adam Opel, then Germany's largest producer. By 1933, the combined sales of Vauxhall and Opel were, for the first time, greater than the foreign sales of GM's American-made cars, but perhaps GM's greatest overseas triumph occurred in Australia, where the company arrived with a team of about thirty engineers and production experts in 1946. In 1948 the Holden, a small car specially de-

signed to appeal to the largest group of Australian consumers, was
sold for the first time. At the end of the Fifties, GM was not only the
fifth-largest European manufacturer, but had also devastated BMC
in Australia. Not until 1960 did GM decide to produce a full line of
cars in Europe, however.

By contrast, Chrysler owned nothing, or next to nothing. There was
a small manufacturing plant in Kew Gardens in London where about
four thousand trucks a year were assembled, a tiny assembly plant in
Antwerp and an insignificant car-and-truck operation in Australia. In
Detroit, Chrysler Export, a small group working on the third floor of
company headquarters, continued to operate much as it had before
World War II. The Export Division still relied on its foreign distributors, most of whom were burghers in their own country. The conservative Financial Department rode herd over the group, with the senior financial officer, B. E. Hutchinson exhorting his men not to accept
"wooden nickels." Irv Minett, who later headed the International Operation, remembers that the Export Division "wouldn't have taken
Swiss francs for a spare tire."

Like much of the rest of Chrysler, the Export Division was a tightly
run duchy, dominated by Cecil B. Thomas until his sudden death
from a leg injury in 1956. Shortly after the conclusion of the study by
McKinsey Company (see Chapter Three), Tex Colbert heeded the advice of the outside consultants and made a couple of offers to overseas
companies. He was sternly rejected by Rolls-Royce, whose management insisted that it would remain forever British, and by Heinz
Nordhoff, the head of Volkswagen. Nordhoff told Colbert that an acquisition by Chrysler would be impractical, since most of the company's shares had been widely distributed by the German government. The death of Thomas left a vacuum, since the details and extent
of the Export Division's activities were almost entirely unknown to
senior management. In 1958, Bill Newberg decided to make a decision, one way or the other, on Chrysler's overseas plans. Lynn Townsend was appointed chairman of a study group charged with investigating the activities of the Export Division and examining the
possibility of manufacturing abroad.

Chrysler's choice was limited. Almost everywhere, smaller roads,
higher fuel costs and lower standards of living made American cars as
desirable as a line of elephants. In small, underdeveloped countries,
Chrysler could still afford to start from scratch by organizing and
building a manufacturing plant and establishing a string of dealers. In
countries, especially in South America, where Chrysler had long dealt
through local distributors, Highland Park could buy them out and
control assembly and distribution. Carving a foothold in the more advanced countries, particularly in Europe and Australia, was a far trick-

ier proposition. In Europe Chrysler had to interpret different laws, various taxes and a mosaic of likes and dislikes: the French liked a four-door car, the Germans wanted to clamber into the back seat, the British needed right-hand drive and the Italians speed. The countries were too developed, the automobile industry too advanced, the economies of scale too large, the dealer networks too entrenched, the owners' allegiances too strong, for Chrysler to start from scratch. The only practical route was to purchase part or all of an existing manufacturer—but in an industry where the founders and chief executives are loath to seek a partner or a purchaser until the need is irresistible, the only willing manufacturers were likely to be lame or poor. In Europe, there was a further complication. The United Kingdom's independence from the Common Market would clearly grow following the signing of the Treaty of Rome in 1957. It didn't take long for the study group to understand that in Europe, at the end of the Fifties, there were two markets: the British and the Continental.

In August 1958, Chrysler bought 25 percent of Simca, the company Ford had abandoned earlier in the decade. Chrysler purchased Ford's remaining equity and lined up alongside the other owners—Fiat's Agnellis and Henri Pigozzi, chief of Simca. Simca was the second largest producer in France, even though its profit margins hovered around 1 percent. Chrysler acquired a ready-made distribution network, with Simca selling Chrysler cars and trucks in areas where it had a greater share of the market (Europe, Algeria and Brazil), while Chrysler took on Simcas in the United States and Canada, the rest of Latin America and the Far East. "The 25-percent interest," said Irv Minett, "gave Chrysler nothing. It was neither fish nor fowl." Although Chrysler had representation on the board, Simca continued to be dominated by the interests of Fiat, whose connections with Simca extended back to the Thirties. Between 1959 and 1963, the technical contacts between Paris and Highland Park were so limited that the cost-planning system was developed through an interpreter. Determined to gain a greater voice in Simca management, Chrysler officials scoured Europe for shareholders; finally, in 1963, Chrysler announced that it had attained control of 63.8 percent of Simca, with Fiat retaining 20 percent.

The reaction from the French government, which only four years earlier had urged that, if American investment was going to be made in Europe, it should be in France, was swift and furious. Chrysler's announcement, made four days after President de Gaulle had vetoed British entry into the Common Market, partly from fears of Anglo-American domination, was derided by Treasury Minister Valerie Giscard d'Éstaing, who snapped, "It is not desirable that important sectors of the Common Market's economy depend on outside decisions."

Chrysler's Irv Minett hailed the acquisition and predicted that, "In the perspective of another ten years, it may rank in importance with the purchase of Dodge in 1928."

As Chrysler was building its stake in Simca, Townsend's international task force was piecing together a blueprint for an imposing foreign presence. In September 1958, largely to reduce the time lag that existed in communications between Detroit and Europe, Chrysler International was organized and soon had a staff of two hundred working out of its new headquarters in Geneva. A variety of other brides were approached. In the United Kingdom, Standard Leyland turned down a Chrysler proposal for a variety of reasons, not least of which was the ambition of Donald Stokes, who later became head of British Leyland. In Germany, overtures were made to the Flick family, which controlled Daimler-Benz. Largely because of Daimler-Benz's strength in the truck market (in contrast to Chrysler's weakness), the match seemed suitable. Although the Flicks were unwilling to sell their company, they agreed instead to an exchange of shares, but the deal finally snagged when it became apparent that a share swap would make the German company Chrysler's largest shareholder. There were also some fruitless discussions with the Quandt brothers of Munich, the majority owners of Bavarian Motor Works (BMW).

While the search continued for companies, it became a matter of principle that they would remain unconsolidated. Partly as a sop to nationalistic tendencies, but also because the executive in charge, Irv Minett, strongly supported the notion, the newly acquired companies were largely left to their own devices. As long as Chrysler remained a minority partner, the company endeavored to play the role of sympathetic outsider, leaving major managerial responsibility in the hands of local nationals and expecting that the companies provide the funds for their own growth. Chrysler's gradual shopping spree coincided with major changes in the European market. For the first half of the Sixties, the Europeans did more business than ever before. In the five years ending in December 1966, the number of cars rolling along Europe's freeways and byways doubled. In less than two decades, Italian manufacturers increased production fifteenfold, the West Germans, elevenfold, and the French, sevenfold. Even the British automakers managed to triple their annual output between 1950 and 1967. Between 1965 and 1968, though, the pattern changed. What had been a seller's market turned into a market where the buyer was in control and the smaller, weaker companies, thoroughly dependent on working their factories at capacity, were particularly threatened by the switch. As the market changed and the need for further investments accelerated, Chrysler increased its minority stakes. One sign of the changing mood came in 1967, when Chrysler made its first serious effort to provide overall direction for the overseas operations by splitting the companies into three groups: Europe; Latin America; Far East and Africa. Two countries, Spain and Britain, illustrated Chrysler's deepening involvement abroad.

Spain was one place in Europe where neither Ford nor General Motors was operating at the start of the Sixties. Ford had established an assembly operation in 1920 but, after World War II, had come under increasing pressure from a government that wanted a national industry and a controlling interest in a joint venture. Reckoning that the small Spanish market wasn't worth the bother, Ford fell back on its assembly operation in Portugal. The only foreign manufacturers present in Spain were Fiat (through its links with SEAT), Citröen and Renault. There was, however, one Spanish company that had greater aspirations. Barreiros Diesel, S.A., had started as a small repair business after the Spanish Civil War and had expanded by modifying Russian gasoline engines, which were mounted on secondhand chassis. By the mid-Sixties the company, under the direction of Don Eduardo Barreiros, one of four brothers, was engaged in large barter deals with Middle Eastern countries, particularly Egypt, where it exchanged vehicles and spares for cotton. In 1961 it had entered into a licensing agreement with AEC Ltd., a British heavy-duty truck manufacturer, to marry AEC-designed buses with Barreiros engines.

Barreiros, who came from the same province as General Franco and hunted grouse and pheasant with the Generalissimo, had unconcealed desires to become the Henry Ford of Spain. However, his company needed money to start producing automobiles and to fend off the challenge from the heavy trucks of the state-controlled competitor, ENASA. Barreiros approached Britain's Jaguar and Rootes and even General Motors, but each time withdrew from signing an agreement for fear of endangering his control of the business. Chrysler's proposal had distinct attractions. In return for a minority partnership, the Don would receive financial support and a production line for both the Dodge Dart and the Simca. For Chrysler, the deal brought access to a country Ford had found inhospitable, lower wage rates and a base for exports to the European community. However, the difficulties of managing an efficient business in Europe were dramatized by the connection between Barreiros and Simca. Simca shipped kits to Barreiros which, in return, supplied engines and transmissions for Simcas. Similarly, the body stampings sent to Spain were made in France from imported Spanish steel.

The subtle task facing Chrysler's managers quickly became apparent. Chrysler, for example, insisted that the Spaniards work normal American business hours rather than break for the traditional Spanish siesta. An effort to consolidate Barreiros' books with those in Detroit failed when it was learned that the modifications made to the Spanish bookkeeping were against Spanish law. General Franco himself presided over the opening of the expanded Spanish plant, but even his presence could not persuade Spaniards to buy the Dodge Dart. Snapped up by government officials for use as a limousine, it was too luxurious and too expensive (more than double the price of the next most expensive car) to gain popular acceptance. An advertising campaign based on the slogan "Dart is Power" failed because in Spain the literal translation from the English implied a lack of sexual drive. In 1969, six years after some Darts had been exported from Detroit in knockdown form, they were still awaiting assembly in Spain.

At the time of the initial agreement with Barreiros, another proud European automobile family was looking for support. Lord Rootes of Ramsbury (Billy to his friends) was, like Eduardo Barreiros, an ebullient entrepreneur. As British as Yorkshire pudding, and fond of women and shooting, Billy Rootes and his brother Reginald founded a car sales company which, by 1926, was the largest distributor in Britain. Two years later the brothers decided to start building cars themselves and began to gobble up troubled companies. With a small share of the British market (10 percent in 1939), Rootes looked abroad and began one of the early sales organizations in Latin America. He established the first Australian car plant in 1946. In the United Kingdom, particularly after Austin and Morris merged in 1954 to form the British Motor Corporation (BMC), Rootes had a tough time. With the arrival of BMC's spectacularly successful Mini at the end of the Fifties, and after Ford bought out its British shareholders, the going got even worse. In contrast to Ford (which had purchased Briggs Motor Bodies) and BMC (which had taken over Fisher Ludlow), Rootes was strapped for money and dependent on suppliers for body production. Rootes was especially vulnerable to strikes against his suppliers, and the company was not helped by shoddy marketing. The large number of brand names—Hillman, Humber, Singer and Sunbeam—was enough to baffle even the sharpest of buyers. Shortly before Chrysler's approaches, Rootes had started the production of the Imp, a small car designed to counter the Mini. It represented Rootes's attempt to enter the low-priced market, but it arrived five years later and was poorly designed. The front-wheel wells, for example, chewed chunks out of the passenger compartment. With its arrival, Rootes, which had always concentrated on higher-priced models, acquired a reputation for unreliability and tawdry workmanship. The Imp was manufactured at a new 1.6-million-square-foot plant in Linwood. A new town twelve miles northwest of Glasgow, Linwood was part of Clydeside which, along with Merseyside and South Wales, had been earmarked by the British government for further investment by the automobile industry. Located in the middle of a stern, unyielding part of Scotland where the workers and management were more used to the relative freedom of the shipyards, Linwood had been built by government decree and was, in a country that measures distances in tens rather than hundreds of miles, 250 miles away from Rootes's main factories and even farther from the richest markets. In addition, Rootes's professional managers were often at odds with the proprietors. There was snobbery among the dealers, some of whom acted as distributors, and the wage structure and bargaining procedures were uncoordinated. Market share had slipped from 11.5 percent in 1955 to 9.5 percent in 1961.

Billy Rootes had long been connected with Chrysler, partly through a Dodge dealership that sold trucks assembled in Kew Gardens. The talks about a partnership were conducted in great secrecy at his London apartment in Fountain House on Park Street. Rootes gave his servants the day off so that he, along with sons Geoffrey and Brian, could hash out final details with Chrysler's representative. On June 4, 1964, just a week after Rootes had made loud public denials of a possible sale, Chrysler acquired 30 percent of Rootes's voting shares and 50 percent of Rootes's non-voting shares. Chrysler's limited British operations were to be merged with the Rootes organization, and the U.S. purchaser promised no major changes. In Britain, where the intrusion of the American company was not greeted with enthusiasm, the deal protected jobs while Rootes was given access to Chrysler technology. Under the terms of the agreement, Chrysler was bound to apply to the British government if it wanted to increase its holdings.

Within a year, Chrysler made application, purchased more shares, faced further losses and plowed over $40 million into equipment and the acquisition of a steel-pressing plant near Linwood. In 1967, Chrysler informed the British government that it required voting control to safeguard any further investments. For the Labour government, Chrysler was an intractable problem. Having opposed the American challenge originally, the Wilson government was hard pressed to present a coherent strategy. An alliance of Rootes and British Leyland in a nationalized automobile industry was unpalatable because of the layoffs that would be involved and the lack of assurance about the future of Scotland's Linwood plant. Anthony Wedgwood Benn, then the Minister of Technology, defended the government's decision to permit Chrysler complete control by telling his fellow Members of Parliament, "The Government did not believe that Rootes by itself was a viable organisation with or without Government money, owned or not by a British company. If we had nationalised Rootes we should have been left . . . with a company which, in technological terms, was not on a scale which could survive at a critical time."[6] Chrysler's proposal for majority ownership was approved in early 1967 and the government itself, through the freshly formed Industrial Reorganisation Committee, invested over $30 million in Rootes.

Chrysler was a complete neophyte in international business. One of the early staff reports on prospects in Britain remarked with surprise that the British drove on the left-hand side of the road. Many of the officials sent overseas were unfamiliar with the language or the customs of the country to which they were assigned. Stranded abroad, the Chrysler men were often left to work out the troubles of international business by themselves. Few had heard of, let alone understood, the intricacies of hedging in the foreign exchange markets. Therefore, when the Peruvian peso was suddenly devalued in 1967, Chrysler got battered while General Motors survived unscathed. For most of the Sixties, Chrysler took out none of the traditional political and credit insurance available for products exported from the United States. Unlike General Motors or Ford, which had traditional career progressions through their overseas subsidiaries (it was normal for the GM manager of Brazilian operations to be promoted to Opel in West Germany, for example, and then to Detroit to head overseas business), Chrysler men hopped about all over the place. Despite Townsend's efforts to build worldwide staffs gradually, Chrysler's management was spread too thin to support the extraordinary demands of the burgeoning empire. John Day, Executive Vice-President, Defense and International Group, who spent eighteen years abroad for the company, winding up in charge of Chrysler Europe, noted, "We were quite a naïve company in international business. We were a group of real novices competing with a bunch of professionals."

The experiences in Latin America during the Sixties showed that mere presence was no guarantee of success. In Peru, the first year of production, 1965, was by far the most successful. Chrysler's plant twenty-five miles south of Lima was struck by two misfortunes in quick succession. First, the Humboldt current moved farther offshore, decimating the local anchovy fishing industry, then the most vibrant part of the Peruvian economy. If the departure of the anchovies was one disaster, the departure of the obliging Fernando Terry government was another. Overthrown in 1968, the government, which had eagerly sought foreign automakers, was replaced by one more anxious to set up workers' committees and expropriate entire industries.

In Brazil, Chrysler, as part of its agreement with Simca, took over the company once run by the French automaker. The company was a mess. Its one line of cars was powered by a derivative of Ford's 1932 V-8 engine and the mixture of engines rolling off the line was determined by the quality of castings delivered by a local supplier rather than by skilled planning. Only when the castings were machined would Chrysler workers discover the quality of the finish. If the casting was rough and coarse, the men would slip a sleeve into the holes and trundle out a small displacement engine. If the casting was all right, the Chrysler Esplanada would be powered by a large displacement engine. It was not surprising that many of the engines had an alarming tendency to blow up after as little as four thousand miles. In 1967, Chrysler bought International Harvester's fully integrated plant which included a foundry, stamping plant, engine plant and assembly line, and Brazil came to represent the single largest investment in South America, larger than other commitments made in Colombia, Venezuela and Argentina. Although the dealer network was streamlined in the mid-Sixties (one dealer had not sold a Simca in two years), the lack of a small car appropriate for the local market, the manner in which the Dodge Dart was pitted against the Volkswagen Beetle and the failure of Chrysler's truck to achieve the desired market share all meant that the Brazilian operation was never properly cleaned up.

The entire South American operation, running full tilt, would have been hard pressed to satisfy half the annual capacity of one of Chrysler's U.S. assembly plants, and their private problems, together with the troubles in Europe, remained concealed for the better part of the Sixties. One thing was clear: Lynn Townsend had remained true to his promise to try to turn Chrysler into a worldwide automobile company.

At home, despite a hiccup in 1966 and the beginning of 1967, when budgets were cut, employees laid off and spending postponed, Townsend seemed to have the touch of a mechanical Midas. At the beginning of 1968, Chrysler's pistons were pumping faster than ever. The 1967 market share had climbed to over 16 percent. There were audacious murmurings around Highland Park that the production lines wouldn't slow until Chrysler had captured a quarter of the market and had eclipsed General Electric as the nation's fourth largest manufacturer. Townsend, it seemed, had performed marvelous surgery on Chrysler's entire operation, from the lengths of vinyl sold to Samsonite to the new assembly plant in the middle of Illinois. The balancing act was delicate—a nudge too much and Chrysler would have been burdened with excess capacity, idle plants and a hefty overhead—but Townsend seemed to have avoided that. He had raised production by an average of 150,000 units a year and the plants were fully loaded. In the summer of 1968, production seemed headed for the ceiling of 1.75 million units and company president Virgil Boyd noted, "If we get off to a strong fall, the sand in the hour glass will start running out and a decision about extra capacity would have to be made." The buoyancy of the summer was reflected in capital spending plans of $300 million for 1969, compared to the $200 million spent in 1968 and the $191 million expended in 1967. The plans included a new styling building in Highland Park, a new air-conditioning plant in Bowling Green, Kentucky, three new parts depots, expansion of the Kokomo transmission plant, the De Witt gear plant and the Trenton engine plant. Even the production of window vents in Perrysburg, Ohio, was going to be boosted. Most importantly, in September 1969, Chrysler decided to build a brand-new assembly plant in the heart of Pennsylvania at a place called New Stanton, where 200,000 cars a year were to start rolling in 1970. With a projected work force of four thousand, it was the biggest new industry in the Pittsburgh area since World War II.

No one was complaining. The New York *Times* applauded and remarked, "If the Chrysler Corporation's silver cloud has a murky lining, it is a hard one to detect. Almost every move made by Lynn Townsend and his management since 1961 seems to have been the correct one."[7] Industry analyst David Healy agreed, remarking, "You don't have to like 'em, but you do have to admire 'em."[8]

The results were built on a precarious foundation, though. As it takes months and years for the wisdom of decisions in the automobile industry to become apparent, so it is with mistakes. The cars that were about to be introduced for the 1969 model year had their roots in 1965, a time when peculiar things had started to happen to Lynn Townsend. The Chrysler chairman and the rest of the company's officers had first become aware of what lay ahead the day they jetted to Atlanta to launch the 1969 cars. After a sobering committee meeting in Detroit, where gloomy forecasts for the coming months had been discussed for the first time, the mood aboard the Falcon jet resembled a wake. Life was turning sour, yet the inexorable rhythm of the industry had a few months to catch up. Chrysler, the executives knew, was running on fumes—but for the newsmen who greeted them in Atlanta they had nothing but smiles and glad-handing jests. Chrysler, the executives predicted, was heading for its most profitable year in history. They were right: 1968 ended with earnings of $6.23 a share—but the Michigan state fairgrounds were stacked full of unsold cars.

CHAPTER FIVE

"We're Shipping Junk"

The American people really want an Imperial that gets 40 miles to
the gallon, doesn't pollute and costs $1,500.
                    —Lynn Townsend, Detroit *Free Press*, August 10, 1975

Every morning when Lynn Townsend arrived at his Highland Park
office, he was greeted by a small three- by five-inch card, which he
carried around in his wallet for the rest of the day. The shipping report, which carried four sets of numbers, breathed the details of
Chrysler's operation. It told the chairman how many units were scheduled to be shipped that month, the number shipped the previous day
from all the North American assembly plants, the cumulative total of
shipments for the month and the balance remaining for the rest of the
month. Before he started the day's work, Lynn Townsend always
knew how much cash was on hand. Around noon he would usually receive a call from the Sales Division reporting retail deliveries in the
field, and late in the afternoon he was handed a detailed shipping report: a summary of each plant's output, a report on new orders and a
report that compared orders, production and retail deliveries. Townsend would take less than an hour to comb through the summaries

and the more detailed breakdowns. By around 6:30 P.M., he would be heading for his home in Bloomfield Hills. "I have two hundred thirty-four thousand people working for me," he used to remark. "If I've got to work an extra two hours there's something wrong."

Lynn Townsend could tell a lot from the numbers. When times were good they whispered reassurance. When times were bad, they yelled bloody murder. Everything that Townsend had done was judged every few hours, on every working day of the year, by those numbers. It was as if Lynn Townsend were a priest to whom the vice-presidents, the division managers, the sales managers, the zone managers, the plant managers—all the elaborate hierarchy of an automobile company—confessed daily. There was nothing more holy in Chrysler than the long, tidy rows of numbers. These told Lynn Townsend what he wanted to know: volume.

Townsend would run his finger up and down the reports, wondering why the Belvidere assembly plant had not met its shipping target, why production was slow at Lynch Road or why Plymouth Dusters were selling poorly in the Southwest. Lynn Townsend's ability with numbers had been what had gotten him the job in the first place. It was an essential skill in modern management. Chairman George Love had noted, "It used to be possible to control the company through personal contact. But when a company gets this big you no longer know all the people. You can't see that so-and-so is loafing, so you need a man for whom figures live. You control the company by a knowledge of figures."[1] Lynn Townsend was just such a man. The reports were what stirred him. If something was amiss he could spot it right away. He was rather like a man who knew what a well-engineered carburetor should look like, but who felt he didn't need to understand what went on inside. He knew that it should gleam like a round pot and that it should mix air and fuel together and feed them to the engine in the right quantity. Just as he didn't know the intricacies of the float bowl and the metering jet, the fast-role lever and the power piston, the seal idle compensator and the vacuum break control, Townsend didn't understand what went on in various parts of the company. He didn't realize that changing the air pressure and the fuel flow could do so many nasty things to all the little springs and screws inside a carburetor that very soon the engine would start to splutter.

If something was amiss, Townsend could spot it. "The boys knew that Lynn Townsend knows the figures and why something did or did not happen,"[2] Townsend himself said. With or without his top executives, he could adjust the production schedules, the shipping schedules and the sales targets. "Sales just aren't made; sales are pushed," Townsend would say. The changes made in the quiet of his office would begin to stir the company. They would put pressure on the vice-presidents, who would pressure the division heads. The head of automotive sales would know that he would have to come up with a good excuse if he didn't meet his sales targets. In the "war room" at Highland Park, the charts of market share for each model, which hung on the walls, would be watched nervously. In the plants, the managers would be grimly determined to meet their production targets and the zone sales managers would concentrate on shoving the new cars onto dealers. Gradually the pressure from the top would filter through the company, spreading to the gray metal desks in plant offices and to the shiniest floor in the farthest-flung dealership. For a time, particularly during the early Sixties, when the domestic market was expanding, the pressures were concealed and the company responded. When times changed, when executives misjudged the styling of a car, when a recession hit or when the oil embargo caused the rafters to shake, the implacable pressure began to send ripples through the company. Pretty soon, the pressures started to make Chrysler crumble. Lynn Townsend never seemed to understand how delicate his creation was —how easy it was to bend a company entirely out of shape.

Lynn Townsend came wrapped and wreathed in pressures that weren't all that different from those bearing down on any executive in an industry prone to cyclical disturbances. As president, and later as chairman, Townsend was accountable to directors who sat on boards of other major corporations and knew well how to bid farewell to a sloppy executive officer. The board, for example, felt very strongly that Chrysler should maintain a steady and regular stream of dividends to prime the financial markets for new stock issues and keep the price of the stock healthy. Most of the stockholders didn't care about anything apart from the stock price and dividends, either. In 1967, after net income for the first quarter had fallen to forty cents per share, its lowest level in five years, Townsend told reporters as he left the annual meeting to "make that forty cents look big." The stockholders didn't mind. One informed the meeting that he had "just got back from Hawaii with beautiful pineapples and beautiful girls" and sunnily ordered his fellow shareholders to stand and give the directors an ovation. They duly obliged.[3]

Impression was vitally important. Wall Street analysts would always be peering critically at the financial statements, ever ready to offer caustic comments or slap "sell" recommendations on the stock. The press meanwhile would lap up the ten-day sales reports, the quarterly reports, the half-yearly reports and the annual reports and readily transfer the latest tidbits, regardless of the longer-term trends, into apocryphal tales of doom or glory.

Townsend, along with his other executives, had private financial reasons for building and shipping as many cars as possible. "There's no question but that there was every incentive in the world for management to churn out everything they could before December thirty-first in order to show a big year, big profits for bonus purposes," Rockwell's Robert Anderson explained. "That would have an impact on the stock price which would boost the options up. We made pretty good money on stock options. We made pretty good money on bonuses too." At Chrysler there was an extraordinary amount of incentive, far too much incentive, to make each year the best possible. Although the disease is common throughout most American companies selling consumer goods, it was ironic that the pressure for short-term gain would help to destroy one of the companies which (with the annual model change) had helped to teach all Americans to expect better things year in and year out. To please the stockholders, the directors, the press and, not least, his own bank balance, Lynn Townsend could only look one way, and that was up.

Lynn Townsend also exerted personal pressures. In his prime he was intimidating: six feet, two inches tall and topping 195 pounds. He was fierce, had a mind that ran as smoothly as Valvoline, and could suddenly add a vicious bite to his booming voice. "Lynn Townsend," says Irv Minett, head of Chrysler International until 1970, "had a Jekyll-and-Hyde personality. He could be charming and he could be a bastard."

By every usual measure, Lynn Townsend had good reason to be pleased with himself. He had, after all, taken over the helm of Chrysler at forty-two, which made him an executive adolescent compared to his peers at General Motors, who generally reach the most senior positions when they are in their fifties. "I was really over ten years ahead of my time," Townsend later recalled. His grand Olympian view seemed successful. Unit capacity had risen from 1.2 million units a year in 1963 to 2.2 million in 1969. Chrysler's market share in the United States had been raised from 10.3 percent in 1962 to 18.1 percent in 1968. Worldwide sales had tripled to $7.4 billion while Ford's had risen by about three-quarters and General Motors by just over half. Tricks like the 5-50 warranty and the blue-and-white Pentastar had been smashing coups. He had made himself a multi-millionaire from salary, bonuses and stock options; he had even decorated the cover of *Time*.

However, a darker, sullen side began to emerge in a way that still puzzles his former colleagues. "Something happened to the man in the middle Sixties," Rockwell's Anderson recalled. "He turned into a different guy. His outlook, his approach, his ability to take counsel and advice changed. He became short-tempered, a little heavy on the martinis from time to time and unfeeling about people and the things that he would say to them in front of groups. I don't know what brought it about, but things began to crack. He almost changed personalities." Most of the people who worked close to Townsend noticed the change sometime during 1965, while he was still president of the company. Townsend himself reckons that any change happened later and was entirely due to his elevation to the chairmanship when George Love retired on January 1, 1967. "Sure I changed," Townsend admits. "I quit being the Chief Operating Officer. I changed because my job changed."

Even before Virgil Boyd, the man recruited from American Motors to beef up the sales force, was promoted to the presidency, colleagues remember that Townsend began to pay less attention to daily affairs. He began to dabble in regional fund-raising for the Republican party, and in March 1969 he became chairman of the National Alliance of Businessmen. His mind, he admitted, began to drift toward other careers. He never had intended to stay with Chrysler until he turned sixty-five, and now he started to contemplate the possibility of teaching at a university. Although he was never offered a position as a head of a federal agency, Townsend, like other men in similar positions, wondered about running for the U. S. Senate. One thing Townsend knew: he didn't want another job in business. "Once you're the chief executive officer of a company the size of Chrysler," he observed, "you've had the course."

Inside the company, he struck colleagues as distracted and bored. For a company that had always revolved around one man, the change was alarming. Chrysler, like so many other large companies, made nonsense of all the managerial textbooks, which emphasized the role of committees and ridiculed the notion that individuals could still influence changes. Townsend now used to arrive at the design and styling studios to make judgments about new cars, said colleagues, without appearing to have read the briefing books that accompany the model's development. He adopted a cavalier attitude. When he traveled, especially to press previews, he began to drink and, on occasion, the martinis got the better of him. When he drank, he tended to get mean or mournful. The old Detroit press hands still remember Townsend sitting down at the end of an evening during the 1972 new-model preview at Missouri's Lake of the Ozarks resort and pouring his heart out to them while Dick Muller, his personal public relations man, looked on helplessly.

He wasn't afraid of humiliating his high-ranking executives. He would play one off against the other and at Officer Council meetings ridicule a recent decision as "stupid." On one occasion, after the Navy League had presented mess jackets to Lynn Townsend for contributions to business, there was a reception at Chrysler's suite in the

Waldorf Towers. Townsend was explaining to a group that the Defense operation was only a small part of Chrysler when Tom Morrow, who then ran Defense, interrupted to note that his group did provide a lot of profit. Townsend looked at Morrow, reached into his pocket, pulled out a handful of small change, held it out in the palm of his hand and sneered, "Yeah, this much!" At private clubs in Detroit, before a roomful of automobile men, Townsend would occasionally call the man who in 1970 he handpicked to become president of Chrysler, snap his fingers and order: "Johnny, get me a drink!" As Lynn Townsend went, so went Chrysler. "Lynn Townsend might be a good example of why a chief executive officer shouldn't run an automobile company for more than ten years," observed former Chrysler treasurer William McGagh, who was in fact an admirer of the chairman.

Life at Chrysler, as at the other automobile companies, had a predictable rhythm. Every few weeks top executives would gather and plot out budgets, product plans, sales targets and production schedules. Usually—especially during the Sixties, when the car market kept expanding—the basis for most of the decisions depended on the projected share of the overall automobile market estimated by the company's economists.

At crucial production scheduling meetings, the first thing invariably stenciled in was the goal for earnings per share, which was decided by the chairman and the president. Once the earnings figure had been settled on, the numbers were allowed to dribble through the outlined income statements. To achieve the earnings targets, sales had to reach a certain level. "We were always too aggressive on penetration," R. K. Brown, the third-ranking Chrysler executive between 1976 and 1979, observes. "We'd look at the numbers and say, 'Last year we got twelve percent of this market segment, so this year we'll shoot for thirteen and a half!' We had already started building too many cars. If the segments got warped, or the market went down, we'd end up with cars without dealers' names on them." For sales to reach the projected levels, Chrysler had to build and ship the appropriate number of cars and trucks. To provide the volume that brought the earnings, the shipping schedules had to be met. "Shipping schedules," past Chrysler executives recall like a Greek chorus, "were always the top of the bottom line." No matter how much lip service was paid to the whims of the consumer, Chrysler's production and shipping targets were the results of decisions made by a few men: the nine members of the Operations Committee, which was ruled with an iron hand by Lynn Townsend and later John Riccardo. "Lynn Townsend," said one former subordinate, "would always boost shipping targets." And Tom Killefer, who left Chrysler to become chairman of the United States Trust Company in 1976 but remained as a director, said, "Lynn

Townsend's policy was always to stack cars like cans of beans on a shelf."

It wasn't surprising that, at Chrysler, cars were treated like baked beans or shampoo. Volume was what propelled the company through most of the Sixties, and without the proper volume Chrysler was doomed. Townsend used volume as a financial weapon, partly to compensate for the disadvantages of relatively small size and to keep the plants running smoothly, but also to keep pressure on the salesmen and dealers. To maintain volume, Chrysler took to building cars that weren't specifically ordered by the dealers. More than anything else, the practice of building cars "for sales bank" rather than strictly to dealer order helped to make Chrysler buckle. If the sales bank had been watched with the sharpest of eyes, there was a slim chance that the practice might have paid off. But once over-optimism, impetuosity and avarice got the better of Chrysler executives, the sales bank brought disaster.

Townsend wasn't unaware of the importance of dealer orders. With the advent of computers, he did more than any previous Chrysler chief executive to tie the factory closer to the sales offices. In 1962, work started on a Corporate Information Processing Center tied in to a net of seventy-one computers, all designed to speed messages between the dealers and Highland Park. Before a group of financial executives in Dallas in 1964, Townsend explained that sales reflected the consumers' judgment of a company's products, engineering, manufacturing, quality and even image. "It is crucially important," he said, "for management to see the word on sales performance as rapidly and as completely as possible." In 1965, to help spot the latest changes in sales patterns, Chrysler installed what was lavishly described as "the most modern customer order system in the automotive industry." Each of the forty-two regional sales offices was equipped with a simple keyboard to record orders. In Detroit, the information was recoded for IBM computers, which automatically rattled out production and delivery schedules and reduced the lag between order and production by as much as seven days. Before the start of the 1969 model year, some changes were made in the system to allow the regional computers to communicate directly with the large machines in Highland Park. Chrysler's dealer ordering system, at least in theory, didn't differ very much from the one used at General Motors and Ford. Every month the dealer would be visited by a zone sales manager, who would request orders for cars. A dealer had to maintain a spread of cars and couldn't plump for the hottest-selling machine, but otherwise had complete freedom to choose engine size, upholstery and all the other options. Only during the "build-out" period at the end of a model run was the dealer compelled to take options. The zone sales manager would leave a dealership with firm orders for cars to be built within thirty days, tentative orders for cars scheduled for production within sixty days and projected orders for ninety days. When the dealer orders failed to arrive in the desired quantities, Chrysler built for sales bank.

General Motors' Alfred Sloan had recognized the problem of building cars for an inventory at the beginning of the Twenties. He later wrote, "In those days the General Managers tended to be optimists, as most executives in the selling end of the automobile business were and perhaps still are. They always expected that sales would increase and thereby bring inventories into line. When the expected sales failed to materialize, a problem arose to which there could be no entirely pleasant solution. Hence we learned to be skeptical of expectation of increased future sales as a solution to a rising inventory problem."[4] Chrysler's senior managers still qualified as optimists at the end of the Seventies and were long used to getting rid of thousands of cars. In lean periods, the sales bank turned Detroit into an open-air parking lot. Travelers on the Amtrak train to Chicago, which swept by some of Chrysler's favorite storage areas, used to joke that they could tell the size of the company's executive bonus pool by the number of cars lined up—in inverse proportion. Cars would languish in quarters rented from Ford in Highland Park. Large lots next to the Jefferson Avenue plant would be stuffed with cars and trucks. Over the years, Chrysler became one of the most reliable tenants of the Michigan state fairgrounds, where cars sometimes filled every available inch. They would be squeezed in between the trees that peppered the parking lots, ranked alongside the grandstand and occasionally filling the oval inside the trotting track. When Detroit was full, the unsalable goods spilled into Canada, where the Windsor Raceway was prey to the elements as well as the news photographers who were dispatched with dismal regularity to record the visible signs of Chrysler's recurring misery.

The sales bank was like a deadly worm chewing at Chrysler's innards. Everybody knew it was there; everyone could feel it gnawing at the company, and nobody was able to get rid of it. Lynn Townsend remained unrepentant about the way Chrysler used to build to sales bank. "You cannot sell automobiles without having an inventory," he said. Under Townsend, the sales bank was both a result and a cause of the tremendous pressure that eventually perverted the company. The production scheduling, aimed in part at the sales bank, put appalling pressure on the factories, which were forced to build and ship cars of sorry quality. It sometimes even forced men to choose between losing their jobs and performing acts that verged on the illegal. Because the sales bank was little more than an expensive tool for forcing cars onto dealers, it destroyed Chrysler's marketing network and allowed the dealers to control the actions of the factory. It ended by digging deeply into Chrysler's profit margins—precisely what it had been designed to prevent.

In theory, the sales bank was sound enough. If practiced properly, building cars for an inventory isn't harmful. The Japanese manufacturers, for example, largely because of the time it took to ship a car to overseas markets, didn't worry too much about dealers' orders. Although Ford and GM liked to insist that they built each car strictly to the order they received, some (though the proportions are closely guarded secrets) were built simply to iron out kinks in production runs. For Chrysler, as the smallest company, and therefore more prone to costly fluctuations, the sales bank made more sense. Indeed, there were periods of three to seven months when the company built strictly to dealer order. Under Townsend and Riccardo, though, about half the cars produced in an average year were built without a dealer order.

From the start of the automobile industry, Detroit had been at the mercy of seasonal and cyclical fluctuations. Walter Chrysler himself (see Chapter Two) met them by refusing either to keep the plants open when orders slowed or to pay workers during the annual model change. During normal years, retail sales through the fall and spring usually equal or exceed production. After Christmas and toward the end of the model run, they slacken and production schedules have to be altered accordingly. In addition, suppliers generally complete their production several months before the end of a model year and start making the bits and pieces for the cars to be introduced the following October. By the end of March, a supplier has to choose, if orders don't arrive, between scrapping ordered parts or building on sheer speculation. It's the slowdown in production, often entailing the temporary closure of plants, that Lynn Townsend was determined to avoid. "You'll never learn how to build a quality car with the plant down," he would snap.

In the years before World War II, Townsend's predecessors had an easy time controlling inventory. If the orders didn't arrive, they slammed the factory gates. After the war, the increasing sophistication of labor contracts made temporary closures expensive. In 1955, the UAW (see Chapter Three) won a guaranteed semi-annual wage and from 1967, the automakers agreed to make contributions to the SUB fund, which, together with State Unemployment Compensation, paid laid-off workers 95 percent of their normal take-home pay. For Chrysler, the company with the thinnest cash flow, the consequences of lengthy closures were serious. With the plants closed, the labor costs were almost the same as when they were running full tilt, even if dealers weren't buying any new cars. "You're doing quite a bit," Chrysler's former executive vice-president R. K. Brown later recalled, "if you can skate through without shutting the plants."

The advantages of building for sales bank, of smoothing out flows within the factory and balancing the assembly lines, had been emphasized by the proliferation of parts and cars that took place during the Sixties.

In 1959, there were three well-defined markets: low-, medium- and high-priced. By 1969, there were seven segments: compact, intermediate, standard, medium, luxury, plus high- and low-priced specialty cars. Even by 1965, when the industry had barely reached the middle of its surge, a Yale physicist calculated that since Chevrolet offered 46 models, 32 engines, 20 transmissions, 21 colors (plus nine two-tone combinations) and more than 400 accessories, the number of different Chevies available was greater than the number of atoms in the universe.[5]

Chrysler proliferation grew right along with the rest of the industry's. In 1949, the U.S. public had been able to run their hands over 205 different cars. Aided by computerized ordering systems, the line in the showrooms had grown to 244 by 1960 and reached 370 in 1967.[6] By virtue of sheer arithmetic, the smallest company was bound to lose. Yet Chrysler merrily joined the spree, seeking not only to match GM and Ford, but also to infiltrate parts of the market previously ignored. In 1962, Chrysler produced 93 styles; by the 1967 model year, Townsend had subdivided Plymouth and Dodge into four different price lines and rolled out 160 styles.

The grand choice and the marketing paradise brought a staggering explosion of costs to the industry. The expansion of models meant more than just a small growth in the number of parts. It brought an entirely new world. At Chrysler, where the engineers were not only harried but also determined to design special parts for particular cars, the troubles were even worse. One internal survey estimated that it cost Chrysler an average of $10,000 a year to style, manufacture, order, deliver, store and assemble any part. The company was ordering thousands of new parts. In 1962 Chrysler carried around 12,000. Four years later the number had ballooned to 21,000 and by 1970 it had reached 75,000. The new parts clogged up the aisles in the plants, overflowed out of the doors and frequently had to be stored in boxcars, for which the company had to pay demurrage. Chrysler was almost in two businesses. One assembled automobiles, the other stored parts. The vast range also dug into the profitability of the Parts and Sales Service Centers, which had to stock more parts than they knew what to do with. About the only concession that Chrysler made to this newly created complexity was a computerized inventory system that linked seventy-seven of the major independent suppliers, twenty-six Chrysler parts plants and the assembly lines—and that didn't start to make a dent in the costs.

By the end of the Sixties, workers at Chrysler's Eight Mile Road stamping plant were having such difficulty separating window regulators for different models that, to tell them apart, the workers ended up spraying them with paint. At the newly purchased speedometer plant in Ann Arbor (which also supplied parts to Buick), workers couldn't understand why Buick had only two speedometer parts while Chrysler had 22. An inquiry revealed that Chrysler's stylists, when they modeled the clocks on mock-ups from which specifications were taken, had stuck pieces of paper (to signify the meters) at distances that pleased the eye. The resulting crucial gap between the trip meter and the mileage counter affected the gearing of the entire mechanism. For a time, the faceplates on the radios in the Chrysler and the Imperial were so similar that it almost took a microscope to tell the difference, but, on close examination, it turned out that the modeler had given slightly different twirls to the lettering. There was no shortage of other examples. In 1970, Chrysler was making 156 different engines, 72 different side-body lamps, 69 rear axles and 17 shapes of door handles. There were even 11 kinds of seats for Plymouth and 13 for Dodge. The cars also managed to gobble up 93 shock absorbers, though it took only 11 Delcos and 13 Monroes to service the entire fleet of cars on the road. In a supposedly high-volume business, the parts factories were running off some batches that were no bigger than a thousand.

The production schedules for the staggering choice (composed frequently of a mixture of dealer and sales bank orders) thundered down to the manufacturing plants, where they became the horrible benchmark by which all performance was judged. Like everything else in the auto industry, the pressures in the plant had a special rhythm. The pressures built toward the end of each quarter (when the companies release their quarterly sales statistics), toward the end of the model run (so that showroom floors could be cleared for the new cars) and toward the end of the year (when the books are closed and the bonuses decided). In the plants, toward the end of each quarter, the manager would hurry to meet his allotted production schedule, book what the trade calls "the manufacturing profit" and shuffle the responsibility to the sales and distribution department. For thanks to a quirk in the way that the industry keeps its books, once cars are "shipped" to dealers, the factory can book its profit on the wholesale price (the price sold to dealers) regardless of whether the dealers have any customers.

Robert Anderson remembered, "It was 'drive, drive, drive' during the last quarter. It was 'Here's your quota! Get 'em out the door!'" As head of manufacturing, he rarely slept during the last two nights of every quarter. "We'd sit in Hamtramck making phone calls to all our plants and field offices across the country and when we'd find some-place to ship a car we'd ship it to get it off the line. These cars weren't bought on the last day of the quarter; they were just shipped." Tom Killefer observed, "There was just too much pressure. It emanated from the top."

On occasion, Lynn Townsend himself used to drive down to High-land Park and pace the corridors while his officers herded cars out of the plants. One former executive recalled, "We didn't have a Christmas holiday. We'd just ship, ship, ship. The heat was intense." The same man once telephoned Townsend, who was staying at the Bel Air Hotel in Beverly Hills before attending a Rose Bowl game that Chrysler was sponsoring. He told Townsend that all the cars in a par-ticular quota had been shipped and that it was perhaps time to ease up. The Chrysler chairman simply retorted, "Ship 'em." The disease was contagious. While working in Canada John Riccardo, who in later years used to yell at his staff, "You guys don't know how to sell," resorted to even bolder tactics. Irv Minett, then head of Chrysler Can-ada, remembers one big drive to push the cars out of the factories. Checking with Riccardo, he asked whether the cars had been shipped and was told, "There's not a car left at Windsor." There wasn't. The cars had been shipped and the lots were empty, but the cars were all sitting in the storage lots belonging to the sales zones, scattered across the country.

Every conceivable trick was used to tear cars out of the assembly plants. Chrysler was just playing a game of mirrors with the profit statements. Frequently, cars ordered for a month following the end of a quarter were preshipped so that the profit could be booked. Even if the cars ended up sitting in shunting yards in Tuscaloosa, they were, as far as the factory was concerned, sold. "Profits were borrowed from the next quarter and at the end of the year from the next year," a Chrysler executive recalls. "It was numbers masturbation. We stroked ourselves until we felt good." At Dodge Main, there were always about 250 cars stashed in stalls along the production line because they needed extra attention. Toward the end of each quarter, the stalls were stripped and the cars shipped. "We'd work overtime to do it," says one current Chrysler official, "and then the workers would sit around for three or four hours the next day with nothing to do."

Dan Popa, formerly head controller at Dodge Main, a man inti-mately connected with the shipping cycles, admits, "We shipped cars at the end of a quarter we never should have. In the last hour of over-time work on an end-of-quarter shift, we'd ship out hundreds of dogs." Sometimes the quality deteriorated to such an extent that the lines were stopped. One engineer (now retired) made some spot checks. He discovered a Plymouth sitting at a Detroit railhead with no engine mountings, the engine just resting on the frame. Buttonholing Riccardo at lunchtime in a suburban restaurant, the executive told him, "We're shipping junk!" On this occasion the line was stopped until the problem was sorted out, but mostly the pressure was just too strong to resist. Dan Popa says men went to every conceivable length to meet their quotas. "We dummied up orders to get the cars out and then bring them back in again. Out of Hamtramck, two or three thousand would go out on a fake order at the end of a quarter, or about 5 percent of the quarterly output. We knew they'd be coming back and then into the sales bank." In their desperation to pretend that cars stored in the sales bank were actually sold, sales officials used to resort to a number of tricks. Anxious to lower the sales bank, they used to place unsold cars on "finance hold," which took the pressure off the sales force, even though the cars never budged. Normally the financial subsidiary used to slap "finance hold" on cars sold to dealers who had exhausted their credit and weren't able to pay for any extra cars—but in times of despair, when the sales bank was large, the sales department would slap between 5 percent and 10 percent of the cars in "finance hold." Frequently, in order to lower the sales bank, Chrysler Corporation would sell cars to Chrysler Leasing at the end of a quarter. The Chrysler Leasing official would accept an invoice for the car while the leasing company would wire the money to the parent firm. The cars, meanwhile, stayed put. "There was no need to move the cars," an executive who participated in the scheme explained, "because the sale was the most important ingredient in the whole picture." Often, too, leasing officers would engage in more innocuous cat and mouse games to help balance out the ten-day sales reports. After a large transaction was completed, the leasing company operators prepared "retail delivery cards" which, once fed into a computer, record the sale of a car. After a major deal was closed, the leasing officials would hold onto the cards to balance the sales figures until given parental permission to feed them into the computer. "We were robbing Peter to pay Paul," said one former leasing official in a resigned way. "It was obvious that sooner or later we'd end up getting a sore Peter."

Thanks to the sales bank, Chrysler had to bear a whole range of costs that don't appear when every car built has a home. Storage space had to be found and rented. The inventory had to be financed—a cost that rises as interest rates climb. After the cars had sagged up to their axles in the snow, ice and mud of a midwestern winter, they were frequently in a dreadful state. One middle-ranking manager remembers spotting a sales bank car near the Mound Road plant "where there were weeds growing inside on the carpeting." Squads regularly roamed the lots, recharging batteries, pumping and changing tires, replacing broken windshields. All these costs tended to soak up the eventual profit.

The miserable pictures of these cars standing exposed in the cold of winter or the heat of summer hardly conjured up an image of a company dedicated to providing cars with top-quality finishes. Consequently the cars were difficult to sell to dealers, who naturally preferred machines that had recently rolled off the assembly lines. Furthermore, the programming department was reluctant to spike the cars destined for the sales bank with all of the profitable options usually ordered by dealers. It made no sense to install air conditioning in a car destined for the backroads of the Pacific Northwest or Northern Canada. The only way that the cars could be moved out of the sales bank was by the offer of juicy rebates, so that Chrysler usually ended up conducting a fire sale. Finally, if the sales bank built up to such a degree that the entire company was swimming in cars, there would be no alternative but to do what should have been done weeks before: close the plants. "The sales bank," remarks Jerry Pyle, a rosy-cheeked enthusiast recruited by Lee Iacocca, "is like Dachau. It's hard to describe until you walk through it and then it hits you in the stomach."

The most serious result of the sales bank was the destruction of Chrysler's marketing network. The fate and shape of the dealers is central to the story of the corporation, for though Chrysler, in its own way, came to solve most of the problems connected with production, it was unable to conquer the headaches associated with distribution. The perversion of the dealers was insidious. It wasn't something sorted out at a policy meeting and described in a terse memo. It grew from within and was rooted in the years after World War II, when Chrysler, rather than cope directly with dealers, had relied on its wholesale distributors to do the bartering. With its competition directly controlling their dealers and with the sales information from the showrooms becoming increasingly valuable, Chrysler struggled to follow suit. Yet Chrysler, under Colbert, Townsend and Riccardo, never really fathomed out how to sell cars; they merely forced them on the dealers. Unless an automobile company is able to exert firm discipline over its dealers, it runs into all sorts of trouble, for, as a rule, the dealer network can live quite happily off a lower volume of sales than the manufacturer. Lynn Townsend puts it quite simply: "The manufacturer needs a higher volume to survive than the sum of all the dealers." From this cold truism, a battle developed between the factory (anxious to boost its volume and sell as many cars as possible) and the dealers (who, once assured of profits, could afford to wait until they got the deal they wanted). Often as not, with the factory trying to force cars from the sales bank onto its dealers, the entire network erupted in anarchy. The dealers ended up virtually running Chrysler's Sales Department.

Unlike their counterparts at GM, Chrysler dealers have long been an unruly bunch. The trouble sprang largely from the value of a Chrysler dealership compared to a Chevrolet or Cadillac outlet. The GM and Ford dealerships are larger and healthier, they stock greater inventories (which increase the chance that a customer will find the dream car) and they are less dependent on financing from banks.

The GM and Ford dealers also enjoy a better relationship with the factory and there was a general recognition that their fates were tied together. Even at Ford, which had its own troubles bringing order to its Lincoln-Mercury dealers, it was understood that the factory representative would pester and badger dealers on everything from the color of the bins in the repair bays to bookkeeping controls. The discipline had led everyone to higher profits. As a small-volume producer, Chrysler was caught in an extraordinary vicious circle. Because it was small and relatively unprofitable, it was often unable to attract the most qualified entrepreneurs; because the dealers were fragile, the factory had a hard time boosting its volume. R. K. Brown, who spent his entire career at Chrysler in sales, noted, "The factory and the dealers were antagonists, yet they were lying in the same bed." By contrast, no small part of Volkswagen's success at the end of the Sixties, when it accounted for well over half of all imports, was its tightly controlled dealer network. The company laid down the size, layout and appearance of a dealership and specifically forbade plastic streamers. It even stipulated how many parking spaces should be allotted for the service department and a clean lunchroom for mechanics. Unlike Chrysler, VW's management had one great advantage: demand for the Beetle far outstripped supply.

The conflict was often bitter and cruel. If volume and earnings goals were to be reached, Chrysler needed the help and support of every dealer it could muster. The company's only real recourse against an obdurate dealer was the cancellation of the franchise; that was the dilemma Chrysler never solved. "If a dealer won't order thirty to sixty days in advance, what do you do?" asked Townsend. If the company brought down the ax, it went against all the pressures from the executive suite. A canceled franchise cost sales, antagonized customers and allowed a dealer, particularly if his showroom occupied a prize spot, to join a competitor. Former Chrysler treasurer William McGagh bluntly acknowledged, "The dealers could tell us to go to hell and we couldn't get anybody else." Eventually the sales bank, designed to help sales, rebounded viciously. When it first ballooned—to 60,000 units in 1966—the dealers were caught off guard by the vehemence with which the factory pushed sales. With relatively low interest rates, financing the extra inventory was no great burden. The dealers didn't need a second lesson, though, and by the end of the Sixties, the relationships between the factory, the sales managers and the dealers were completely askew. The sales managers, rather than tending to the dealers' needs and offering business advice, ended up prostituting themselves. In what came to be known as the "push-pull" program, the factory would push a combination of sales bank cars and retail cars onto the dealers. The dealer meanwhile would wait and pull the most favorable terms out of the factory. The incentives offered when the factory got desperate were super for the dealer. He could afford to wait until the right "pots and pans" program turned up. Rebates would be offered on cars and there would be extra if he ordered a certain number of cars. If a salesman played his cards right, he could even furnish his home with sofas and tables and beds offered as sales incentives. There was barely a gimmick that Chrysler didn't use. In a good year, a dealer might make $70,000 from the incentive programs alone.

For talented sales managers, the work was demeaning. No man worth his salt stayed very long, for every time the sales bank mounted the district managers would be summoned to hotel or motel rooms where they would be put in the "tank" or "tub." When the senior management had been too optimistic about sales or the models were stodgy or the economy had faltered, a district manager could expect to spend two weeks of every month, eight hours a day, penned in a room in a Holiday Inn. There—along with a dozen colleagues and among the plastic coffee cups and cigarette ends—armed with a quota, he would spend the day wrangling with dealers. The sales bank ended up turning sales into a grading game. One other victim of the sales bank was Chrysler president Virgil Boyd. In 1967, aghast at what the sales bank was doing to Chrysler's marketing organization, Boyd told all his managers and dealers that the practice of building for sales bank was at an end, but, as Irv Minett observed, "Everybody is opposed to smallpox, but it was difficult to find a vaccine." R. K. Brown recalled trying to curtail the practice, but eventually discovered, "The sales bank was like holding a McDonald's franchise and then finding out that hamburger is poisonous. It's difficult to switch to eggs."

Boyd, a likable enough man whose greatest strength was with dealers, was never able to make the switch. Had he succeeded in getting rid of the sales bank, Chrysler would have been left to ride the viciously capricious swings of the market, and Lynn Townsend, who was trying to bring stability to an unstable company, wanted nothing to do with that. The cars designed for 1969 sealed Boyd's fate. Faced with immediate cunsumer resistance, Townsend, instead of slowing production, decided to rely on pressure. Years later, the Chrysler chairman explained his own recipe for extracting a company from a slump. "We are optimistic and we are pushers and you push very hard while you can, but once the market turns, you put your helmets on and ride it out." So, though 1968 ended with record profits, the number of cars in the sales bank grew and grew. Chrysler was building its own monster. By February 1969, the unchanged production schedules had driven the factory and dealer inventory to 408,302 cars and Boyd was made the scapegoat for a policy he wanted no part of. Attended by polite public pronouncements, he was shunted into the specially created position of vice-chairman and later retired at the age of sixty, taking with him a gift from his colleagues for his ranch in western Nebraska: a Black Angus bull named Pentastar CCC.

Walter P. Chrysler. *Credit: Chrysler Corporation*

Walter Chrysler (in car) with his successor as chairman, K. T. Keller; engineer Fred M. Zeder; and finance officer B. J. Hutchinson. *Credit: Chrysler Corporation*

Lester L. "Tex" Colbert in 1951. *Credit: Junebug Clark*

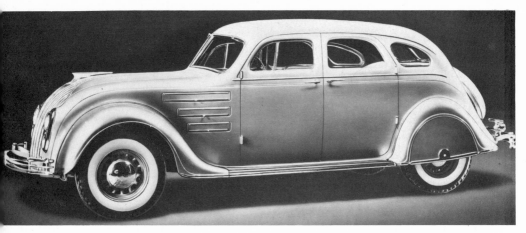

The 1934 Chrysler Airflow. *Credit: Chrysler Corporation*

The 1949 Chrysler Royal. *Credit: Chrysler Corporation*

The 1957 Chrysler New Yorker. *Credit: Chrysler Corporation*

Churning out cars from Dodge Main, February 1951. *Credit: Junebug Clark*

Lynn Townsend, handing over the management of Chrysler to John Riccardo (left) and Gene Cafiero (right). *Credit: Chuck Ternes*

The Chrysler "sales bank" stacked up at the Windsor (Ontario) Raceway, spring 1975. *Credit: Junebug Clark*

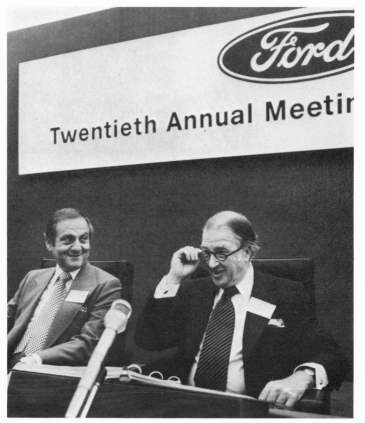

Lee Iacocca (left) as Ford president in happier times, with Henry Ford II, May 1975. *Credit: Junebug Clark*

Henry Ford II announces the formation of the Office of the Chief Executive, promoting Philip Caldwell (right) to vice-chairman over president Lee Iacocca (left), April 1977. *Credit: Junebug Clark*

John Riccardo the day he announced the hiring of Lee Iacocca—November 2, 1978. *Credit: Chuck Ternes*

Lee A. Iacocca. *Credit: Junebug Clark*

CHAPTER SIX

"Negligence, Incompetence, or Manipulation?"

Chrysler didn't have the luxury of passing up any automobile market in the United States.

—Lynn Townsend

Rooted, like everything else, in decisions made several years earlier, 1969 was an unmitigated disaster. With cars piling up in the Michigan fairgrounds, the dangers of chasing after volume became painfully apparent for the first time. Despite Lynn Townsend's campaign to make Chrysler a full-line producer, the results, by 1969, were curiously lopsided. Constantly working with short-term goals to stimulate sales, Chrysler was ringed with the exhaust of the drag strip, loaded with unappealing large cars and, perhaps most painful of all, had no hold on the extremely profitable personal luxury car field where Ford, with the Thunderbird and the Mark, was battling GM's Buick Riviera, Olds Toronado and Cadillac Eldorado. In the rarefied luxury segment, where GM took about three-quarters of the sales, the Imperial ran a sorry third behind the Cadillac and the Lincoln.

It was cruelly ironic that Townsend's goals of higher volume, steadily increasing earnings and higher dividends—all the tried and tested fruits of American business—were largely at odds with his desire to improve the balance and stability of the company. Since "conquest sales" (capturing sales from other brands) were so difficult to obtain, adding volume entailed chasing after a fad or a blip on a sales chart. It was a complicated and tricky task, since Chrysler's size and its relatively weak financial position prevented it from jumping at a chance lest the gamble prove too costly. Yet chasing the opposition and galloping into particular segments brought other problems. It meant that signals and directions were always changing. Although Lynn Townsend, during his redesign at the start of the Sixties, had taken pains to stress that Chrysler's cars would henceforth be consistent, conforming in style from year to year and remaining in line with other makers, the reality of the chase made nonsense of the promise. The race at Chrysler inevitably started when the competition was already kicking up the dirt.

Only one thing was consistent, and that was the emphasis placed on solid, durable engineering. It was the theme played by Walter Chrysler, K. T. Keller and Tex Colbert. Lynn Townsend took up the refrain without missing a beat. Townsend was determined not to allow anyone to forget that engineering was as synonymous with Chrysler as "A car for every purse and purpose" was with General Motors. Almost every advertising campaign lauded engineering features and executives constantly played on Chrysler's "engineering excellence." When money ran low, when recessions intervened and when the oil shocks arrived, though, the task became infinitely more difficult. Thinking back to the experience of 1966, when the market lapped up a selection of restyled large, C-body cars, Chrysler pinned great hopes on its 1969 large cars. Ford and General Motors had tooled their plants to produce two types of car, but four of Chrysler's eight assembly plants were solely devoted to the production of the new large cars: the Dodge Polara and Monaco, the Chrysler 300 and the Imperial, and the Plymouth Gran Fury.

The launch was a catastrophe. Insufficient time was left for the preproduction checks; glitches in a revised computerized-ordering system meant that the orders weren't being followed correctly. Cars were being dispatched to the wrong cities and things deteriorated to such an extent that two hundred opulent New Yorkers rolled off the line like rubber-mat specials with standard transmissions, no radios, no power steering or power brakes and no air conditioning. Complaints poured in from the dealers, who were quick to echo the sentiments of wary customers: the flares on the rear fenders were too obtrusive; the trim was unattractive; the wheels made the cars look bowlegged. For the 1969 model year, the market for the C-bodies fell by 7 percent while the market for all U.S. cars grew by 6 percent.[1] In 1970, the company tacitly acknowledged the troubles, restyling the cars with a wider track, lower front ends, shorter rear ends, and changed grilles and trim.

Even without the C-body cars, Chrysler had built itself into trouble. The introduction of Ford's new Mustang and Cougar and GM's Firebird and Camaro in the mid-Sixties had brought a roar to every alley. Chrysler had quickly oiled specially souped-up cars for the stock-car circuit, peeling hemi-headed Plymouths and Dart GTs out of the pits and entering the National Hot Rod Association circuit with race-car driver Richard Petty,[2] but Chrysler hesitated before jumping full-blast into the new sports car market and then, after the competition was established, made the decision to follow. The result: until the fall of 1969 the Barracuda (the answer to Ford's Mustang and GM's Firebird) was little more than a Valiant with a twist in the rear. "It was an abortion," said one Chrysler official. Even the 1969 arrival of the Challenger, six years after the Mustang had set Detroit on its ear, was rushed. The engineering department had compensated for lack of time by playing safe: adding weight and beefing up the brakes, axles and transmission. The Challenger entered the market just as it was beginning to wane. The market for sports cars fell from 11 percent of the car market in 1967 to 7 percent by 1970. Ford and GM had entered the power market with some semblance of modesty, endeavoring not to alienate their traditional customers. Chrysler seemed to believe that muscle was the next best thing to gasoline. Suddenly, half the company's cars seemed to have flared nostrils and rubber-burning tires. A special "Dodge Rebellion" marketing campaign was launched, featuring the blond Pam Austin,[3] cowgirls and other youthful trappings—all of which must have surprised Dodge's dour band of customers. Youngsters were tantalized with ads announcing what a beautiful screamer a Charger was and were urged to "Buy 440 cubes worth of rippling muscle." So deeply did Chrysler enter the hotshot market that it didn't really retreat until the fall of 1974.

As the market turned, Townsend and his executives next found themselves facing the problem of whether to build a small car. The demand for small cars had not disappeared with the appearance of the compacts at the beginning of the Sixties. For a time, Detroit had seemed successful. Chevrolet's Corvair, Plymouth's Valiant, Dodge's

Dart and the Ford Falcon succeeded in driving back the imports from
10.1 percent of the market in 1959 to 4.9 percent in 1962. The manufacturers misread the enthusiasm of the American consumer and happily interpreted the success of the lean, trim compacts to mean that
there was a demand for anything bearing an American label rather
than a permanent demand for small cars; only social misfits, Detroiters
willingly believed, wanted small cars.

Ford's experience with its own plans for a small car echoed through
the Sixties. Convinced that the imports, particularly the Beetle, could
only be beaten by a genuine small car, Ford decided in 1959 to launch
a car, dubbed the Cardinal, that would have a four-cylinder engine,
feature front-wheel drive and be a mere five inches longer than the
Volkswagen. The Cardinal was scheduled for introduction in the fall
of 1962, but with the massive success of the compacts, Ford, even
after the advertising brochures had been printed, abruptly canceled
its U.S. production plans in the spring of 1961. The success of the
compacts was somehow interpreted as an invitation to fall back into
the comfortable habit of prodding buyers toward plusher and more
expensive models. Before long, the freshly cut compacts were growing
larger and larger until they eventually popped right out of the niche
for which they were originally designed. By 1969, the Falcon had
grown by three inches and gone up, without any inflationary pressure,
$300 in price. The Plymouth Valiant, between 1960 and 1975, grew 16
inches and gained nearly five hundred pounds. Apparently bitten by
the success of the sporty Mustangs, Camaros and Firebirds, the companies allowed their compacts to slip into a market where the elderly,
the less-educated and the poor browsed.

By 1968, though, the American automakers had been yet again
rudely awakened by imports. Through most of the middle Sixties, the
success of the foreigners, who rose from 5.1 percent of the market in
1963 to 9.3 percent in 1967, was greeted with the same reaction they
had received in the late Fifties: Detroit simply shipped in more cars
made by their foreign subsidiaries, dismissing domestic production on
grounds that the market was too small to allow all three to turn a
profit on cars priced below $2,000. UAW president Walter Reuther re-
peatedly asked both Kennedy and Johnson to promote legislation that
would free manufacturers from the strictures of antitrust law and permit them to pool their money and jointly produce one small car. Indeed, Reuther told GM's chief labor negotiator that the nation's largest carmaker should produce a small car. Seaton was quick to retort
that his company resented the union's intrusion into its strategic
planning.[4]

By 1968, when imports captured one-tenth of the entire market (the
Beetle outselling its nearest foreign rivals by better than six-to-one),

the U.S. industry recognized that there was a demand for small cars (which it disparagingly called "subcompacts"). However, there was a severe case of inverted snobbery to contend with, as Robert Anderson, who had recently left Chrysler, pointed out. "You can buy a VW for $1,700 and you are assured of being regarded as a sharp, brilliant guy for not spending money on an American car with planned obsolescence. But if you spend $1,600 on a cheap American-built car you are just a cheap guy. How do you compete with that attitude?"

General Motors, Ford and American Motors had their own ideas about how to tackle the imports. Ford was the first to clearly signal its intentions when, as early as 1967, it placed tooling orders for the Maverick, a two-door, sporty sedan which appeared in the spring of 1969 and marked Detroit's first tinny blow at the invaders. The car, which cost Ford $45 million, displayed no technical innovations and was unmistakably American. It shared the same basic components with the Mustang and the Falcon, and even the name had been tested before, on a 1959 Willys Jeep: the Maverick Special. It was almost two feet longer, twice as powerful and, at 2,500 pounds, 700 pounds heavier than the Beetle. American Motors, meanwhile, introduced the Hornet, a restyled Rambler, in the fall of 1969. GM, not previously inclined to reveal much of its internal discussions, trumpeted its decision to build a small car. In October 1968, chairman James Roche used the opening of the fifty-story GM Building in midtown Manhattan to announce work on a subcompact specifically designed for American tastes. The car, code-named the XP-887 and later named the Vega, would not, said Roche, be "a pocket-size version of any other car." It would be priced at the level of the Beetle, weigh less than 2,000 pounds and be built in the most automated assembly plant in the United States, the sprawling Lordstown plant, which stretched across the Ohio countryside.

Convinced that the subcompact market was too large to ignore, GM and Ford clanked ostentatiously forward, but Chrysler refused to budge. Townsend and his men believed that not only would their share of the subcompact market be too small to ensure a profit, but that existing demand could easily be met by shipping cars from overseas. At the end of the Sixties, when it was enjoying a share of the market it has never regained, VW's net profit margin was less than half that of GM and lower than either Ford or Chrysler. The evidence was unmistakable. "It's pretty stupid to go ahead with a chauvinistic display of patriotism when the cost features aren't there," financial officer Tom Killefer told a group of market analysts.[5]

Although Ford and GM had quietly borne the shortcomings of their captive imports, Chrysler continued to pin its hopes on the British-made Sunbeam and the French Simca 1100. However, both of these cars had been banned from the United States during most of 1968 because they failed to comply with federal safety standards, and the previous sales figures weren't encouraging. Combined sales of Rootes and Simca rarely had exceeded 20,000 cars a year and were sold by a mere 740 dealers, compared with the 1,070 for VW, 5,940 for Ford and 6,400 for Chevrolet. Chrysler was sorely hampered by production difficulties in the United Kingdom (see Chapter Seven) and, by the fall of 1972, had halted imports of the Simcas and the Cricket (the successor to the Sunbeam). Chrysler was scorched by President Nixon's August 1971 decision to impose a temporary surcharge on imports. Sales of the Cricket had slumped to just over 13,000 for the first nine months of 1972; there was a strong and more profitable demand for the Simca 1100 in West Germany, and it was considerably cheaper to ship the cars there.

To bolster the imports from Europe, in 1971 Chrysler concluded a joint venture with Japan's Mitsubishi Motor Company, then a subsidiary of Mitsubishi Heavy Industries, which made everything from Nikon cameras to supertankers. In return for purchasing 35 percent of the Japanese automobile company, Chrysler earned the right to import Mitsubishi's subcompact Colt, first sold in early 1970. (The general plan was to sell 60,000 Colts and 60,000 Crickets a year.) The secret negotiations with Mitsubishi proved to be a lingering embarrassment. The Japanese were eager for an agreement: they would gain access to some of Chrysler's technical advances, the American dealership network and Chrysler's investment, which would permit an expansion of their factories. Although the talks between the two companies had been hampered by the characteristic foot-dragging of the Japanese government, there was no mistaking Mitsubishi's sincerity. There was also no mistaking the Chrysler delegation's sincerity. They firmly believed that Highland Park was willing and able to buy 35 percent of the Japanese company. Lynn Townsend himself, having done little homework, traveled to Japan and, with some typical intimidating bluster, attempted to speed up negotiations with the Prime Minister and the head of MITI. It came as a great shock to the Chrysler chairman to find, after the agreement had been all but signed, that there was not enough cash to foot the bill. He dispatched another Chrysler official to Japan to explain the embarrassing predicament to Mr. Yoichiro Makita, president of Mitsubishi. Although Chrysler and Mitsubishi eventually smoothed over the trouble publicly (Chrysler purchased 15 percent of Mitsubishi, deferring the other 20 percent), the shoddy dealing was never forgotten by the Japanese.

Although Chrysler publicly stated that its reluctance to make small cars was purely due to economic considerations, there was also an added element. Lynn Townsend fervently believed that Americans would no more tolerate small cars than they would summers without air conditioning. In the summer of 1968, he noted, "Our economical Valiant (15′ 8″ long and priced at $2,300) is in our opinion the best low-priced automotive value that you can obtain."[6] There was considerable concern within Chrysler that production of a subcompact would damage sales of Chrysler's successful compacts. As late as 1973, the Chrysler chairman insisted, "The subcompacts are just too small, the American people won't climb into them. They have to give up too much in creature comfort. Even a compact is a little small . . . I would think that probably the most popular car size you'll see fifteen years from today will be like our intermediates today. But you're still going to see a hell of a lot of big ones."[7] Nevertheless, Chrysler went to great lengths to placate the press, which was asking increasingly biting questions about Chrysler's plans for a small car. Townsend took every opportunity to deplore GM's and Ford's decision to announce their plans for small cars in advance of the launch. On one occasion, he bent the rules of the game even further. At the 1969 preview for the '70 model year, knowing full well that he would have to counter irritating questions, Townsend gathered a group of executives in his hotel suite, talked briefly about the possibility of a small car and later baldly told reporters that Chrysler was indeed planning to build a small car.

Chrysler did study plans for a small car, and even gave it a code number: R-429; it required all new sheet metal and a new front suspension. By the summer of 1969, though, such plans for an entirely new small car had been abandoned and attention shifted to the "25," a smaller version of the existing compacts. In September 1969, Chrysler announced that it would begin production of a subcompact in the spring or early summer of 1971.

At Chrysler, the pressures from above, the need for quick returns and limited market-share prospects simply didn't allow room for much of a gamble—let alone a mistake that could cost well over $100 million. Ironically, Chrysler, in part for the wrong reason, was saved from a premature plunge into the subcompact market. In 1968, subcompacts totaled 1.5 million units, which—if Chrysler had gained a 20-percent share—still would not have made the company any profit. Indeed, given more pessimistic projections, Chrysler would have been hard pressed to keep a single small-car plant running. Even during the first small-car boom in 1974, when subcompacts took 17.4 percent of a 9.7-million-unit year, Chrysler could have sold perhaps 150,000.

Ultimately, the wisdom of Chrysler's decision to abstain from producing subcompacts was demonstrated by the experience of GM and Ford with the Vega and the Pinto, respectively. By the time the Vega was launched, it was 382 pounds heavier and almost $200 more expensive than its nemesis, the VW Beetle. The car was scarcely helped by near-anarchy at the Lordstown assembly plant, by a weak aluminum engine and by a defective carburetor. The Pinto had combustible problems of its own. By 1977, when the Vega was phased out after GM had manufactured 1.9 million of them, and by 1980, when Ford dropped the Pinto after 3.4 million of them had been built, neither company had made a penny's profit on the ventures. More seriously, the public had accumulated lasting doubts about Detroit's ability to make a decent small car.

Persuaded on small cars by the logic of the numbers, but still searching for additional volume, Chrysler entered the truck market with a vengeance. Trucks had been the ugly stepdaughters of the automobile industry, condemned to barns, country roads and construction sites. Four-wheel drive had been a feature provided only by Jeep and International Harvester. At the turn of the Seventies, however, light trucks, and especially vans, took on a new spirit. Young men's fancy for roaring muscle cars turned to trucks. Like most automotive fads, the popularity of trucks and vans first showed up on the West Coast, where they became popular for surfing and beach parties. So, during the first half of the Seventies, Detroit found itself faced with an entirely new opportunity offering all sorts of tempting profits: the consumer truck market.

Like the rest of the industry, Chrysler was caught by surprise at the market's rapid growth. Between 1970 and 1977 the truck market grew at an average annual compound rate of 9 percent, compared to 2.3 percent for automobiles.

Within the truck market, the popularity of the newfangled vans grew at a faster rate than that of pickups. In 1970, pickups grabbed 70 percent of the market, compared to 56 percent in 1977, while vans grew from 16 percent to 22 percent, small imported Japanese pickups from 3 percent to 10 percent and sports utility vehicles from 5 percent to 7 percent.

Chrysler just kept on trucking. In 1969, the company had 7.3 percent of the truck market and lost $25 million on truck sales. By 1972 it was turning a profit of $100 million on trucks and by 1976 had 14.6 percent of the market. Chrysler dropped its heavy-duty and medium-duty trucks (which had deteriorated into little more than an assembly operation) to concentrate on the more versatile versions. Dodge maintained its position in the recreational vehicle field, where it generally managed to supply more than three-quarters of the chassis used for motor homes. In 1972, it managed to top an 85-percent share of that segment. A new Club Cab pickup offered space behind the front seats for fishing rods and guns or just plain jump seats. Wooden bars were strapped onto the pickups, the sides were daubed with exotic twirls of paint and the angry-looking machines were called Warlocks. The Dodge street van came with a tinted bubble in the back, exhaust pipes thick enough to ventilate a small power station and an interior wide enough to take a queen-size mattress. Youngsters soon discovered that the vans were better than dimly lit country lanes. Sitting high above the ground, the macho Dodge pickup, the Ramcharger and the Plymouth Trailduster had tires ringed with aggressive white lettering and became another generation's hotrods. Buyers could easily spend more on options than on the truck itself. For the more socially minded, the vans formed part of a new vocabulary, "the van-pool." By 1975, one-fourth of all vehicles produced by Chrysler in the United States were trucks.

Compared to investing in an entirely new small car, trucks were cheap. They had to be, for by 1970 Chrysler had scarcely any money. The increase in volume, the plethora of models, the new plants and subsidiaries, the aggressive marketing and the thrust overseas sopped up enormous amounts of money. When Lynn Townsend took charge of Chrysler, he had inherited a balance sheet that was virtually clear of debt and had plenty of room for new stockholders. In 1960, long-term debt (in absolute terms) was $250 million below the levels at GM and Ford. By 1970, it had ballooned to $791 million, and the debt-to-equity ratio had risen from 14 percent to 37 percent, while the ratios at GM remained unchanged and Ford's had altered only marginally. At the end of the Sixties, Chrysler had expanded the outstanding shares by one-third, tripled the stockholders' equity—partly thanks to the 5.6 million shares issued in 1965 in the third largest offering ever—and, astonishingly, carried more debt than General Motors. Lynn Townsend had spent Chrysler into oblivion.

Although Townsend liked to tell reporters that John Riccardo in 1970 occupied the same position Townsend had occupied in 1960, it was a grossly unfair comparison. In 1960, Townsend didn't have to cope with the costs of government regulation and was able to borrow enormous sums. Riccardo and Gene Cafiero, though they refrained from even alluding to it in public, had been left with an empty till. At the very time when Chrysler needed every single penny, it was strapped for funds.

The results were catastrophic. Against the background of sharply declining expenditures during the first slump at the beginning of the Seventies, and during the second, which lasted from the fourth quarter of 1973 into the beginning of 1975, it's easy to understand why Chrysler lost so much market share during the Seventies. The auto industry's capital spending falls into two categories: the long-term commitments made for factories and other equipment that will last for more than one model, and the short-term spending for tools, presses and all the other pieces needed for a particular year's models. In both areas, during both downturns, Chrysler's spending plummeted. For the three years 1970–72, Chrysler's spending on plant and equipment was $457 million, compared to $306 million for 1966 alone and $375 million committed in 1969. Spending in 1971 reached the lowest level since 1963, though the company was selling 1.1 million more units. During the same period, GM and Ford stepped on the gas.

Chrysler's precarious position didn't go unnoticed by the financial markets, and a panic on Wall Street brought the company to within a whisker of bankruptcy. Late on the afternoon of June 19, 1970, the Nixon administration stunned the financial community by reneging on its pledge to guarantee $200 million in loans for the Penn Central Transportation Company. By June 22, the gigantic Eastern railroad had filed for bankruptcy and a petrified Wall Street was scouring its books for other companies that had recently lost money and had large amounts of commercial paper (short-term IOU's) outstanding. Chrysler fit the bill. It had lost $27.4 million during the first quarter of 1970 and Chrysler Financial had more than $1.5 billion of commercial paper. Within days, investors fled from anything vaguely connected with a Pentastar and only a massive rally by the banks saved Chrysler from following the Penn Central. Chrysler's Tom Killefer flew to Washington to ask the chairman of the Federal Reserve Board to help matters and open the discount window. Dr. Arthur Burns would hear of no such thing. Jabbing his pipe at Killefer, a courtly Rhodes scholar, Burns retorted: "You're trying to politicize the Federal Reserve Board of the United States and turn this country into a Latin American banana republic."

John McGillicuddy, the thirty-nine-year-old vice-chairman of the board of Chrysler's lead bank, Manufacturers Hanover, didn't see things in quite the same light. Jetting around North America with Townsend, Bill McGagh and Gordon Areen (president of Chrysler Finance), McGillicuddy cajoled Chrysler's major lenders into a rescue package. An additional $180 million was added to Chrysler Financial's existing line of credit (this deal moved so fast that the finance company was drawing on its new line even before all the banks had been contacted). The banks bought the $150 million of receivables that the financial subsidiary had bought from American Motors, and Chrysler injected $100 million of its own. Several months later, in a highly unusual gesture of support, McGillicuddy issued a statement observing that "Support of Chrysler and its principal subsidiaries has rested and will continue to rest on their ability to demonstrate their credit worthiness."[8] Lynn Townsend had a reassuring thought of his own: "Chrysler," he asserted, "is no Penn Central."[9]

Troubled by a national slump, Chrysler picked out its own mournful melody, and soon there was talk of fresh cuts to come. John Riccardo brittley talked about running "a drum-tight organization," laid off six thousand white-collar workers and withdrew from the U. S. Labor Department's JOBS program, designed to aid the hard-core unemployed. To get through the gloom, Chrysler took on another $200 million of debt and cut the dividend from the $2.00-per-share paid out between 1966 and 1969 to 60 cents. "We were borrowing to pay the dividend," Tom Killefer remembered. Soon even the teeth of Chrysler customers started to rattle, with quality deteriorating so much that Byron Nichols, a Chrysler vice-president, was given a special beat: dissatisfied customers were invited by full-page newspaper advertisements to call Nichols—"My man in Detroit"—and voice their complaints. In the summer of 1971, more cuts were made: the Los Angeles assembly plant, which was building only 35,000 cars a year, though it had a capacity of 110,000, was buttoned up for the final time. Lying in the foothills of Pennsylvania's Laurel Mountains, the New Stanton plant became a delicate thermometer of corporate health. A corrugated aluminum-and-steel frame sheltered a floor the size of thirty-six football fields while cows and horses browsed in an adjoining field. In 1969, Chrysler had hung a "help wanted" sign from an old farmhouse across the road from the plant and 18,000 applicants clogged the rural two-lane road for miles. Through 1970 and 1971, New Stanton stood silent and empty, the floor covered with dust.

As the auto market recovered, so did the prospects for the completion of New Stanton. By the middle of 1973, the manufacturers were so pressed to meet demand that they took to shipping parts by air to avoid interrupting production, and in August 1973 Townsend announced that New Stanton would be finished in time to launch Chrysler's replacements for the compact Dart and Valiant. In 1975, the decision was reversed again. The next major announcement about New Stanton was its sale in 1977 to Volkswagen.

The UAW, a shrewd judge of strength, closely monitored Chrysler's renewed vigor and, in 1976, announced that it would strike the third automaker for the first time since 1964. Chrysler offered the union the largest possible gain with the least amount of pain. As with the dealers, Chrysler could never bargain with the union from a position of strength. The company did not have the resources to weather, let alone emerge from, a lengthy strike as GM managed to do in 1970. Yet by insisting that it was a full-line producer, that all its cars matched anything the competition had to offer, that its managers were nimbler and smarter, in short, adopting all the airs and graces of a dignified member of the Big Three, Chrysler could never argue convincingly that it had private worries and deserved tender treatment. In 1970, when the union for the first time selected Chrysler as a twin strike target with General Motors, UAW chief Leonard Woodcock emphasized the ambiguity. "If you want to run with the pack," Woodcock warned Chrysler, "you can't run with the pack and at the same time tell us you have special problems."[10]

It became immaterial that Chrysler sold fewer cars, had lower earnings and eked out smaller profit margins than its competitors. The different levels of productivity between the automakers have long been obscured, partly because the companies have been loath to disclose the details and partly because it was convenient for the union to dole out equal treatment. Indeed, the union based its assessments of productivity increases on the auto industry as a whole, rather than on individual companies' experiences. Those claims themselves (certainly not quibbled with by the companies) tend to show that the union has not, as its critics love to argue, priced itself out of a job within the confines of the American economy. Between 1958 and 1978, consumer prices rose by 134.3 percent, output in the industry by 113 percent and union wage levels by 234 percent. Even at Chrysler, wage levels, contrary to popular belief, have stayed fairly constant as a percentage of total operating costs. In 1960, total wage costs (which included fringes and pensions) came to $695.7 million or 23.3 percent of total costs; in 1970 they accounted for 25.5 percent of total costs and in 1975, at $2.739 billion, they were only 23.3 percent of all costs.[11]

The United Automobile, Aerospace and Agricultural Implement Workers of America—as the union's full name implies, had long been accustomed to coping with the differences that existed between industries. For example, the union's aerospace workers had always enviously ogled the settlements won by their brothers in the Big Three. However—aided and abetted by the ambiguity of Chrysler's management—the union was not prepared to recognize the differences that existed *within* Detroit. The only distinction the UAW seemed to draw between the companies was their comparable bargaining strength. There was an entirely understandable (if theoretically abhorrent) reluctance to extend that difference to its logical extremes: lower wages, lower benefits and lower pensions.

By the start of the 1970s, the union had become something of a victim of its own success. Auto workers generally lived in the suburbs; they owned cars and televisions, lawnmowers and snowmobiles, mobile homes and summer cottages. The monument Walter Reuther designed for himself along 850 acres on the shore of Black Lake in Northern Michigan told a similar story. Built on land bought from a Detroit advertising magnate, the $23 million education and recreation center, a quiet blend of cedar, birch and fir, was designed for reflection—not action. In the central foyer, bronze-and-venetian-glass plaques depicting the arrangement of the heavens at Reuther's birth are arranged around a fireplace.[12] The younger breed of auto workers, the union leaders moaned, didn't possess the same commitment shown by those who sat down in the Fifties. "The younger people might listen, but they don't believe," a local president mused. "They only think of coming to two meetings every three years. At the first they want to know how much we are asking for, at the second they want to know how much we got."

At Chrysler the tensions were even more acute. For a start, the company employed the best-organized skilled tradesmen—designers and tool-and-die men who jealously guarded their wage differentials. More importantly, there was far greater racial tension within the Chrysler plants than in GM or Ford factories. Even at plants in St. Louis and Belvidere, the bias against blacks was pronounced, while at Hamtramck the work force was a combustible mixture of blacks, Poles and southern whites. The resentment was partly due to frustration, for though the UAW has one of the better records for promotion of blacks, they still have precious little representation. "I got off the production line, it's like a cotton field in 1850," one black worker at the Mack Avenue stamping plant complained.[13] Toward the end of the Sixties, DRUM (the Dodge Revolutionary Union Movement), a violent group of black communists, made matters even worse with their plans to topple both the union and the company. Whites, especially at the Detroit plants, took to walking to their cars in groups for safety. Much of the pressure for early retirement came from men anxious to leave the danger of the plants. Those who remained almost all packed a gun or a knife or a length of pipe with their lunch. Art Hughes, Doug Fraser's administrative assistant for sixteen years, observes, "Inside the Chrysler plants there was just about every kind of problem you could imagine." Bets were taken on anything: on numbers, horses or football games. Loan sharks roamed the plants and musclemen ran protection rackets threatening to slash fellow workers' car tires if money wasn't handed over. Prostitutes openly worked the plants and dope peddling soon became impossible to police. There were, at one time, so many transvestites at the Huber Foundry that they even asked for special lavatories.[14] The daily tensions, the strains of the inner city, were worsened by the cyclical swings in the auto industry. When the order books filled, the aisles at the plants tended to get clogged with machinery or parts. When times were slow, health and safety were neglected and oil slicks, puddles of water and machines dripping grease became common. Every now and then the atmosphere became too highly charged. In July 1970, James Johnson, a thirty-six-year-old black employee at the Eldon Avenue axle plant, pulled an M-1 carbine from his trouser leg, loaded it with a thirty-round banana clip and killed a jobsetter and two foremen, one of whom had suspended him for insubordination. A year later, he was found innocent of murder on grounds of temporary insanity. During the trial one juror cried out, "Did you see the cement room in that plant? Working there would drive anyone crazy."[15]

Chrysler's cycle of misery returned with a vengeance between 1973 and 1975. This time the shock was more severe and the damage more permanent. Like the previous reversal, which had started in the fall of 1968, it began with the introduction of a redesigned series of large cars. Chrysler ran what was fast becoming a familiar course. Sales fell; layoffs were ordered; plants were closed; capital spending plans were postponed; dividends were sliced; the financial subsidiary found itself excluded from the public debt and commercial paper markets and had to sell nearly $400 million of receivables to a group of banks while the parent company sold more debt and hastily rejuggled its lending lines. Chrysler, as before, entered the doldrums before the other automakers and, when the recession started in late 1974, found itself faced, once more, with a smaller share of a declining market.

In the middle of 1973, Lynn Townsend was expressing his customary optimism and projected sales of 14.5 million cars and trucks for the United States by the end of the year.[16] Then Chrysler was smashed by a mixture of appalling luck and slovenly management. As dealers paraded the new $200 million line of full-size cars before the public in October 1973, war broke out between Israel and Egypt and the oil-producing countries of the Middle East began a four-month embargo on sales to the United States (see Chapter Seven). Chrysler reacted to the ensuing fuel crisis by cutting spending on tools, plants and equipment from $629 million in 1973 to $466 in 1974. At General Motors, meanwhile, spending increased from $2.1 billion in 1973 to $2.5 billion in 1974.

The real damage, however, was wrought in the fall of 1974 and much of the blame rests squarely on the shoulders of Chrysler's managers, who, in their eagerness to believe that the nation had recovered from the oil shock (which it indeed appeared to have done), once again pressured the Chrysler plants. As late as September 1974, Lynn Townsend foresaw a good fourth quarter. Despite some acrimonious squabbling at lower levels of management, nothing was done to temper the optimistic production schedules that hurtled out of the executive suite—but within less than ninety days, the course of the industry changed abruptly. In August 1974, cars were being produced at the rate of 9.5 million a year. By November, the nation was dropping into a recession, unemployment had risen to 7 percent and auto production had plummeted, in what was the severest shift since the Second World War, to an annual rate of 6.8 million. Townsend was at his vacation home in Hawaii when the cars started to pile up in the Michigan fairgrounds. The UAW's Douglas Fraser snapped that the absent chairman was like Nero and that, together with John Riccardo, he was "guilty of negligence, incompetence or manipulation." By the end of November, Chrysler had a three-month supply of cars, compared to slightly less than two-month supplies at Ford and General Motors.

Swinging away from running plants at capacity, Townsend and Riccardo quickly improvised a rescue plan that was one of the most severe ever seen in Detroit. Perhaps the only cuts faintly comparable were those made by Walter Chrysler shortly after he joined the Maxwell Company at the beginning of the Twenties. Townsend insisted that he wanted to shrink the company to a size where it could remain profitable even in a market that bought only 6 million cars and trucks a year. "We are not going to permit ourselves to go on rosy forecasts of the future," he said.[17] Several of the full-size Plymouth Fury models were dropped and plans to close the Jefferson Avenue assembly plant were only shelved after vehement protests by the UAW, the City of Detroit and the State of Michigan. In a move that left an especially bitter taste, workers, because of plant closures, were deprived of their Christmas and New Year holiday pay, which saved the company $19 million. Top executives took a 50-percent pay cut for a few weeks; white-collar employees were forced to take part of their 1975 vacation in 1974 and for over four months one or more of Chrysler's assembly plants were closed. By Christmas, Chrysler had dipped into $250 million of an emergency line of credit. It was no coincidence that Chrysler refrained from issuing its traditional year-end message. In an effort to spur sales, a warranty program was expanded to offer free repairs on almost any part for twelve months. One company insider called the announcement, "The biggest break for traveling salesmen since the farmer's daughter," while other mordant wags joked that the warranty lasted, "For 12,000 miles or until the company goes out of business—whichever comes first."[18]

Only with the introduction of the Car Clearance Carnival by former baseball catcher Joe Garagiola during the January 1975 Superbowl did Chrysler begin to sell the cars that it never should have built. The almost total closure of Chrysler's operations had a serious effect on its product programs. The Aspen/Volare compacts scheduled for the fall of 1975, the L-body Omni/Horizons due for the fall of 1977 and the large R-bodies planned for 1978 were all affected. The impact on the Aspen/Volare, premium-priced successor to the durable Darts and Valiants, was felt first. The stockholders were no more pleased than the company's employees and, at the annual meeting, the corporate Pentastar was, for some reason, mounted on a black rather than a blue background. One stockholder, perhaps sensing that 1975 would be the first time that no dividend was paid (even in 1933 dividends were paid for two quarters), angrily stated, "You don't go to a doctor to have a will drawn up. You don't go to a lawyer to have a leg set. Therefore you shouldn't go to an accountant to build a car."[19] Lynn Townsend disagreed. On Friday of the Fourth of July weekend, he announced his intention of resigning from Chrysler the following October 1 and recommended to the board that they select as his successor John Riccardo, a fellow alumnus of the accounting firm of Touche Ross. Townsend advised the directors to name Gene Cafiero president. Riccardo and Cafiero were Townsend's choices from start to finish, and their selection underlined the validity of Alfred Sloan's terse observation that "The perpetuation of leadership is . . . the greatest challenge to be met by the leader of an industry." To those who questioned his judgment, Townsend retorted, "At this level of management it doesn't make a difference what your background is. We don't design or build cars at this level. We set the objectives and policies and monitor their progress." Although it went unnoticed in the rush to meet deadlines, the press conference at which Townsend presented his successors contained the seeds of trouble. Riccardo, announcing a program to redesign all the Chrysler models by 1980, told the reporters crammed into the claustrophobic press center, "We will have broadened our appeal by competing in all new segments of the market as they develop." Meanwhile Cafiero proceeded to outline another strategy. Explaining that Chrysler would not try to match its competitors in every class and would develop new cars from fewer platforms, he noted, "Our strategy is to try . . . to be a General Motors in whatever segments of the market we choose to compete in." As Cafiero warmed to his topic, Riccardo pointed to the back of the room, abruptly interrupted his colleague and proceeded to take another question.

Cafiero and Riccardo were not only heirs to the top two posts in the company, they also inherited the fat purses and bonuses which had consistently upset junior executives during Townsend's stewardship. Although Chrysler's top men received dramatically less than their counterparts at GM and Ford (while hourly workers received the same as their counterparts) that fact was quickly lost in the bitterness.[20] Managers alleged that Chrysler lacked the stern bonus allocation measures of GM, that too much money went to too few men, that the prospect of a large bonus score influenced decisions. One senior manager remembered, "I went to many meetings where the only discussion was about how decisions would affect the pocketbook." To outsiders, it seemed that Chrysler's top men went to every length to reward themselves. In 1972, for example, the formula governing bonuses was changed to allow payments as soon as profits exceeded $51 million, rather than $116 million. Doug Fraser charged correctly, "It's simply a gimmick to give highly paid executives even more money without extra efforts."

Like many other chief executives (including Lee Iacocca) Townsend surrounded himself with familiar faces—and for him, both Riccardo and Cafiero were familiar. One past executive noted, "He jiggled people a lot, and usually the people he jiggled were his friends." Part of the reasons for the frequency of the management changes was Chrysler's thin layer of top-flight managers. There were never the battalions of corporate officials that line the halls at GM or Ford. There was never a predictable career pattern. In an effort to overcome this weakness, executives were given a quick trip around the company, but the journey was so rapid that the film was blurred and no frame was ever given time to develop. Townsend's Technicolor star was always John Riccardo. He had studied economics at the University of Michigan before joining Townsend's alma mater—Touche Ross. Following Townsend to Chrysler, where he started as an International Staff executive in 1959, Riccardo thereafter leaped up the organization every year, serving in two Canadian posts, two Dodge Division posts and a Chrysler-Plymouth position before becoming Vice-President for Marketing in 1966. A year later, he was Group Vice-President for Domestic Automotive Operations and a member of the board. It had taken John Riccardo eight years to reach a position that would have taken thirty at General Motors.

CHAPTER SEVEN

Under the Law

With bushy, white Mephistophelian eyebrows that turned up like cats' whiskers and the impressive title of Director, Research and Materials Engineering, Charlie Heinen was a caricature of the quintessential corporate villain. Little in his railing denouncements of Washington bureaucrats who foisted safety devices, clean air and fuel economy standards on the greatest single industry on earth would have suggested he was anything else—yet Ralph Nader himself singled out Heinen as one of the honest mavericks in Detroit by alleging that Charlie got "the cool treatment" from industry colleagues for promoting a pollution-reducing "Cleaner Air Package" in Chrysler cars during the early Sixties.

Ralph Nader soon stopped singing Charlie Heinen's praises. After forty-seven years with Chrysler, Heinen was still a maverick, but hardly a Naderite. There were bitter edges to his account of three decades of jousting with smog, fuel efficiency, shoddy research, devious politicians and deadening bureaucracy. The man who left Highland Park in July of 1980, after a career that included participation in the Manhattan Project and a leading role in the identification of automotive air pollutants, had the sparkle of a dedicated—if, at sixty-three, aging—revolutionary. He was committed to the challenge of unmasking false and incomplete data, banning "so many stupid extrapolations of one-point pieces of information" and re-instilling a sense of cost in

American life. "We may," he admitted, "lose a corporation in the process. But we've got to do it."

By the time John Riccardo took over as chairman of Chrysler, regulation had become an inextricable factor in the automobile business. In fact, with the debate on fuel economy standards well in progress, Detroit may have been heading into the final, debilitating swing of the pendulum-like pattern of American regulatory policy. Just ten years earlier, in the twilight of Detroit's heyday, there had been almost no regulation. Chrysler was on the upswing under Lynn Townsend; Ford, riding the merchandising genius of a young division general manager named Lee Iacocca, was making Mustangs at home and money all over the world; General Motors was in the midst of its greatest financial performance in history—a 25.8 percent return on investment and a 10.3 percent return on sales.

In New York, though, publisher Richard Grossman was preparing to launch *Unsafe at Any Speed*, Nader's bombshell analysis of the Chevrolet Corvair and its propensity to roll over on sharp corners. Nader's opening sentence, a remarkable black-mirror image of an industry that prided itself on its contribution to man's progress, was to capture a dissident mood and begin an erosion that would not be arrested for more than fifteen years. "For over half a century," wrote Nader, "the automobile has brought death, injury and the most inestimable sorrow and deprivation to millions of people."

In the years since that first sentence was read by millions of Americans, Ralph Nader's anonymous career as a Connecticut product liability lawyer grew into an empire of quasi-governmental consumer action groups and the American automobile industry has watched its profits, as a percentage of both investment and sales, decline. For a crucial while, they even disappeared.

Industry apologists suggested that concern for auto safety emanated from a small circle of fanatics and a few politicians in search of an exploitable issue—but as the annual death toll on the nation's highways climbed through the early Sixties, with each successive holiday weekend marked by new records, the alarm spread. At the outset of the 1965 Fourth of July weekend, the New York *Times* editorialized, ". . . automobile accidents are as familiar as the common cold, and far more deadly. . . . Fifty thousand Americans will lose their lives in automobile accidents this year—almost as many as were killed in World War I. Several hundred will be killed this holiday weekend." The *Times* editorial ended with a prescient warning: "The responsibility lies with the industry. If Detroit does not exercise it, Washington will—and should."

There had already been hearings on auto safety in Washington by the time those words were written. And by the time *Unsafe at Any*

Speed was published, more hearings were about to get underway. Nader not only criticized General Motors for the design of the Corvair, he presented a litany of charges against Detroit, ranging from callous neglect of passenger safety and the intentional pollution of the air to an array of monopolistic practices. His book was a catch-all for criticism; it was effective not only because of its timing but because Detroit was walking blindly and naïvely into its trap. Despite protestations of responsible self-policing, the compelling evidence suggests that very few auto executives were willing to put thought or money into occupant safety, exhaust control or fuel efficiency before outside forces pushed them into it.

The irony was, as Charlie Heinen once said, that the industry equally naïvely ". . . developed all the technology necessary to regulate ourselves. . . . We established what we were guilty of and then we established the solutions." The implementation of those solutions, after 1965, was wrenched from its control and applied with almost senseless disregard for prudent business management. Not until the entire industry was losing billions of dollars in 1980 did the pendulum again begin a slow return toward rational consideration of economic, as well as consumer and environmental, well-being.

Since the first American was killed by an automobile in 1899,[1] it has been obvious that the horseless carriage was a weapon to be reckoned with. The carnage—in relative terms—actually peaked in the flapper days of the Twenties, around the time Scott Fitzgerald's poor Myrtle Wilson was killed by the stylish yellow coupe so badly driven by Daisy Buchanan along the road from New York back to East Egg. As the population of both cars and people exploded, so did the death toll. In 1965, more than 49,000 died on American roads.

Harry Truman had called the first national traffic safety conference in 1946. It recommended that "Motor vehicles should be progressively designed and constructed for safer operation and maximum protection from injury in an accident." Detroit's idea of safety protection was to make sure the brakes worked and the vehicle could be maneuvered sufficiently to avoid collision. The venerable National Safety Council lectured the country on safe driving habits, but the industry continued to build big, heavy and increasingly powerful cars.

In 1952, a Cornell University study produced statistics showing that seat belts similar to those used in airplanes had a notable effect on reducing injury in car crashes. A sharp-eyed Ford man, Robert S. McNamara, took note of the Cornell study and offered to contribute substantial sums to further research. He was refused by academics wary of a compromising association with Ford. McNamara appealed to GM and Chrysler, but only Chrysler contributed. GM's recalcitrance prompted Ralph Nader to accuse GM brass of conspiring to get

McNamara fired at Ford for breaking the silent pact and trying to, as Nader wrote, "replace stylist pornography with engineering integrity."

In fact, McNamara led an unprecedented promotion of safety features on Ford's 1955 models, armed with safety door latches and impact-absorbing steering wheels as well as optional sun visors, seat belts and padded dashboards. The cars lost significant market share that year to the unarmed but stylish Chevrolets. That was reason enough to shelve the idea for the new models introduced in the fall of '56. Ford began outselling Chevy again, confirming Detroit's honored maxim, "Safety doesn't sell."

The contention that the cost of building safety into cars was not recoverable on the sales sticker grew into a philosophy of mandatory standards. Dismayed by the Ford failure, various state legislatures, notably New York's, dictated safety requirements. First came anchors for seat belts in 1961, then the belts themselves in 1964. Even at GM, meanwhile, some engineers were warning executives that their cars' safety features were inadequate.

In 1965, Senator Abraham Ribicoff, who had dabbled in auto safety as governor of Connecticut, held hearings in his Executive Reorganization Subcommittee of the Senate's Government Operations Committee. A certain amount of acrobatic logic was needed to justify padded dashboards as a proper subject for nine senators charged with reviewing the structure of the executive branch of the federal government, but the hearings proceeded and drew considerable attention.

By the second round of sessions, held in February 1966, Nader's book had insured a packed house. The predictable recommendation of the National Safety Council's Howard Pyle was for the enforcement of existing laws and no new legislation. Pyle testified that the Government Services Administration already had sufficient power to specify padded dashes, recessed instrument panels, collapsible steering columns, shatter-proof windshields, standard bumper heights and dual-operated brakes on all government vehicles, but his testimony failed to cut the charged atmosphere of the hearings.

Next to Ribicoff on the committee was New York Senator Robert Kennedy. Orchestrating testimony from his adopted home state, Kennedy elicited from State Senator Edward Speno, a leader in Albany's efforts to set New York safety standards, the observation, "There is a certain rigidity of thinking that I have encountered in this industry. . . . They don't want anybody outside the industry to tell them what to do."

After opening witnesses had established that Detroit, despite its vast wealth and technical resources, was unwilling to build safe cars, the stage was set for the drama of February 10, 1966. General Motors, in one of the classic displays of their early political naïveté, announced that they would make dual braking and collapsible steering standard on all 1967 models. The ungainly attempt to absorb the impact of Ralph Nader's expected testimony failed. At the hearing, before a hushed, attentive audience, Nader called the auto "the greatest environmental hazard in this country" and the "first man-made cause of death." He spoke of children skewered and torn on "the dagger fin of a Cadillac" and of passengers dying in collisions as slow as five miles per hour. He spoke of Detroit as an "intransigent, unified industry that produced millions of little pollution factories on wheels and refused to apply the necessary remedial engineering to clean them up."

Occasionally, conservative Republican Senator Carl Curtis would interrupt with feeble baits and probes, but Nader prevailed, condemning the annual model change, which he said cost the customer $700 but gave nothing in return, psychoanalyzing automotive advertising, which he said incited aggressive behavior, and complaining that independent scientists were being denied access to industry data on the feeble excuse that the numbers were proprietary information. The industry, he charged, was "uniquely outside the law," while its products affected everyone. Quoting the old Roman adage, "Whatever touches all should be decided by all," Nader urged wholesale governmental regulation of the automobile business in America.

"Safety measures that do not rely on or require people's voluntary and repeated cooperation," reasoned Nader, "are more effective and more reliable than those that do." It was a logic that was to pervade regulatory thinking for the next fifteen years.

The Corvair, according to Nader, embodied General Motors' callous disregard for human life and of the industry's arrogance. The "extraordinary tendency for rear-end breakaway behavior leading to uncontrollability and rollover" of the rear-engine compact was easily reparable for a paltry $15 per unit, he said—yet GM allowed 750,000 extant copies of 1960-through-1963 Corvairs to run loose on the nation's roads. Years afterward, there were still automotive experts who insisted that Nader's engineering analysis of the Corvair was a sham and that the car was no more dangerous than the beloved VW Beetle —but General Motors' reaction to the charges rendered those arguments futile.

By the time Nader's book was published, GM was already the defendant in over one hundred lawsuits worth some $40 million in potential damages, stemming from Corvair accidents. Company lawyers were compiling a list of certain product liability lawyers whose names kept reappearing on court documents across the country. There was evidence that information and expertise were being exchanged through newspaper and legal journal ads. GM's legal department,

headed at the time by Aloysius F. Power, feared that there was a conspiracy afoot to promote litigation. Since Nader was touted as an expert witness and legal counsel, Al Power and his staff believed that
they were fully justified in investigating him as part of the corporation's defense.

The job of ordering a detailed investigation of Nader fell to Eileen
Murphy, a veteran GM staffer. During the subsequent congressional
probe, GM's corporate counsel took pains to see to it that Eileen
Murphy never testified about her involvement, but from the existing
record, it seems apparent that Ms. Murphy approached the task with
unusual zeal. She hired a Washington law firm and a New York private detective agency to probe Nader's background, under the pretext
of conducting a preemployment check.

Ribicoff's hearings were only on temporary adjournment when news
stories broke accusing GM of nosing into Nader's sex life, tailing him
across the country, generally harassing him and violating his privacy.
Confronted, GM executives at first denied the charges categorically.
Then, in a carefully worded press statement released the night of
March 9, 1966, the company admitted that it had "initiated" a routine
investigation through a reputable law firm to "determine whether
Ralph Nader was acting on behalf of litigants in Corvair design cases
pending against General Motors."

Under questioning back at the hearings, general counsel Power was
led to admit that the accuracy of the release hinged on the use of the
word "initiated." Power acknowledged that, although the investigation's intent may have been limited when it began, it had grown to
include harassment and invasion of privacy far beyond the bounds of
a routine preemployment check.

Nader, the scheduled opening witness on March 22, 1966, was late
that morning, and James M. Roche, GM's president, was unlucky
enough to be present. Although his reputation had been spotless going
in, Roche emerged that day as an arch-villain.

"I deplore the kind of harassment to which Mr. Nader has apparently been subjected," Roche said bravely at the outset—but after
Robert Kennedy elicited an admission from Power that the March 9
press release was indeed a sham, Roche stumbled lamely. "This is certainly not like General Motors, Senator Kennedy," he stammered. Replied Kennedy, with characteristic charm and cunning, "I like my General Motors car, but you shake me up a bit."

The import of Roche's admission would shake the auto industry to
its roots and probably cost Detroit $35 billion over the next fifteen
years.[2] It certainly contributed substantively to the financial weakness
of Chrysler. Whatever thin thread of credibility remained between
Detroit and Washington broke that March morning. Thereafter, Ralph

Nader's testimony was taken as gospel. The halo was nearly visible when he pledged all royalties from *Unsafe* . . . to the furtherance of automotive safety research. Asked by Kennedy why, if not for fame or fortune, he worked, Nader performed an unrehearsed soliloquy that insured his place as a folk hero of the Sixties:

"When I see, as I have seen, people decapitated, crushed, bloodied and broken, and that is what we are really talking about in auto safety . . . I ask myself what can the genius of man do to avoid it? And frankly I think this country and the auto industry are abundantly endowed with the genius of man to provide an engineering environment of both highway and vehicle which will protect the occupants from the consequences of their errors and which will avoid the very perpetuation of these errors in the first place by a humane automotive and highway design. . . ."

Expounded at a time when the boundless "genius of man" was visibly permitting America to reach for the moon and simultaneously rid the earth of poverty, Nader's philosophy was a fitting prologue to an era dominated by new rules and government bodies that would change the relationship of the public and private sectors more profoundly than at any time since the creation of the income tax.

After the Ribicoff hearings, the National Traffic and Motor Vehicle Safety Act of 1966 came together quickly and was signed into law by Lyndon Johnson on September 9. It mandated the inclusion of dual brake systems, anchorages for shoulder safety belts, flashing emergency lights and impact-absorbing steering columns on 1967 model cars. Nader himself later wrote with satisfaction, "With nearly unprecedented rapidity, a major unregulated industry was brought under the law."

In the next few years, equipment that should have been standard on all automobiles finally became so: in 1966, laminated shatterproof windshields; in 1967, collapsible steering columns that would not impale drivers in collisions. Dr. Donald F. Huelke of the University of Michigan Medical School later advised that "Anybody who drives a car older than a 1967 model is a damn fool."[3]

With the law creating an independent government agency to monitor the auto industry's safety standards and establish new ones as it saw fit, it wasn't long before tensions developed. While Ralph Nader complained that the first National Highway Safety Bureau, directed by Dr. William Haddon, was "weakened by self-inflicted understaffing and inadequate engineering talent," Henry Ford II griped that the new standards set forth by the agency were "unreasonable, arbitrary and technically unfeasible." Ford warned that implementation could shut the whole auto industry down. The two positions were not necessarily contradictory. Indeed, the auto industry was forever complaining that standards were based on inadequate information. Nader complained in 1972 that the Safety Bureau's budget of $46 million in 1968 and $99 million in 1970 left it "limping along." No less valid was the industry's complaint that since the agency acted with the full force of the law behind it, nothing less than fully documented and carefully considered policy would do.

The heart of the safety issue lay in the fundamental philosophical question of who is responsible for the protection of man against himself. Dr. Haddon viewed auto safety as a matter of protecting the occupant as if he or she had no control of destiny. A passenger in a car, reasoned Haddon, was like a "teacup in the mail." The objective for the automobile should be to get passengers to their destinations unbroken. This approach was the logical extension of Ralph Nader's arguments before the Ribicoff hearings.

The "teacup" theory had some limitations in practice. Any number of independent agencies and companies have designed and built so-called "Experimental Safety Vehicles" (ESVs) that incorporated every known impediment to injury—from accordion-like body frames to collapsible fuel bladders. These utterly womb-like vehicles are intended to keep even an alcoholic bent on suicide from harm. Despite repeated claims by the appropriate government agencies that, once mass-produced, these cushioned cars would cost no more than standard Detroit fare, the extra equipment and specialized material would unquestionably have added hundreds if not thousands of dollars to car prices while penalizing fuel economy and performance.

A number of devices designed to protect occupants made sense. By the time safety standards were under consideration for mandatory use, there was no doubt that shoulder-harness seat belts inhibited injury significantly—but there was also no doubt that not all drivers were willing to take the few seconds and trifling inconvenience needed to "buckle up" their seat belts. Surveys taken during the 1970s suggested that fewer and fewer people were using belts. By 1977, surveys were saying that only about one person in six bothered to wear belts on the road.

There has never been much question that "seat belts save lives." The University of North Carolina Highway Safety Research Center surveyed real accident data and concluded that seat belts reduced serious injuries by as much as 50 percent and fatal injuries by perhaps 75 percent. A Swedish study in the late Sixties failed to uncover a single death caused by nearly 29,000 accidents at speeds up to 60 mph where occupants were strapped in. Limited studies by GM in the United States suggested much the same result.

More than a dozen nations require automobile passengers to wear seat belts under penalty of fine and/or removal of insurance coverage,

with significantly positive results. The United States has steadfastly refused. In 1972, a Department of Transportation lawyer insisted that
the government could not legally require belt use. "We can regulate
the vehicle and its equipment," he said. "The states retain the right to
regulate its use. If belt-wearing is to be required, the individual states
must be the ones to require it."[4]

Despite some nominal threats to withhold federal highway funds
and despite a few erratic attempts by some states to pass laws, by
1981 there still was none on the books. Most observers agree that this
legislative reluctance was based less on the conviction that the courts
would overturn such laws than on the presumption that seat-belt laws
would be politically disastrous and difficult to enforce. By a political
process of elimination, the onus of protecting the individual fell not on
the individual, not on the government, but on the automobile industry.

The concept of a "passive restraint" system was a natural one for
private industry to develop on its own, since it combined the salable
attribute of convenience with the moral virtue of safety. Indeed, that
is just what happened. Air bags were not the invention of the National
Highway Traffic Safety Administration but of engineers at Eaton Corporation, an automotive supply company in Cleveland, Ohio. NHTSA
discovered air bags in 1969, several years after Eaton, working with
Ford, and Allied Chemical, working with General Motors, had initiated product development.

Air bags are theoretically ingenious. Nestled in unobtrusive canis-
ters under the dashboard (or under the front seat for rear passengers),
they lie in wait for an accident. When a collision occurs, sensors alert
the bag, which is inflated by a burst of sodium azide within a fraction
of a second. As described by the Insurance Institute for Highway
Safety, a Washington lobbying group, the air bag "gently, buoyantly
spreads the force of the crash evenly across the protected crash occupant's body, rather than concentrating it harmfully at a few points [a
disparaging reference to seat belts]. During the critical split second
of the crash, the bag becomes an energy-absorbing shield between the
protected crash occupant and the hazardous, hard, sharp interior
structure that the occupant otherwise might smash against."[5]

Clean up the copy a bit and it would fit neatly into a sales brochure.
Indeed, such descriptions of the air bag typified government propaganda throughout the 1970s, curiously paralleling the increasing restriction of advertising claims by private industry by the Federal
Trade Commission and the Federal Communications Commission.
The same rules did not apply to government promotional efforts on
behalf of the air bag, despite some of the most contradictory data in
the history of product testing.

However ingenious it may be in concept, the air bag is a complicated device. Expected to lie dormant for the life of the car—as long
as eight or ten years—before performing its duties with microsecond
timing, it requires an extremely high degree of precision. Not only
must it work precisely when needed, it must *not* work at any other
time. NHTSA's soothing sales pitch gave the public an image of a
giant pillow that arrives magically between passenger and windshield
in time to accept the human body with loving softness while violence
is perpetrated beyond. Actually, the air bag is—necessarily—a fairly vicious beast that explodes in the first microsecond of impact, knocking
the occupant back against the car seat with awesome (but evenly distributed) force. Almost as quickly as it appears, it must disappear
again, deflating into a benign rumple of canvas on the floor of the car.

In the vast majority of instances, to the credit of Eaton and Allied
Chemical engineers, the air bags built over the past decade have
worked as advertised. In a head-on collision, they are clearly superior
to any other existing form of occupant protection, and there are plenty
of grateful survivors who had quite forgotten about their air bags
until they appeared in time to save their lives—but there have been
problems that are real and deserving of more discussion than NHTSA
deemed appropriate. The problems are not insoluble and may indeed
be overcome satisfactorily in the early Eighties, if sufficient road testing precedes their mandatory installation in automobiles.

Above all, the evidence suggests that air bags, if they succeed, will
do so in spite of, not because of, federal mandate. Eaton's and other
designs had barely left the drawing boards when John Volpe, Secretary of Transportation in the first Nixon administration, called for
their use in 1969. The industry began fighting the idea almost immediately, at least partly because of what had grown to be a knee-jerk resistance to more regulation, especially at a time when exhaust emissions were emerging as a new target of regulators. Part of the
resistance was based on the recognition that the industry knew very
little about air bags, how much they might cost and who would be
legally liable if they didn't work.

Washington again called Detroit recalcitrant; Henry Ford called air
bags "a bunch of baloney." Lee Iacocca, Ford's chief operating officer,
ordered his PR staff to write to every governor, pushing for mandatory seat-belt laws on the reasoning that a requirement to use seat belts
was no different from a requirement that drivers with poor eyesight
wear glasses. Iacocca hoped that his proposal to use seat belts would
allow the government to satisfy its mania for protecting people from
themselves, without resorting to the use of an untested if promising
system and without tangling with the constitutional issue of states'
rights. At Ford, they called it "Interlock."

Very simply, Interlock prevented a car's ignition system from working until the seat belts were connected. "It wasn't well conceived," Iacocca later admitted, "but at Ford, we were so anti-airbag that we would have stood on our heads." He and Henry Ford went right to the Oval Office on Interlock and even ended up on the infamous Nixon tapes, albeit hawking safety systems rather than obstructing justice.

The industry was not united on Interlock. Naturally, the American Seat Belt Council, the trade organization for belt manufacturers, favored anything that perpetuated the sale of their webwork. The Japanese importers endorsed it. Ford lobbyists buttonholed administration aides, but at hearings in November of 1971, GM and Chrysler testified against Interlock while Ford and AMC supported it. The Ford side won. In May 1973, Claude S. Brinegar, Nixon's current Secretary of Transportation, wrote: "After a thorough review of the issues, we have concluded that the public benefits from the Interlock system will outweigh the costs." As of the following August, proclaimed NHTSA, all new cars had to be so equipped.

It was a total disaster. Even before introduction day, executives were back-pedaling at full speed, some beginning to admit that Interlock was likely to have some mechanical difficulties, and that drivers, already dissatisfied with many conventional ignition systems, were unlikely to embrace this one. AMC's Gerald Meyers, then a group vice-president, said that even the basic car radio had a 5-percent failure rate, and that the 3-percent failure rate anticipated with Interlock would mean hundreds of thousands of problems.

Even Ford tried to squirm out of its own device through the courts, but lost at the appellate level in Cincinnati. At its preview for the 1974 models equipped with Interlock, Chrysler actively promoted mandatory seat-belt use, as Iacocca had first proposed. Emile Grenier, the Ford engineer who claimed to be the inventor of the system, began a one-man crusade to stop Interlock, calling it "potentially lethal."

They were right to have been worried. The Interlock was widely resented by the public, and mechanical problems abounded. Besides, the ingenious American driver took little time to figure out myriad ways to "fool" the system. Some could be circumvented simply by connecting the belt before sitting down. Others could be rendered useless by attaching one end of the passenger's belt to the opposite end of the driver's. The hardest to beat were only the most exasperating. Cars wouldn't start if even as much as a small bag of groceries were on the passenger side, even if the driver were alone and properly strapped in, since any weight on the front seat signaled the Interlock to cut off the ignition.

Within a year, Congress, led by Republican congressman Louis

Wyman of New Hampshire and prompted by an avalanche of protest mail, was preparing legislation to repeal Interlock. On October 27, 1974, thirteen months after it was introduced, Interlock was terminated by an act of Congress and was replaced by an innocuous, albeit annoying, warning buzzer (lasting no more than eight seconds) to remind occupants to buckle up. Not only had Interlock failed to win the hearts and minds of America, it also had developed considerable resentment toward the wearing of seat belts.

Meanwhile, valuable time in which the air bag could have been further refined through field testing and development had been lost. Engineers at Eaton continued to worry about reliability—especially for a product that might be ordered into production on short notice by the federal government. Unreliability could well mean liability. What would happen, for instance, if an air bag went off under routine conditions, triggered not by a dangerous collision but by a pothole? Who is liable if a driver is stunned by an exploding bag, loses control and has an accident that would not have occurred had it not been for the air bag? What protection is there for small children in the back seat whose bodies slip around the protection of the bag and slam lethally into the side windows? Who is liable for the passenger who turns sideways at the moment of impact in reaction to the impending collision and subsequently suffers a wrenched back as a result of a collision with the air bag at an awkward angle?

In its propaganda, NHTSA chose to ignore data that indicated that such problems were possible, if not likely. The manufacturers—who, unlike the government, would be legally liable for such catastrophes—had no choice but to try to resolve them and to do so under the severe pressure of time.

The cost of air-bag installation and replacement, for which the government would also not be accountable, was in constant dispute. NHTSA originally said air bags could be built and installed for $75. Eaton, which built them, said the cost was more like $200. By 1980 NHTSA was claiming that the bags shouldn't cost more than $300, while the manufacturers were saying it couldn't be done for less than $600, with replacement costs more like $1,000. As inflation continued, the numbers kept going up, but the gap remained unresolved and unexplained.

General Motors, because of the forceful enthusiasm for air bags of former president Ed Cole, was once an active proponent. Indeed, during the early Seventies, GM offered air bags as options on Buicks, Cadillacs and Oldsmobiles at $400 apiece, which the company said was $200 under cost. Out of the millions for whom the option was available, only 10,000 customers ordered them, and GM dropped the option in the 1976 model year.

Beyond public reluctance to purchase air bags, the industry was facing a growing body of evidence that air bags, while effective in front-end collisions, were virtually useless in equally common side collisions. The evidence suggests clearly that air bags are effective overall only if accompanied by seat belts. Chrysler's Roy Haeusler, an absolute safety fanatic who was known to drive around Detroit not only strapped in with a crossover harness seat belt but also encased in a motorcycle crash helmet, said NHTSA was "dishonest" for suggesting that air bags alone were safer than belts.

William Coleman, Gerald Ford's Secretary of Transportation, took the most reasonable approach toward air bags, recommending that the industry field test 500,000 of them before any government mandate was considered. However, Brock Adams, Coleman's successor under the Carter administration, scrapped the test program and simply mandated "passive restraints" beginning in the 1982 model year. Air bags were no longer specifically mandated because Volkswagen had demonstrated that a "passive seat belt" system could be installed in two- and four-passenger cars. By attaching the upper end of the belt to the door, VW could force the driver and passenger to climb in underneath the shoulder harness and be buckled up without lifting a finger. That relieved some pressure and allowed NHTSA to rule that passive belts were suitable alternatives to bags.

A large percentage of American cars are designed to accommodate five or six passengers, so that at least one person has to sit in the middle, where a passive belt is impossible to install without subjecting the occupant to a giant game of vehicular "cradle." For these cars, bags are the only choice—and will continue to be, if the six-passenger car survives fuel-economy laws.

In late 1977, a message was delivered to the government, but it was a message that apparently went unread: Eaton, the company that had pioneered the air bag, announced it was dropping out of the business. Chairman Del DeWindt explained that, after thirteen years and $20 million in investment, his company had "nothing but bruises to show for our efforts." The government had grossly politicized the air-bag market and had so telescoped what one Eaton executive called the "natural cycle of product development" that it was no longer a safe bet. Where unhurried testing might well have worked the kinks out of the air-bag system, federal involvement had rushed development, then postponed it, and the government constantly overpromised, through its huckster promotion, what really was an untested concept.

By 1981, it remained likely that air bags would someday be a part of the American automobile, and most of them would work. What Eaton said in 1977 was that they could have been a part of the American automobile by the end of the Seventies if the government had left industry well enough alone.

Air bags are but one safety requirement forced into error. Since its inception, NHTSA has mandated and set standards for hundreds of pieces of equipment, from the commonplace components one would expect to find in any car, like windshield defrosters and even wipers, to concealed headlamps that must rise in a specified time period. Nearly as controversial as air bags are NHTSA's bumper standards, which are set to withstand impacts up to 5 mph without allowing damage to the body of the car. Like most standards, the bumper requirement had some basis. In the Sixties, when style was everything, Detroit built bumpers that were easily damaged themselves and so close to the underlying metal of the car that they were useless. NHTSA's first 2.5-mph bumper requirement resolved this, but fender-benders on the street showed that the cost of replacing a 5-mph bumper was greater than any savings derived from having one in the first place. NHTSA, needless to say, claims otherwise. But as the *Wall Street Journal* dramatized in a March 4, 1980, examination of NHTSA's testing methods, NHTSA's credibility is very much an issue in itself.

Despite totally contradictory evaluations of the damage done to a car in an NHTSA crash test conducted in Arizona, the agency used the results to support its 5-mph bumper standard. The $300,000 testing program appeared to have been poorly designed and badly executed. Even one of the independent appraisers used in the evaluation told the *Wall Street Journal* that it was "a Mickey Mouse type operation all around." Yet NHTSA persevered, claiming that its standards would save car owners $11 to $29 over the life of the car. It is no wonder that automakers complain about cost/benefit losses. That same bumper cost the manufacturer about $50 per unit more than the bumper it is designed to replace, and it's a safe bet those costs will be passed on to the consumer, who will have no choice but to pay for NHTSA's standard.

Throughout the Carter administration, meanwhile, the teacup theory remained alive and well in Washington. Carter's team at NHTSA began rating cars according to their crash-worthiness. Congress funded NHTSA to test all foreign and domestic vehicles to see what the likelihood of serious injury or death to occupants would be in a 30-mph barrier collision. NHTSA director Joan Claybrook, an alumna of Ralph Nader's consumer watchdog school, took the standard one step further and conducted crashes at 35 mph. Sophisticated dummies were used in place of people. (There was a time when the auto industry, for want of a better idea, used cadavers, and some automakers, in an attempt to simulate children, once used small pigs as crash victims.)

Driving new cars at 35 mph smack up against a solid wall, NHTSA examiners ran elaborate tests, including films replayed in slow motion, to see what happened to the dummies inside. Because it would be inordinately expensive to crack up a couple of hundred of each model, the agency sacrificed true statistical accuracy for a closer look at a one-shot wreck. Dozens of makes—only one of each—slammed against the barrier and NHTSA staffers ran in to survey the carnage. The results were fascinating—and, critics argued, meaningless.

The Volvo, the personal choice of Joan Claybrook because of its reputation as a solid, safe vehicle, was among the models that flunked, their "occupants" deemed critically injured and/or killed. Contrary to some scientifically sound rules of thumb that big cars, because of their extra weight, are safer than small cars, standard models like the Mercury Marquis and Chevrolet Impala flunked too. So did all the popular small Japanese cars. In every instance, of course, the cars were built according to NHTSA's own specific minimum standards. Yet some domestic small cars, including the Chevrolet Citation, Ford's Mustang and Chrysler's Plymouth Horizon TC-3, all "passed," meaning that their dummies didn't die.

Even Ms. Claybrook was "surprised" by the results—especially on her Volvo. The Japanese protested vigorously that the test itself was flawed. Despite the opportunity to crow about a government-supported advantage they had over the Japanese, who were at the time ripping through their markets, the American producers said little to contradict the protests of Toyota and Nissan. Indeed, General Motors' Vice-President for Environmental Activities, Dr. Betsy Ancker-Johnson, a relative newcomer to Detroit who held a Ph.D. in physics, called the crash test "a fraud upon the public," and argued that NHTSA could turn right around with clean versions of the exact same models and come up with exactly the opposite results. NHTSA's barrier tests, she claimed, were so far removed from reality as to be meaningless. In actual automobile accidents, the exact position of each occupant, the angle of the impact, and the relative size, weight and degree of immobility of the object or objects hit comprise a jumble of uncontrollable variables.

The French automaker Renault, which has been developing its own crash tests in Paris for nearly thirty years as well as keeping close track of thousands of auto accidents in the real world, found NHTSA's methods equally absurd. Philippe Ventre, a Renault executive on duty in the United States with American Motors, observed that the U.S. system of running cars up against a flat, immobile surface at exact perpendicularity revealed far less about the structural integrity of a car than an impact at some angle. "In France," said Ventre, "we have cars that do very well [in accidents] on the road but very badly against the [NHTSA] wall. Frankly, I would rather be in a car that did well on the road but badly on the wall than a car that did badly on the road but well on the wall."

Even vehement critics of NHTSA do not fault the agency for trying to develop a proper measure for structural integrity, and indeed, NHTSA did not claim to have perfected the system. Nonetheless, they not only persisted in ramming cars up against walls at spectacular expense—both for the cars and for the sophisticated electronic devices and dummies—they persisted in publicizing the results, knowing full well that the measures used were at best preliminary. After each round, reporters were summoned and told which cars flunked and which passed—a production comparison claim that would never have been tolerated from a private company.

Automotive pollution emerged as an issue no more suddenly than safety. In the early 1950s, Californians were already concerned about the role of cars in Los Angeles' smog problem—but just as auto safety exploded in a particular socio-political atmosphere in the mid-Sixties, so auto emissions, as a piece of the environmental movement, reached a flashpoint around 1970.

"Automobiles account for at least 60 percent of the nation's total air pollution," charged columnist Colman McCarthy authoritatively in the January 26, 1970, editions of the Washington Post. "In the smog belts of some cities, car pollution is as high as 92 percent. Each year, automobiles dump into the air, and potentially into the lungs, more than 90 million tons of pollutants."

Just ten days earlier, the New York Times had pronounced in an editorial that General Motors chairman Ed Cole's promise to clean up car exhausts by 1980 was "simply not good enough." Barked the Times: "The thought of inhaling foul air in the streets for ten more years is not merely unpleasant; it is unacceptable."

Even Fortune, traditional defender of big business and reasoned arbiter of industrial dispute, sounded a note of concern in its February 1970 issue, duly observing that "in many U.S. cities, motor vehicles are the cause of 75 percent of the noise and 80 percent of the pollution."

April 22, 1970, was officially christened Earth Day. Congress even recessed to allow members to reap the political spoils of participation. Hundreds of thousands took part in what was described as "almost a pagan holiday . . . festive and faddish; yet it touched the American imagination with a memento mori, a vision primitive as trilobites and novel as the idea of a windless, uninhabited earth orbiting on."[6]

New York's Fifth Avenue was closed to traffic for two hours. At the

University of Wisconsin, 58 separate programs were staged, including a dawn "earth service" of Sanskrit incantations. Students at Florida Tech tried and convicted a Chevrolet for poisoning the air. Companies struggled to salvage some respect by announcing new, environmentally harmless products to celebrate the occasion, only to be condemned by militant environmentalists as exploitive.[7]

One ambitious politician who picked up pollution and ran with it was Maine Senator Edmund Muskie, later to bid unsuccessfully for the Democratic presidential nomination and eventually to serve as Jimmy Carter's last Secretary of State. Muskie convened clean-air hearings, marshaling an amazing battalion of statistics that were quoted as gospel for years. These alarming numbers—all expressed in tonnages of poison spewed across the earth—certainly seemed to justify immediate action. Muskie himself warned in a September 1970 speech in New Jersey, "Unless we act and act now—the smog alerts throughout this country will become death watches of the grimmest kind."

Following a virtual kangaroo court, Muskie's Clean Air Act was signed into law in December of 1970, demanding of the automobile industry a 90 percent reduction of hydrocarbon and carbon monoxide emissions by 1975 and a 90 percent reduction on oxide of nitrogen emissions by 1976. "You could have knocked us over with a feather," recalled Chrysler vice-president Sydney Terry. "Those standards were a complete surprise."

Surprise? Where did those numbers, very specific ones indeed, come from?

They were the culmination of all available information collected by the National Air Pollution Control Administration's Bureau of Criteria and Standards, under the direction of Dr. Delbert Barth. By congressional mandate, Barth had assembled all the studies ever done on what automobiles produce from their engines and tailpipes and what these emissions do to the human body. Barth assumed a few things: that by 1990, the number of motor vehicles would more than double; that they would increase in concentration not just where populations increased but everywhere equally—meaning, for instance, that they would more than double in cities like New York and Los Angeles; that the effects of the various substances emitted from automobiles would be the same as they were in laboratory settings. He took the most conservative estimates of health effects gathered by the Department of Health, Education and Welfare in the heat of the clean air movement and he added an occasional statistical cushion to boot. He used the worst recorded incidents of air pollution in Los Angeles and Chicago, multiplied them times the number of cars he had assumed would be on the roads everywhere and came up with an aggregate figure for the amount of pollution he expected would be aloft in two decades. From that gruesome number, Barth subtracted what he considered to be safe maximum levels for each pollutant. The remainder was construed to be the total amount of pollutants that should be removed from the automotive exhaust production of America by 1980. Even Barth never claimed that these figures were exact.

Senator Muskie, prompted by a zealous committee staff, rounded Barth's reduction percentages upward to an even 90 percent. Then, on the reasoning that Detroit was fully capable of any achievement if sufficiently pushed, Muskie cut the time frame in half, demanding that the standards be met by the mid-Seventies rather than the far-off Eighties (the original deadline). "The numbers," wrote Charles Burck in the June 1973 issue of *Fortune,* "were arbitrary and were adopted with little serious thought." Observed the *Wall Street Journal* somewhat more snidely in a May 21, 1973, editorial: "The auto emissions standards written into the Clean Air Act of 1970 were based on the best scientific evidence available at the time, which is another way of saying they were scribbled on the back of an envelope."

Subsequent studies and a more dispassionate examination of the Barth criteria have indeed shown that Muskie's standards had very little basis. First, they were based on studies that were often scientifically questionable. Second, it was incorrectly assumed that the industry could meet them without much difficulty. Third, they were presumed to be accurately and consistently measurable, a presumption long since demonstrated to be wrong.

Air pollution research, like air pollution itself, grew up in the Los Angeles basin. Auto industry defenders are quick to note that the first Spanish explorers labeled Santa Monica Bay the "Bay of Smokes," suggesting that L.A. smog had been a problem long before the internal combustion engine was invented.[8]

Clearly, the automobile contributed something to the haze. As early as 1952, Dr. A. J. "Arlie" Haagen-Smit of the University of Southern California discovered that "smog" was a synthesis of sunlight, of which there was plenty in L.A., and various chemicals, some of which were emitted by automobile exhaust systems. It was this synthesis, theorized Haagen-Smit, that caused eye irritation. During the next decade, Haagen-Smit was able to develop the single greatest contribution to automotive environmental science in history—largely by cooperating with other scientists and engineers from government, on the one hand, and the petroleum and automobile industries on the other.

Some of the best engineers and scientists in the business—on both sides—made up a group of less than fifty who put together all the basics of auto emissions. One of them was Chrysler's Charlie Heinen. They identified hydrocarbons, carbon monoxide and oxides of nitrogen as the potentially harmful components. They learned to distinguish between "smog" and ozone and to identify their different effects. They learned that emissions interact and must be studied together. They ascertained quickly that what comes out of a car's tailpipe has a great deal to do with how the car's engine is tuned as well as how the car is driven, and in what kind of weather. They figured out that by ventilating the crankcase of an engine, they could remove 20 percent of the harmful fumes in one swoop.

"It was kind of an 'over-a-drink' type of relationship," recalled Charlie Heinen. "We were technical people after technical objectives. . . . The contact was extremely close. We had not added the hordes of lawyers, politicians and political activists. It was being handled as an engineer's job, with a slight political irritation."

The Californians were by no means pushovers. They set the nation's first meaningful air pollution standards back in 1959 and were later exempted from federal standards because their own were tougher.

California also provided the industry with a glimpse of political turmoil to come. After earnest research, Charlie Heinen and other auto engineers working with Haagen-Smit on smog went up to Sacramento to lay out what they thought was the problem to a joint session of the state legislature. "We damn near got our heads knocked off," recalled Heinen. The expectations were high. "They wanted a device, a magic box, a tomato can they could put at the end of the tailpipe that got rid of the smog miraculously."

Heinen and company tried to dispel the notion of a quick fix; they also suggested that, because Northern California didn't have a smog problem, there was something other than automobiles at work.

Charlie learned that politics don't necessarily have anything to do with reason. One California official from Los Angeles visited Heinen in his hotel room on an evening before a hearing. "Charlie, I know you're right," he said. "But tomorrow I'm going to let you have it in public because this isn't going to go across with my people. They don't want to hear that kind of stuff. They want a solution and they want the automobile industry damned."

"He was true to his promise," reported Heinen. "He cut me up in little bits."

California's actions drew federal attention. Congress authorized a study by the Surgeon General which was released in 1962 and brought about the first Clean Air Act in 1963, primarily a call for more information, which in turn led to another act, passed in 1965. In 1966, in the midst of Washington's safety blitz, the federal government broadened its powers and the scope of its interest in air pollution and passed standards for 1968 model cars.

Apparently forgotten in the hysteria of pollution phobia during the

Muskie hearings were the reductions in auto emissions already accomplished. Before Muskie's standards were ever written, by Detroit's count, 80 percent of the hydrocarbons, 70 percent of the carbon monoxide and more than a third of the oxides of nitrogen emitted in uncontrolled auto exhausts had already been removed. By Washington's post-Muskie standards, the achievements were less impressive but substantial nonetheless.[9]

The Clean Air Act of 1970 roundly demanded 90 percent fewer hydrocarbons, carbon monoxide and oxides of nitrogen anyway. Muskie's standards, which were to be enforced by the new Environmental Protection Agency (EPA) created by Richard Nixon the same month the Clean Air Bill passed, called for no more than 0.41 grams per mile of hydrocarbons (HC), 3.4 grams per mile of carbon monoxide (CO) and 0.4 grams per mile of oxides of nitrogen (NOx). The numbers were, of course, meaningless to the American people, but nightmares to men like Charlie Heinen, who knew what they meant.

Not only were the numbers frightening, but the methods of testing to determine whether cars were up to snuff were at best primitive. Nixon's agency at least cleared the bureaucratic decks of the conflicting work of sixty separate government agencies and twenty congressional committees—each of which had a mandate to meddle in auto emissions—but the Environmental Protection Agency gathered under its wings awesome administrative power over American industry.

EPA immediately went to work setting up enforcement of the government's standards. The agency devised an elaborate test to measure emissions. Chrysler contended that "It is beyond the capability of the present analytical equipment to measure these concentrations (ten-to-one in EPA's "Constant Volume System") accurately, and small variations are magnified into seemingly large total emission variations." Both Ford and GM concurred, saying that variations were as much as 50 percent on the same car, depending on atmospheric conditions alone.[10] Ultimately, the manufacturers were left to determine their own results—fully documented, of course. In the engineering labs and prototype garages in Highland Park, in Dearborn and at GM's Tech Center in Warren, automotive engineers burned a lot of midnight oil and scratched heads trying to meet and measure Muskie's curious numbers. There was often bitterness aimed at Washington bureaucrats seen punching out at four-thirty or five o'clock while some Detroit engineers went weeks without seeing their families, but there were also flashes of humor, albeit engineers' humor. "We have a new test at the end of the line," one Chrysler emissions man quipped. "A technician opens the hood and pours a bucket of water into the engine compartment. If any leaks through onto the floor, we've left something out."[11]

At higher levels, the lines of battle were drawn. In the fall of 1969,

the Justice Department ruled that the auto industry could not exchange information on pollution control on grounds that such sharing
was anti-competitive. "I could no longer talk to Charlie Chayne," said
Charlie Heinen, who had worked closely with Chayne (his counterpart at General Motors) and others in setting up the California studies. "I could," he qualified, "but not about quite a few things and not
without a lawyer at my side. . . . After 1970, we didn't go anywhere
without a lawyer."

Sydney Terry, a Chrysler vice-president who dealt with Washington during those years, called the Justice Department decision "purely
political" and "a charade from the beginning." The ruling was the result of a suit filed by the Justice Department in the lame-duck days of
the Johnson administration and represented reversal of a policy established in 1958. The original policy allowed exchanges of information between the various companies on the reasoning that reduction of
air pollution was a common societal goal and beyond the realm of
competition. A decade later, the assumption in Washington was that
Detroit's engineers, if allowed to exchange information, would only
conspire to stifle progress against pollution control.

The Attorney General of Illinois filed a conspiracy suit against the
Big Four, charging them with deliberately withholding information
and equipment that could clean up the air, dating the alleged conspiracy all the way back to 1953. "The motives range," recalled Heinen.
Some were less interested in establishing reasonable standards to control pollution than they were in simply ridding the country of automobiles. Groups even advocated the complete ban of internal combustion
engines by 1975. Not everyone had thought through the consequences
of their positions. Within a matter of several years, America had become a nation of environmentalists.

Once again, Detroit displayed its political naïveté. Charlie Heinen
may have learned a small lesson from his experiences in California,
but apparently not enough of one to make him control his candor. On
April 9, 1969, while Washington was busily collecting numbers to con-
demn Detroit, Heinen presented a paper at the New York City meeting of SAE, the Society of Automotive Engineers. It was a progress report on emissions control, an analysis of the empirical studies of the
effects of pollutants and, in Heinen's words, "a paper that questioned
whether we weren't letting this thing get out of hand." Its title, however, was typical of Heinen: "We've Done the Job—What's Next?"

One of the saddest things about that paper was that practically everyone in the country read the title and practically no one read the
paper. "It was rather dull, if you please," said Heinen, "a technical
paper." Ralph Nader addressed an Ann Arbor audience that included
one of Heinen's eight daughters and cited as a typical example of in-

dustrial arrogance Charles Heinen of Chrysler, who had written the "classic example of industrial pornography."

That evening, Heinen's daughter was besieged with phone calls from campus friends asking if they could take a look at her daddy's porno. Heinen remembered the incident as a psychological milestone. "I felt at that point that it was our duty to fight from here on in."

The Muskie standards shocked the industry far more than any safety standards. "We were bewildered, used to thinking we were the most advanced technical industry in the world, used to going out if there was a problem, putting on our overalls and fixing it. Since then," said Heinen, "we learned what it means to be regulated, to answer questionnaires, to have government give some third party a grant and then have them come tripping through here to get educated . . . then to have our own information sent back, turned around and used against us."

The greatest frustration was in knowing that Muskie's numbers were wrong, but being unable to break through the wholesale bias to get that message across. Chrysler was the most vocal about what they considered to be the injustice of the standards—largely because John Riccardo was incensed by them and Charlie Heinen was not going to roll over and play dead. The company put together a full-page advertisement spelling out what was wrong with the standards, why they couldn't be met and what the public was going to end up paying—as much as $1,300 more per car after 1975, the ad said. Heinen went into John Riccardo's office the morning before the first ads were to appear to warn him that the company was going to get crucified for its efforts. Indeed, in the circles of the most fervent environmentalists Chrysler was reviled for its efforts—but mostly they were ignored.

Attention was largely limited to journals sympathetic to business.[12] These efforts were aided again by Chrysler, where Research and Editorial Services staff member Charles H. Connolly, with Charlie Heinen's guidance, accumulated all the work that had been done on air pollution and health effects and put them into book form.

Air Pollution and Public Health[13] took Del Barth's studies and assumptions and reexamined them alongside some studies and facts that somehow had been ignored during the Clean Air hearings. There was hardly any information in Connolly's book that was not available to the government, yet it suggested some vastly different results.

Barth's conclusions, Connolly argued compellingly, were far from inevitable, given the information available. One of the foundations of the Muskie carbon monoxide (CO) level of 3.4 grams per mile (gpm) was the résumé of a study done by Stanford University Medical School's Rodney Beard and George Wertheim indicating that people with a carboxyhemoglobin (COHb) level of 2 to 2.5 percent—that is, a blood absorption of CO at that level—showed a slightly impaired sense of sound duration. The HEW résumé concluded that those blood levels of CO were "associated with adverse health effects." Using another HEW estimate that cars produced 97 million tons of CO in 1969 and multiplying the worst concentration levels on record times the number of cars he expected to be on the road in ten years, Barth arrived at a per-car maximum emission level of 15 parts per million (ppm) for CO. Connolly's book questioned whether carbon monoxide from auto exhausts could be reasonably expected to raise the blood level of the chemical very much and whether raising it affected people adversely. He noted that J. R. Goldsmith of the California Department of Public Health had observed that cigarette smokers took in CO concentrations of between 400 and 475 parts per million, absorbing up to 54 percent, and had concluded that more CO was put into the human bloodstream—even of exposed nonsmokers—by cigarettes than by traffic jams.

As for the impairment of senses, scientists have demonstrated that it results more from the disturbance of the blood's COHb equilibrium than it does from any particular exposure level. Dr. John Schulte of Ohio State had done a number of studies on CO levels that produced results out of line with the Barth assumptions. Sailors on Navy nuclear submarines who had been exposed to average concentrations of 35 to 45 parts per million for 72 to 120 days showed no effect on their performance of duty nor any differences in health from an unexposed control group. Moreover, observed Connolly, despite numerous attempts, no one had been able to duplicate the Beard/Wertheim results of audio impairment using the classic "double-blind" method of checking experiments. Despite these facts, the government set an exposure level of 9 parts per million over 8 hours, not to be exceeded more than once a year, as its standard for auto emissions of carbon monoxide.

As for that frightening figure of 97 million tons of CO coughed into the atmosphere by automobiles, Connolly offered some perspective. According to tests done by Argonne National Laboratory and reported in *Science* magazine in July 1972, nature produces some 3.5 *billion* tons of carbon monoxide annually through the decay of matter—more than 35 times the output of all internal combustion engines.

Similarly, Connolly noted that nature, through the decay of plants and animals, produced a billion tons of oxides of nitrogen each year—a concentration of 0.25 to 0.5 parts per million—as well as 500 million tons of nitric oxide and nitrogen dioxide—an average concentration of one part per million. Man, by contrast, produced 24 million tons worth of oxides of nitrogen (NOx) in 1969. Automobiles accounted for less than 9 million of those tons.

"I remember howls of laughter in the editorial pages when we said that," recalled John Riccardo in a speech given in 1979. It wasn't until as eminent an authority as the Bureau of Naval Research, corroborated by studies done at Washington State University, reiterated that, as Riccardo said, "Mother Nature, all by herself, really does violate the EPA's standards for clean air, just as we have said all along."

Oxides of nitrogen can indeed be dangerous. Farmers know to stay only briefly in a silo where fermented grain can produce concentrations of 500 parts per million. The American Congress of Governmental and Industrial Hygienists recommended a maximum prolonged exposure of 5 ppm. But the Muskie standards called for emission levels that would keep NOx levels at almost half a part per million, one-tenth the tested exposure recommendation.

The only study supporting the NOx standard, wrote Connolly, was done by Dr. Carl Shy of the Health Effects Research Division of the old Air Pollution Control Administration. Shy set up four control quadrants in Chattanooga, Tennessee, and tried to measure the rate of illness among schoolchildren according to their exposure to NOx. The trouble was, some of the so-called "control areas" had NOx levels that were sometimes higher than those in uncontrolled areas. In mid-experiment, one quadrant experienced a flu outbreak. Shy's measuring devices were questioned for accuracy. Even if these severe operational difficulties are disregarded, the results of the study were only marginally significant.

While Tennessee schoolchildren determined the NOx levels for Congress, California high school cross-country runners helped set the hydrocarbon (HC) standards. There are hundreds of different hydrocarbons—twenty identifiable ones coming out of an automobile exhaust pipe. Each has a quantifiably different effect under measurably different circumstances. Some can irritate the eyes; some may have long-term health effects. As with other emissions, the total output of hydrocarbons from cars is but a fraction of those produced by forest fires, burning leaves, swamps and coalfields.

The study cited by Barth and used by Congress measured the times of the Los Angeles high school runners according to their exposure to photochemical oxidants, only one ingredient of which were hydrocarbons. As noted, Los Angeles air is made up of many elements and their interactions are as significant as their individual makeup. Nevertheless, the fact that higher concentrations produced slower finishing times was taken as a sign of HC's harmfulness. Barth and his people ran the numbers through their macro-calculators and deemed that 0.41 grams per mile per car was enough for Americans, with no allowance made for pollution from forest fires, coalfields, and decaying life forms. "To the extent that [other] sources are uncontrollable," wrote

Barth, "the restriction of the motor vehicle would have to be increased." In other words, Detroit would just have to make up for the inequities of nature, since nature was beyond federal control.

Other scientists looking at the data used by Barth came to opposite conclusions. Dr. Frank Spizer of Harvard Medical School concluded in 1970, the same year Barth recommended exhaust controls, "If one was to consider only the available epidemiologic data which have attempted to associate photochemical pollution and respiratory diseases in man, the only conclusion which could be drawn would be that the currently observed levels of pollution are *not* harmful to man."

What a close examination of the data does show, however, is that cigarettes, far more than cars, are harmful. In the concentrations considered most dangerous for carbon monoxide, oxides of nitrogen and aldehydes (a hydrocarbon), cigarettes have been shown to be the primary source. Any attempt to control the emission of these substances from cigarettes to the degree Washington has demanded from cars would shut down the tobacco industry permanently.

Connolly's book should have been absorbed by more people than a handful of journalists and the preconfirmed auto-industry critics of government regulation. In 1973, the year of its publication, a moment of truth arrived. In order to meet Muskie's standards, Detroit had to have the tools in hand at least two years before production. By then it was apparent that no one in the industry could meet the total allowable output of slightly more than 4 grams of the three controlled-emission substances. Muskie's Clean Air Committee mulled over the alternatives. Congressmen, mostly lawyers by trade, made judgments the only way they knew how: by compromise. Syd Terry recalls one meeting where a group of senators, aides and lobbyists batted around the CO standard—0.4 gram per mile versus 1.5—and compromised at 0.6 or 0.8. New York senator James Buckley walked into the room and, apparently sensing how meaningless it all was, suggested: "How about just rolling some dice?"

William Ruckelshaus, Nixon's appointee as head of EPA, used his prerogative to delay each of the 1975 and 1976 standards by one year, but he set intermediate standards that were tough enough to force Chrysler to change its entire approach to pollution control in midstream.

Through the Sixties, Chrysler had been working toward lower emissions through the engine itself—fine-tuning the carburetion and combustion cycles to reduce pollutants. Since CO and HC levels can only be lowered by improving the efficiency of the combustion process, while NOx levels actually increase with higher combustion efficiency, Chrysler engineers knew they were up against a tough problem, but they were convinced that, given proper time, they could develop an engine that would control all three.

Ruckelshaus' interim standards effectively scrapped the project. Once again, compromise prevailed over scientific evidence. General Motors had designed a system for treating exhausts *after* combustion, as they emerged from the tailpipe. A canister attached to the exhaust pipe oxidized fumes. At GM, these "catalytic converters" were ready for market.

The converters did have several drawbacks: they cost the industry an aggregate $15 billion to produce and install; they required rare noble metals, platinum and rhodium, to do the oxidizing, and they required lead-free gasoline. Since the oil industry used lead to raise the octane level and hence the power of gasoline, that last restriction dictated to the oil industry that they spend at least $4 billion converting their refineries to the production of no-lead gas.

"We said that unleaded gasoline would cost much more than leaded gas," John Riccardo reminded an audience in a 1979 speech, "and that the catalyst would continue to need exotic metals from Russia and South Africa. It's 1979, and the unleaded gas costs 4 to 8 cents more a gallon than leaded gas. That's costing the United States almost $2 billion a year in needless inflation. The automobile industry is also importing more than 1,600,000 ounces of platinum and rhodium a year from South Africa, and by 1981, the cost of precious metals required for catalysts will add another $1.5 billion every year to inflation as well as to our negative balance of payments."

Such costs might have been justified if there had been no other options, and the loss of research effort would have been significantly smaller if a company other than GM had come up with the catalytic converter. Ford, which had been working on a stratified-charge engine to beat the countervailing effects of CO and NOx, had to shelve its work in order to catch up with GM on catalysts. Chrysler, which had rested all its hopes on a similar lean-burn system, had no choice but to abandon ship and swim along with GM and Ford. "We were going to do it all with that engine," lamented Syd Terry. "And we would have been able to eventually, had we had enough time. But we had to completely change the course and go to the catalyst in a heck of a hurry in order to meet the new standards." American Motors was simply unable to meet the standards in-house and, with the help of Wisconsin senator William Proxmire, in whose state a large AMC plant and work force resided, was granted a waiver and permission to buy its emissions technology and equipment from General Motors. Catalysts presented numerous headaches once they were installed in cars. In California, all manufacturers had trouble getting certified. The first 91-octane no-lead gas caused engine knock, driving many owners to break the law forbidding the use of leaded gas in catalyst-controlled cars. (Once contaminated by lead, catalysts are rendered useless.) Nonetheless, many drivers—one government survey said as many as 14 percent—continue to destroy catalysts by using the more powerful leaded gasoline. Functioning catalysts were suspected of emitting dangerous sulphuric acid mist.

Problems, costs and all, catalysts became a way of life between 1975 and 1980 and proved to be the only way to meet the final standards for 1981. The tragedy of the catalyst, however, is a variation on the theme of the air bag and one that would play a more insidious role in the government's fuel-economy standards: By scheduling standards *not* according to technology but according to goals alone, the government actually inhibited development and slowed progress. One reason the Japanese manufacturers have achieved so much in emissions control— in some instances surpassing American technology—is that their government has encouraged multiple research and set standards *not* according to what they wanted but according to what the companies could achieve. A Japanese representative in the United States voiced astonishment over U.S. regulatory policy. "In Japan," he said, "there would be no regulation until the government was sure the companies could meet the regulation. But then," he stressed, "there would be no loosening at all. It would be fixed."

Sadly, the American experience with emissions standards has been different. Chrysler and Ford were virtually torn from promising research efforts to meet frantic and ill-advised requirements. They simply could not afford to do both. Government and industry played brinksmanship for six years. Muskie's draconian numbers were postponed again and again because the industry could not meet them, and each new head of EPA came up with a new formula for interim standards.

"We were told by the government and the press at least once a month that some foreign company or some exotic engine already met the Clean Air Act's emissions standards," said Riccardo in an admonishing "I told you so" speech. "All Detroit needed was to have its feet held to the fire." By the end of the Seventies, no volume-production car could meet Muskie's numbers, and even in 1981, despite highly sophisticated electronic engine control devices *in addition to* catalysts, there were still cars—Japanese and European vehicles among them—that do not meet those original standards and for which the U.S. government grants routine waivers.

It was not until long after emissions regulations were set in stone that a number of experts began admitting publicly that those regulations might be more than was necessary for the protection of public health. Even some regulators, once retired from politics, have suggested that the standards they enforced were unnecessary. In August of 1979, as Chrysler prepared its survival plan for the Treasury, former EPA administrator William Ruckelshaus, the original enforcer of the 1970 Clean Air Act, recanted. He acknowledged that neither he nor anyone else knew then whether those numbers could be justified, and he urged that the government ". . . launch a serious and credible program to understand where we will be in terms of human health when the standards are achieved and further, what are the implications for public health if we fall short of the current goals."

Kenneth Mills, a former EPA engineer, quit EPA in 1972 because he realized that the agency's standards were too stringent. A relaxation of even the interim standards for 1980—themselves below the Muskie levels—would have "no measurable adverse effect on the health and welfare of the population as a whole," said Mills.[14]

"All these guys suddenly got religion," said Lee Iacocca wryly during the loan-guarantee debate. "Where the hell were they when we needed them?"

Washington's regulatory agencies have never accepted Detroit's arguments that regulations cost the smaller manufacturers more and thus have contributed to the industry's problems. During the Chrysler debate in Congress, NHTSA, representing the regulators, sought to refute Chrysler's claim that it had been regulated into its financial crisis. NHTSA argued that investment in the auto industry was always roughly proportionate to the size of the company and that, though GM and Ford might spend more to meet regulations, that was largely because they had more models, engines and transmissions to bring up to standards. But the agency did not acknowledge that the full-line marketing approach taken by the three largest manufacturers made volume runs the biggest differential in costing—not individual nameplates. Most of General Motors' basic car lines are sold by at least four of the five car divisions (i.e., the X-car is basically the same whether it's labeled a Chevy Citation, a Buick Skylark, an Olds Omega or a Pontiac Phoenix, and the regulatory standards that apply to one apply to all and can be spread over the cost of all four). Chrysler, by contrast, has only two nameplates competing in the same compact market —the Dodge Aries and Plymouth Reliant—so the costs of the same standards must be divided between them.

The agency's contention that economies of scale occur at relatively low production volumes, achievable by Chrysler as readily as by Ford and GM, rests largely on a study done by New York University's Lawrence J. White[15] that has already been refuted. White based his conclusions on the assumption that body panel dies wear out after 400,000 stampings, meaning that, for those parts, 400,000 was the maximum run over which the cost of the dies could be spread. GM has since demonstrated that its dies can survive up to 4 million stampings.[16]

NHTSA's case before Congress was a study in extended sophistry. The agency argued that the original Highway Safety Act did not focus on the automobile as a "culprit," citing its programs for safety education, road devices and anti-drunk-driving campaigns—as if these programs somehow counterbalanced the vast expenditures demanded of a private industry.

The agency argued that its "Advanced Notice of Proposed Rulemaking" system gave Detroit every opportunity to present its case on various proposed standards. However, NHTSA failed to note that, for the thirty-nine standards and hundreds of proposals, subsequent hearings produced only two substantive changes in those regulations.

NHTSA's presentation offered an analysis of industry trends that showed Detroit's sales measured in constant dollars while leaving profits in inflated dollars in an effort to show how well the industry has done, despite regulations. No mention, of course, was made of the relentless decline of profit margins that left Detroit's Big Three with less than half the return on sales during the 1970s—even in the relatively good years of the early Seventies—that was achieved during the preceding decade.

While categorically dismissing Chrysler's claims of "huge capital investments" required to meet their standards, the agency was mute less than nine months later when the Carter White House offered to reduce the stringency of *a single 1984 high-altitude emission standard* for a potential saving of *$500 million* in order to help Detroit through its financial doldrums. That single, relatively minor standard was the equivalent of a complete four-cylinder-engine plant that might have added 300,000 small cars to the American market.

The entire NHTSA testimony was designed to isolate Chrysler from the rest of the domestic auto industry and show that the company was simply the victim of its own poor management. In October of 1979—before an internal memo at Ford leaked, showing that the number-two automaker was losing $1 billion on its North American automotive operations; before American Motors was forced to throw itself into the arms of France's Renault to avoid bankruptcy; and before the entire domestic auto industry piled up some *$9 billion* in operational losses in a single year—that was a plausible argument.

As long as Detroit was making money, industry arguments that regulations were putting at least some of the companies in jeopardy fell on deaf ears. During the late Seventies, especially after the corporate fuel-economy standards were passed into law, each company accelerated its efforts to educate the public about the costs of regulation. Ford estimated, for instance, that the last 14 percentage points in emissions improvement cost them better than twice as much per point as the previous 16 percentage points and seven times as much as the first 65 points. Chrysler figured the steep cost curve another way: removing the last five grams of pollutants from the tailpipe to meet the 1981 standards, they said, was costing them one hundred times as much as removing the first thirty-seven grams.

Industry accounting methods were ill-equipped to show the total financial impact of regulation. It was all but impossible, for instance, to separate the regulatory-cost factor in the construction of an engine —part of which might have been charged off to fuel-economy standards, part of which (perhaps even the same part) might have been attributable to emissions standards and all of which simply made up the cost of building the engine. Chrysler had to re-analyze its books from 1974 to 1979 at Lee Iacocca's request to identify extraordinary costs associated with safety and emissions. The finance staff concluded that some $360 million had been spent, over five years, just on those standards. After other non-vehicle standards, such as Occupational Safety and Health Administration (OSHA) and plant-level EPA standards, were added on, as well as the sheer paperwork and labor costs involved, Chrysler had spent some $700 million over those five years.

Only General Motors, realizing in the early Seventies that regulations were here to stay, restructured its cost reporting in order to identify total regulatory costs. Between 1974 and 1979, for those same five years, the giant automaker logged $4.7 billion in accumulated costs to meet safety, emissions and noise standards. And when OSHA, plant-level EPA and paperwork were tacked on, the expense total climbed to $8.1 billion. GM was careful to omit any expense related to fuel-economy standards, since these were readily construed as marketable improvements.

The numbers—either because they were too complicated or too big to have any meaning to the average citizen—had no impact. More often than not, they were met or at least neutralized by arguments such as Joan Claybrook's oft-repeated contention that there is no way to put a price on human life or the pain and suffering of those injured in an automobile accident or afflicted by some chemically caused disease.

Nor is there a way to measure the toll on people earning a living in the auto industry. Frustration and anger are common among thousands of perfectly honest, well-raised midwestern engineers—the kinds of straightforward individuals who used to carry slide rules in high school and who never smoked in the boys' room. At Chrysler, during the '75 cutbacks, there were days when the only engineers left on the payroll were working on government emissions standards and a number of others were coming in on their own, without pay, to keep a product program alive. "We're working in a constantly changing environment of laws," complained former Chrysler design chief Richard G. MacAdam. "The bastards won't stay still. It's irresponsibility based on complete naïveté." Fred Bolling, a Ford materials engineer, simmered over the waste engendered by regulatory policy. "You can't do the best job if the rules aren't the best rules," he reasoned. "And you can't do the best job if the rules keep changing."

"Pretty soon you're willing to compromise at anything you can do physically and still maintain production," said Sydney Terry about the industry's final submission to regulation. "If you get into the hassle of going to court, then you keep on building cars which eventually have to be fixed retroactively. All the marbles are on the side of the regulators."

"One thing that cannot be quantified," concluded Charlie Heinen before he left the business in July of 1980, "is the deadening effect of having to go through all the red tape. It leaves you angry when you first see it, then just limp so you don't give a damn."

Over the years, by trial and error, Washington's regulators have improved, if only because they accumulated more working knowledge of the real-world constraints—but the pattern of cross-purpose policy-making has, if anything, gotten worse as more and more regulations have been piled on. Safety standards promulgated by NHTSA often add unnecessary weight, which hurts fuel economy. Emissions standards stole another 10 percent from the average car's fuel efficiency, and in the case of diesel particulate standards still under consideration, they may even prohibit outright the use of an entire technology that promises a major contribution to aggregate fuel savings. To be sure, trade-offs are inevitable—but, too often, the trade-offs are made with insufficient or even no justification.

Throughout, regulatory policy has rested on the assumption that the industry, as big as it is, was fully capable of paying the full price of clean air and safety, regardless of the merit of the standards themselves. The assumption itself is the child of the Camelot years of the 1950s and '60s, when American business ruled the world and a myth of invincibility surrounded American free enterprise, epitomized as it was by the multinational corporation.

Ralph Nader argued before the Ribicoff committee that "whatever touches all should be decided by all." But he did not address the question of who should pay for the social benefits incurred. Chrysler, in an attempt to justify its request for government aid in 1979, presented what Public Affairs Vice-President Wendell Larsen called "a philosophical threshold question: if the purpose of the regulations was to meet general social goals rather than goals of either the purchaser or the manufacturer, was it proper for society to impose the tax for meeting the goals solely on the purchaser and the manufacturer? Might not one argue that meeting general social goals is the responsibility of society in general?"

The questions were never answered in the course of the Chrysler debate. The economics of regulation dictate that private enterprise pay for the cost of social goals and then pass these costs on to the consumer. No account was taken of the social impact of these higher costs, although some of the same public officials who advocated this system of regulatory cost allocation vehemently opposed all attempts to allow gasoline prices to increase, on the grounds that higher gas prices were an unfair burden on the poor. Such inconsistencies have seldom sparked public debate.

Ironically, as the Reagan administration took office in January of 1981, the danger loomed that the pendulum would once more swing back too far in the other direction: that the legitimate need for environmental monitoring would be overwhelmed by the push for economic recovery. Even in bloodied Detroit, it is recognized that harmful chemical effects not discernible by human senses must be monitored and kept in check by some authority.

Safety and emissions standards did not, in and of themselves, bring Chrysler to its knees. Evidence of poor management decisions, lack of organizational discipline and any number of penalties inherent in the company's relative size argues against such claims. But a conspiracy of factors—unintentionally devastating in effect—clearly included federal regulatory and energy policy, the impact of which would not be felt until Detroit was hit with the full cost of fuel-economy standards.

John Riccardo embodied Detroit's attitudes and reactions toward government regulation. He was, as colleagues often noted, aggressive and persistent in his opposition to federal intrusion. He fought tooth-and-nail throughout the early years, naïvely believing that because he had evidence for his case, he would prevail. Because he inevitably led with his chin, because he was all too often emotional and sometimes abrasive in his dealings with public officials, and because he was fighting from a position of weakness within his own industry, he lost.

In 1978, on one of his many journeys to Washington, Riccardo led a Chrysler contingent into the offices of the Federal Trade Commission. In one of the classic ironies of Washington-Detroit relations, the FTC was deeply involved, along with the Justice Department, in an investigation to determine whether General Motors had an unfair advantage over its smaller competitors. Riccardo was pleading to be excluded from what was an elaborate, time-consuming and costly exercise requiring thousands of hours and some $13 million in expenditures from Chrysler—one of the firms the investigation sought to protect. Chrysler, argued Riccardo, was having enough trouble competing with GM without throwing away precious resources on the probe. The response was, in effect, "Go away and stop complaining."

Riccardo's team left, but as they did so they warned that they might indeed go faster than Washington imagined possible. Within a year, Riccardo was back—this time pleading for his company's very existence.

CHAPTER EIGHT

Under the Gavel

There was no question, following the outbreak of the Yom Kippur War in October 1973, that the energy shortage in the United States was real. It would be at least a year before conspiracy theories developed around rumors of oil tankers lined up just outside New York harbor, waiting for oil prices to rise. America sat in cars during the winter of '73, waiting hours in the frozen predawn darkness of Chicago, Pittsburgh and Detroit for portions of precious fuel—some doled out in maximum $3 or $5 lots, others for a minimum of $8 or $10. "Topping off" emerged as an image of personal greed. Those older than fifty revived images of the Depression soup lines, while the under-thirty remnants of the Sixties' Consciousness III generation condemned the lines as symbols of America's addiction to fuel, growth, greed, crass commercial waste and profligacy. There was no more identifiable symbol of sin, however, than the full-size, two-ton, air-conditioned automobile, powered by an eight-cylinder engine with automatic transmission, that swilled gas at a gallon every 10.5 miles of ten-lane enviro-destructive highway.

Motor vehicles consumed the most conspicuous share of oil—some 40 percent as of 1973—and before the creation of the Department of Energy in 1977, the terminal moraine of facts and figures about energy was none other than the Environmental Protection Agency, which happened to be coming off three mutually unsavory years of jousting with the automobile industry.

The U.S. auto industry's fuel-economy average for 1973 was 13 mpg, the lowest in its history. This was partly caused by Detroit's relentless surge toward bigness, horsepower and comfort. However, federally mandated safety equipment had already added nearly five hundred pounds per car, and the necessity to "detune" engines to meet emissions standards had cut another 10 percent from average fuel efficiency. Nonetheless, EPA and the Department of Transportation, reporting to Congress a year after the embargo began, concluded that the fuel efficiency of American-made cars and trucks was "significantly less than the state of the art."[1] If all those little foreign cars people were buying could get good mileage, there was no reason American technology couldn't produce the same.

Besides, reasoned the report's authors, concentration of fuel conservation policy on the automobile itself would avoid the messy business of trying to change human behavior. At least it was recognized that Americans themselves were no less wasteful than their autos. Car owners used their vehicles for short trips that easily could have been made by foot or bike, duplicated journeys to buy items that could have been bought on a single trip with some forethought and drove alone in six-passenger commuter cars on an almost daily basis. Inherent in the report's recommendations was an assumption reminiscent of the debate on auto safety: that Americans are somehow incapable of or at best unwilling to help themselves. Improving by mandate the fuel efficiency of cars rather than people was tantamount to a "passive restraint" of American profligacy—an air bag for oil consumption.

The government agencies argued that mandating better fuel economy would not burden the auto companies. They contended that a better miles-per-gallon rate was a natural selling point, since it meant lower operating costs for car owners. Unlike a tax on gasoline or on engine capacity and vehicle weight (the so-called "gas guzzler tax"), fuel efficiency standards would not directly penalize the consumer (read "voter"). Washington deemed the plan as an ingenious blend of political expediency, national policy and enough ideological consistency to placate conservatives worried about governmental intrusion into the free-enterprise market. It was, after all, a carrot-and-stick approach: instead of dictating specific mileage figures for specific cars, the government would dictate only one number and let free enterprise determine how best to achieve it. In the best tradition of federal acronymetry, Washington dubbed it Corporate Average Fuel Economy, longhand for CAFE.

Proponents even professed to believe that the system would benefit the "little guys" in Detroit. Here at last was a genuine opportunity for dedicated engineers to desert the war of chrome, trim and subliminal advertising, return to their garages and develop some of those ingenious fixes that everyone knew were languishing on the R & D shelves like so many gas hogs in a showroom. The nimble mechanics of Chrysler and American Motors could surely outmaneuver the pornographic stylists at General Motors and Ford and return economic balance to the industry.

Having firmly established the soundness of the approach, CAFE advocates had only to plug in the right numbers and send Detroit on its way. Take the desired aggregate number of gasoline gallons to be saved, divide by the number of cars on the road times the number of miles driven and add the resulting mileage improvement number to the existing mileage of cars on the road. It was a classic example of public-policy logic.

The trouble with the CAFE formula was that it failed to take into account either the industry's technical ability to meet the standards or the cost of meeting them even if they were technically feasible. The Ford White House, picking up the pieces of a major automotive recession brought about by the oil embargo, had asked the carmakers what they thought they could achieve by the 1980s. The Ford administration was at least willing to set mutually agreed-upon standards and set them voluntarily.

Because of the gas panic and the subsequent shift to small cars in 1974, Detroit's fuel-economy average rose a full point, to 14 mpg, without significant technical change. By merely changing the "mix" of cars they bought, the public improved the industry's CAFE (though they wrought disaster financially). General Motors, which was well along anyway in its own program to improve the fuel efficiency of its fleet for the Eighties, told the government it could project a 45 percent improvement by the end of the decade. Since GM was farther behind on fuel efficiency, with a 1974 CAFE of 12, the government accepted those numbers and set an overall industry improvement goal of 40 percent. There were a few knee-jerk protests from Detroit, but no one doubted it could be done—and done cost-efficiently.

At the time, General Motors became a popular subject of commercial obituaries. Its dinosaur fleet of full-size cars gathered dust throughout 1974: unit sales fell 27 percent, earnings plunged 60 percent and, by the end of the year, nearly a quarter of its work force was idle. However, six months *before* the Yom Kippur War, in early 1973, the Executive and Finance committees on the company's fabled fourteenth floor had pieced together a long-term strategy to address the possibility of dwindling fuel resources and rising fuel prices. Top executives decided then to "down-size" each of their basic model lines, starting with full-size cars in the 1977 model year and proceeding to intermediates in 1978, compacts in 1979½ (a mid-model-year or spring introduction), a second mid-size body classification in 1980 and the subcompact line in the spring of 1981. By 1978, at which point the full-size cars and intermediates would have been trimmed 600 to 1,000 pounds each, the company would have reached the Ford administration's goals.

The strategy, even in hindsight, was ingenious. With the continuing American preference for big, six-passenger cars and the obvious reluctance of the American government to use fuel-price increases as an incentive to conserve, GM was preserving as much of the big-car look and capacity as possible while reducing weight and hence the need for power. By down-sizing their fleet gradually, from the top down, they could create the relative illusion of size while at the same time not overburdening the automotive tooling industry, which would be called upon to build the tools to make smaller pieces for the new cars.

It was also a stunningly expensive strategy. Vast accumulations of earnings over the years typically allowed GM to remain free of short-term debt. But its down-sizing scheme—then underestimated even at $15 billion over the next ten years—had to be paid for no matter what the market did to cash flow. When the downturn of 1974–75 cut into earnings, the company was forced to borrow $600 million from its banks to keep the program going.

The oil embargo did spark two "crash" programs at General Motors: blueprints for the subcompact Opel Rekord from the company's West German subsidiary were shipped in, Americanized and built as the Chevette, and a luxury "skin" with appropriate interior baubles was pulled over the GM basic compact platform and dubbed the Cadillac Seville.

Congress wasn't about to buy voluntarism, however. It mandated a 20-mpg CAFE by 1980 as part of the December 1975 Energy Policy and Conservation Act, giving Detroit twenty-one months to start producing a fleet that averaged 18 mpg for the 1978 model year. The standard itself was not alarming. What was disturbing was the establishment of yet another precedent-setting federal mechanism to measure and dictate standards. From then on, the pattern developed predictably.

As required by law, the newly charged federal agencies solicited industry opinion on what sorts of standards were achievable beyond 1980. By 1985, Chrysler suggested, it might be able to reach a fleet average of 23.6 mpg. "GM and Ford weren't too far from that figure," recalled Syd Terry. The government, approaching the problem from a macro-policy goal of oil conservation, pushed for a complete doubling of the 1974 industry average, jumping from 14 to 28. In conference committee, the number was haggled down to 27.5. "Nobody had any idea what you had to do to get that average," said Terry. "Nobody had any idea what the fleet average was in any other country. They just didn't know! It just came out of the air—the cigar-smoke-filled air!"

The change of government brought about by the 1976 election made matters worse for Detroit. A number of zealous consumer advocates were moved into key administration positions. EPA's Erik Stork was eased out for being too soft on Detroit. An ambitious Washington state congressman named Brock Adams was named Secretary of Transportation, and his new Director of the National Highway Traffic Safety Administration was one of the best and the brightest graduates of Ralph Nader's legion of activists—Joan Claybrook.

Left undetermined by Congress in the 1975 Energy Act were the incremental standards Detroit would be required to meet between 1980, when they would have to average 20 mpg, and 1985, when CAFE would culminate at 27.5. Logic, of course, suggested a straight-line approach: 21.5 in '81, 23 in '82 . . . 27.5 in 1985. One of the Carter administration's first actions in 1977 was to accelerate the requirements in the early years in order to goad Detroit into action. It was a way to dramatize the importance of energy conservation. The 1981 standard would therefore be 22 mpg; in 1982 it would be 24 and in 1983, 26. Then the increments would relax to 27 in 1984 before that last half-mile per gallon.

The industry was outraged, labeling the system "front-loading." Engineers and executives protested that they weren't even sure they could meet the 1985 standards on a straight line, let alone at the accelerated pace. "Front-loading," they said, would only aggravate what was already a severe technological lag. "Give or take half-a-mile per gallon," griped Ford Motor president Lee Iacocca, "the European owner field, where fuel is two to three times as expensive, where the standard of living has been consistently lower and where by necessity for thirty years auto manufacturers have concentrated on small, fuel-efficient cars, averages only 24. That's all the little Fiats of Italy and the Mercedes get. But not to be outdone, with that good ole Yankee ingenuity, we're going for broke."

For all the periodic pronouncements in the mid-Seventies that the big American car was at last dead, the market—even in 1974—did not have a very clear message about fuel economy and vehicle size. Imports—which, with rare exceptions, were small, fuel-efficient cars—were the first beneficiaries of the sudden shift in the spring of the year, but it was too sudden even for them. Caught by surprise by the American-market panic and wholly reliant on long supply lines back to Europe and Japan, Toyota, Datsun, VW and others simply couldn't match demand. The market, impatient and increasingly hesitant to buy any car, turned away. By year's end, import sales in the United States had dropped to a four-year low. GM, Ford and Chrysler had a

variety of small cars in 1974: the Chevy Vega, Buick Skyhawk, Ford
Pinto and Maverick and Chrysler's highly efficient Dodge Colt and
Plymouth Arrow. The two giants kicked up production to maximum
and Chrysler pulled every Colt and Arrow it could out of the Mitsubishi pipeline. Strangely, the cars didn't sell. GM president E. M.
"Pete" Estes blamed it on the Americans' lack of small-car sales experience, but that excuse seemed specious. Part of it was price. Suffering
across the board, the manufacturers desperately stuffed their little cars
full of lucrative options to make up for lost profits from big-car sales.
The public resisted. Alfred Sloan, Jr., and the currency-cheap imports
had conditioned them too well to associate small size with a small
price tag.

By December 1974, dealer gimmicks were signaling the end of the
small-car boom. Most Americans have long since forgotten, but Harvard Business School marketing students are annually reminded of the
thirteen San Diego Ford dealers who ordered 150 red-white-and-blue
"Inflation Fighter" Pintos, matched the cars' colors with salesmen's
outfits and put on a dandy small-car circus. An Atlanta Toyota dealer
gave Christmas trees away to anyone who test-drove one of his little
Japanese numbers. Then, on Superbowl Sunday in January 1975,
Chrysler launched its "Car Clearance Carnival" with Joe Garagiola
hawking a modern industry first: direct customer rebates.

Lynn Townsend's massive overbuild the previous fall left a wide
array of models on Chrysler's rebate list, but the most prominent cash
giveaways were attached to small cars—the compact and durable
Dodge Dart, the Plymouth Duster and, of all things, leftover 1974
Dodge Colts from Mitsubishi, among the most fuel-efficient cars on
the road.

GM and Ford got suckered in quickly. The industry rebate lists
comprised a roster of just about every small car made in America:
Pintos, Mavericks and Mustang IIs from Ford, Vegas and Omegas
from GM and AMC's boxy little Gremlins. The imports didn't join in,
but that was no sign of success: Datsun dealers were sitting on a four-
month supply of cheap little gas-sippers. As early as 1976, the small-
car share of the market had slipped back under 50 percent. Macho but
gas-guzzling four-wheel-drive off-the-road vehicles began a sweep of
the market, and "sin bin" vans filled the void last left by the rubber-
peeling "muscle cars" of the late Sixties. They at least partially
reflected buyer efforts to wriggle out from under power-constricting
emissions standards that did not yet encompass the light-truck market.
AMC's little cars sat on dealer floors while buyers snapped up proud
Jeep Cherokees and Wagoneers that got 10 to 13 mpg.

Public surveys and market research offered little explanation. Beta
Research Corporation of Syosset, New York, conducts annual auto

market studies, sponsored by *Newsweek* and used by the industry as a standard marketing tool. In 1975, while 59 percent of the sample felt that Detroit should make smaller cars and 77 percent felt that horsepower should be cut down, only 23 percent said they were likely to *buy* a small car, even if gas prices increased or fuel was in short supply. By 1977, half as many advocated smaller cars and less horsepower, and only import owners listed fuel economy high among their priorities. The market and the law were pulling Detroit apart. The case was not proved until 1979–80, but the source of the disparity, quite clearly, was federal energy policy and the price of gasoline.

As far back as 1959, the United States government had protected the nation's domestic oil industry from cheap foreign competition by holding the imports to 18 percent of the market. By 1971, domestic production had clearly peaked; Texas and Oklahoma crude were becoming increasingly difficult and expensive to extract. The trade-off facing the Nixon administration was whether to suppress domestic production by unleashing the cheaper imports or to accept higher fuel prices at a time when inflation was an increasing worry. Nixon went with cheap oil, and by the outbreak of the Yom Kippur War, 30 percent of all oil consumed by Americans came from overseas.

The effectiveness of the embargo itself demonstrated to the Arabs the stranglehold they had over the West, encouraging them to continue to use oil as a weapon. By the end of the embargo, world oil prices had risen from $2 a barrel to $8, but the U.S. government, anxious to avoid economic destabilization, held gasoline prices to considerably more moderate increases. After the gas lines had dispersed, Americans were still only paying between 55 and 60 cents a gallon.

There was widespread recognition, however, that conservation was essential if the country was going to avoid greater disruptions. John Sawhill, Nixon's energy czar, recommended a $1-a-gallon tax on gasoline, following the example of European countries. Even the auto industry agreed that price increases would be necessary, though Detroit felt that oil price ceilings should be lifted gradually rather than in one jarring leap.

In January 1975, Gerald Ford imposed a $2-per-barrel surcharge on imported oil as a relatively mild discouragement. The Administration had obviously focused on price as the simplest weapon against demand, a rather elementary economic conclusion. It turned out to be a political nightmare.

By 1975, with oil flowing freely once more and the big oil companies raking in enormous paper profits from the rapid increases in world market prices, Americans rebelled against the scare of the embargo. Conspiracy theories abounded and Congress picked up the scent. By mid-year, with Democratic candidates coming out of the woodwork to take on President Ford in the campaign ahead, everyone had a theory about the great oil rip-off and a scheme to protect citizens from it. Henry "Scoop" Jackson of Washington, an acknowledged expert on energy, promised that America would be paying no more than 10 cents a gallon higher for gas by 1980, a price hike that would put a gallon of regular unleaded at less than 70 cents.

In a fit of partisan rage, Congress slapped down Ford's surcharge. Incredibly, as part of the same comprehensive bill that mandated a fleet average of 27.5 mpg by 1985 from Detroit, the legislators established an oil price ceiling that actually rolled back the price of oil by $1-a-barrel. Ford, faced with a certain congressional override if he vetoed the bill, signed it four days before Christmas 1975. To cope with its artificial pricing, Congress further established a labyrinth of oil categories, the base of which was a three-tiered market with "new" American oil priced at $8.65 per barrel, "old" oil capped at $5.65/bbl and an uncontrollable world price then at $11.28/bbl. Over the next four years, the tiers would breed sub-tiers and exceptions and so many variations on a theme that even the Department of Energy experts were caught numerous times not understanding their own rules.

As William Tucker, a contributing editor of *Harper's* magazine, wrote in one of the most cogent analyses of the auto/energy drama of the past decade, "Immediate decontrol in 1976 would have raised the price of gas by less than 10 cents per gallon at worst."[2] Instead, from 1975 through 1978, the price of gasoline at the pump in the United States rose in total only 12 cents and in uninflated dollars *actually declined* by several pennies per gallon. Little wonder that by 1976, automotive insiders were comparing the GM subcompact Chevette to Ford's market disaster of the Fifties, the Edsel, or that the confidence in the market acceptability of "down-sized" big cars in the late Seventies was so shaky that both GM and Ford were looking for the shortest possible fashion models so that their cars would look bigger in relation to them.

In 1974, when the big-car market was taking a beating in the midst of the first gas shortage, *Fortune's* Charles Burck wrote that "the consumer's swing away from big cars has already done more to get the manufacturers moving than any enactment could have done. What's more," he warned, "legislation that is not carefully thought out could do more harm than good."[3]

In November of 1978, the Department of Transportation's house think tank in Cambridge, Massachusetts, the Transportation Systems Center, issued a report entitled "The Effects of Federal Regulation on the Financial Structure and Performance of the Domestic Motor Vehicle Manufacturers," singling out CAFE requirements as by far the most expensive of a series of expensive federal mandates.[4] The report estimated that "manufacturers will have to turn over almost all their capital assets . . . perhaps $60 to $80 billion in eight years." The unprecedented financial burden, suggested the report's authors, "will take place according to a regulatory schedule which is divorced from market economics and the cyclicality of business."

Not surprisingly, the report focused its analysis on Chrysler, which was already exhibiting some dysfunctions, in part because of the financial squeeze. Clearly unable to pay out-of-pocket for the necessary technology required by the regulation, Chrysler would be forced to increase its debt dramatically and would dig itself into a financial hole from which it might not be able to emerge.

No less than four independent studies undertaken during the late Seventies, before the Iranian crisis and subsequent oil-price explosion, reached essentially the same conclusions. The most pervasive criticism of federal policy was contained in "Energy Conservation and the Passenger Car," sponsored by General Motors but pointedly unedited by the company.[5] Indeed, GM, long under the shadow of antitrust prosecution, could not have been terribly pleased by one of the essential conclusions of the study: contrary to the wishful thinking of NHTSA and Congress, the mileage requirements would *not* enhance the competitive opportunities of the smaller manufacturers. "The rapid reshaping of product lines and the development of technological fixes has proved to be much more demanding of capital resources than [was] ever imagined by either government agencies or the automakers themselves," said Harbridge House, a Cambridge "think tank" that authored the study. "The burden of this development falls somewhat disproportionately on the smaller full-line companies. The largest firm in the industry, General Motors, enjoys a greater ability not only to generate the necessary funds from both internal and external sources, but also to apply those funds efficiently over a larger unit of output."

The penalty for not keeping up with GM's technological advances, predicted Harbridge, was a disproportionate loss of market share. A shift of 2 percent in market share is little skin off GM's back at 59 percent. But the same two points taken from Chrysler—from 11 percent to 9 percent—would (and did) spell financial disaster.

NHTSA disputed the conclusions of this and other independent analyses, claiming that there was no historic evidence of market-share shift in favor of the bigger companies. Indeed, through 1976, there was little sign that GM was gorging itself at the expense of its smaller competitors, but the record thereafter showed a steady disintegration of the market positions of Ford, Chrysler and AMC, the stability of GM and the astounding advance of the Japanese. Then again, it was

NHTSA's estimate that the entire cost of the fuel-economy laws to the industry would be no more than $200 million.

By early 1979, the evidence was mounting that CAFE was engendering a number of negative side effects not anticipated by the lawmakers. Because they were required to meet a specific timetable—and an accelerated one at that—the automakers found themselves extending their product development cycles well beyond the traditional three and a half years. The most obvious way to reduce gasoline consumption was to use smaller engines. Moving from the tried and tested eight-cylinder block down past six to four required completely new tooling and, in many cases, new plants. That in itself was a five-year project.

In order to relieve the new smaller engines of as much weight as possible, new lightweight materials had to be found and then tested to see if they provided sufficient durability under driving conditions, to see if they meshed properly with other pieces and adhered satisfactorily, and to see if they met existing and impending safety standards. Glass thickness, for example, had been the same in the industry for years, until the need for weight reduction made engineers rethink the gauges they'd been using. The thinner glass had to be fully tested against wind and collision pressure; then all the surrounding pieces that held the glass in place had to be redesigned to match the new gauge.

The sudden new demands on the machine-tool industry that supplied the equipment to make engines and parts caused a backlog that only grew thereafter. Because automakers all over the world need such tools, and since the new American cars were becoming closer in size to European and Japanese models, the competition for contracts extended machine-tool makers to their limits. What was a two-year lead time for major machine orders grew to three and four. Ironically, machine-tool orders are used by the government as a leading economic indicator. Because such orders increased dramatically in the automotive sector, the statistics misleadingly suggested business optimism when, in fact, the demand was utterly divorced from market dynamics and certainly devoid of any optimism.

The extension of lead time and the forced utilization of new and relatively untried systems and materials dramatically lowered the confidence of the manufacturers that what they were spending billions on would be accepted by the consumer or even function properly five to seven years hence. By mid-1980, programs for as far ahead as 1985 and '86 were set in stone and unalterable without severe economic penalty.

The mileage standards, divorced as they were from market demands, placed artificial parameters around the range of models. Assuming continued low fuel prices and little consumer demand for fuel economy, Detroit calculated its CAFE requirements around a mix of products weighted toward the largest cars possible, to meet what was perceived as the demands of the market. Thus, inordinate amounts of money were spent designing cars of maximum size with a minimum protraction of weight and size range. Arvid Jouppi's river (see Chapter One), however, would inevitably be narrowed as the mileage standards grew higher. The ability of the smaller companies to find space along the river and fish for customers would become increasingly limited. As each corporation spent more and more money covering bets, less and less money would be available for what Harvard Business Professor William J. Abernathy called "epochal research"— the quest for major technological breakthroughs that have historically changed the dynamics of industry.[6]

American Motors, increasingly stifled by regulatory costs, opted in the late Seventies simply to bow out of the race for technological development and buy into new systems as others developed them. Beneath the hood of every single AMC passenger car at the turn of the decade lay an engine made by either Pontiac or Volkswagen. Chrysler, already forced by emissions standards to abandon a promising "lean burn" pollution-control system, would soon find its once-heralded turbine program on paper only.[7] Ford, by the end of 1980, would be struggling to keep a breath of life in its PROCO project (for "Programmed Combustion," a variation on the stratified-charge technique of handling both mileage and emissions control within the combustion cycle). Only GM, with its vast resources, could continue a broad range of epochal research into advanced automotive power sources. As Maryann Keller, a Wall Street automotive analyst, noted, "The curious result of the government-mandated programs is that, in the end, the rich will be richer and the poor will be poorer."

Riccardo's Chrysler clearly was on the poor side of the ledger. In North America, he faced the enormous advantages of General Motors, exacerbated by the new law. But even GM's lead at home seemed a pale concern compared to the overall competitive advantages coming from the eleven smaller producers perceived in Detroit as an industrial monolith dubbed "Japan, Inc."

Before World War II, Japan, like many countries, had looked to Detroit for guidance on every aspect of automobile design and production. The first Toyota, built in 1935, bore an uncanny resemblance to the Chrysler Airflow, and a '37 Datsun would not have looked out of place tooling down Fifth Avenue. However, out of the rubble and poverty of the postwar period came the historic irony of having to build an entire industry from scratch, thereby gaining the advantages of brand-new plants designed for an environment in which fuel was scarce and expensive while consumers were unable to afford more than minimal amenities. For the first decade after the war, the Japanese concentrated on trucks, for rebuilding their country, and motorcycles, for the very limited private transportation market. The first postwar cars were so flimsy that the Japanese themselves used to joke, "Buy two, one for each foot."[8] Not until the entire Japanese highway system was spruced up for the 1964 Olympics, with the long-awaited arrival of hard-won affluence, did the industry begin to expand.

The first tentative venture into automobile export to the United States came in 1958, when Toyota sold all of 274 cars and Datsun a mere 52. For nearly a decade, the offer of Princes, Daihatsus and Izuzus in the booming, energy-abundant and ever-expanding American market was met with understandable condescension from both the public and Detroit. GM, Ford and Chrysler executives were more than glad to allow flocks of Nikon-clicking Japanese engineers into their massive plants to learn how the unconquerable Yankees did it.

No one balked as the U.S. government gave Japan billions in aid, surplus industrial tools and advice. No one questioned Japan's favored trading status or the pronounced policy of protectionism established by the tiny recovering nation. The United States, after all, had won the war and emerged as the most powerful nation on earth—so powerful that she could afford to concede advantages to the vanquished and indeed had an obligation to do so if she expected the Japanese to recover and rejoin the industrial world. Japan was more than welcome to pick some of the excess fruits of the American market.

Even in 1973, when the Japanese exported some 800,000 cars and trucks to the United States, Detroit didn't mind. American automakers that year had sold an all-time-record number of cars and trucks—more than 14 million—with the help of their Canadian subsidiaries. There was some concern during the fuel crisis of 1974, when the Japanese jumped to a million units, because their products were not only cheap but fuel-efficient. The gas scare subsided quickly, though, and in 1975, Japanese imports receded to 800,000. Thereafter, however, the Japanese manufacturers launched an invasion that will go down in commercial annals as one of the phenomenal successes in international business. In 1976, Japanese imports jumped to 1.4 million; in 1977, they were up to 1.6 million; by 1979, they had topped 2 million and in 1980, their 2.5 million unit sales accounted for better than one out of every five cars and trucks sold in America. Over a five-year period, their sales tripled, increasing annually by 320,000 units on average. While Chrysler, Ford, GM and even small-car specialist AMC laid off as many as 313,000 auto workers in production cutbacks throughout the slump of 1979–80, Japanese workers put in steady overtime building cars for the U.S. market. While exports accounted for less than 30 percent of Japanese production in 1973, they made up 56 percent of production in 1980. Thirty-five years after Hiroshima, the Japanese surpassed the Americans in motor-vehicle production and did so by the whopping margin of 40 percent.

Contrary to the common perception, Detroit did not ignore the Japanese until they realized they were being done in. Even when they were still making money, back in 1976 and '77, executives at Ford were beginning to air concerns about the trade advantages exploited by the Japanese producers. When the domestic market plunged into the small-car segment in 1979, Ford—this time echoed by Chrysler, AMC and, to a limited extent, even GM—began to cry out for its very survival. Ford argued that U.S. trade policy was giving the U.S. car market to the Japanese and petitioned Washington for relief.

The nub of the American industry's argument was that the United States is the only industrialized nation that does *not* protect its auto industry from foreign competition through duties and non-tariff trade barriers. Common Market countries have duties ranging from 11 to 14 percent; Australia requires 85 percent of the vehicle to be manufactured locally or else it imposes a 58 percent duty; Canada, except for its production pact with the United States, imposes a 14 percent duty. Most Third World countries have either strict local content requirements or prohibitive duties as high as 95 percent. The Japanese, while they have over the years gradually dropped formal tariffs and direct foreign investment bans at home, maintain a commodity tax on automobiles that is 15 percent on small displacement engines and 20 percent on larger engines. The 15-percent tax covers cars under 2,000 cc, a 1,700-mm width and a 2,700-mm wheelbase; the 20-percent tax covers anything bigger. Only the smallest American subcompacts, such as GM's Chevette and Chrysler's Omni and Horizon, qualify for the lower rate. In addition, the Japanese burden imports with weight taxes, dealer acquisition taxes, a host of special vehicle modification requirements and individual vehicle inspection as each car is registered in Japan.[9] Altogether, the technical and administrative changes required for entry into Japan serve to double the price of an American car from its home-market price. Thus, a 1980 four-door Chevette, one of the least expensive cars made in the United States (generally priced under $5,000) and small enough to qualify for the lower 15-percent commodity tax, ended up with a Tokyo sticker price of nearly $10,500.

To make matters worse, Japanese law prohibits dealers from carrying more than one line, making it impossible for low-volume imports to "piggyback" onto high-volume Japanese franchises. With little volume, lots of paperwork and guaranteed high prices, there has been little incentive for a Japanese to open a foreign-car dealership in his country. It's not surprising that the Japanese manufacturers have enjoyed a 99-percent market share at home.

By contrast, the United States exacts a single 2.9-percent duty on imported cars, the lowest in the world. No Value-Added Tax (VAT), which could be deducted under international trade agreement (GATT) for cars being exported to other countries, exists in the United States. The Japanese tax their own cars with the same 15-percent to 20-percent commodity levy placed on incoming cars, but exempt their own manufacturers from the tax when the cars are being exported. Thus, a $5,000 Toyota cost $750 less upon leaving Japan than it cost in a Tokyo dealership and, shipping costs and preparations notwithstanding, usually ended up costing less than $200 over its home-market price in an American showroom.

To be sure, the commodity tax differential cannot be construed as a direct penalty, since it affects retail prices equally on both ends—but because the revenues accruing to the Japanese government help pay for such general benefits as national health insurance and at the same time relieve corporations of what would surely be higher direct taxes on profits, they do indeed constitute an advantage to the Japanese producer . . . or, perhaps better said, a *dis*advantage to the American producer. And as for the non-tariff barriers, as Neil Goldschmidt, Jimmy Carter's able and respected second Secretary of Transportation, put it: "We cannot have companies overseas perceiving that what's theirs is theirs and what's ours is half theirs."

There is danger in overplaying the one-on-one imbalance of U.S./Japanese auto trade. Even if it were completely open to American autos, Japan would not provide a very lucrative market. Only in 1980 did the entire Japanese car market reach 5 million units—roughly half the American total. And with extremely limited land and a stable population level, it would never provide much promise to foreign competition. Moreover, until the sudden shift in American production to small, fuel-efficient cars, the prospect of selling more than a handful of full-size, V-8-powered American products for use on those tiny island roads was about as likely as selling fur coats in the tropics.

There is, however, one distinct advantage gained by the Japanese, first through wholesale protectionism and later by more subtle impediments. Japanese automakers have been granted the comfort of developing an industry free from the pressures of competition. U.S. antitrust laws prohibited such comfort on the presumption that the industry would only have exploited its captive market and reaped excessive profits. The Japanese appear to have recognized that their competition was not in Japan but in the rest of the world and that their auto manufacturers needed the time and the profitability at home to catch up. In the huge American economic arena, where resources have been plentiful until recently and the market itself seemingly boundless, the importance of this global perspective as a framework for policy has all too often been missed.

"To an American," wrote Peter Drucker in *Fortune*, "the most visible aspect of Japan's position in the world economy is its trade surplus with the U.S., especially in automobiles, steel and consumer electronics. To the Japanese, however, the most visible aspect . . . is its trade deficit overall and its heavy dependence on imports of fuel, agricultural products and raw materials."[10]

Drucker, who has spent much time studying the Japanese culture and economy, observed that the Japanese have concentrated on the development of a program of mercantilism designed to help pay for the island nation's chronic dependence on imported energy and raw materials. Japan imports 99.7 percent of the petroleum it uses—much of it from the politically volatile Middle East. More vulnerable to the whims of OPEC pricing than any other industrialized nation, Japan must establish a healthy surplus in the trading of high-technology, value-added goods. Drucker emphasized that Japan's greatest concern was that it had become too dependent on the export of cars, steel and appliances, products of older industries on the wane and overly labor-intensive. Just as the United States and Western European nations were losing their competitive edge to the Japanese in these industries, so the Japanese feared the emergence of Taiwan, South Korea and eventually China as cheap-labor competitors. Others suggest that Drucker overplays this alleged concern for cheap labor from emerging nations; they say that, ironically, like the Americans a generation earlier, many Japanese dismiss the Koreans and Taiwanese as being eons behind them in technology and capitalization and therefore not to be feared as competitors.

In any case, MITI, Japan's Ministry of International Trade and Industry, symbol to Westerners of "Japan, Inc.'s" central coordination, was unable during the 1970s to steer its industries into the truly high-tech, education-intensive products such as computers, pharmaceuticals, medical electronics and telecommunications, according to Drucker, and was essentially against the massive expansion of the auto industry. Although Drucker illustrated the strains within Japanese society, the overriding message of his piece was that there *is* a consensus within Japanese society and, more importantly, a general acceptance that there *should be* a consensus.

Perhaps the Japanese auto industry did explode in spite of MITI's discouragements, but explode it did, drawn into the energy-inspired small-car vacuum of the American market. It is frequently argued that Toyota, Datsun and other Japanese cars performed so well in the U.S. market solely because American manufacturers failed to anticipate the changing market. This argument credits the Japanese manufacturers with more foresight than is warranted, though. They had been building small cars exclusively for more than thirty years and would therefore have been prepared for a market shift in the United States whenever it occurred. So, for that matter, were the European manufacturers, who built their automobiles in the same environment as the Japanese. Yet Volkswagen—the only foreign manufacturer besides the leading Japanese makers, to achieve substantial market share in America—made only modest gains during the late Seventies after losing its corporate shirt in the U.S. market in the early part of the decade. Altogether, European cars just barely held their own in the United States from 1976 through 1980, at about 600,000 units, while the Japanese tripled sales.

The principal difference was price, which, coupled with product quality, translates into "value for the money." Following the Nixon administration's decision to abandon the Bretton Woods agreement and float the dollar, the currencies of most industrial nations soared. The value of the German mark, for example, jumped from just over 20 cents to nearly 60 cents, taking the price of the VW Beetle with it. Since achieving a market share of 7 percent in 1970 by selling more than 580,000 cars—most of them $1,900 Beetles—Volkswagen's share plunged to under 3 percent, almost bringing down the parent company in 1974. VW's modest success since has been largely the result of its decision to build cars in the United States in order to avoid further currency deterioration, plus its development of a well-conceived marketing strategy to sell Rabbits, Dashers and Sciroccos as high-quality, high-priced, up-scale automobiles in the $6,000 to $12,000 range.

Contrary to Ford Motor Company's allegation that the Japanese have managed to maintain an "artificially weak yen," the fact is that the yen appreciated to almost the same degree as the mark. Moreover, while the Japanese carmakers have enjoyed lower labor costs, those costs have been rising at a faster rate than have U.S. auto-industry labor costs. Yet throughout the 1970s, Japanese importers have managed to keep the prices of their cars sold in the United States between $200 and $500 below the prices of comparable American models while they substantially increased the value of the cars themselves.

The disheartening (to the Americans) message of the comprehensive study completed by Neil Goldschmidt's Department of Transportation in early January 1981 was that the Japanese manufacturers averaged a cost advantage over their American competitors of between $1,000 and $1,500 per car landed in the United States. Thus, contrary to a popular Detroit belief that the Japanese suffered lower or even negative profit margins in order to gain market share, it was the Goldschmidt Task Force's conclusion that—even with shipping costs and with tariffs and taxes aside—the Japanese have been enjoying a thick cushion of profitability that has allowed them to maintain their final sticker-price advantage with little regard to the fluctuations of the yen.

In the late Seventies, the American manufacturers' near-total transformation of their facilities to build smaller cars only increased the Japanese cost advantage. The 1978–85 payout by U.S. manufacturers, estimated at $80 billion, would have to be recovered from the sticker price. Toyota, Datsun and Honda, their four-cylinder-engine plants already in place, had only modest capital requirements to keep abreast of world market demand. While GM, Ford and Chrysler faced a major production overhaul, the Japanese needed only a tune-up. What was already a significant competitive advantage seemed certain to become an overwhelming one.

Even more astounding than the Japanese cost advantage, which could easily have been used to widen the pricing gap even beyond what is already a significant margin, has been the Japanese emphasis on product quality. Instead of pocketing the profits, as many would expect Detroit to do under reversed conditions, the Japanese clearly pumped more money back into their products. Not only had those teams of Japanese engineers gleaned the best manufacturing and design techniques from the Americans in the formative years; the Japanese designers were able to piece together the kinds of cars and car features to meet American consumers' wishes.

Forced to second-guess demand for options and accessories to circumvent the disadvantage of a five-thousand-mile supply line back to Japan, Toyota and the others learned to load their cars up before shipping them out. Although every Datsun and Honda dealer carried a modicum of base-price, stripped-down models to lure consumers into their showrooms, most cars came loaded with FM stereo radios, air conditioners and other options American manufacturers traditionally tack on afterward. The Datsun 810 even carried a voice synthesizer to remind drivers to close their doors.

Gimmicks aside, the Japanese made certain that every automobile represented maximum quality. "Fits and finishes," the Detroit-spawned phrase used to describe the quality of paint jobs, the alignment of doors and the flush of window gaskets, almost invariably met standards expected of few cars except $40,000 custom-built European gems. Nissan hardly invented microprocessors, but the company built them into every car and exploited their advantages sooner than all but the luxury-class American nameplates. Toyo Kogyo, makers of Mazda cars, stuck with the irksome Wankel rotary piston engine (invented by Germans) long enough to make it work, whereas VW, Mercedes and even GM gave up. Honda's CVCC (Combined Vortex Controlled Combustion) stratified-charge engine was able to meet U.S. emissions standards nearly a decade before most other manufacturers could. After years of concentration on only a few basic engineering and design concepts, the Japanese industry was able to fine-tune its products just as the Americans were being forced to junk their old blueprints and start all over again.

Nearly every type of survey taken after 1978 reflected the appreciation of the American consumer for Japanese achievements. The Los Angeles market research firm of J. D. Power & Associates polled a representative sample of 5,000 Americans who owned cars and found that 52 percent rated the quality of Japanese products "good" or "excellent" versus 47 percent for European cars and only 20 percent for American-made cars. Perhaps the greatest testament to Japanese quality was a *Ward's Auto World* poll of 236 American automotive engineers—48 percent, or nearly half of them, felt that Japanese cars were better built than any others, including their own.

After years of blissful ignorance under the protection of a two-tiered world market, Americans began in the late Seventies to examine what it was that was making the Japanese so successful. The tides turned, and teams of American automotive engineers descended on Japanese plants to see what their secret was. What they found was an astoundingly improved variation on the very theme they themselves originally wrote.

Basic production principles were the same; many of the dies and machine tools were manufactured in places like Cincinnati, Ohio. Technologically, there was little evidence of significant innovative advantage. Japanese cars, like American, German and Italian cars, were still running on internal combustion engines, rubber tires and gasoline —but beyond these basics, the differences overwhelmed the similarities.

Labor costs in the Japanese auto industry were considerably lower than in Detroit. But those who cite high American union wages as the cause of America's industrial decline overstate the case. Total labor costs, concluded the Goldschmidt Task Force, ran about $11 an hour in Japan versus $18 in the United States, including the Japanese system of government-paid health insurance, lifetime employment, willingness to underwrite mortgages for Japanese workers and the virtual cradle-to-grave benefits of company association. However, Japanese wages, according to Citibank data, rose 212 percent between 1970 and 1978 while American wages rose only 90 percent—and, despite highly publicized contract gains during the decade, the UAW-won wages remained a relatively stable percentage of manufacturers' costs.

Where the Japanese enjoyed their greatest labor-related advantage was in non-economic benefits. Cultural differences were undeniable.

"They no longer sing the company song before each work shift at Toyota," observed *Time* bureau chief Ed Reingold, who had the advantage of observing Detroit for seven years between tours of duty in Japan.[11] However, an identification with and loyalty to their companies, coupled with meticulousness and a sense of mission, have long distinguished Japanese blue-collar workers from their counterparts almost everyplace else in the world. Certainly nothing in American experience can touch the tale of Takuya Sakai, captain of the *Fuji Maru,* who attempted *hara-kiri* and eventually slit his throat after discovering on arrival in Los Angeles harbor that more than two hundred Subarus on board had been water-damaged in transit.

In U.S. auto plants, a "low" absenteeism rate still hovers around 10 percent. In Japan, they don't even bother keeping statistics, but it is estimated that absenteeism runs something under 1 percent. Company baseball teams and a full range of recreation facilities, company songs, calisthenics and an inherent sense of honor have done much to ensure a dedication on the job that translates into manufacturing advantages impossible to measure in P&L statements. But beyond these are concrete and wholly replicable methods of maintaining consistent workmanship. Ironically again, it was American experts who taught the Japanese how to involve workers more meaningfully in production. William Edwards Deming, a U. S. Census statistician, introduced the Japanese to the statistical techniques to measure quality and has been honored by the "Deming Award" given each year to the company making the greatest strides in quality control. Now it is the Japanese who have re-exported the concept of the Quality Control Circle— regular meetings of workers and supervisors to hash out the best ways to produce the best products in the most efficient manner. By the early Eighties, each of the American companies had adopted in its own fashion the Quality Circle system, though none goes as far as allowing a single assembly-line worker to stop production simply by pulling a cord if a problem is observed.

Although Japanese executives were loath to admit it on the record, there is little doubt that they questioned the quality of cars produced by American hands. Japanese customers have demanded more of their cars and their workers have learned to produce accordingly. Japanese manufacturers who contemplated construction of plants in the United States were especially reluctant to adopt the traditional adversary relationship between union and management that has characterized American labor relations. They feared the rigidity and the workplace bureaucracy as much if not more than they feared higher wages.

Slowly, based on the experience of the few Japanese companies who did build plants in the United States, the fear of poor workmanship has dissipated. Honda, which began with a motorcycle assembly plant in Ohio, and Kawasaki, which has been building motorcycles in Nebraska, found the quality convincingly similar to Japanese quality. They were further encouraged by the experience of Volkswagen in Pennsylvania, where the quality of Rabbits was deemed equal to if not better than the quality of Rabbits built back in West Germany. Despite myths that absolute productivity in the U.S. industry is poor, American output per worker is still superior and, according to Robert Cole of the University of Michigan's Center for Japanese Studies, the American worker is no less committed to his job than the Japanese worker. The major difference remained the absence in Japan of the adversarial union/management relationship.

Probably even more important to the Japanese advantage than labor costs and union relationships was the relationship between manufacturers and their suppliers, wherein a greater number of parts are parceled out to suppliers than in the United States. In Japan, the difference between the wage rates on an auto assembly line and in a supply plant is usually greater than the difference between the compensation of a university graduate and a high school dropout.

Also, Japanese auto manufacturers keep close tabs on their suppliers. More often than not, supply plants are set up right around assembly plants like satellites, thus eliminating the complicated and expensive materials-handling systems burdening American manufacturers. Proximity not only cuts costs; it allows for closer monitoring of quality and precise inventory control. Toyota's "Just in Time" parts delivery system not only lowers carrying costs, it allows for fewer stockroom workers as well as shipping, receiving and inventory-control personnel.[12]

Suppliers, by tradition in the Japanese industry, have been brought in on design and quality-control decisions sooner and more readily than in the United States. One-on-one cooperation, plus mutual supplier-manufacturer loyalty, are the hallmarks of the Japanese system, in contrast to the cutthroat competition that has branded American supplier-manufacturer relations. As a result, the quality of parts delivered to Japanese assembly plants has tended to be better than in the United States. Both Volkswagen and Kawasaki reported having initially bad experiences with their U.S. suppliers after opening U.S. plants in the late Seventies.[13]

On their expensive home turf, the Japanese have learned to build plants as cheaply as possible, too. A Ford executive, according to Time's Reingold, was startled to learn that an engine plant in Japan cost only $350 million instead of the $500–$600 million Ford had figured it would have to spend on an equivalent plant in the United States. Less durable construction accounted for $200 million of the difference.

Automation has been amply utilized by Japanese manufacturers, with little of the trepidation from workers experienced in other industrialized countries. At Nissan's famous Zama plant, where 110 of Japan's 10,000 industrial robots and limited-sequence manipulators are installed, workers have even given nicknames to their mechanized co-workers. Automatic arms fill tanks with gas and radiators with water, but contrary to some exaggerated reports, the Zama plant does employ some two thousand human beings per shift as well. Nonetheless, not until Chrysler's aging Newark and Jefferson Avenue K-car plants and Ford's Wayne Escort/Lynx facility were decorated with Unimates and Robogates in the summer of 1980 had capital, man and machine combined to form such an efficient *ménage à trois*.

Combined with these cultural, managerial and technical advantages, however, has been the fundamental benefit of economies of scale. Simply stated, the Japanese produce on average more cars per plant than anyone else in the business. GM, Ford and Volkswagen (and until 1978–79, Chrysler) have had their capacity spread out over many continents. For the Americans, of course, it was a necessity for them to build automobiles appropriate to foreign markets, but the Japanese carmakers, until politics entered the picture, steadfastly maintained all their production at home and concentrated on fewer body styles. Honda, for example, built just three basic body styles in just two plants in Japan—each with an annual capacity of 800,000 units. In 1980, GM's U.S. volume of four-cylinder subcompacts was only a quarter the size of Toyota's domestic production. Unencumbered by the two-tiered world market and unwilling to test their managerial techniques in other cultures, the Japanese manufacturers were able to achieve what Lynn Townsend was always looking for: volume.

The United States was not alone in bearing the brunt of Japanese success. Indeed, the almost frantic concern in Europe over the growth of Japanese car sales disproves the theory that a uniquely American flaw exists. During the same period in which the Japanese tripled car sales in the United States, they gained an astounding fivefold increase in West Germany, long considered the home of technical excellence. In Detroit's view, it is more than coincidental that the West Germans, next to the United States, have the industrial world's most liberal trade policy, with no barriers beyond the standard EEC 14-percent duty. Yet the five-year climb from under 2 percent to over 10 percent of the auto market prompted the newsmagazine *Der Spiegel* to intone, "The industry has a vision of horror: that the Japanese may achieve with automobiles the success they have had with their cameras, watches, sound equipment and calculators."[14]

The Europeans were not about to be industrially usurped. France effectively stopped the Japanese simply by informing them unofficially that they could have no more than 3 percent of the French market. Italy was lucky: back before Japan developed its expertise, the Japanese themselves initiated a bilateral ceiling of no more than 2,000 cars going either way. The Japanese had been concerned that their then-fledgling market was vulnerable to Italy's little Fiats, but when the tide turned, the advantage rebounded to the Italians. Great Britain, long the dumping ground of the world's auto exporters because of its own competitive dysfunctions, finally negotiated a 10.8-percent market-share limit for the Japanese in 1975. The common denominator for these nations and also for virtually every Third World country was a recognition of the importance of maintaining a viable domestic automotive industry as a matter of national interest. Only the United States, with its laudable if naïve adherence to the principles of free trade, seemed to ignore such considerations. The Japanese have been accused of, and in some cases found guilty of, dumping products in the American market. So it was not without precedent that many in Detroit, *sotto voce*, continued to accuse them of dumping automobiles as well. After a decade of losing market share to the Japanese television industry, during which time all U.S. firms except his own company were driven to manufacture offshore or to leave the business altogether, Zenith Corporation chairman John Nevin finally put together a case showing that the Japanese were dumping color TV receivers into the United States—only to have the American government let the Japanese off the hook, ostensibly for diplomatic reasons. Robert Anderson, Rockwell International's chairman, was one who opted out of the TV business rather than fight the Japanese. "You don't have to be very smart, when you're selling product below cost and making it in Taiwan, which has cheaper labor rates than Japan, and they come in and *still* undersell you," said Anderson, "to know that you'd better get the hell out of that business. That's just what we did. But how the hell," wondered Anderson, "do they get out of the automotive business?"

By the fall of 1977, despite the veneer of profitability that had accompanied his two years at the helm, John Riccardo faced the very real prospect of being forced out of the automotive business—unless he could find a way to finance his way out of the coming crisis. Money for new product would have to be spent in order to meet federal standards—twice as much annually as Chrysler had ever spent on product before—but pressure from the low-priced, high-quality Japanese cars prevented any of the American car companies from recovering those costs through substantially higher prices. GM and Ford had the financial resources to survive a rough period, and their overseas operations were richly rewarding. Riccardo had slim resources, and overseas operations that only drained money away. Once again, his choices were far fewer than those of his wealthy neighbors.

He could "skinny down" domestically, leaving the company with only a few car lines concentrated in the small end of the market, bereft of diversities such as real estate, sailboats and air conditioners. That way, even if the small cars didn't generate much profit, they would meet the law and match the cars being built by Chrysler's European subsidiaries—thus allowing the company the one remaining advantage of sharing parts and tooling across the Atlantic. But who would buy the ancient facilities designed to build big, eight-cylinder cars, vans and light trucks, when the market of the future was for small vehicles? Chrysler's profits were far too slim to make use of the depreciation advantages of writing the old plants off—and stockholders were certain to protest the sale or closure of assets that were making money today, whatever value they might lose in the future. Riccardo knew that the stockholders—and even Wall Street—wouldn't stand for such austerity when dividends and portfolio value were at stake. He needed resources from somewhere. The one salable commodity he had at his disposal was also the greatest drain on current profits: Lynn Townsend's creation in Europe, by then more than halfway through its second decade.

By 1977, Chrysler's management had discovered overseas that if everything went well they made modest returns, but if everything went badly they suffered enormous losses. Until 1970, Chrysler had made little effort at coordination of its three European companies, largely because the executive responsible, Irv Minett, was a staunch believer in local autonomy. After John Riccardo became president, the policy changed, Minett was replaced and a drive was started toward integration of product planning, dealers and staff among the renamed companies: Chrysler United Kingdom, Chrysler France and Chrysler España.

The creation of Chrysler Europe was the easiest task. Even Ford hadn't established Ford of Europe until 1967, and it soon had found that closer connections between its European operations—however desirable—were tricky to achieve. The metric measure used on the continent, for example, didn't match the British standard measure and resulted in hoods that didn't fit properly. Although Ford of Europe quickly began using its own small shuttle airline to ferry executives between different parts of the company, it wasn't until 1969 that it introduced the first car specially designed for sale all over Europe: the Capri. The Fiesta, launched in 1976, was the first car that embodied the effort to achieve integration. The engine blocks were made in Dagenham, the transmissions and axles in Bordeaux, carburetors in Northern Ireland and engine machinery in Valencia. Assembly was split among factories in the United Kingdom, Spain and West Germany.

At the beginning of the Seventies, Chrysler was also hamstrung by a distinct shortage of cash. Capital spending (see Chapter Five) had been drastically cut in the United States and, though Chrysler had plunged into Europe, it had committed less money than either General Motors or Ford. At the end of 1971, GM had invested $1.097 billion overseas, Ford $1.556 billion and Chrysler $626 million. Meanwhile, Chrysler's British company had become an almost perpetual drain on revenues.

The problems elsewhere were minuscule next to the headaches associated with trying to conduct business in the United Kingdom during the Sixties and Seventies. Labor unrest at Chrysler was no worse than at other British manufacturers. Even Ford, massively successful in the United Kingdom, wasn't immune to tremendous fluctuation brought on largely by labor unrest. At Ford, profits went from a low of minus $42 million in 1971 to a plus $220 million in 1977, but for Chrysler, which slipped from being the third- to the fourth-largest manufacturer in a country that barely had the means to support two, Britain was cancerous. Between 1966 and 1976, Chrysler U.K. enjoyed only four profitable years, worth a cumulative $27 million in profits, compared to $188 million in losses during the remaining years. Chrysler had saved Rootes from oblivion with its initial purchase in 1964, had combined with the British government to bail it out in 1967 and thereafter teetered on a tightrope.

The 1960s and '70s were scarcely ideal times in which to establish a beachhead in Britain. The country failed to offer either domestic or foreign manufacturers a market with the vigor and vibrancy of most other European nations. Only Italy contrived, between 1966 and 1975, to create a less hospitable climate for growth. During the nine years, the annual growth rate for cars in the United Kingdom was 1.3 percent, compared to 3.4 percent in West Germany, 2.1 percent in France and 8.6 percent in Spain.

As part of the arthritis generally afflicting Britain, government policy and labor relations turned Chrysler's Rootes into unremitting agony. Some of the troubles in company plants made the factory portrayed in Peter Sellers' film *I'm Alright, Jack!* look positively industrious. In 1970, for example, the introductory year for the Avenger (the only specifically British model introduced between 1965 and 1975), more than 20 percent of planned production was lost to work stoppages. For American managers, the British trade-union system was especially baffling. Much of the authority on the factory floor rested with shop stewards, and the myriad different unions each had private political biases, demands and needs. No sooner was a dispute in one of the three main Chrysler plants settled than another broke out. Wildcats became a way of life and, in 1973, the worst year for industrial relations, 90,000 vehicles (or 22 percent of potential production) were lost. Between 1973 and 1975, short stoppages, lasting under four hours, averaged one a day. As a multinational corporation, Chrysler appeared to be a potentially bountiful victim of industrial disruption; it failed to dispel the image by making repeated and empty threats to withdraw from the United Kingdom or suspend investments. "Time and again we'd go to the brink and blink," recalled John Day, a former head of Chrysler Europe. "That was the unforgivable sin."

Although government regulations were never the specter they became in the United States, government policies during the years in which Chrysler attempted to salvage its British operation were scarcely conducive to a stable auto industry. A succession of Labour and Conservative governments were inevitably at odds about the virtues of hire-purchase controls, purchase taxes (later value-added taxes), special car taxes, a duty on gasoline—all of which had abrupt effects on car sales. Policies aimed at minimizing the lurches of the British economy and the stanching of wounds in economically depressed areas also hampered Chrysler.

Rootes's plant in Linwood—which was easily the greatest drain on the British operation—came to epitomize much of the poor planning, regional jingoism and sheer bloody-mindedness that wracked other parts of the country—but Chrysler, because of its agreement with the British government, was effectively prevented from closing the plant.

The troubles in the United Kingdom during 1974–75 were harbingers of events to come in the United States. Sorely hampered by under-investment, Chrysler U.K. in 1973 had a mere $2,300 in fixed assets per employee while the Spanish subsidiary had $5,700 and the French $4,550 per employee. Over 14 percent of the machine tools used to produce the Arrow's power train in 1975 were between twenty-four and thirty-three years old, while the bulk were between fourteen and twenty-three years old. A British government report estimated that while an efficient plant should produce between 250,000 and 300,000 cars a year, Chrysler's two plants had a total capacity of 365,000 between them. Chrysler U.K. had a small share of a declining market where it was up against stiff Japanese and European competition. Little wonder that the overall slump of the mid-Seventies had a devastating effect on profitability. By June 1975, Chrysler's share had fallen to a pitiful 4.7 percent of a market that had itself shrunk 25 percent the year before. In 1974, Chrysler U.K. lost more than $35 million and another $71 million in 1975. It had become swamped in debt and was begging Detroit for loans. By the end of 1975, Highland Park had contributed $80 million to its cranky subsidiary, in part because the British banks refused to supply more funds unless they were guaranteed from Detroit.[15]

The approaches to the British government for assistance were played gently at first but rose quickly to a crescendo. In March 1975, the company asked Finance for Industry (an agency formed to provide loans for commercial projects) to help restructure the choking debt load. Three months later, Chrysler approached the British Department of Industry for money. By the end of October, against a dismal backdrop in the United States, Chrysler decided to rap on the door of Number 10 Downing Street. At his first board meeting as Chrysler chairman, John Riccardo won permission to confront the British. No sooner had the Chrysler directors adjourned in New York than Riccardo and Gene Cafiero boarded a corporate jet and flew to London.

The approach was no longer delicate or diplomatic, and provided Fleet Street with a choice opportunity to unleash screeching headlines. The Chrysler men, labeled "Gunslingers from Detroit," were accused of coming armed with "muggers' cudgels" while the tabloid *Daily Mirror* pointedly asked: "Does Mr. Riccardo think the Chrysler Company is the world's most deserving charity?" Prime Minister Harold Wilson complained that John Riccardo was holding a pistol to the head of the British government. He was. In the other hand, though, Riccardo held an outright offer to give Chrysler U.K.—lock, stock and liabilities all thrown in—to the British government, *plus* some $70 million to cover that year's expected losses. "The ultimatum was," said corporate counsel Paul Heinen, Charlie's younger brother, "either you take it or we liquidate." In retrospect, Chrysler would have been far better off liquidating.

The Wilson government was facing a litany of horrors similar to those that later confronted the Carter administration. With British unemployment running at its highest levels since the Thirties, there was the immediate prospect of another 55,000 people joining the unemployment lines, with increasing social security payments and added tax losses. The Linwood plant provided another wrinkle. The ruling Labour Party, its hold on the region already threatened by the grassroots Scottish Nationalist Party, was reluctant to show any further steeliness. The closure of Chrysler U.K. also threatened Britain's balance of payments since, in 1974, 30 percent of the company's output had been shipped to Iran as knockdown kits.

"By no stretch of the imagination," a British government report later concluded, "can the events leading up to the agreement with Chrysler be said to form a glorious chapter in the history of the government's industrial relations."[16] Under the terms of the agreement, the British government agreed to provide $325 million between 1976 and 1979 for possible losses, capital expenditures and loan guarantees. For its part, Chrysler kicked in $126 million to cover further losses, waiver of loans and interest, and launch costs on new cars. The agreement also called for 8,200 layoffs, most of which were to take place at Stoke and Ryton, not at the farflung Linwood plant. Meanwhile, in language uncannily similar to the 1979 Chrysler Loan Guarantee Act, the British government claimed the right to appoint two directors and receive quarterly statements. Chrysler was forbidden from making substantial alterations to the business, from making loans to outside companies and from disposing of subsidiaries without consultation with the government. The dividends paid to Detroit were not to exceed the repayments of government loans, and there was to be employee participation in planning agreements.

Compared to Britain, France was a smashing success. Even with Chrysler U.K. slowing them up, the French and Spanish subsidiaries performed respectably. The French company was paying dividends, while the Spanish company had repaid $40 million in loans. The success of the French company, where there had been no work stoppage for thirty years, assured it the dominant position of Chrysler Europe. Between 1967 and 1975, the French company was profitable for every year, apart from 1974 and '75, when the auto industry worldwide was in the doldrums. In a country where the government steadfastly supported domestic producers, Chrysler's achievement was not to be underestimated. Benefiting from the high degree of integration at the Poissy plant, Chrysler France was being supplied by some of the British plants.

Once the Spanish company started shipping cars to France in 1972, Chrysler Europe began to take on the trappings of a coherent organization. There were still expensive glitches. Even in 1976 and 1977, there was still individual product planning in the three companies. Part of the agreement with the U.K. government, for example, required Chrysler to ship cars from Paris to its Ryton plant for final assembly. The cars, by the terms of the agreement, were priced at and even below cost to help the British company. The French company, meanwhile, had to rent an outside facility to box the cars and could have shipped a fully assembled car to Britain for the same cost as it shipped the kits. In addition, though the lines at Poissy ran at the rapid pace of 127 cars an hour during parts of 1976 and 1977, the French company was too small by itself to battle the European giants.

However, it was the amount of money needed to fill the cupboards of the French and Spanish companies with new products which, more than anything else, made disposition of Chrysler's European assets attractive. Since Chrysler had first wandered overseas, the changes that had made foreign business riskier were causing anxiety at Highland Park. After the 1971 decision by the Nixon administration to float the dollar, Chrysler had been prey to enormous currency shifts. The company was also being battered by nationalistic cries abroad and a desire, especially in South America, for local ownership and control. Although the potential costs of conducting business abroad were a heavy burden, the amount of time consumed by the troublesome companies was an even greater burden. Said William McGagh, "The parent was hurt more by the attention required of high-level management overseas than by investments." It was not unusual for senior managers to spend two weeks out of every three months away from Detroit.

Even before Lynn Townsend departed, there were hints of what, over the ensuing five years, turned into one of the largest corporate auctions in history. The rumors of change began farthest from home—in 1974 in Australia, where Chrysler had slipped from its traditional third place and started to make appeals to the Australian government and Japanese manufacturers for help. By 1980, Mitsubishi, Chrysler's erstwhile junior partner in the East, owned the Australian company, which made sense since, by then, nearly 80 percent of the cars sold through joint Chrysler/Mitsubishi dealerships were Japanese.

Also in 1974, under strict orders from the Peruvian government, Chrysler agreed to sell 51 percent of its interests there to local investors by 1989. A year later, the Argentinian government followed suit and Chrysler drew up a plan to sell 60 percent of its equity in Fevre Argentina to the government for $30 million. As long as Townsend remained on top in Highland Park, talk of selling the bulk of the overseas operation was stifled, but after he left, the empire soon began to crumble.

First to go was the Airtemp Division in the United States, sold to Fedders at a $55 million loss and leaving a string of messy litigation that dragged into the next decade. Toward the end of 1976, Chrysler arrived at an agreement with Illings Ltd., a subsidiary of South Africa's Anglo-American Group, on a joint venture. Chrysler's South African company, which had lost $6 million in 1975 and had a capacity for a meager 30,500 cars and trucks annually, was merged with Illings (importers of Mazda cars and Mack trucks) and renamed Sigma Ltd. Before the end of the Seventies, Chrysler had agreed to sell off its remaining 25-percent share of equity.

The turn of the decade found Chrysler stripped of all its Latin American subsidiaries as well. Volkswagen walked off with Brazil; Venezuela and Colombia went to GM. At home, the real estate company brought $50 million from a Kansas firm, ABKO. Pieces of property around the country were auctioned off bit by bit, but nothing compared with the one great disposition that would sound the final retreat from world competition—the sale of Chrysler Europe.

The first hint came in October of 1976—days after Lynn Townsend stepped down. The original germ of a deal was floated to Chrysler by an official of the French government interested in the availability of Chrysler France. The first prospective buyer was Régie Nationale des Usines Renault, then the leading French carmaker and wholly owned by the French government—but this same government source suggested that it would be preferable to have private, rather than public, capital involved. Peugeot, newly under the leadership of Jean-Paul Payrare and anxious to fend off what was perceived to be a coming onslaught by General Motors and the Japanese, was the logical candidate. Dining with Peugeot officials in Paris, John Riccardo was guided in the direction of President Valerie Giscard d'Éstaing and came away with an understanding that the French government would not object.

Peugeot had its own objections, though—first to Chrysler's offered price, which was roughly double the book value of the entire European operation at more than $1 billion, and second to the all-or-nothing package that included, to Peugeot's chagrin, Chrysler U.K. "We made it clear that it was no deal unless it was everything," said Riccardo.

The deal sat on ice for over a year, going through what Riccardo described as a "sifting-out period." What it was in reality was a sifting-*in* period wherein Peugeot came to realize that the British cash sump was simply going to have to come along. Peugeot's—and France's—intense desire to expand quickly to stay in the diminishing pack of worldwide competitors eventually wore down opposition to the inclusion of the U.K. operation.

In January of 1978, Cafiero and the head of Chrysler's Paris office, Joe Ris, reported back to Highland Park that Peugeot wanted to reopen talks, but little happened until July, when Riccardo and Cafiero met in New York with Peugeot's François Gautier and Roland Peugeot. Before the session was over, the four men had hashed out five essential points, including the acquisition of Chrysler U.K., the exchange of Peugeot stock and the general notion that the two companies should continue to do business with one another in the future. Originally, Riccardo was to have become a member of Peugeot's board of directors, but the U. S. Federal Trade Commission, which was none too pleased with the whole idea of Chrysler's 15-percent ownership of Peugeot, ruled that he could not.

After the New York meeting, it took all of two weeks of intensive negotiations in Paris, New York and Detroit to pull the package together. When it was finally announced during the second week of August, it was, surprisingly, a complete surprise. Corporate counsel Paul Heinen was convinced that the deal would be exposed twice in the final days—first when he looked out the window of Chrysler's corporate jet as it taxied down the runway at Pontiac's PDQ airstrip on the way to Paris and saw the electronic billboard lit up with "GOOD LUCK CHRYSLER!" and again in France when it was discovered that their highly secret discussions were taking place next door to ABC's Paris bureau.

"A thunderclap in the world of the automobile," Paris's *Le Monde* called the announcement. Chrysler got $230 million in cash to pump into its product program at home and 15 percent of Peugeot's stock, then worth some $200 million. Peugeot took on a bundle of organizational problems and $400 million in Chrysler debt, but became, in the process of adding Chrysler's 726,500 annual car sales to its own 800,000 and Citröen's 685,000, the number-one automobile company in Europe, with some 2.2 million units of sale a year, worth some $12 billion.

After a final all-night session in Paris, the Chrysler and Peugeot negotiating teams flew on Payrare's corporate jet to London's Heathrow Airport in order to sign the deal on British soil, where tax advantages for Peugeot would be enormous. Shortly after 9 A.M., as air travelers scurried obliviously around them and flight information echoed through the crowded terminal, Peugeot's ebullient attorney Peter Paine pulled a table out into the middle of the passageway and orchestrated the signing of the biggest deal in modern automotive history. With the stroke of his pen, Jean-Paul Payrare became chief executive officer of the third-largest automobile company in the world in terms of units of sale. With the stroke of *his* pen, John J. Riccardo lopped off 25 percent of Chrysler's capacity and ended Lynn Townsend's dream that Chrysler would one day become an independent, multinational, full-line producer of automobiles.

What was left was Canada, essentially an extension of U.S. operations, and Mexico, an astonishingly successful operation that was known as the "General Motors of Mexico." (Indeed, Chrysler Mexico was so attractive that General Motors itself was constantly pestering Chrysler throughout 1980 to sell it to them. Chrysler refused on the defensible grounds that its profits were sorely needed against enormous U.S. losses and its components were thoroughly integrated into U.S. production.) Riccardo postured that the 15-percent ownership of Peugeot qualified Chrysler as an international company, as did the 15 percent Chrysler still held in Japan's Mitsubishi. Still, it was clear to most that Chrysler was not the same company it had been.

At least the debilitating drain on cash and time seemed at an end. Riccardo could now concentrate on Chrysler's domestic operations. He could also begin in earnest to go after what would become Chrysler's most important acquisition—Lee Iacocca.

CHAPTER NINE

The Egg Man

Shortly before three o'clock on Thursday afternoon, July 13, 1978, a tall, nattily attired man with a pronounced Neapolitan nose supporting stylish wire-rimmed glasses emerged from the northeast corner suite on the twelfth floor of Ford Motor Company's world headquarters and walked resolutely across the plushly carpeted corridor. The focal point of his sharp features was an inscrutable, thin smile—the faint, fixed grin of a gargoyle—well-worn in the service of masking moods.

At the request of Henry Ford II, the occupant of the larger suite on the southeast corner, an appointment for that hour had been confirmed the previous day. As he entered the outer room, Lee Iacocca looked briefly through a secretary's door out over Michigan Avenue to Ford Motor Company's massive Dearborn, Michigan, complex of offices and plants. Everywhere above the thick deciduous greenery, familiar blue ovals inscribed with the single word "Ford" crowned buildings and entrance signs—a constant reminder to more than half a million employees, from the president on down, that it was "Mr. Ford" whose name was still on those buildings and "Mr. Ford" who still sat in that twelfth-floor corner suite.

Iacocca, Ford's ninth president, had reason to suspect he was about to be fired. Even before the three o'clock appointment had been made, William Clay Ford, a vice-president of the company, had warned him privately that he feared his brother was about to bring down the ax. Then, Iacocca had been specifically disinvited to the normal penthouse gathering of the company's board of directors—a gathering less formal than the regular monthly board meeting to follow Thursday morning. As president, he had every reason to expect an invitation to the penthouse. "That," he recalled, "raised my antennae a bit."

Thursday morning, prior to the full board meeting, he received a phone call from Keith Crain, publisher and editorial director of *Automotive News*, the industry's trade magazine. "Say it isn't so," Crain had said straight away. Iacocca didn't have to ask "what" was so, nor could he say any longer that it wasn't. Crain had been getting signals that this was to be the week. Although Iacocca would not deny the imminence of his departure, Crain hung up with the impression that this intense man, so used to controlling his own destiny, thought he still might somehow control it again.

Waiting in the middle of the three-room suite at the appointed hour were the Ford brothers. Henry, the chairman, waited behind his uncharacteristically modern desk, where he kept an ominous computer terminal from which he could call up data on virtually anything and anyone in his $43 billion industrial empire. Iacocca remembered him as looking "nervous." Across the room, Bill Ford, younger than Henry by seven and a half years and thinner since he had given up drinking, fidgeted openly.

What it was exactly that Henry Ford said to Lee Iacocca that afternoon has slipped into the realm of personal recollection. It may well have been taped, for Henry was known to keep a Nixonesque record of office transactions. The New York *Times* and other media reported that Ford explained his decision with a petulant "Let's just say I don't like you." Within hours of the meeting, Iacocca told two national magazine correspondents that the boss had lamely—if tunelessly—offered that it was "just one of those things." It is doubtful whether anything as blunt as "you're fired" ever passed Henry's lips. In the end, recalled Iacocca more than two years later, whatever the wording, "It was his mean, vindictive way of saying, 'You've become too powerful.'"

The meeting was civil, but understandably tense. No voices were raised, though Bill Ford made sure he was present in case this confrontation between two of the most volatile and strong-willed executives in American business got out of hand. Henry's reasons for ending the longest tenure of any Ford president were imprecise, resting only vaguely on the notion of unsound planning in recent times. Iacocca—who, Bill Ford thought, was holding onto a belief that he could prevail—marshaled before him all the details of his stewardship, countering Henry's vagueness with precise evidence of his success—and loyalty—over the years. He reminded Ford of his 1975 rejection of

Iacocca's $3 billion product program that would have kept Ford abreast of GM's front-wheel-drive and down-sizing programs. He pricked him with the fact that it was under his operational leadership that Ford had just emerged from its second consecutive year of profits topping $1.5 billion each. "The way things are going lately," predicted Iacocca, "you'll never see a billion-five again."[1]

"Lee was a complete gentleman," recalled Bill Ford. He had built a case for himself on the facts, coolly and logically. Bill Ford, though visibly upset, said nothing to interfere, realizing that nothing he or Iacocca could do would change the outcome of the meeting. "There was," he remembered, "no room for logic."

The three—two Ford brothers and the man who had run their company's operations for the better part of a decade—ended their meeting after forty-five minutes. Bill, the youngest of Henry Ford I's three grandsons and the least inclined toward the car business, tried to console Iacocca, whom he admired greatly, as they left Henry's suite. Bill Ford had been looking forward to working with him in the Office of the Chief Executive, to which he had just been appointed. If it was any consolation, he offered, "Nobody has ever laid out my brother like that. Nobody's ever given him the dressing down you did." The outcome of those forty-five minutes could not be denied, though. Iacocca turned to the younger Ford. "But Bill," he observed quietly, "I've just been fired."

The abrupt dismissal of Lee Iacocca as president of Ford shocked the industry, captured the attention of the international business community and made headlines all over the globe. Its precipitousness suggested dark deeds, corporate subterfuge and office infighting on an epic scale—a thrilling contradiction of the dull image of professionally managed technocracies that had come to dominate postwar America. It also presented John Riccardo with a thrilling and serendipitous opportunity as he contemplated the awesome problems his Chrysler Corporation faced. Suddenly, one of the great modern masters of the automotive world was out of work.

The dismantling of Iacocca's power at Ford began long before Henry's final pronouncement in July 1978. In April of 1977, using the management consulting firm of McKinsey & Company as executioner, Ford announced the creation of the Office of the Chief Executive (OCE) and elevated a quiet, fifty-seven-year-old Harvard Business School graduate named Philip Caldwell to the rank of vice-chairman. Henry Ford explained that the new arrangement provided "a vehicle for some Ford to sit in that office when I retire at sixty-five." Thus it was widely accepted that the OCE would be used as a transitional conduit through which young Edsel Ford, Henry's only son, who was just twenty-eight at the time, could be groomed for leadership. While

Edsel was learning the business, his Uncle Bill, whose primary interest in life was his ownership of the Detroit Lions, could serve as titular Ford.

All that was possible with Lee Iacocca as president. Ironically, according to his friends, Iacocca always had had a clear understanding that he would never "head" Ford Motor Company; that he would always be no more than a loyal lieutenant who would "manage" the company. It was apparent, though, that the OCE was also created to insure that Iacocca would never succeed Henry Ford as chief executive. Following his angina attack in 1976, Ford had become more aware of his own mortality and had developed an abiding concern over the matter of succession. He had determined at some point that Lee Iacocca was not the man to follow him.

Detroit was rife with rumors about precisely what it was that had turned Henry against Lee, a man he had personally brought to the top. Indeed, the speculation stirred the nation. Walter Cronkite mused on his evening broadcast from New York, "It sounds like something from one of those enormous novels about the automobile industry."

Some said it was a matter of taste. Ford, after all, was a patrician, raised in Grosse Pointe splendor on an isolated estate with its own yacht haven and acres of manicured lawn. Educated at Hotchkiss in Connecticut and Yale (though he was denied a degree for turning in a paper written by someone else), Henry Ford was worldly, sophisticated and thoroughly at home in the best New York and London clubs. Iacocca, by contrast, was a product of middle-class America. He had fought his way to the top. Although he, too, could lay claim to a touch of Ivy League, his was a master's degree in Mechanical Engineering from Princeton, paid for by a scholarship. At the time of his firing, the local press carried quotes from an unidentified representative of the Ford family suggesting that Iacocca was "pushy" and "lacked grace."

Oddly, over the years the two men came to be ostensibly similar in manner. Both were hard-driving, tough-talking, cigar-smoking individualists with a penchant for disarming—sometimes brutal—candor. Iacocca, at the true peak of his Ford career after he launched the Mustang in 1964 at age thirty-nine, once said that he was particularly happy at Ford because of Henry Ford. "He's an easy guy to get along with," the young Ford Division general manager rhapsodized. "I've never had any trouble with him. Some guys have. He calls a spade a spade. He wants you to be blunt, and I happen to be blunt. We don't try to Alphonse and Gaston each other. We don't try to beat around the bush. We both like to cut through red tape. And I happen to think this is a great way to operate."[2]

Both typically used the vocabulary of longshoremen, and not always just with the boys—but somehow, for Henry Ford it came off as old-shoe Establishment, Hotchkiss dormitory crudeness laced with charm, while for Iacocca it was street talk.

During his tenure as Ford president, Iacocca grew into the vestments of power given him by Ford. He was, according to some former colleagues, quick to use the perquisites available—corporate jets, New York hotel suites, minions to do his personal bidding. Some say that Henry, who was thoroughly accustomed to doing the same and then some, resented Iacocca's ready assumption of what he saw as his personal rights. Moreover, it has been suggested, Ford always favored fellow patricians, but Iacocca was soiling the robes of power on crass, nouveau-riche cronies, some of whom Henry viewed with obvious distaste. It was, if true, an invidious distinction—but Henry Ford II may well have come to see an uncomfortable reflection of himself.

Others say it was simpler. Henry saw Lee's star rising at an alarming rate throughout the Seventies. He was accumulating a cadre of loyalists at Ford that was running deeper and deeper into the organization. He had courted 6,700 dealers and won their confidence. His earthiness notwithstanding, he had won the respect of the patricians of Wall Street. All too often, Ford executives and the top officials of major automotive supply companies, seeking top level advice or action at Ford, would come to the twelfth floor in Dearborn and turn left toward Lee Iacocca's office instead of right toward Henry Ford's. Even outside directors, curious about one aspect or another of company business, would go to president Iacocca rather than chairman Ford.

The chairman even resented what he perceived as Iacocca's own public relations loyalists at the company. Walter Murphy, executive director of Ford's worldwide public relations staff, was, in Henry Ford's view, Iacocca's spokesman. On the night following the fateful meeting in Ford's office, Murphy received a 3 A.M. phone call from Henry Ford himself, demanding to hear whether or not Murphy "liked" Lee Iacocca. When the astonished Murphy answered "yes," Ford fired him on the spot.

Once, in 1971, a Ford executive from Grosse Pointe, Henry's neck of the woods, came to Iacocca and gave him a confidential warning. That Sunday, following a rash of complimentary publicity, Iacocca had been the cover subject of the New York *Times* Sunday Magazine. "As a friend," he said, "I'm warning you. Henry doesn't like that." Iacocca protested that Ford cars were prominently featured and, besides, he wasn't seeking the publicity. "You're getting too high a profile," said the Grosse Pointer.

The advice was not heeded. Iacocca was and is a driven man, incapable, as he would admit, of going at half speed. "I wasn't trying to take on the Ford hierarchy," he said later. "I was always the good boy."

Henry obviously didn't think so. In 1975, Ford ordered an "internal audit" of Iacocca that expanded into a broad investigation of his conduct. It was widely rumored that Ford suspected Iacocca was conniving with an old personal friend, New York travel czar William Fugazy, who had what some competitors claimed was a stranglehold on the Ford Motor Company travel and dealer sales-incentive business. According to published reports at the time, Ford spent $1.5 million on the probe, questioning as many as five hundred executives and lower-level managers both at Ford and at agencies doing business with the company, searching for substance to rumors of questionable personal conduct. Fugazy complained that he was being harassed by Ford investigators, but asserted flatly that no irregularities had been uncovered. Iacocca declared simply, "I'm clean."

Public persons rarely escape their own indiscretions—as Henry Ford well knows after his arrest on drunk-driving charges in California in 1976 with Kathy DuRoss, the former model who was his companion at the time and eventually became his third wife. The incident was marked by his famous retort, "Never complain; never explain."[3] Iacocca, for all the rumors, was never caught in an indiscretion and has emerged—not only from Ford's internal audit but from countless informal probes by tenacious newsmen—with a clean slate. The most that has been substantiated is that he drinks scotch and wine moderately, spends most evenings in town at home with his family and plays a distinctly minor-league brand of penny-ante poker on Friday nights.

The internal audit sealed a distrust between Ford and Iacocca. The split became increasingly obvious. "Decisions were made abruptly," recalled one insider. "Tension was a part of every meeting with the two." Iacocca grinned publicly and held on, but by June of 1978, when Bill Ford was named to the Office of the Chief Executive, further diluting the president's once-penultimate power, Iacocca found himself unable to salute and abandon thirty years of hard work. He didn't want to be just another marketing specialist and he certainly didn't want to report to Phil Caldwell. While Henry was off on a trip, Iacocca met with some of Ford's outside directors—notably George Bennett, president of Boston's State Street Investment Corporation— with whom he had developed a good rapport. It is unclear who initiated the meetings, but it is clear that Iacocca was not prepared to go gently into the dusk of corporate bureaucracy.

There was indeed disgruntlement among many of the nine outside board members over Ford's new scheme and Iacocca's obvious demotion. When Henry returned, he faced some serious questioning, and he didn't like it. In fact, according to some sources who were rela-

tively close to the events that July, Henry blew up. He felt that Iacocca was now conniving behind his back, and if ever there were
doubts that Iacocca should go, they vanished. On Wednesday, July 12,
Ford met with the Organization Review and Nominating Committee
of the board, which was made up, with the exception of Ford himself,
entirely of outsiders. It was far from a rubber-stamp meeting, and
Ford was apparently able to get his way finally by resorting to an ultimatum: "It's him or me." There was, of course, little choice. By the
time the decision to fire Lee Iacocca would have come before the
board, it was a *fait accompli*.

Henry Ford was not without troubles of his own at the time. New
York lawyer Roy Cohn, whose infamous career had begun as the
Commie-baiting counsel to Senator Joseph McCarthy in the Fifties,
had filed suit in the spring of 1978 on behalf of Ford stockholders,
charging Ford with what Cohn termed "the pettiest forms of graft":
overseeing if not indulging in the taking of kickbacks from suppliers
and using company money for his private perks. Cohn claimed that
Henry Ford regularly used his New York apartment at the Hotel
Carlyle for personal stays but had the company pick up the tab. Cohn
charged that Ford had no compunction about landing the corporate
jet, at thousands of dollars' expense, for something as trivial as buying
a pack of cigarettes for a friend. More ominously, Cohn threw in that
Ford was involved in an international bribery scandal in which $1 mil-
lion was paid to an Indonesian general in 1975 in exchange for a $29
million telecommunications contract for Ford's aerospace subsidiary.

Some Ford defenders suspected that Cohn was getting his information from Cristina Ford, Henry's estranged second wife, then in the
midst of protracted divorce procedures. Others suspected it was an
embittered Iacocca, whose friend Fugazy also happened to be a friend
of Cohn's. Cristina claimed she had no dealings with Cohn and would
never cooperate with him. Iacocca and Cohn, though both knew Fugazy, had themselves never met. Cohn and Fugazy, moreover, were
having a falling out at the time.

Cohn's suit, as well as related inquiries by the Justice Department
into the Indonesian bribery charge, never got off the ground. Ford
and Cohn settled out of court, with the company paying legal fees in
exchange for an official statement from Cohn that neither Henry Ford
nor any other company executive was guilty of wrongdoing. It was, in
effect, a draw.

There was also the growing Pinto scandal. The explosion-prone subcompact had been linked with some two dozen deaths and had drawn
more than sixty multi-million-dollar civil lawsuits as well as one celebrated criminal trial later held in Winamac, Indiana. Although the
National Highway Traffic Safety Administration had forced the recall

of 1.4 million Pintos and identically designed Mercury Bobcats, it was never resolved satisfactorily whether Henry Ford or Lee Iacocca—or any other Ford executive for that matter—was derelict in failing to correct the problem. Both men publicly expressed misgivings about the car and concern about evidence that it burst into flames if struck from the rear. Iacocca claimed he recommended that Ford install a longer filler pipe for the fuel tank to prevent leakage, after he learned that the existing filler pipe was ripping out on impact, allowing gasoline to spill over the car. Ford's lawyers, he said, quickly nixed that idea, warning that repair would be tantamount to an admission of guilt. "That's the trouble with lawyers," said Iacocca. "A businessman's instinct is to cut the losses, solve the image problem immediately. Theirs is to guard some goddamn legal principle." Ford's attorneys used questionable courtroom tactics in some of the early civil suits. "When I heard about that," recalled Iacocca, "I said, 'We're in the soup.'"

Although both men apparently agreed on the Pinto, the course the company took was in another direction. Moreover, that was one of the few things Henry Ford and Lee Iacocca could agree upon during those final few years. More than likely, the fight over the small car to replace the Pinto in 1978 or 1979 rubbed a healthy dose of salt into the wounds.

Iacocca depended heavily over the years on a young product-planning engineer named Hal Sperlich, recognizing in him a knack for picking the right concept for the market. Sperlich was especially strong on small cars. It was he who, more than any other individual in a massive worldwide corporate effort, was responsible for the design of the 26-mpg subcompact Fiesta, Ford's prototype "World Car," designed internationally, sourced internationally and finally assembled in Spain.

High on the success of the Fiesta, Sperlich and Iacocca dreamed up a scheme to Americanize the car and build it in the United States as early as 1978. "We called it a 'blown Fiesta,'" Iacocca later recalled. Taking the basic wheelbase and frame dimensions of the little European car, Sperlich "blew out" the sides to give it the inside room Americans demanded. "It was a sporty little sonofabitch," said Iacocca wistfully.

Iacocca saw the Japanese onslaught about to begin. He saw even little Chrysler with a front-wheel-drive subcompact, the Omni/ Horizon, in the works, utilizing Simca technology. Insiders knew GM was well on its way to putting the front-wheel-drive X-car on the market sometime before the end of the decade.

With Sperlich's design, he made a pitch to Henry Ford for a front-wheel-drive subcompact program scheduled for the 1979 model year, but Ford, already squeamish about the better-than-$1-billion investment thrown into the Fiesta, said no to a project that was, at its cheapest, a quarter-billion-dollar enterprise. Specifically, Ford, according to Iacocca, was unwilling to gamble such money on the new facilities needed to build the necessary four-cylinder transverse engines and transmissions.

Iacocca didn't give up. On his own, he went to Japan and met personally with Mr. Soichiro Honda. The two men worked out a deal. "I'll never forget it," said Iacocca. "Three hundred thousand power packs—transmission with the engines hooked up, $711 apiece, delivered in San Francisco. I said, 'I'll take it!'" He returned to Dearborn and laid the package in front of Ford. According to Iacocca, the chairman's reply was frosty and final: "No Japanese product is going under a hood with my name on it."

So ended the "blown Fiesta" project and, with it, apparently, Hal Sperlich's career at Ford. Sperlich, like Iacocca, was a maverick, brilliant but equally prone to argument and overstepping the bounds of corporate protocol. Iacocca liked and could make use of such a free spirit, but Sperlich, with his growing monomania for small cars, got himself squarely on the wrong side of Henry Ford. "In 1974 and '75," Sperlich later reflected, "Henry got really worried about the company —and I was the guy who was always talking about spending money. Then he got sick [angina] and realized he might not live forever. I guess he decided to purge the company of anybody who wasn't going to be quiet and obedient . . . I was pushy."

In an eerie precursor to Iacocca's own dismissal, Ford called Iacocca in one autumn afternoon in 1976 and told him he wanted Hal Sperlich out of the company. Iacocca asked why. Ford said he wasn't entitled to ask that; it was personal. "Must it be today?" asked Iacocca, pleading that it was already three-thirty and he was due to fly to New York at five. "Then you have an hour and a half to fire him," Ford shot back, according to Iacocca, "or you're fired."

The job of informing Sperlich that his ostensibly brilliant twenty-year career at Ford was over fell to William O. Bourke, who, in addition to being Sperlich's boss, was the "heavy" put in place to keep Iacocca in line. Iacocca felt no resentment toward Bill Bourke, knowing that such tactics were vintage Ford. After all, Iacocca had served for two years as the "heavy" to keep Semon "Bunky" Knudsen honest during his short tenure as Ford president after Ford stole him from out of the General Motors hierarchy. "Bourke was a good auto man," Iacocca would later say. "He worked his ass off. I respected him."

In the spring of 1980, Bourke himself was asked to take "early retirement" at age fifty-seven, when Henry Ford II gave up the chairmanship to Philip Caldwell and Ford International chief Donald Pe-

tersen got the presidency instead of Bourke. It was Bourke, the
dismissal implied, who was designated to take the blame for Ford
Motor Company's miserable market performance in the 1979–80 recession—a performance that was in no small measure due to Ford's lack
of small cars.

But in November of 1976, Bourke did his job: he fired Sperlich as
ordered. Just as he did some twenty months later with Iacocca
directly, Henry Ford left the impression that there had been something, some one terrible act, that had sealed Sperlich's fate. Perhaps
there was. Or perhaps some pattern of insubordination or independence (there is a fine but important distinction between the two in
Detroit) convinced Ford that Sperlich was not the "team player"
needed in Dearborn. Sperlich asked for an audience with Ford and
continually pressed for a reason. All Ford would say, like someone
pleading the Fifth Amendment at a congressional hearing, Sperlich
recalled, was that it would be "best for you and best for the company"
if he just left.

Hal Sperlich did not take long to land on his feet. Gene Cafiero,
president of Chrysler Corporation, invited him to lunch in a private
dining room on the second floor of the Detroit Athletic Club. Several
such meetings later, Sperlich signed on. In March of 1977, he was
named Vice-President of Product Planning and Design in Highland
Park, becoming in a sense, an automotive John the Baptist for the
coming of Lee Iacocca.

In Detroit, they speak in reverent tones about the "real" automobile
people: the old tycoons with gasoline running in their veins, engineers
with a feel for cars and people and how to bring them together. In the
modern era, when sophisticated management techniques surpassed
those attributes as the prerequisites for reaching the top, Lee Iacocca
was one of the very few acknowledged to have a touch of octane still
in his blood. Since high school he had wanted to be in the car business
—and since high school, he had worked toward his goal.

Nicola (Nick) and Antoinette Iacocca brought Lido Anthony into
the world October 15, 1924, and raised him in a brick row house in
Allentown, Pennsylvania. Nick Iacocca was devoted to his son. He had
come to America from Benevento, between Rome and Naples, in 1902,
established himself in the country and gone back in 1921 only to
marry Antoinette Perotto. They honeymooned in Lido Beach, outside
Venice, before coming to America. A daughter, Delma, was born first,
followed two years later by the son whom they named for their honey-
moon spot.

Lee grew up surrounded sporadically by wealth. Twice in his
eighty-four years, Nick Iacocca made and lost a modest fortune. He

started one of the country's first car rental agencies, "U-Drive-It," in the mid-Twenties and made enough money to invest in the local real estate market. He was wiped out by the Depression, then made and lost another bundle when he used cash generated from a pair of fast-food restaurants and an Allentown movie house to get back into real estate.

Nick was a tough disciplinarian who hammered home to his son the classic notion that whatever it was he chose to be, he should be the best. Excellence was a matter of course. In third grade, Lee's sense of discipline lapsed: He walked on stage in a class play in the lead role of king, chewing on a stick of gum handed him by a girl offstage. As a result, he got a report card grade of 50 that session and his father, unable to comprehend such failure, punished him severely and never forgot the incident. Nick never, ever, hit his son, but he made him suffer considerable anguish for occasional shortcomings.

Fortunately, Lee had the capacity to meet his father's standards. He was an achiever. His grades, the gum-chewing incident notwithstanding, were always good. He was popular, quick-tongued, brash and smart. In tenth grade, he contracted rheumatic fever and had to give up sports. Doctors told his family that his heart was not damaged, but that he should be careful and avoid an insurance physical for ten years. The disease forced him to rechannel his energies into schoolwork and debate. It also gave him a 4-F classification during World War II and a skittishness—if not outright hypochondriacal concern—about his personal health. Said a friend, "Lee gets a cold and he's going to die."

Graduating twelfth out of a high school class of more than a thousand, Iacocca went to nearby Lehigh, partially on a state scholarship won on the basis of his high grades and partially on his father's proud fortunes. He graduated, class of 1945, with a grade-point average of 3.53—good enough to win him the addendum on his degree "with high honors," of which he remained fiercely proud.

With his degree in engineering, Iacocca heard about and applied for a fifty-man training program at Ford Motor Company. His father had always rented Fords and Lee had driven a used one back and forth between Lehigh and home. No sooner was he accepted in the program than he heard about the offer of Wallace fellowships at Princeton University. Told by the Ford recruiter that the training program would still be there when he got back, Iacocca went off to Princeton to get his master's degree in Mechanical Engineering. But when he had taken his degree, he returned to find in charge of Ford's recruiting effort a new man who had never heard of the promise to save him a spot. Undaunted, he talked his way into a fifty-first opening and packed off to Dearborn.

At that time, which coincided with young Henry Ford's courageous salvaging of his grandfather's company from the hands of henchman Harry Bennett and the brink of bankruptcy, Ford had an infamous introductory program for incoming engineers and management known as "The Rouge Loop Course." The company's main plant on the banks of the River Rouge had every element of the automotive manufacturing business on location—from iron-ore boats unloading at the foundry through final car assembly. The "Loop Course" put young university graduates through each phase and reputedly left them with a broad appreciation of the total business of making and selling cars.

Iacocca took the course, which was later phased out, and prepared himself for the life of an automotive engineer, but his ambition and need for human contact got the best of him in the midst of a boring, post-"Loop" stint working on a clutch spring at engineering headquarters. Frustrated, he asked to get out of engineering and into sales. His unorthodoxy was unappreciated, and he left Dearborn to go back to Pennsylvania.

He finally worked his way into Ford sales through a man who would become what one old Iacocca friend would describe as "Lee's father in the Ford Motor Company." Charles R. Beacham was a tough bull of a man from Georgia who never lost his native drawl. Beacham hired Iacocca as a truck salesman for the Chester, Pennsylvania, assembly plant sales office because he figured the young engineer could talk the technical language potential truck buyers needed to hear.

Iacocca very quickly demonstrated the qualities of imagination and initiative. He was soon selling cars as well as trucks, and with near-evangelical fervor. Once, he personally drove a Pennsylvania dealer's entire stock of used cars around the countryside, using owner registration lists to determine who had the oldest cars and were thus most likely to consider replacing them. Within three weeks, Iacocca had helped clear the lot.

He began holding evening training courses for area dealers to teach them new selling tricks. He'd secretly tape a salesman's pitch and play it back before the class to demonstrate strengths and weaknesses. At a district sales meeting, Charlie Beacham gave a little sermon about the differences between the ordinary salespeople and those who did that little bit above and beyond the job expected of them. There was one man, said Beacham, who belonged in the latter group: Lee Iacocca.

Iacocca's fertile mind was a henhouse of sales gimmicks. One captured attention at national headquarters. To push slow sales at the launch of the 1956 model year, Iacocca boosted a "$56 a month for a '56 Ford" campaign in Pennsylvania. Sales indeed climbed upward; Robert McNamara heard about the slogan in Dearborn and ordered it nationwide. Lee Iacocca's name was in circulation.

Some of Iacocca's eggs didn't hatch. In Philadelphia once, he decided to dramatize Ford's new padded dashboards, part of McNamara's celebrated safety campaign in the mid-Fifties, by dropping eggs from a ladder onto dismantled dashes. They were supposed to bounce gently and remain intact. Four eggs, two of them missing the padding altogether, broke before a fifth held together as advertised. It's not certain whether word of that fiasco reached Dearborn or not.

When he first hired on in Chester, Iacocca began dating a red-headed Ford receptionist named Mary McCleary, whom he would frequently bring home to Allentown on weekends. Mary could seldom talk Lee into staying in Chester. Only after Iacocca was promoted to the eastern district sales office in Washington did he decide it was time to marry Mary McCleary. Barely settled into their new house, the Iacoccas got word from Charlie Beacham, the man responsible for Iacocca's fast early rise, that they would be going to the home office in Dearborn.

Before he left the East, however, Iacocca learned some elements of human behavior that would shape his managerial style. Under Beacham, he'd traveled the eastern seaboard (Beacham had advised him to simply go by "Lee" when meeting "good ole boy" dealers in the South, rather than fool with "Iacocca"). Before long, he'd recognized that the local sales force would lapse into easy habits unless prodded. They'd make their rounds weekly, concentrating on successful dealers, dining leisurely and talking about good times, rather than making the uncomfortable calls on the troubled franchises. Iacocca made his salesmen draw up weekly lists of whom they would see, forcing them to tackle the tough problems. At the beginning of the next week, he would check to see how they'd performed and whether they'd brought about any improvement at the weaker outlets. In Dearborn, and later at Chrysler, the concept of periodic review would become a way of life.

Charlie Beacham was Assistant General Manager of the Ford Division when he called Iacocca to the home office in November of 1956. Another newcomer to Dearborn arrived that same snowy day, a fellow named Gar (for Elgar) Laux (pronounced "Low"). Laux had been brought in to set up a new "field sales operation" for the Ford Division. "I saw another young guy walking around the lobby of the Dearborn Inn," recalls Laux, "so I walked up and asked him if he was with Ford." Laux had heard about Iacocca. Most people in the field had because of the "56 for a '56" campaign. Laux recalled him as a "sharp young guy, a guy who'd say it like it was, very direct." Laux got to know that style well: He worked directly under Iacocca for twelve years at Ford and was one of the old Ford men brought out of retirement when Iacocca began the restructuring of Chrysler twenty-two years later.

Laux remembered Charlie Beacham, too. He was one of the most demanding men in the business and toughest on those in whom he saw the most promise. "One day Beacham called me in," recounted Laux. "He chewed me up so badly that I finally got up and said, 'Mr. Beacham, I don't have to take that from anybody, and I'm leaving,' and I turned around and headed for the door. Just as I got to the door, he said, 'Laux, come here. Sit down.' He said, 'If I didn't think you had it in you, I wouldn't give you the goddamn time of day. Now get the hell out of here.'

"That's in effect how Lee operates. He would bust your ass if he thought you could do it or could do it better. He won't fool around with you if he doesn't feel you've got it. If he's really through with you, he'll almost ignore you. . . . Some people enjoy firing people. Lee doesn't like that at all. He'd rather just get the guy out of his way, find something else for him to do. If you go to him and say: 'I don't think so-and-so is doing the job and we ought to get rid of him,' Lee will always ask, 'Have you talked to him? Have you sat down and gone over his weaknesses with him? Have you given him a shot at it? . . . Is there somewhere else you can use him?'"

Iacocca learned how to deal with people from Charlie Beacham. He would eventually broaden his repertoire of ways of handling those who worked for him, but he always held to the basic maxim that a good manager milked a minimum of 100 percent from his charges. "On that," said Laux, "he is ruthless."

Charlie Beacham didn't have to drive Lee Iacocca very hard. Iacocca drove himself and others with him. He first handled trucks for the Ford Division and, while he did, everybody in the division seemed to be talking about trucks. Another Detroiter who met Iacocca on his first day in town was *Life* magazine's Detroit Advertising Sales Manager Burns Cody, who watched his career as a friend for better than two decades. "His first truck assignment brought Ford truck leadership," said Cody. "In fact, Lee did as much for the American truck business as anybody."

When Iacocca moved from trucks to cars, he took the excitement with him. Beacham moved on to corporate sales, but Iacocca continued to race up the Ford Division ladder. He was Assistant General Sales Manager by the autumn day in 1960 when Henry Ford II called him personally and asked him to come over to headquarters right away. Iacocca arrived and met the chairman among a small cluster of top Ford executives that included Arjay Miller and Robert McNamara. When he left the meeting, he was general manager of the Ford Division, the second-largest operating entity in the business, behind

GM's Chevrolet, selling 80 percent of the cars made by Ford Motor Company in the United States, as well as all its trucks, with a work force of 13,454 people. He was just thirty-six years old, though, according to a career plan he had once drawn up, a year late in reaching the position.

The new Ford general manager used his Beacham-taught toughness to counter questions about his age. His reputation as a no-nonsense manager spread quickly. He gathered a group of loyalists around him and drew from them, as Beacham taught, the maximum. Among those in the early days were some who went on to high positions in U.S. industry: Hal Sperlich, who rose again at Chrysler; John Nevin, who later became chairman at both Zenith Corporation and Firestone Tire and Rubber; and Donald Frey, who took over Bell & Howell.

Iacocca preached the virtues of youth as well. He recognized the emergence of the postwar baby boom as a consumer generation. Ford advertised heavily in hotrod and teen magazines, sponsored "hootenannies" at university campuses and got back into competitive racing. Indeed, there were some who looked askance at Iacocca's quick move into racing. In the late Fifties, auto manufacturers had agreed to stop sponsoring races as a gesture to automotive safety, and Iacocca's "Race 'em on Sunday; sell 'em on Monday" promotion was viewed as being somewhat analogous to a widow dating too soon after her husband's funeral.

Iacocca pushed market research heavily. Just as he had with dealers in Pennsylvania, he went that one extra step. Convening a group of his young hotshots known as the "Fairlane Committee" for weekly evening meetings at the Fairlane Motel in Dearborn in 1961–62, he drew up a demographic picture of the new American automobile market and planted the seeds of a new car to match it.

At the time, Ford executives were dropping plans to build an all-new front-wheel-drive two-seater sports car, the Cardinal, in the United States, though the program continued in both Germany and the United Kingdom, but Iacocca was in the midst of creating a larger, rear-wheel-drive entry from the Cardinal for the sport field. Ford had been losing market share during the early Sixties—some say because of Robert McNamara's overly cautious approach to styling. Iacocca's new small car was an attempt to grab that share back, targeting the growing legions of the young who would command the automobile market for the next decade.

Contrary to the "all new" hype that surrounded the car, the Mustang was an automotive mutt, pieced together from parts borrowed from the existing Ford Falcon as well as others, but assembled ingeniously with a low, flat hood and sleek, sporty lines. As he would do later with the luxury Mark, Iacocca cross-sourced from every conceivable product—in a sense, building a new car out of stock. "Christ," said an old colleague still at Ford, "he was like a rug merchant."

"Lee is in many ways a huckster," said Matt McLaughlin, Iacocca's Assistant General Manager of the Ford Division at the time. The year he introduced the Mustang, he managed to get his face—and the car— on the covers of both *Time* and *Newsweek* the same week. It was a master-stroke of public relations, credited largely to Walter Murphy and Robert Hefty of Ford public relations, who played the two news-weekly staffs off one another with delicate skill, hinting but never promising exclusivity.

The Mustang's launch was also helped in no small measure by Lyndon Johnson's election year tax cut. Twelve months after the car was launched, Americans had purchased 418,000 of them—a record that would stand until the launching of General Motors' X-car in the spring of 1979. Before that Year of the Mustang was out, Iacocca had been promoted to the "Glass House" World Headquarters, where he took over in January 1965 as Vice-President, Car and Truck Group, heading up North American automotive operations.

Iacocca lost some of the public visibility that had marked his years at the Ford Division, but he was certainly well known—and feared— within Ford Motor Company. He drove underlings hard and pushed into a variety of new car programs. There were always small cars associated with Iacocca—the Mustang, of course, and later the Pinto and the Maverick—but he had no qualms about pushing big cars, too. Using his "rug merchant" technique of minimizing the use of expensive new parts, Iacocca guided the development of a luxury car at Ford to compete with GM's profitable Cadillac. By "re-skinning"—that is, putting a new design of sheet metal over the basic frame of a Thunderbird—Ford's Lincoln-Mercury Division created the Lincoln Continental Mark series that, until the Iranian crisis of 1979, was one of the most profitable lines in the history of the car business. "One year," recalls Iacocca, "we made $800 million on the Mark—net."

In October of 1967, Iacocca jumped a notch closer to the top, taking over as Executive Vice-President, North American Automotive Operations, a title that gave him control of the majority of Ford Motor Company's total worldwide business. By then, his system of quarterly reviews was in place throughout much of the company's operations. It was, along with Henry Ford's own nurturing of Ford's dominant international business and Robert McNamara's legacy of strong internal financial controls, one of the major contributions to Ford's success in the 1960s and 1970s.

Ford men referred to it as Iacocca's "black book," a token of awesome power. He kept one on every executive working directly for him and expected those executives in turn to keep books on people who reported to them. The most powerful ingredient of the quarterly review system was its reliance on self-evaluation. At the beginning of each fiscal quarter, Iacocca would go around to each executive to review the previous quarter as well as set goals for the coming one. Each was asked what his or her (though there are very few female executives in the auto industry) objectives were for the coming quarter and then asked to prioritize them. In the review portion of the meetings, Iacocca recalled the executive's past goals and then measured them against actual results. "There were an awful lot of wet palms around the first of each quarter," recalled one veteran of the system. Iacocca was never known to let up on someone who had fallen short. If they had been unable to achieve certain goals, Iacocca wanted to know why. If the problem was in someone else's department, he wanted to know why the problem wasn't communicated. If the shortfall was strictly the fault of the executive himself, Iacocca would force him to reassess what he was capable of achieving. Perhaps he should set his sights lower next quarter. Perhaps he needed help from others. Perhaps he was just plain in over his head. "If he's a good manager," explained Iacocca, "four times a year he's got to come into the barrel and report. . . . Sometimes they can't wait to tell you 'cause they told you what they were going to do and they knocked hell out of it. They can't wait to tell you 'cause they know it'll get 'em a raise . . . and it will."

There were times when the quarterly review system smoked out an executive who'd been misplaced or, perhaps, as the "Peter Principle" theorizes so accurately, simply had been promoted beyond his abilities. "You have guys after four quarters come in and say, 'I can't do it. I'm over my head. I hate the job and I never wanted it. Take me off.' And you do," said Iacocca. "It's better than canning him."

The system didn't always fit every job or department. It was relatively easy to evaluate manufacturing jobs. An assembly-plant manager had obvious goals to achieve: so many products a day or a month, a certain level of quality, a minimum of rejects, etc. A salesman in the field either handled his customers' complaints or he didn't. "An executive engineer?" hypothesized Iacocca. "Repairs-per-hundred, cost and weight objectives: you've got him by the nuts." But staff functions, public affairs? Iacocca admits it's not easy to quantify these functions in a way that makes evaluation meaningful to all concerned, but when presented with new functions that didn't permit clear measurements, Iacocca responded, "Give me time. I'll find a way." His philosophy: "If you can't grade a man, you can't follow him at all."

It took Iacocca four or five years to get the system humming at Ford: to get executives at lower levels to understand and adopt the system effectively and to keep it from falling into bureaucratic stagnation—a danger with any system in a large organization.

There were other management systems over which Iacocca rode herd at Ford. One of his favorites was a list of the ten biggest winners and ten biggest losers among all the operations within the company. Every function was measured according to its own profitability, and if it couldn't be measured in terms of monetary profitability, then Iacocca figured out another way to measure it. Every plant manager knew whether his plant was making or losing money for the company or whether the parts he was responsible for building cost less than what they could be purchased for outside. The "winners and losers list," as Iacocca called it, was known to all. "Everybody knew and everybody carried them around. If there was a list of a hundred, you didn't want to be in the bottom ten too long. Sooner or later I'm going to ask you 'When are you selling it off?' or 'Give me a program to get profitable. Give me all your alibis and excuses, fine. But give me a program.' To me, that's basic. A department store would say 'We're losing our ass in that boutique over there. Close it!' They're departmentalized. So are we. All businesses are somewhat the same."

Despite the wholesale institution of Iacocca's style in Ford's automotive operations and Henry Ford's apparently growing confidence in him, his rise was suddenly short-circuited in 1968. Semon "Bunky" Knudsen had been an executive vice-president at rival General Motors. Not only was it a tradition at GM for the company to promote from within—executives there tended to reciprocate by remaining loyal to the firm. Traditionally, there has been very little "jumping" from one auto company to another, and General Motors epitomized what defenders labeled constancy and what detractors called inbreeding. Moreover, Knudsen was second-generation GM. His father, William Knudsen, had been president, and his name was almost as revered as that of Sloan or Durant within the corporation. But in one of the most talked-about switches of the decade, young Bunky abandoned the GM ladder and came over as Henry Ford's fourth president, the company's eighth.

It may have been the first indication of Henry's misgivings about Iacocca—but the manner in which Knudsen came to and went from Ford offered more insight into Henry's peremptory style than it did into Henry's estimation of Lee Iacocca. Within a year, Knudsen was dismissed, told by Ford that "It just didn't work out."

Iacocca said that Henry had set him up as the "heavy" to keep Knudsen, an outsider, in line. But it also befits Iacocca's own personality and driving ambition to have accepted that role with gusto. In any event, there was little love lost between Knudsen and Iacocca. After Bunky was fired, the most prevalent rumor had it that Iacocca had undermined Knudsen during his entire tenure and that Henry did little to smooth over their differences. The Detroit *Free Press* accused Iacocca of "gloating" over Knudsen's firing. Ironically, it would seem that the two former Ford presidents had more in common than either seemed willing to admit.

It took Henry Ford about a year to replace Knudsen, but when he did, it was a tribute to Iacocca's tenacity. The only person Iacocca could not help signaling that something momentous was about to happen on December 10, 1970, was his father Nick. His parents beamed with pride as Iacocca told a crowd of reporters in Dearborn that Henry Ford had just given him "a helluva Christmas present"—the presidency of Ford Motor Company.

In the early Seventies, Iacocca dutifully played his role as spokesman for Henry. He was, in an industry that almost universally resented government intrusion, the most vocal and articulate critic of safety and emission regulations. He used his considerable oratorical skills everywhere, including the Oval Office, where he badgered Richard Nixon and his aides into abandoning the air bag in favor of Interlock.

His power at headquarters began to dwindle, though. Iacocca wanted his protégé, Hal Sperlich, to move into the presidency of Ford of Europe. Henry said no and put Bill Bourke in the job, where he worked for Philip Caldwell. Sperlich was still responsible for the product development of the prototype "World Car," the Fiesta, but Caldwell headed up the complex manufacturing scheme that allowed the car to be assembled in Spain and sourced in a variety of countries. By the mid-Seventies, Iacocca was losing influence over corporate decisions. He was overruled on small cars as well as on the "down-sizing" plan to parrot General Motors' efforts at easing the American buyer into smaller cars with gradual size and weight reductions. Under Henry's jealous rule, Iacocca's loyalists within management found themselves sorely tested and increasingly reluctant to speak out on his behalf. Henry's name, after all, was still on the building. After July 13, 1978, those who admired Lee Iacocca and wished to remain in the employ of Henry Ford learned to keep it to themselves.

His swift execution left Lee Iacocca numbed. He was, as he described it, "walking on eggs" for months afterward. Ford gave him ninety days to clean up his affairs—until October 15, his birthday, when he would reach the age of fifty-four. Cleaning out his desk and removing his personal belongings would hardly take three months, but Iacocca had to negotiate with Ford's chief legal counsel, Henry Nolte, over severance terms, stock options, pension rights and all the other details of recompense that had accumulated after thirty-two years on the corporate payroll.

Millions were at stake. Iacocca thought Ford owed him roughly $2 million. Nolte held him to $1.5 million and a noncompetitive clause that forbade him from joining any other automotive company if he was to keep his stock and severance. Iacocca questioned the competitive contingency for stock he felt he had earned as outright compensation and balked at the withholding of the last $500,000. Friends urged him to sue—not just for the money but for his reputation—but Iacocca declined.

He spent minimal time in the "Glass House" after mid-July. The nominal perquisites of his old job were still at his disposal—a car, a company suite at the Waldorf in New York and a corporate jet, for example. He used them as perches from which to view his future.

Hardly a businessman alive wasn't aware that Lee Iacocca was in the job market that summer. Offers came within days of the execution. His reputation as a top operations man easily overrode the inevitable rumors of malfeasance. Most approaches were exploratory. They ranged from major automotive suppliers to one of the leading aerospace companies. Two business schools dangled their deanships before him. Iacocca scoffed at the *New York* magazine report that he had fifty-five offers of chief executive officer positions that summer, but admits to about a dozen serious inquiries ranging from cushy jobs with cash-rich *Fortune* 500 firms to equity offers in hot entrepreneurial outfits. Charles Tandy of the Fort Worth-based Tandy Corporation, owner of the Radio Shack chain, cornered him one day to explain how he was getting on in years and needed help; how Iacocca, with his marketing skills, was perfect for the company and how he could write his own ticket. Iacocca later mused over that particular offer when he picked up the paper one morning to read that old Charlie Tandy had died of a heart attack within the year.

From abroad, Renault's Bernard Hanon, in the midst of negotiations with American Motors over the joint production and marketing arrangement that eventually verged on an outright takeover of AMC, discussed various positions Iacocca might take with Renault—either as a board member or something more. Iacocca might have ended up as top man at American Motors Corporation, facing an entirely different —if not almost as tough—set of problems.

He soon got a letter from an old contact—Gardner Wilson Heidrick of the esteemed Chicago executive "headhunting" firm of Heidrick & Struggles. Iacocca flew over to Midway Field in the Ford plane and met Heidrick for lunch at the venerable Chicago Club. Iacocca explained that he was, of course, anxious to get back into action; that he knew he'd get off the ground that much faster in the automotive business he knew so well. The two laughed over what proved to be an historical irony: two decades earlier, acting as an agent for none other than Lynn Townsend's Chrysler Corporation, Heidrick had approached young Lee Iacocca to see if he'd be interested in an executive vice-presidency there. Iacocca had said no then, but he'd also expressed a general interest in anything Heidrick might come up with wherein he could run his own show sooner than he might at Ford.

It didn't take Iacocca long to conclude that what he wanted most was to get back into the automobile business. As broadly applicable as his marketing skills might be, they were, for him, built around a love for cars. He was not a very diversified man. He'd done some things for the Boy Scouts and was, because of his wife's long affliction, an active member of the American Diabetes Association and related groups; he was a trustee of Lehigh—but almost everything else he did revolved around either his family or the automobile business. He lived and breathed cars. Even working for an automotive supply company like Dana or Bendix or Budd couldn't have satisfied him. "I had to be in the mainstream of the car business," he recalled. "That's where I'd spent my life. What the hell. It's like a guy saying 'Gee, you're a good musician—you can play the piano. Why don't you try the saxophone?'"

There was a third alternative: he could retire. In his last six years with Ford, Iacocca had earned an aggregate $4.2 million in salary and bonuses—including two recession years when no bonuses were awarded. His severance from Ford included $400,000 in cash, $22,500 a month for a year from the day he left, retirement benefits of $178,500 annually until he reached age sixty-five and $175,000 every year thereafter. He owned a large condominium in Boca Raton, Florida, as well as his fifteen-room split-level house in Bloomfield Hills. He could have dabbled at golf and tennis, fished off the Florida coast and consulted—but he was not yet fifty-four years old and the forces that had driven him all those years at Ford remained a part of his constitution.

The first call from John Riccardo came in early August. Iacocca was at home. Riccardo wanted to get together and talk. The two men had, of course, met, but Iacocca claims he knew very little about Riccardo. "Like all guys in the auto business," they saw one another at Motor Vehicle Manufacturers Association (MVMA) meetings, Economic Club of Detroit luncheons and the like. Their daughters went to the same convent school and the Iacoccas had met Mrs. Riccardo socially. "But once you get out of [downtown] Detroit," Iacocca explained, "you never get to know other auto people well because everybody has always been so fearful that if you're seen playing tennis or going fishing, you must be talking anti-trust. Pete [former GM president Elliott M.] Estes is almost my goddamn neighbor. We like him and his wife, but the only time we could have dinner was between July fifteenth and the date I joined Chrysler. That's the only time I was not a competitor."

Iacocca knew little about Chrysler before that summer. He had heard rumors that Riccardo and Cafiero were having a "battle royal" at the time. He knew through the usual industry intelligence what Chrysler was building and planning for the near future. He knew their reputation for engineering and believed it. "If you needed a good transmission man or a good air conditioning man, you came to Chrysler." And in the Sixties, Iacocca did just that, stealing ten or so top young talents out from under Lynn Townsend's nose not long after Townsend had tried to steal Iacocca from Ford. He knew Hal Sperlich, of course, but since Sperlich had gone over to Highland Park, the two had spoken only occasionally and had not talked much about Chrysler.

Within days of Riccardo's call, Iacocca heard from another Chrysler man: outside board member J. Richardson Dilworth, manager of the massive Rockefeller family fortune in New York. Dilworth knew Iacocca mostly by reputation. He too had followed the drama in Dearborn with interest and knew peripherally of the dispute between Iacocca and Henry Ford, but it cast no shadow on Dilworth's appraisal of Lee Iacocca as a businessman. He knew Henry Ford well enough to know that Ford was capable of peremptory actions that didn't necessarily signal chicanery or incompetence on the part of his victims. Moreover, a man who knew the Ford scene rather well had telephoned Dilworth to see if he and other Chrysler directors might be interested in getting together with Iacocca.

Arrangements were made for a meeting in New York in mid-August. The Waldorf-Astoria, as it would be several more times, was the setting for a very general discussion of the automobile business between Dilworth, Iacocca and Wall Street lawyer Louis Warren, another Chrysler board member. The Chrysler directors came away extremely impressed with the scope of the ex-Ford president. It was clear to them that Lee Iacocca had the wherewithal to give Chrysler the product and marketing expertise that was lacking, but Dilworth, like other outside directors at Chrysler, had a particular fondness and respect for John Riccardo and was squeamish about approaching him with the notion of bringing in a man of Iacocca's caliber. There was a consensus by then, though largely unspoken, that Riccardo was a fine human being and a tireless worker, but less than an automotive genius. The company's outside directors were well aware of the "bean-counter" image of Chrysler management at a time when much more than accounting was needed to pull the company through.

Fortunately, Riccardo himself let his directors off the hook. He was by then determined to get Lee Iacocca. The match was perfect. "It

was John who did it all," said a company insider. "John perceived the
need for change. If it weren't Iacocca, it would have been somebody
else." Although Riccardo personally refused to discuss the differences
between himself and Gene Cafiero, those around him were well aware
of his determination to get someone else to run the company's operations while he threw himself into negotiations with the banks and the
government.

Riccardo would more than admit that Iacocca was his idea. "I
picked Lee for the company," he emphasized. "It was my suggestion
that we hire him." It is indicative of the obviousness of the choice,
however, that at least three outside directors came to the same conclusion independently and almost simultaneously.

Riccardo presented his scheme to the board's Executive Committee
and, a short time later, in August of 1978, they approved his plans to
approach Iacocca. On a hot August afternoon, three men arrived separately at a suite in downtown Detroit's Pontchartrain Hotel, which
overlooks the river. Board member Dick Dilworth was there more or
less as a token representative of his colleagues—a tacit statement that
Riccardo's overtures had directorial approval and were serious. Riccardo did most of the talking that afternoon. He outlined in rough
form his idea of bringing Iacocca in as chief operating man. Iacocca
mostly listened. He told Riccardo right away, however, that he could
do nothing until after October 15 because of his severance terms with
Ford. Riccardo's skin-level emotions showed: he was disappointed and
said so. He had hoped to present a complete arrangement to the full
board at the October board meeting, around the first of that month.
Iacocca repeated that it was out of the question. He was bound to
Ford at least until then, and in reality until November 1, when he
would officially go off the payroll.

The two met again at the Pontchartrain, this time without Dilworth.
They began, intellectually, to circle one another. All was done with
elaborate security, not only to keep the automotive press corps off the
scent, but to keep both Ford and Chrysler executives in the dark.
Touchiest of all was the necessity of keeping Gene Cafiero blissfully
ignorant until the matter was resolved, one way or the other. Chrysler
vice-president Wendell Larsen, a former Army Intelligence officer,
made all the meeting arrangements and saw to it that the group aware
of the negotiations remained as small as possible.

As ignorant as Iacocca had been about Chrysler prior to mid-July,
he was rather serendipitously well prepared for his talks with Riccardo. After one meeting, Riccardo told a colleague in Highland Park,
"He knows more about us than we do; he's had Salomon Brothers do
some work on us."

Indeed, in his ruminations following his departure from Ford, Iacocca had pondered the possibility of an international consortium of smaller auto firms to compete against General Motors and the Japanese. Once or twice, he'd met with his old protégé, Hal Sperlich, and the two had tossed around the general theory of industry realignment. They even created an imaginary car company and dubbed it "Global Motors."

The world auto business, they assumed, would filter down to somewhere between a half dozen and a dozen competitive consortiums and/or fully integrated firms. There would be General Motors and Ford headquartered in the United States, "Japan, Inc.," as they referred to the entire Japanese fleet of companies, the Germans as an interlocking national group, at least one French-based group, and only a few others who would survive on their abilities to preserve economies of scale through joint ventures and other arrangements.

"Global" would be one of the consortiums. Taking Chrysler, with its engineering strength, as a base, the company would bring American Motors into the fold and work out a marketing and parts exchange deal with one of the major European companies—Volkswagen, perhaps, or Fiat, or Renault. American-engineered automobiles would run on German or Italian or French engines and joint dealer networks would be able to match the market penetration of the American giants. The truck business would be relegated to the AMC division, essentially its Jeep facilities.

Renault president Bernard Hanon's inquiries had piqued Iacocca's interest in the "Global" concept, and through John Gutfreund at New York's Salomon Brothers, he arranged for the investment banking house to do some research into the pros and cons. Salomon's biggest concern, according to Iacocca, was the prospect of an antitrust challenge. The investment analysts saw Fiat as a strong European possibility for such joint activity, but questioned how the U.S. government would feel about the merging of AMC and Chrysler into an operating arm for a foreign manufacturer. Others had pondered the marriage of the two smaller American companies in the past, and antitrust had always been the stumbling block.

In the process of examining the possibility of such a consortium, Salomon drew up evaluations of each of the companies under consideration. Thus, when John Riccardo began making his pitch, Lee Iacocca had a surprisingly up-to-date independent appraisal. Under current market conditions, Salomon said, the company was in tight shape, but Chrysler had just sold a large chunk of preferred stock without much difficulty and Salomon predicted that they would "skinny through."

Influenced strongly by the cross-examination of Salomon's Lee Higdon, Iacocca had forged a list of ten specific questions about

Chrysler's future, which he presented to Riccardo at their first of two meetings in a room at the Northfield Hilton, on Interstate 75 just south of Pontiac. Most of them centered on how Chrysler planned to get the money needed to execute an ambitious product program for the Eighties. At the second Northfield Hilton meeting, Riccardo tried to give him some answers. Iacocca remarked to him that the billion-dollar K-body program to replace the compact Aspen/Volare was "an expensive mother." He pressed Riccardo for his own forecast outlining where the money would come from. "They were banking on doing a lot of things," he recalled. "They were banking on getting profitable quick." Iacocca didn't doubt Riccardo's sincerity; he simply saw in the projections an unusual amount of optimism glossing over a lot of risk. "It wasn't John concealing anything from me," he recalled later. "But in looking at it, I thought, 'Oh boy! Not much cushion here!'"

By October, the meetings were getting more and more frequent. Some were held in Riccardo's home; some were at the Iacoccas'. Lee's wife, Mary, knew that he was discussing a job at Chrysler, and at some point he told his older daughter, Kathi, then a student at Middlebury College, but he kept it from Lia, his younger daughter, because she was still in high school locally with many classmates from car-company families. That was too high a risk.

Occasionally during his casual personal meetings with Hal Sperlich, during which "Global Motors" was tossed around, Iacocca picked up odd bits of information about Chrysler. Sperlich was by no means briefing him and was utterly unaware of the talks going on with Riccardo, but he would occasionally refer to Chrysler as a benchmark. From Sperlich's remarks, Iacocca pieced together that Chrysler was certainly a lot different from Ford. Apparently statistics, so readily ordered up and immaculately maintained at Ford, were hard to come by at Chrysler. Sperlich indicated that he sometimes had to do his own research.

By October, Iacocca and Chrysler were in earnest negotiations; it was clear to both parties that the deal was workable. Hewlett-Packard co-founder Bill Hewlett, who chaired the board's Compensation Committee and who had had a number of phone conversations with Iacocca after Riccardo and Dilworth had established contact, began drawing up a package for the ex-Ford president. Since it was clear that the minute Iacocca signed on at Chrysler he would forfeit his severance package at Ford, Hewlett had to come up with $1.5 million up front. It was no bargain for either side. From Iacocca's point of view, the money merely replaced what he would lose at Ford, adding not a penny more. He had been making $360,000 a year at Ford and said he'd take the same from Chrysler. The only trouble was, John Riccardo, the chairman, only made $340,000. It didn't take Hewlett and

Riccardo long to agree to an equalization package that gave John Riccardo an instant $20,000-a-year raise.

If there was any real bargaining, it was not over money—it was over power. Riccardo had in mind a chief operating officer role for Iacocca that would last for two years. He knew Iacocca eventually wanted the chief executive position. He had wanted one all his life. Two years, Iacocca told Riccardo flatly, was too long. He wanted the job as soon as possible. They compromised at one year, agreeing that on November 1, 1979, Lee Iacocca would succeed Riccardo as chief executive officer.

On October 15, the day he officially signed off as president of Ford, Iacocca signaled Riccardo that he could go ahead and draw up a package. In fifteen days, Iacocca would go off the Ford payroll and, except for his pension and his ownership of more than $3 million worth of Ford common stock, he would break all ties with what had been until then his only employer.

Prior to the November 2 meeting of the Chrysler board, at which the Iacocca package would be presented for official approval and subsequent announcement to the public, Iacocca met with the full Executive Committee at the Chrysler suite in New York's Waldorf Towers. Once again, secrecy was paramount. The directors waited in the suite while Lee Iacocca took one elevator and John Riccardo waited out of sight for another. Despite some speculation, including one uncannily accurate item in the "Intelligencer" section of *New York* magazine, the secrecy up until then had been successful. Riccardo, tense as he was from the talks and no doubt apprehensive about the inevitable showdown with Gene Cafiero, entered the elevator in the Towers lobby a safe period after Iacocca and asked for the thirty-sixth floor. "That's funny," chirped the woman operating the elevator. "I just finished taking Mr. Iacocca from Ford up to thirty-six." Riccardo paled, fearing the cover at last was blown.

He needn't have worried. No enterprising reporter had suspected enough to bother quizzing elevator operators at the Waldorf-Astoria, and the operator herself was evidently content that the arrival of two of the nation's top auto executives in her elevator was pure coincidence.

To some of the outside directors, the full implications of Iacocca's arrival at Chrysler didn't dawn until later. Dick Dilworth, for one, had assumed, somewhat naïvely in retrospect, that Cafiero, whose polished presentations at board meetings had always impressed the outside directors, could somehow continue to work for the company along with Iacocca and Riccardo. Bill Hewlett had no such illusion, and neither did John Riccardo.

On the last Friday in October, Riccardo and a handful of top executives met with Cafiero at the old Detroit Club; the Chrysler president was told he would no longer be president. He was given the nominal position of vice-chairman but, with his duties undefined, it was obvious he would be packing up as soon as he could comfortably do so. He was not present the following Thursday at the Highland Park press conference when Iacocca and Riccardo faced flashing cameras and hurried questions from a press corps that had been caught almost totally by surprise. Even the *Wall Street Journal,* which had pieced together the actual deal in remarkably accurate detail for that morning's front-page account, was in no position to contradict Iacocca's facetious description of the long wooing process: "Johnny called me and said 'Why don't you come over and give me a hand?'"

That weekend, Gene Cafiero went to see Iacocca at his home. He had spent the past eight days buttonholing erstwhile friends on the board in an attempt to salvage his job. Dilworth had suggested he talk to Iacocca. Although Dilworth's intent was to avoid his own further involvement at all costs, Cafiero somehow interpreted his recommendation as encouragement. The implication of Cafiero's pitch to Iacocca that Saturday was that the board had gotten rid of the wrong man. Cafiero hoped to stay on and help Iacocca through the transition period . . . a period that just might extend beyond John Riccardo's retirement date. Iacocca, somewhat taken aback by the proposition, replied that the new management arrangement was the board's decision, not his. Nonetheless, Gene Cafiero left Iacocca's home further encouraged that he had planted a new idea in the new chief operating officer's head. To avoid any accusation of subterfuge, he even reported his conversations to John Riccardo, but Riccardo already knew and told Cafiero flatly that he had been right behind him, undoing his every action.

Sometime later, as he was finishing packing his personal belongings, Cafiero paid Iacocca a final visit in his temporary office midway down the executive corridor. He wished him luck, but said he didn't envy him. He outlined Chrysler's plight as he saw it, naturally painting the weaknesses into John Riccardo's corner of management, but Iacocca knew enough by then to understand that the problems were largely operational. That put them squarely in Gene Cafiero's corner. What he did not appreciate then but would soon learn was just how deep into Chrysler's management those problems ran.

For the moment, Iacocca was back on top of a car company. He began his new job the same week the 96th Congress of the United States was elected by calling in the people who now worked for him and ordering his new public relations department to bring in the national press. He was more than ebullient; he was soaring, that old dollop of gasoline coursing again through his veins.

Even his detractors conceded that Lee Iacocca was a marketing wizard. Over the years, he displayed an uncanny knack for "feeling" the market, "sensing" the mood of the public, knowing intuitively, it seemed, what style, size, color and texture would have the broadest appeal. "Lee has an inner feeling about a new car," said Paul Bergmoser, the man who later succeeded him as president upon John Riccardo's retirement from Chrysler. "Lee had perhaps the best feel of the consumer and the marketplace of any top automotive executive in the business," said a former Ford colleague who remained behind in Dearborn.

A psychiatrist would associate Iacocca's marketing powers with a dominant right-brain lobe, where human emotions and artistic talents originate. Indeed, more often than not, colleagues recall Iacocca scrutinizing a proposed new car by running his fingers over the upholstery, opening and closing doors and trunks, examining lines with as much of an artist's eye as an engineer's calculations.

His personality certainly contributed to the image. Prone to drama, short of temper, quick to joke, he tended to dominate meetings whether presiding over them or not. He was a favorite of newspeople because his answers to their questions were seldom guarded, or so it seemed. Usable facts were somehow always stated colorfully. Sometimes he got himself into trouble. Shortly after he took over the Ford Division, Iacocca opined to a national magazine correspondent that Ford Motor Company couldn't have taken too much more of Robert McNamara's leadership. McNamara, whom Iacocca had always praised until after he accepted Jack Kennedy's offer to run the Defense Department, had been neglecting product and leading the company toward disaster, said Iacocca. Fortunately for the new Ford Division head, the quote never made it into print. One of the Ford veterans who followed Iacocca to Highland Park advised a group of them once that they would all have to learn to protect Lee Iacocca from himself on occasion.

Since his intuitive marketing talents dominate his reputation, it is natural that Iacocca was perceived to have few analytical skills and not much feel for money. A number of businessmen who know him more by reputation feared that he was just not the right man for Chrysler: that Chrysler needed a penny-pinching cost control expert who would, as one chief executive said, "cut the suit to fit the cloth." Some middle-level managers at Ford sneered that all Iacocca knew how to do was design and sell cars . . . as long as someone else was there to sign the check.

Those who were close to him at Ford saw his skills differently. Former colleagues quickly noted that his greatest marketing successes—the Mustang and the Mark—were pieced together from pallet loads of existing components at minimum development cost. "He's got the kind of combined product sense and financial sense that allowed him to do that sort of thing for a long time," said one. Financial staffers who worked for him at Ford maintain that Iacocca was as facile with numbers as any high-ranking Ford executive. The acid test was his acumen in the 1974–75 downturn, when he engineered $1 billion in cuts from corporate operations without damaging product programs.

Since Iacocca began receiving massive public exposure from his role at Chrysler, some former Ford colleagues and underlings griped privately that he was taking more credit for product success than was his due, while ignoring his role in some of the flops. Indeed, he wears the title "Father of the Mustang" most comfortably, though he admits when pressed that Hal Sperlich, Don Frey and others played major roles in the development of the car. He even on occasion laid claim to the Fiesta, a project for which at best he had oversight responsibility, but he seldom brought up his near-parallel role with the infamous Pinto, except to contend that he recommended fixing it. "Lee cherry-picks," admitted a Ford executive who basically sympathized with Iacocca. "All brilliant guys do, to their own advantage."

There were plenty of businessmen who were ready to dismiss Lee Iacocca as a bully and a huckster, a con artist whose maverick style they considered inappropriate for the heady atmosphere of New York's financial community or within Washington's wily cadre of policymakers. Even some who praised his breadth of talent voiced doubts about his ability to fulfill the role of a major chief executive officer. A portion of these critics merely reflected Henry Ford's precipitous judgment. Most of the others simply didn't know Iacocca.

Indeed, Lee Iacocca was inclined to do some things differently. For the most part, he dressed, looked and acted like the quintessential big businessman, but he was neither careful nor conservative. His friends ranged as widely as his mind. New York investment bankers and even some of his close Detroit pals looked askance at some of the people to whom he remained stubbornly loyal over the years. Fugazy was the name most often mentioned. "Lee has the quality of being very close to a certain group of friends," said one of them, Burns Cody. Some were old high school chums from Allentown. Some were famous, like New York's Terence Cardinal Cooke or Attorney Edward Bennett Williams. Some were plain unpredictable. "He does all his entertaining at home," said Cody. "At one of his parties, you might see anybody from a masseur to the shoeshine guy from Ford."

He regularly captivated clusters of bankers or congressmen with his rapid-recall knowledge—not only of cars but of virtually anything—yet he was chronically prone to indiscretion. He was known for eruptions that smack of irrational response. Still, final decisions proffered

almost inevitably reflected surprisingly dispassionate analyses, explained in coolly logical language. Little wonder that distant subordinates in both the Ford and Chrysler hierarchies could recall vividly
what in many instances were their only contacts with Iacocca as one-
dimensional violent outbursts and onerous orders that left men shak-
ing. "Lee is like Lynn Townsend in that sense," a Chrysler veteran
noted once. "He is a man you want to please." It was a powerful but
dangerous executive tool.

The contradictions notwithstanding, Lee Iacocca carried with him
to Chrysler a net reputation as a true master of his trade, though as
one Chrysler director observed with a wry smile, "He is a very unusual piece of business."

He would find in the years ahead that he would need to draw upon
every ounce of his good reputation to shore up Chrysler's bulkheads.
Some would say the effort drew out the worst in him—the pugnacious,
abrasive ego that would drive him to put his face on Chrysler TV ads
and to write feisty complaint letters to the *Wall Street Journal, Fortune* and other publications that took on the philosophical issue of the
Chrysler bailout. Many others would conclude that no one else in
American business could have done it . . . if it could be done at all;
that Lee Iacocca would take Chrysler as far as any businessman could
in the face of a conspiracy of events that cracked the American industrial foundation itself.

In November of 1978, before even Lee Iacocca knew the extent of
Chrysler's problems, even his critics and foes could not question the
judgment of business's most ruthless arbiter, the New York Stock Exchange. Two factors were at play in the movement of Chrysler common stock on November 2: John Riccardo's gruesome revelation that
the company had lost a record $158.8 million in the third quarter, and
Lee Iacocca's arrival as president. Chrysler closed for the day up 3/8
at 10 7/8.

CHAPTER TEN

Starting Over

Lee Iacocca wasn't even sure where Chrysler's headquarters was. He knew it was somewhere off the Davison Expressway, which runs across the northern edge of Detroit and the enclave of Highland Park, but he'd never noticed how close the motley campus of brick and concrete buildings was to the intersection of the Davison and the Chrysler expressways. On a couple of occasions, he'd been driven by a Ford chauffeur to the K. T. Keller Building for industry meetings on labor negotiations, but until that morning in November, his first day on the job as president of Chrysler, he'd never paid much attention.

His attention focused rapidly in the ensuing weeks. The process was hastened by one of his first and most alarming discoveries: the finely tuned reporting systems that existed at Ford, and which he had assumed existed in every big company, simply weren't there. In his first full week, he asked department heads to give him a rundown on operations—how many cars the company made and sold, a list of every plant and product from bumpers to battle tanks, how much they cost and how much they were making or losing. The information he got was haphazard and heavily oriented toward ledger accounting rather than what he was used to: cost control and management by objective.

One look at the organization chart and he grew more concerned. The most obvious structural curiosity was the position held by R. K. Brown. Brown was charged with running both manufacturing—the

oversight of one hundred thousand people in more than forty plants—
and sales. One man was managing the alpha and the omega of the car
business at Chrysler, but nothing in between.

Theoretically, Brown was Gene Cafiero's executive officer in charge
of Chrysler's total automotive line operations. Frank Anderson ran
manufacturing for him, with four vice-presidents reporting to him for
the various categories—General Manufacturing, Stamping and Assembly, Quality and Safety. Engines and Castings were lumped together
under veteran Steve Sharf. Mexico, Canada, Service and Parts reported directly to Brown. Funny groupings, thought Iacocca.

Engineering, by tradition, was off by itself under Dick Vining. It
made sense to have product engineering and planning report to
Vining directly, but Iacocca was puzzled to see that purchasing, apparently separated from manufacturing, also reported to engineering.

All the staff functions—public and civic affairs, personnel, general
counsel, comptroller, auditor, treasurer—reported not to Cafiero, but to
Riccardo above him. Curiously, so did Chrysler Leasing Corporation,
a natural adjunct to sales, and Chrysler Realty Corporation, that un-
natural adjunct to the automobile business.

There were two committees: an unwieldy thirty-one-member
"Officers' Council" that met bimonthly for briefings, and Riccardo's
Operations Committee, consisting of Cafiero as vice-chairman; Bill
Blakeslee, non-automotive operations; Don Lander, international
(such as it was by then); Lars Larsen, public affairs; Ed Doyle, the
comptroller; treasurer Bill McGagh; engineering chief Dick Vining;
and the ubiquitous R. K. Brown. (By early 1981, twenty-seven months
after Iacocca first reviewed Chrysler's organization chart, only one of
the nine Operations Committee members, Larsen, was still with the
company, and the configuration was radically different.) In all, it was
not the kind of organization chart one would find in a business school
textbook.

Coming in, Iacocca had assumed that there would be specific problem areas to attack. Chrysler's quality-control problems were well
known. He arrived right in the midst of the late launch of the R-body.
He suspected that there were purchasing problems because of Chrysler's reputation among suppliers as an inefficient buyer of parts.
His merchandiser's eye told him that the styling was stodgy on many
of the cars. He had no idea, though, that these and other shortcomings
were mere symptoms of a deep organizational disease. "My greatest
disappointment," he said later, "was starting from scratch."

Riccardo had given Iacocca *carte blanche* over operations—the role
of Mr. Inside—while the chairman continued to play Mr. Outside with
the banks and the government. He even allowed Iacocca to smoke ci-
gars in meetings—for Riccardo, a major capitulation. The standing rule

had been "no smoking" during any of Riccardo's staff gatherings until the new president, Riccardo at his side, walked into the first Officers' Council meeting after his arrival to a standing ovation by the other executives. "That's a precedent," Riccardo laughed. Looking down at Iacocca's glowing Monte Cristo, he added sheepishly, "I guess we'll change the rules on smoking too."

Within the first month, Iacocca knew he was going to have to turn the company upside down, ridding it of methods that were either anachronistic or disintegrated beyond repair. In one of his darker moments he growled, "This company took twenty-five years to become decadent—I mean rotten to the core."

Not three weeks in office, Iacocca ordered a massive reshuffling of the organization chart. R. K. Brown was relieved of his duties as executive officer and given Chrysler's marketing portfolio. Service and Parts stayed with him; so did Chrysler Canada. Dick Vining, in whom Iacocca immediately recognized an engineer's eye combined with plant experience, became one of the few old-line Chrysler officers to advance immediately under Iacocca. His new title would be Executive Vice-President for Manufacturing and Purchasing, with Assembly and Stamping, General Manufacturing, Engine and Casting, Manufacturing Engineering, Vehicle Quality and Reliability, Purchasing and Operations Planning all reporting to him. "Dick was one of the guys early on I felt would be one of the mainstays here," said Iacocca.

As for Brown? "A nice fella; nice guy, really. Never could get riled; mild-mannered, old-shoe type. He was cast in that organization way over his head with both Sales and Manufacturing. He tried to divert his time from one to the other." Iacocca paused, looking for the positive side. "I think a lot of dealers like him. He had a good relationship with dealers."

It was no surprise that Hal Sperlich emerged from the shuffle with more power. From his position as a vice-president for Product Planning under Vining, Sperlich rose to a group vice-presidency and took charge of Product Planning, Design, the Engineering office and the Program Timing office—in short, the whole scope of the company's product development. An Iacocca man, a small-car man, was overseeing Chrysler's cars for the Eighties.

John Day, who had run Chrysler's European Automotive Operations until they were sold out from under him, moved over to take control of Non-automotive Operations, including the Defense Division and the XM-1 turbine tank program. Don Lander, once captain of an enterprise spanning five continents, continued to run Chrysler International, though the company was actively working to spin off as much foreign business as possible for cash.

One of the intended by-products of the reorganization was the isolation of operations so that they could be examined individually for flaws. Under Sperlich, Program Timing could be coordinated with product development. Under Vining, the entire manufacturing process could be isolated from product development on the one hand and sales on the other. Iacocca was laying the corporation open for surgery. In the end, it was the total system that would have to work. Shuffling executives around the organization chart wasn't going to solve the problems.

The assumption among automotive writers during those first few months was that Iacocca's monomaniacal objective was to "get back" at Henry Ford for firing him, using Chrysler as a weapon. Sitting about the horseshoe bar of the dimly lit Detroit Press Club, reporters reveled in conjuring up scenes of night raiding parties into Ford's executive suites, the planting of moles deep inside Henry's organization and streams of talented auto men signing on in Highland Park to the accompaniment of gloating Chrysler press releases.

Iacocca was indeed deeply resentful of his treatment by Henry Ford, but he was far less interested in getting even than he was in getting control of his own car company, where he could call the shots and be his own Henry Ford. If he could "take a little out of Ford's hide in the process," as he used to say, all the better. Eventually he did steal some good people from Ford, though not as vindictively as imagined. It did not take long after his arrival before he was frightened by Chrysler's precarious condition and became desperate for help. He turned to men he knew, who in turn knew the same systems and business shorthand he had used over the years. In the beginning, there were three of them he went after—each already retired from Ford and each with a particular skill and an experienced eye to catch the flaws.

Hans Matthias was a quality-control specialist. He had spent a career at Ford cleaning the bugs out of the automotive manufacturing process, finally retiring in 1972 as vice-president in charge of manufacturing for all North American Automotive Operations. Though he had been in the United States since he first arrived from Mannheim in 1934, he never lost his German accent, which colored the constant flow of technical aphorisms: "Design and process must be capable of meeting design intent"; "Get it right the first time through"; "Don't schedule inventions . . ." After forming a manufacturing consulting firm along with a group of fellow automotive retirees, Matthias has become something of a quality-control guru around Detroit.

During fifteen years at Ford, Matthias had worked for Lee Iacocca, and he remained one of the many Ford men swept into that special circle of loyalty. In December of 1978, the phone rang in his Farmington Hills condominium. "Come give us a hand on quality," beckoned

Iacocca's familiar raspy voice. Matthias signed on for one year at half time, strictly as an outside consultant. Iacocca was careful to present him to Vining, an old-line Chrysler man, not as some storm trooper brought in to dictate a new order but as a consultant who would report to Vining right after the first of the year.

Paul Bergmoser was known as a purchasing man in the trade. He had spent thirty years with Ford in "materials control," an arcane discipline that requires the kind of toughness, bargaining ability and sensitivity to quality shared by first-rate housewives, department store buyers and theatrical agents. It was his job to get the best possible deal for Ford each time the company bought parts and materials from outside suppliers, to determine whether the company would be better off buying a given part or building it inside the company, and, ultimately, to goad the myriad suppliers into furnishing Ford with what it wanted, when it wanted it, at the lowest possible price.

Bergmoser was good at his job—some say too good. On the inside, admirers like Lee Iacocca called him a disciplinarian, "a goddamn Prussian general," as he once applauded him. On the outside, Bergmoser was feared by some as a rough, ruthless slave driver. He was one of Iacocca's key lieutenants, his Vice-President for Purchasing. But in 1976, when he turned sixty, he retired to Palm Springs, California. There he stayed with his wife, Yvonne, visited occasionally by three grown children, until he got the call.

"Bergie, I'm all alone in Chrysler," Iacocca said. "It's different from Ford in organization and philosophy. I have nobody to reach for." The proposal was fairly harmless: a stint of a few months as a consultant on purchasing matters, examining Chrysler's material traffic patterns, the systems that tie an automobile together, taking stock of the purchasing operation and measuring it against what Lee Iacocca was used to. On January 1, Paul Bergmoser left the warmth of Southern California and returned to Detroit for a little while—he thought.

Gar Laux had worked directly for Iacocca for twelve years at Ford. He was Division Sales Manager when the Mustang was introduced. While Lee Iacocca was credited for revitalizing the Lincoln-Mercury Division, it was Laux who ran it, as general manager. A genuinely warm, shoulder-grabbing type, Laux was a consummate "dealer man," able to cajole the best out of thousands of Ford or Lincoln-Mercury franchise operators, most of whom he seemed to know by name.

The arrival of Bunky Knudsen at Ford in the late Sixties not only had stalled Iacocca's career temporarily, it had brought Laux's to an end. He left the company after sixteen years at age fifty-one and took a job as head of the Dallas Chamber of Commerce. Five years later, however, Laux was back in the car business. He and Arnold Palmer, *the* Arnold Palmer, formed a partnership in Charlotte, North Carolina, and opened up a Cadillac dealership. With rare exceptions, a Cadillac franchise constitutes a license to print money. Margins are more than healthy and, as one cynical competitor once put it, "The extent of salesmanship for the average Caddy dealer is to pick up the phone and listen as his rich client says 'Herb, I'd like a blue one this year.'" With Arnold Palmer's name and Gar Laux's ability, the Charlotte franchise was, to say the least, lucrative. Laux did well enough to buy the local ice hockey franchise and to live very comfortably in one of the nation's nicer small cities.

After a few informal phone conversations about dealerships and whether or not there was any good marketing talent around for hire, Laux flew to Detroit and dined with Iacocca. They talked about marketing and sales people from Ford days, the kinds of men Iacocca wanted to straighten out yet another mess at Chrysler. Eventually, they talked about Laux taking some time himself to look around and see what was needed—a few months, nothing that would jeopardize his business with Palmer. By February, Gar Laux was officially a consultant. By spring, he was in charge of sales and marketing, hooked as a full-time executive and once again working for Lee Iacocca.

The three Ford retirees were brought in to trouble-shoot, but Iacocca saw quickly that Chrysler's financial system needed more than consulting. There was nothing, he observed, resembling the committee structure that marked the way both General Motors, following its Alfred Sloan blueprint, and Ford, in more streamlined fashion, operated. Clearly lacking at Chrysler was the oversight function that committees provided. Jobs were being done without anyone to examine their efficiency or to question whether the job assignment even matched the desired goal.

The irony of Chrysler's organization at the time Iacocca took over operations was that it lacked the one discipline it had so often been accused of overdoing. "They talked about 'beancounters,'" scoffed Iacocca. "Chrysler had nothing *but* financial controls, they always said, because of the background of their top people. No. They had *accounting* controls, *auditing* controls. But financial controls to help the operating people run their business? God, if they're there, I still haven't found them." Said Paul Bergmoser after his first year at Chrysler: "I have a terrific accountant's report that tells me we lost a billion dollars. What I don't have is an analysis to tell me *how the hell* we lost a billion dollars."

To restructure the controller's office at Chrysler in a manner suited to his own methods, Iacocca needed new and permanent blood. "I needed guys who knew what you meant by having financial controls." This time, he went right into the heart of Ford Motor Company's famed finance staff for his first real steal. The man who had built Ford's financial control system was J. Edward Lundy, a contemporary of McNamara and Arjay Miller, one of the original "whiz kids," whose square features and brush cut reflected the Air Force discipline he instilled in Ford's financial ranks. As luck would have it, Iacocca had undertaken a review of Lundy's staff in search of high-potential young managers less than five months before he was fired. From out of his infamous black book, he pulled some names and ran five or ten of them by Lundy. The "sleeper" in the group, Lundy said, was the forty-three-year-old president of Ford's Venezuelan company, Jerry Greenwald.

Greenwald, a Princeton graduate in economics, had been somewhat of a maverick at Ford, pressing his bosses for an opportunity to get out of the elite financial corps and into operations. He'd finally won his chance in 1976 when he was given Venezuela. Over the next two years, the subsidiary nearly tripled sales and increased profits tenfold, running Ford's market share in Venezuela from 28 percent to 37 percent—the highest car and truck market share of any Ford subsidiary.

By December of 1978, however, the stampede was over and it was time to consolidate gains. Life was "comfortable" for the Greenwalds. They lived in an impressive hacienda up against a mountain in Caracas; the temperature was seventy degrees in winter and Jerry was a big fish in a little pond. When they arrived home one evening from a party to find a phone message from Lee Iacocca, Glenda Greenwald immediately sensed a threat to their established comfort. "Don't call back," she said.

Greenwald called anyway. Over the next four months, in phone conversations and in meetings from Miami to Las Vegas, Iacocca pitched him a deal. As with all those he recruited, he imparted a keen sense of adventure. Greenwald was particularly reluctant to give up the line position he had won in order to take Iacocca's offer to be Chrysler's controller—to be typecast again as a numbers man—but Iacocca won and, in April, Greenwald told his superiors at Ford that he was about to jump ship.

For a day and a half, he was questioned and cajoled in Dearborn, right up the line to president Philip Caldwell. When he finally made it clear that he was indeed leaving, "things became very formal very quickly." Interestingly, the man who seemed to understand most clearly what he was doing was Henry Ford II. What appeared to impress Ford most was Greenwald's suggestion that the chairman think back thirty-five years to a time when Ford himself had picked his grandfather's company off the ropes, put together a new team and turned it around. Of all the arguments he presented to Henry Ford that day, that analogy alone seemed to touch him, Greenwald thought, and make him understand.

It was painfully clear by the first quarter of 1979 that almost everything was wrong with Chrysler's management structure. It was, chortled Iacocca, "like Italy until 1860. It was these little states—duchies.
They would not report to central authority." The winners, few though
they were by then, did not want to be tainted by association with the
corporate body. Belvidere, the Omni/Horizon plant in Illinois, wanted
nothing to do with Detroit. Huntsville, Alabama, the elite electronics
plant spun off from the space program, acted like "prima donnas."
The tank plants, nestled safely within a government program, free
from consumer troubles; the highly profitable Mexican subsidiary,
which was the envy of both GM and Ford south of the border; engineering, Chrysler's self-proclaimed elite—all of them claimed special
status. "Everybody had his own little empire," said Iacocca. "Twenty
little companies and nobody to pull them together."

It was a pattern not unfamiliar in the auto industry nor uncommon
in business generally. At Ford, Iacocca recalled, he had faced the
same phenomenon in Europe in the early days of consolidation. Jack
McDougall, later to become Executive Vice-President at Ford, used to
tell him how one department would take its assignment, complete it
and pass it on cold to the next department—"Like taking a rock, tying
it up in a handkerchief and tossing it over a fence." A veteran manufacturing engineer at Chrysler echoed McDougall's experience at
Ford. Criticizing Chrysler's elitist Product Engineering Group for
passing on to Manufacturing designs that were often impossible to
build, he snarled, "Around here, we called R & D 'Release and Develop.' They'd release it; we'd develop it."

Part of the trouble was a residue of Lynn Townsend's penchant for
moving his executives through the system rapidly, creating automotive
dilettantes. Paul Bergmoser determined quickly in his examination of
Chrysler's purchasing operations that "by my standards, purchasing
management was not equal to the task. One of the primary problems
was that so many different Chrysler people have served in so many
different assignments around the world without living as a true professional in any one of those assignments.

"You look at their records," explained Bergmoser. "Two years in
finance, two years in manufacturing, two in purchasing, two in quality
control, finance again. Somebody had the idea that management development was to make everybody a generalist. At Ford, we were dis-
ciplined. Every engineer was not run through the finance office, and
every finance guy was not put in a factory. I found it significant that
the top three people [in the Chrysler Purchasing Department] had
somewhere around six years' experience in purchasing—for the three
of them."

The problems in engineering were quite the opposite. Since the days of Zeder, Breer and Skelton, product engineers at Chrysler had held an elite position within the company. Townsend, whose primary interest after finance was in marketing, left engineers on their own. Riccardo handled them similarly. Cafiero, who had come up the manufacturing side, concentrated on long-term strategy. Somehow, supervision of the company's one source of a positive reputation had fallen between the cracks.

Chrysler engineers, good as they were, had become isolated and unpracticed in the crucial art of "handing off" their work to manufacturing. "We've got a bunch of engineers who've been up on a pedestal too damn long," said one manufacturing man. The pattern, he observed, was for product engineers to go straight from the Chrysler Institute, with its crack curriculum in design and product engineering, to the home office engineering building on Lynn Townsend Drive—seldom, if ever, pausing to pick up experience in the field. "We were constantly going back to them and saying this or that had to be redone because the original specs just didn't work." Virtually every year, he said, a needless argument over the under- or over-crowning of hoods and deck lids took place between the product people and the manufacturing people. Every year, he said, the extra time and expense were written off against manufacturing when, in fact, the fault lay with the design.

At the recommendation of Dick Vining, Iacocca called in a veteran engineer named George Butts from his post as Vice-President for Stamping and Assembly. Familiar with the whole sweep of the manufacturing and basic engineering process, Butts was well suited for quality control. A wide-eyed and tenacious executive who went after assignments like a bull terrier, Butts was a perfect disciple for Hans Matthias—an automotive Luke Skywalker to the old German's Yoda.

The most urgent task was to straighten out the R-body, by then not only badly out of synch with the market but also full of mechanical flaws. Emerging from the Lynch Road assembly plant in fits and starts, the cars were plagued with more than a hundred individual problems. Matthias had Butts single out the top ten, collecting his data from Sales, through which dealer complaints were channeled. Water leaks, wind noise, loose windows and a soft front fascia (a plasticized grille molding) that was too often malformed or off-color were high on the list. Matthias began to trace each back through the process.

A look at independent surveys and other measures of quality showed that the problems were not limited to the New Yorker and St. Regis models. Chrysler's overall warranty costs were higher than either Ford's or GM's. Quality tracking surveys conducted for the industry by Rogers Research showed Chrysler some 30 percent worse than

its two big brothers, measured according to early customer complaints. Flaws sometimes went uncorrected, despite reports, for years.
A faulty sealant on the lift-gate of the basic Dodge truck, for example,
was repeated for at least four model years until Matthias got engineers to work it out.

"On paper, they had a quality-control system," Matthias observed.
"But the thing didn't work because a lot of people were acting as
firemen instead of working on fundamentals." Correcting problems
after the fact was costly, Matthias would say, always adding, "Get it
right the first time through."

Over the years, there was a tendency during staff cutbacks to let go
of people who were not performing essential line tasks. More often
than not, quality-control personnel got the ax. It was not, insisted
George Butts, a matter of intention. He doubted senior management
even knew the cuts were made. As for Gene Cafiero's theory of total
participation in quality control, Matthias was old school. "The risk is
that when everybody is responsible for quality," he said, "nobody is.
You have to have somebody seeing whether the job's been done."
Chrysler, more often the victim of high absenteeism and line cutbacks
during the past decade, tended to shift blue-collar workers in and out
wherever gaps occurred. Under union seniority rules, a senior man
might be brought in from his job at a foundry to fill in on the assembly line—an entirely different process where his seniority was of little
use. Besides, apologies for manpower shortages meant little to the customer whose trunk didn't close. "The customer doesn't give a damn
why you have a problem," said Matthias, "—just that you have it."

The most serious problem Matthias found was attitudinal. Concern
by senior management only filtered down the line sporadically, leading Chrysler workers to conclude that their bosses only cared when
the heat was on. "The whole process starts with a lack of top-
management discipline," he observed. Coupled with the isolation in
which each department operated, the lack of discipline explained volumes about Chrysler's deteriorating quality image. The plant manager
at Lynch Road, Matthias discovered, was quite unaware that some
eight thousand parts, many major components, had been rejected
because they were flawed. His ignorance not only cost Chrysler
money; it guaranteed perpetuation of both the flaws and the laxity
on the line.

Butts and Matthias, with their collection of aphorisms, began
pounding away at the problem. "Don't schedule an invention" meant
that a given part or process had to be proven before it was put on the
schedule for mass production. "First-time-through capability" ensured
processes would be protected from costly mistakes. "Three strikes and
you're out" required that any part that turned up flawed more than

twice in the production process got reported to the vice-presidential level for corrective action. One of the most significant for Chrysler was "Design and process must be capable of meeting design intent." The manufacturing engineer's complaint that blueprints were too often dropped over the fence had to be answered. Matthias installed a system that dictated resolution of any differences between designer and builder before the manufacturing process began. The penalties for not having such a system were myriad.

One of the flaws in the R-body cars was rattling windows. In examining the blueprints, Butts's people found a flange that was originally designed to extend in a straight line across the door panel to hold the glass firmly in place. In the production cars, however, the flanges were always curved. Engineers at the Twinsburg, Ohio, stamping plant were contacted and reported that they'd never been able to make the flange straight; they just couldn't build it as it was designed. The problem was solved only when Butts took the problem all the way back to the original product engineers, who redesigned the piece so that it could be made properly.

Matthias created quality task forces. The window-flange problem was handled by a door task force, made up of seven permanent and six temporary engineers. "They eat, breathe and sleep doors," said Butts, sounding somewhat like a drill sergeant. The door boys, after learning everything there was to know about the R-body door systems, moved over to the K-car doors to apply their newfound knowledge—this time a full fifteen months before scheduled production. There were at least a dozen teams—from "driveability" to "squeaks and rattles"—with more being formed all the time. Each followed what Matthias called his "cradle to grave" approach: they were responsible for their particular systems from the designers' blueprint to the customer's garage, charged with working out every transaction along the way. "We must," Matthias would repeat, "get people off the idea of laying down their part of the job and walking away. We have to keep verifying that it's right all the way through."

Accordingly, outside suppliers were corraled. Approval of the design and process of 516 of the most critical parts of the '81 K-cars was signed after on-site inspections in the plants.

The quality improvement program, like everything else in the auto industry, took months to get off the ground. Iacocca rode herd on it throughout the dark days of 1979 and '80, with some success. By the end of the '80 model year, despite miserable sales, Chrysler's warranty costs were down significantly and its Rogers Quality Tracking Study results were improved by 32 percent over 1978, placing Chrysler slightly ahead of Ford and nearly comparable to General Motors.

The Japanese, whose quality had soared over the past decade, were still ahead, but it was significant that virtually every aphorism Matthias used and every goal he sought to achieve in Chrysler's quality control was reflected in the manner in which each of the Japanese manufacturers had worked to improve quality. Recent studies of Japanese quality-control practices by Americans—notably the University of Michigan's Robert E. Cole—suggested that the Japanese approach to product design, as Cole observed, ". . . is structured to build cooperative relationships with all those who will work with the design, including and indeed especially feedback from production workers."[1]

Cole also found what Matthias had been working on at Chrysler: ". . . because U.S. quality personnel have commonly not had the authority to stop the release of engineering designs and have not reported to the highest levels in the corporation, they have been in a weak position to resist the pressures for shortening product cycle time at the expense of quality."

Aside from the obvious lack of experience in Chrysler's purchasing management, Paul Bergmoser found that the company lacked a reputation for reliability among its suppliers. Smaller suppliers in particular, while they felt they were treated with relative fairness by the company, were often unsure they could count on any continuity of business with Chrysler. Bergmoser discovered that Chrysler had a habit of changing horses in midstream, sometimes deciding on a new sourcing scheme right in the middle of a model year. The result was all too often tit for tat. Chrysler, eventually, could not count on its suppliers for a steady flow of parts.

At Ford, Bergmoser had used a sophisticated material flow system that allowed managers to trace by computer virtually every part, its specifications and quantities. "We could even trace a railcar by number," he claimed. At Chrysler, by contrast, such systems remained unfinished and therefore useless. Because installation of a flow analysis is quite expensive, Chrysler's system started and stopped over the years, according to the company's fortunes and the availability of cash.

It was painfully clear that Chrysler's lack of purchasing control and traffic monitoring adversely affected product quality. Although the purchasing people appeared to drive hard bargains in initial negotiations with potential suppliers, there was no follow-through. At Ford, part of the purchasing job was to see to it that the acquired merchandise met specifications—just as parts made in-house had to meet specs. Understaffed Chrysler just didn't have the slots for quality-control personnel in purchasing. As a result, ill-fitting and otherwise flawed parts flowed into the assembly plants and bad cars rolled out. Chrysler had particular problems with plastic moldings supplied from the outside. The infamous soft front-end fascias on the New Yorker came in from a Massachusetts supplier with bubbles and ripples and sometimes colors that didn't match the rest of the car.

Because Chrysler depended more on outside suppliers than either Ford or GM, it was more vulnerable to such problems—and because it was smaller than the other two, it lacked the purchasing clout needed to keep suppliers in line. Big suppliers in particular, annoyed by Chrysler's inconsistencies, often threatened to discontinue business or simply not renew contracts. Little wonder when, for example, Chrysler changed the design on the side mirror of the New Yorker just weeks before final manufacture and assembly was to begin in 1978. TWR, the Cleveland-based supplier that had made the mirror exactly according to original Chrysler specs, had to swallow $1.94 per mirror in building a revised design, put together on a raw sketch supplied by Chrysler's pre-production team in the Clairepointe plant.

One of Bergmoser's first acts was to restore quality-control people to the purchasing staff. "We think you can afford those people more than you can poor quality," he told the staff.

A second major contribution of both Bergmoser and Matthias, working under Iacocca's mandate, was to restore timing to product development. Even without major changes in the design of power trains— engines and transmissions—the cycle of development is about thirty-three months in the car business. The more pronounced the change in design from an existing vehicle, the longer the development cycle. New parts mean new tools to build those parts. Machine-tool companies must be engaged to design and build the equipment needed to produce these new parts precisely and consistently. Each new part must be fitted alongside other parts to see if the mesh is right, the performance adequate and the durability sufficient. Step by step, the car must be rebuilt, and each step requires adequate time. In the 1970s, Chrysler had a number of lapses in development timing, the most notorious being the late launch of the R-body.

Delays in the program began right at the beginning. Management, right up to president Gene Cafiero, vacillated on basic design decisions. By the time they were made, the program was four months behind. As Bergmoser observed, "You can wave your arms, you can scream, you can even spend premium money, whatever; you can never make up for that lost time."

Promotion for the launch of the New Yorker and St. Regis came out on time, heralded by cocktail receptions in Detroit and at New York's Tavern-on-the-Green, but on introduction day, many dealers had nothing to show customers. "We went out," said Hal Sperlich, "fired our marketing salvo, put people into the showrooms, and *then* shipped the cars. It was terrible." Not until early winter did the dealers begin receiving merchandise in the quantities needed to sell the cars.

"We missed the launch," admitted John Riccardo flatly. Many people at Chrysler blamed Gene Cafiero, the chief operating officer. *"He* missed the launch," charged a former executive. "That's something you just don't do."

In searching through the debris of the R-body catastrophe, Paul Bergmoser found plenty of Chrysler employees who readily admitted they hadn't done their part of the job well, but whose explanations were almost uniformly the same: "Because I didn't have the time to do a good job."

"Basically," said Bergmoser, "it's management discipline." Under the new regime, every executive involved in a program knows when the preliminary, intermediate and final decisions on each of the elements of the car must be made. In January of 1980, Bergmoser was making final decisions on the design of vehicles to be introduced in the spring of 1983. Within a matter of a month, he was "putting to bed" designs for the 1984 model year. Each successive stage of development had a specific date for completion.

The strict control of schedules was hardly a new concept at Chrysler. It has been an integral part of the auto business since Henry Ford I opened the first moving assembly line. It was institutionalized under Alfred Sloan in the 1920s. A Chrysler man who left the company at the beginning of the Seventies was surprised to hear that such controls were lacking. "It wasn't like that when I was there," he protested. "We always had strict schedule controls: a part was made, a sample part approved, it would go to pilot, it would be built. We had dates for everything. . . . Controls have been in existence as long as the auto industry's been around. Without them it would be like being a soldier and not knowing 'hut-two-three-four, left-right-left-right.'" The schedules had not disappeared; they had merely been neglected. It was, as Bergmoser said, "a matter of discipline."

The sales bank and the perverse system it engendered served to eradicate any sense of discipline from the company's sales force. Throughout Chrysler's marketing system, Gar Laux found plenty wrong. As John Riccardo had noted, the sales bank itself was like dope. By 1979, Laux observed, it had reduced dealer relations to little more than a quiz show giveaway contest. Five unwanted cars from the bank could get a dealer a genuine California hot tub. Ten won him a trip to Tahiti and twenty-five would send him around the world.

Another knotty problem was Chrysler's participation in the leasing business. A by-product again of the sales bank, leasing provided another conduit for cars built without specific order, Laux observed. Instead of selling cars by the fleetload to established car rental outfits like Hertz and Avis, Chrysler leased its own products. A very expensive string was attached to every vehicle and, eventually, they all ended up back in Chrysler's lap. Laux didn't appreciate the danger of the policy until after the Iranian oil crisis, when Chrysler found itself the none-too-proud owner of nearly seventy thousand used cars, saddled with millions of dollars in carrying charges—above and beyond the vehicles in the sales bank.

With so little opportunity to sell cars to dealers, Chrysler's sales force had no idea how to work its dealer body. Laux had to institute a training program to teach them the rudiments of a 30-60-90 ordering system.

He also realized early on that Chrysler simply had too many dealers. There were 4,800, compared with 6,700 for Ford and 11,500 for GM. With Chrysler feeding only about 10 percent of the car market, its dealers were averaging only slightly more than 300 cars a year, whereas Ford dealers averaged 500 and GM 600. Chrysler was simply spread too thin.

Even within those shallow waters, the distribution of sales was skewed to a relatively small group of dealers. Six hundred of them handled half the sales generated nationwide, and through a larger group of not many more than 2,000 dealers, fully 82 percent of Chrysler vehicles were sold. That meant that more than 2,500 Chrysler-Plymouth and Dodge dealers allotted among themselves a mere 18 percent of Chrysler Corporation's annual sales volume.

"Some dealers," observed Jerry Pyle, who was, after Greenwald, the first direct steal Iacocca managed from Ford, "are like cockroaches. They don't live particularly well, but they're almost impossible to kill." In hundreds of instances, Chrysler had dealers it would have been better off without. Among them were 196 "company-owned stores" established under Lynn Townsend's Marketing Investment Division (see Chapter Four). Laux was determined to whittle that group down to a minimum. A company-owned store, he maintained, "is just about as unfair a form of competition as I know." By the end of 1980, he had squeezed the number of MID franchises down to a tolerable 35.

Chrysler's overabundance of dealers also reflected a maldistribution of franchises. Little care had been taken, Laux concluded, to spread the wealth and allow enough room for individual dealers to prosper within a reasonable marketing territory. Highways are built, cities grow or shrink and demographics shift; the need to review dealer locations is constant. Chrysler's marketing and sales staff had let it slip. Too often, new franchises were allowed to open inside the territory of existing franchises. In the late Seventies, marketing management acquiesced as a new Chrysler-Plymouth showroom opened in a small midwestern town where another Chrysler-Plymouth dealer had opened his doors just a few years earlier. "They both went broke," said Laux.

The image of the company and, more importantly, its cars, suffered. Because the sales forces for Chrysler-Plymouth and Dodge had been merged into one, the local Dodge dealer did business with the same company rep who called on the Chrysler-Plymouth dealer. There was no sense of distinction between the dealers, and it bled over onto the cars. Buyers never seemed to know that Dodge cars are supposed to be more upscale than Plymouths, just as a Pontiac outranks a Chevy.

"The first thing we did," said Laux, "was to separate the field force. There has to be a definition of a group." With the need for greater efficiency in the manufacturing process, which tended to increase the commonality of parts and blur the physical differences between the compact Dodge Aspen and the Plymouth Volare, for example, it was all the more important to separate the marketing arms of the two divisions.

As elsewhere in the organization, there was almost a total lack of staff to monitor operations. There was virtually no marketing plan at Chrysler. There were, said Laux, "great chasms within the company as far as people were concerned . . . almost a strained relationship between the company and its dealers." There was, Laux concluded quite quickly and sadly, "no discipline in the system."

Changes in Chrysler's quality control, purchasing and marketing were well underway before Jerry Greenwald finally arrived in Highland Park in late April of 1979. He saw quickly that the perceived function of the controller's office was to be an operation that "kept books." Staffers performed financial analysis only on request, and exchanges between financial staff and operating staff were minimal. When there was contact, the tacit assumption was that the finance people were servants of the operating people. "As a result," said Greenwald, "Chrysler has not attracted a lot of strong-willed people over the years to the Controller's side of the business."

Ken Kerr, then Assistant Corporate Controller, tried to explain to Greenwald that Chrysler's financial employees had been raised in a system that didn't demand much of them. Under Townsend, the controller's office was told not to concern itself with analysis, since Townsend and Riccardo had financial backgrounds themselves and could handle any board-level discussions. "They had their own ideas," said Kerr.

John Riccardo made more use of the finance staff, but the rigorous control functions that permeated Ford's and General Motors' financial operations were, at best, scattered around Chrysler—and nothing like the integral part of daily business activity they were at the larger companies.

At Ford, Greenwald had been used to an elaborate system of financial oversight in which every program was subjected to the scrutiny of a number of independent analyses. If the marketing staff was considering a new sales program, there would be a controller there within the Marketing Department with a complete quantitative history of similar sales programs and a report on how they worked and if they worked. The marketing controller would be intimately involved in the development of the program. A staff controller was assigned to play devil's advocate, further testing the program's worth before it came within earshot of senior management.

At Chrysler, the marketing staff put programs together without benefit of such advice, marching in to top management and requesting approval. More than likely, John Riccardo would perform the analysis simply by asking questions, relying on his own memory of marketing programs and his own financial background.

At Ford, periodic reports on the state of operations were produced like clockwork. On a monthly, quarterly and yearly basis, in varying degrees of depth, the books were closed, the data analyzed and projections made for several periods ahead. Keeping such a system both required and encouraged discipline. When actual operating results differed significantly from projections, those responsible had to explain. Once a year, marketing and finance people would sit down and work out how many of each model car and truck they planned to sell according to estimates of what the total market would be and what share of that market the company could reasonably win. A plan for capacity would be mapped out several years ahead, determining what needed to be done to fill those market projections. Finally, the whole strategy for product development and product cycle was built within the parameters of volume and capacity projections—what models would be replaced, what power trains were needed and when. Then all three major plans were melded into one grand operating and financing plan which determined the course the company would take for the next five years. Each year, that operating plan would be updated.

At Chrysler, much of the data required to assemble such detailed operating plans were simply not kept. Greenwald had been on the job for only a matter of weeks when the automotive market simply fell apart under the strain of the Iranian oil cutoff. He was present at a board meeting, not then as a member but in his capacity as Corporate Controller, when a request for an extensive financial report was made. Lee Iacocca turned to Greenwald and asked him to supply the data. Greenwald recalled nodding as if the request were routine but feeling considerable *angst*, knowing as he did that the numbers needed to put such a report together were going to be hard to come by.

Curiously, old Chrysler hands insisted that they *had* systems and that the difficulties that arose when Iacocca's ex-Ford executives moved in were largely the result of differing methodologies. "It was a very difficult time," said Ken Kerr. "Ford forms read down—north to south—while Chrysler forms read across—west to east. The terminology was different. But it was difficult for them as well as for us. I'd say the difficulty was equally distributed."

Greenwald insisted that it was much more than a problem of translation. "With financial controls," he explained, "there's only a ten-degree difference between having the appearance of having them and actually having them. Unless you've lived in one and seen and smelled and tasted the difference, it's awfully hard to know what that last ten degrees mean."

Installing the Ford system meant not only teaching new techniques and a new language, it meant the diversion of personnel at a time in which there was an overwhelming need to cut back. During the first winter and early spring of Iacocca's presidency, some 8,500 white-collar Chrysler workers either received the pink slip or were encouraged without much subtlety to take early retirement. There was no way Greenwald could install a whole new layer of staff financial controllers *and* build a group of controllers within each department. By necessity, the Chrysler finance staff was at least a third thinner than what Greenwald had been used to at Ford. While the modified system could not duplicate the checks and balances achieved at Ford, it was less bureaucratic and more flexible—attributes Chrysler would certainly need during the trying days ahead.

With the beginnings of a reporting system taking shape, Iacocca set about the task of instilling a sense of autonomy into the individual components of the company—this time with an appreciation of their position within the corporation. He began again by breaking the business down to its elements: the seven major systems that make up an automobile, then the eighty-eight subsystems—how each rated against the best in the class in the entire business, including competitors and suppliers, how much each cost and how profitable or unprofitable each was.

"Take our air conditioning business," Iacocca ticked off. Here were optional pieces of equipment costing $500 to $600 apiece—for Chrysler alone, a $400-million-a-year business. It was a matter of asking the most fundamental questions: does Chrysler's air conditioning unit do what it's supposed to do, which is to provide good, clean, cold air on a 100-degree day within three minutes of start-up? Once satisfied with performance, one must assess the costs relative to the competition. "It's not just that GM and Ford will underprice you," insisted Iacocca. "There's a whole group of people out there in the aftermarket trying to make people buy hang-on air conditioners. You've got to earn the right to schedule it as part of your car. You've got to know costs;

you've got to know investments and you've got to know your accounted profit."

It was little different for whole operating entities. The company's Warren truck-assembly plant, for instance, employing more than 7,500 people making vans, trucks and recreational vehicles and generating nearly $660 million in business annually was, Iacocca was told, unprofitable. "Why?" he asked. "Too complicated," offered the manufacturing people. Closer examination revealed that one of those complications was the maintenance of 3,900 different paint offerings for the vehicles produced, among them seven shades of white. "What the Christ!" bellowed Iacocca. "White is white! Creamy white and plain white? Okay! But why do we have seven different whites?"

The rainbow of truck-color offerings might have pleased a handful of picky fleet customers, but it meant hours of down time during which paint guns had to be cleaned and restocked with differing shades. Like the 115 separate rear-driveshaft offerings that divided job lots into volumes too small even to entice an outside supplier to build, it defied every rule of thumb about economies of scale. The task, begun by Gene Cafiero, of simplifying the maze of parts at Chrysler clearly had a long way to go.

Many of the inefficiencies were outgrowths of Chrysler's relative size, but some were self-inflicted. Iacocca, for example, found that Chrysler was in some cases doubling up needlessly. One Detroit-area stamping plant, ostensibly pressing fenders for compacts, was in the habit of changing dies solely to fill orders for a few thousand fenders for export. "They had to shut down all the press lines, take out all the punches and dies and then put them back in," said a bewildered Iacocca. "Productivity gets shot to hell on complexity or short runs. They should be building 500,000 fenders—banging them out. That's how you make money. Too many different pieces in the stamping plants will kill them off."

By the first quarter of 1979, Iacocca had come to the uncomfortable conclusion that Chrysler's problems were so pervasive that salvation was clearly years off. His instinct was to address them as a medical team would handle an incoming chopper of wounded soldiers in a field hospital. "We had to pick the patients who were going to live."

As he had done at Ford during the 1974–75 slump, Iacocca cut all around, but not into Chrysler's future-product program. He could do little but try to ensure that the 1980 Chrysler Cordoba and Dodge Mirada intermediates, due out the following fall, kept to schedule. He perceived immediately that the compact K-body, scheduled to replace the Volare and Aspen in the fall of 1980, was the car that would probably determine the medium-term profitability of Chrysler and came to call the program "the family jewels." Iacocca gave Sperlich almost

free rein to see to it that the car came out on time and right. The
front-wheel-drive compacts were the work of designer Dick Macadam, chief engineer Sid Jeffe and Vining. Iacocca liked it. (There
was very little he could have done if he hadn't.) Actually, Iacocca
abhorred the design of the dashboard and ordered it changed as soon
as possible.

Non-product expenditures, however, quickly came under the knife.
An early victim was Gene Cafiero's $160 million transaxle plant in
Richmond, Indiana. "What the hell do we need a new transaxle plant
for?" Iacocca snapped at Dick Vining during a capital investment review meeting. "We don't," admitted Vining. After the federal government turned down an application for a $250 million guaranteed loan
for the facility, there was hardly a whimper in defense of the Richmond project, and it was killed. The transaxles, automatic front-wheel-
drive components for the K-cars, were built instead at an existing
transaxle facility in nearby Kokomo. "By going to Kokomo," said Vining, "we saved $42 million in investment, $46 million in launching
costs and $30 million in continued fixed costs. All we needed was the
turnaround room at Kokomo." He might have added that Chrysler
succeeded in getting a $50 million federal loan to help expand the old
plant.

The press, with little interest and limited access, paid scant attention to the dreary process of internal cost-cutting, as long as it didn't
involve dramatic staff cuts or plant closings. They focused instead on
Iacocca's alleged night raids into Ford headquarters. Even there, the
pickings were slim in the early months. Matthias, Bergmoser and Laux
were all retirees and couldn't be touted as "steals." Little heed was
paid to the hiring of Eddie Mehrer, the Wixom plant manager who
had kept a tight rein on Ford's luxury Lincoln Continental and Mark
production. Iacocca brought Mehrer in early on to run Lynch Road,
where the R-bodies were being made . . . and being made badly.

No one printed an account of one of Iacocca's more facetious attempts to attract Ford talent, either. Half in jest—but only half—he
had T-shirts emblazoned BORED WITH FORD? mailed anony-
mously to fourteen former colleagues in Dearborn. Most scurried to
hide the evidence, fearing retribution from Mr. Ford and the new
management. Only the bold and singularly irreverent Bennett Bidwell,
Corporate Vice-President for Ford's Car and Truck Group, reacted in
kind, returning his souvenir to Iacocca's Bloomfield Hills home re-
inscribed in Magic Marker: "BORED? NO. PISSED? YES."

None of the fourteen took Iacocca's bait, but Henry Ford II did get
wind of the prank. A mini-investigation was launched at Ford headquarters to unmask the potential traitors.

On March 1, Iacocca announced a genuine robbery. Word that a "major announcement" about Chrysler was about to be made even stopped trading of the company's shares on the New York Stock Exchange. But the surprise had more of an effect on the advertising world than it did on Chrysler's fortunes. At a midday Waldorf-Astoria press conference, the new Chrysler president announced he was signing on Kenyon & Eckhardt to handle $120 million worth of Chrysler business, replacing both Young & Rubicam and Batten Barton Durstine & Osborne on all of Chrysler's car, truck and corporate advertising. "I feel like I just bought the New York Yankees and got myself Murderers' Row," quipped Iacocca.

K & E had handled Ford and Lincoln-Mercury advertising over a thirty-four-year span, producing for Ford's corporate campaign the well-known "Ford Has a Better Idea" theme and establishing Lincoln-Mercury under "The Sign of the Cat." In the Sixties, K & E's Leo Arthur Kelmenson and John Morrissey had worked with Iacocca and Gar Laux on the original Mustang campaign. Ford was to learn that the agency was resigning $75 million in annual billings just three hours before Iacocca told the press in New York.

Y & R had represented Chrysler-Plymouth and had done the corporate ad campaign that featured ex-astronaut Neil Armstrong pitching Chrysler's engineering expertise. B B D & O handled Dodge car and truck business as well as the advertising for the Mitsubishi-made Dodge Colt and Plymouth Arrow subcompacts. Although the hundreds of employees employed by the two agencies in Detroit were stunned by the sudden dismissal, there were private expressions of relief from some after years of rocky relations with Chrysler's old marketing team.

Although the agency switch represented a public relations coup, it also represented a potential contradiction in marketing strategy for Chrysler, or at least a reflection of the financial dilemma the company was facing. At the same time Gar Laux was working to separate the field forces and the images of the Chrysler-Plymouth and Dodge divisions, a single ad agency was taking over the two accounts. Iacocca justified the amalgamation on grounds that the agency was fully capable of developing separate campaigns and that the separation of field forces provided more intramural competition than it did distinction of product image. "The company couldn't afford two agencies for what in effect were the same cars," argued Iacocca. K & E, he said, was a small agency—"one that would go right to the jugular." It was a matter of cutting costs—the total ad budget would be cut from $150 million to $120—and getting "a lean, creative agency with a track record in autos. Only K & E fitted that," reasoned Iacocca. Besides, Leo Kelmenson was an old friend, familiar with the ways and wants of Chrysler's new boss.

As for Kenyon & Eckhardt, it was the old story of a new adventure. The deal gave the agency an unprecedented role in Chrysler's marketing by placing agency representatives on the company's marketing and product-planning committees—and at $120 million, it was the biggest single piece of advertising in the business, next to Campbell-Ewald's awesome $160 million Chevrolet account.

Because of Chrysler's rapidly deteriorating reputation, the need for new marketing and sales talent became high priority. Gar Laux finally bit the bullet and signed on full-time as Chrysler's Vice-President for Marketing, replacing R. K. Brown. Brown accepted Iacocca's suggestion of early retirement gracefully and on generous terms that left him living comfortably alongside a golf course on the California coast.

Before Brown went, however, he opened Iacocca's eyes to the shocking world of the Chrysler sales bank. Iacocca was, of course, aware of the system, but he had never fully understood the extent to which it dominated marketing and even financial policy for the corporation. The revelation came at a meeting with a group of Chrysler dealers in Las Vegas in mid-February. It was also the midpoint of the first quarter and Iacocca was beginning to wonder if the company was making or losing money on the shipment of cars and trucks. Brown and Bill Bivens, his sales vice-president, came to his hotel room with a request to fund a big retail promotion campaign in March, the last month of the quarter. The sales bank included close to 100,000 units, stashed away somewhere with only about thirty selling days left until the books closed.

"When the hell do we sell those?" snapped Iacocca, knowing a potential swing in income of hundreds of millions of dollars rode on the answer. "We'll sell them," said Brown confidently. "Just look at the last ten days of March for the last ten years. That's a spring ritual around here. Everybody goes into the Tank."

"What's the Tank?" asked Iacocca.

Brown cheerfully explained the system: marshaling the corporate sales force, divvying up the bank—100, 200, 500 units each to sell—then dialing through the night to dealers like boiler-room investment salesmen.

"Yeah?" shot back Iacocca. "Well, you never had one *this* big. How the hell are you going to sell 100,000 units in ten days?"

When the last ten-day sales report for the quarter came in, Iacocca was stunned and depressed. "It was the biggest shock of my life that made me almost throw in the towel early." The ritual had been played out. During those last ten days, 66,423 vehicles had been sold, compared to an average of 26,000 for each ten days since the first of January. The dealers had waited for their fix, and it came like clockwork—bargain rates and special deals. It was a clearance sale. "I'd seen them at Ford and I knew that you didn't get money for retail unless you bought wholesale," said Iacocca. "But I thought it was just an occasional program. I didn't know it was a way of life." When interest rates, which determined carrying costs for both the company and its dealers, began to rise dramatically, it became a killer force. It would take a major overdose to make Chrysler go cold turkey.

The turmoil in the months after March of 1979 delayed a number of changes begun in Iacocca's first four months by diverting scarce personnel to the task of winning government aid, but at least the process had begun and, by the end of 1980, new faces were behind almost every executive desk on the fifth floor. Most of the old guard were gone. A few emerged with greater responsibility under Iacocca, but by the time the company was touting itself as "The New Chrysler Corporation," it was indeed in the hands of a whole new management team.

Iacocca's quarterly review system seeped inexorably deeper into the organization and by itself inspired a revolution in attitudes. Jerry Greenwald's Ford-inspired financial control systems began to take root. An old colleague of Greenwald's from Venezuela, Robert S. (Steve) Miller, joined up as Assistant Treasurer and almost single-handedly maneuvered Chrysler through its ordeal with four hundred lenders. Jerry Pyle, another fair-haired young executive stolen off Ford's managerial fast track, dominated the new sales organization, bringing with him Jack Givens. Dick Dauch, a former Purdue fullback, had left the comfort of Volkswagen of America and dragged nearly a dozen young manufacturing managers along with him. Dave Platt gave up a career in Ford Purchasing to join up. Baron Bates, a VW public relations vice-president, returned to Chrysler after more than twenty years. None was a cast-off and all abandoned relatively secure careers. They did it for the thrill and for Lee Iacocca.

Many of those outsiders who thoughtfully measured Chrysler's chances for survival during the two years of crisis that lay ahead admitted that the changes at the top were important, but they were quick to observe that a giant corporate dinosaur does not turn around very easily. It would take years before the mentality of a company Chrysler's size could be changed significantly.

The rude shock of Iran, as much as the new names on the executive suites, accelerated the pace of the massive transformation Iacocca had set in motion. Chrysler's survival depended on the outcome of a race between Iacocca's internal revolution and an implausible conspiracy of external events.

CHAPTER ELEVEN

"The Day the Shah Left Town"

Detroit went into 1979 struggling with the intricacies of the new CAFE game. The degree of difficulty had been raised a notch, to 19 miles per gallon, and the Big Three were all experimenting with ways of fine-tuning their respective averages. There was plenty of small-car capacity, but the little cars weren't selling. Three-month supplies of Omnis and Horizons, 113-day supplies of Ford Pintos and an average of 113 days for domestically built compacts stood in stark contrast to an average of only 36 days' worth of luxury cars. Imported cars had drifted down to 16 percent of the market in December, and the Japanese were back up to a four-month stock of cars.

General Motors started the trend and the others picked up on it: to coax buyers out of bigger cars, or at least into cars with smaller, more efficient engines, the companies began raising the price on larger displacement V-8 engines by hundreds of dollars and offering discounts on anything small and fuel-thrifty. GM was still toying with the idea of converting one Chevette plant back to mid-size production. AMC faced the costly prospect of having to scrap outright some eight thousand four-cylinder engines because, recalled company president W. Paul Tippett, Jr., "We couldn't sell them." Ford, finally on the brink of introducing its down-sized Lincolns and Marks, faced a sudden surge of sentimentality. "Dealers were saying 'Ship us some of those big babies,'" said Philip Caldwell, "'cause they're the last of the big ones.'"

Halfway across the world, a blue-and-white Boeing 727 took a last lazy circle over the city of Tehran and headed east-southeast toward Egypt. Its pilot was Shah Mohammed Reza Pahlavi, and hordes demonstrating in Tehran's streets below were subjecting themselves to another form of tyranny under the religious leadership of Ayatollah Ruhollah Khomeini. January 16, 1979, "the day the Shah left town," as Iacocca would ruefully mark the day, set in motion a chain of events that would virtually seal Chrysler's fate.

Iran, at the time, was providing only 2.5 percent of U.S. oil needs,[1] but strikes in the Iranian fields plus subsequent production disruptions brought about a drop of some 17.5 million barrels in the Middle East pipeline to the United States. Reports at the time predicted a period of "inconvenience" for Americans in the coming year. Jimmy Carter said in a February press conference that "the situation is not now critical," but he warned that "it could get worse."

It did. The new Iranian government goaded OPEC's militant factions into further price increases. On April 1, OPEC crude was posted at $14.54 a barrel. By that time, the embolism created months back in Iran had worked its way through the petro-pipeline to the U.S. market, but the cause of the disruption was considerably more complicated.

Anticipating OPEC price hikes after a comfortable two-year hiatus, the multinational oil companies began building huge stockpiles of fuel during 1977, but even they were not enough to feed the economic boom and the unprecedented surge in American travel that occurred during 1977 and '78. From record levels at the end of '77, U.S. reserves dropped 20 percent by the time Iran was blossoming into full-scale revolution.

As more and more cars on the road required unleaded gas to meet federal emissions standards, demand for unleaded rose beyond the oil industry's capacity to refine it. More crude and newer facilities were needed to make unleaded gasoline, and Department of Energy controls over domestic refining capacity made it difficult for the oil companies to adapt to the new demand. Moreover, because the mandated fuel efficiency of American cars as much as promised a flattening and eventually decreasing gasoline market, the oil companies were reluctant to invest in additional capacity they would not need after three or four years.

The Energy Department also controlled both the balance of fuels produced by the refineries and their eventual allocation. Suddenly concerned that use of available crude for gasoline would preclude production of sufficient supplies of heating oil for the following winter, DOE officials abruptly ordered a shift of refining capacity from gasoline to heating distillates. "All these factors," concluded Robert Stobaugh and Daniel Yergin, writing in *Foreign Affairs,* "amplified an overall oil shortage of 2–4 percent into a nationwide gasoline shortage of about 12 percent."[2]

The problems caused by the confluence of these factors were further exacerbated by the Department of Energy's convoluted system of fuel allocation. The programs for distribution were so confused that even the DOE was unable to predict where, if anyplace, the next shortages would occur. Back in December of 1978, Deputy Energy Secretary John O'Leary had admitted, "It's a real mess and it's caused by our controls. There is no one else to blame."[3]

In April, Jimmy Carter outlined a new energy policy that called for the decontrol of oil prices on a gradual basis, combined with a windfall profits tax to prevent the big oil companies from reaping "obscene" profits from the new high prices. The income from the tax, proposed Carter, would be used to encourage the development of a whole range of alternative energy sources—from shale oil to windmills. Conspicuously absent from Carter's grab bag of alternatives was nuclear power. Not two weeks earlier, the reactor at Three Mile Island in central Pennsylvania had sprung a leak which, following as it did just twelve days after the release of a new Hollywood nuclear-reactor-disaster film entitled *The China Syndrome,* brought about a virtual shutdown of nuclear development in the United States.

While a number of congressional energy experts, including Henry "Scoop" Jackson, were complaining about Carter's scheme to decontrol oil, service stations in the Los Angeles area began experiencing gasoline delivery problems. By month's end, California was a madhouse of gas lines; fights were breaking out as five hundred or more cars and campers lined up for what was feared to be the last gallon on earth. By the second week in May, the California energy crisis had made the cover of *Newsweek,* replete with photos of mimes and brass ensembles entertaining the service station lines and vignettes like the one about the pregnant woman forced to battle for her place in line. Folks in the East and Midwest smiled condescendingly, safe in the knowledge that this was an idiosyncrasy of the West—poetic justice meted out to the profligates of Mellowland. "It's Been Fun," chimed a headline in the New York *Times,* "But California Suspects the Party Is Over."

Californians, on the other hand, screamed that they were being shortchanged on federal oil distribution schedules. Easterners discarded the claim as a campaign bid by California Governor Jerry Brown, who was still aiming to unseat Carter as the Democratic nominee in 1980. Brown did, however, act swiftly against the crisis, following the lead of thirteen counties by instituting statewide odd-even gas rationing (based on the last digit of license plates) as a means of curbing the panic.

Then in June, like Tinkerbell in the children's bedroom, the gas shortage alighted on the East Coast, hitting, of all places, Washington and New York. Suddenly, the energy crisis was real, though no more explainable than when it had blighted the West. As they had in California, gas station owners closed up early and shut down completely on weekends. Ten days before the Fourth of July holiday weekend, 95 percent of New York City's stations were closed Saturday and Sunday. After three weeks of shortages, Washington stores were beginning to suffer economically. D.C. cab drivers staged a one-day protest strike against the alleged inadequacy of a ten-cent-per-mile fare increase. No more than fifty stations throughout the entire state of Connecticut were open the weekend of June 24. The Hamptons, Manhattan's summer respite, were ghost towns.

Gas prices in the New York metropolitan area ranged from $1.05 to $1.60 a gallon; less than sixty days before, 75 cents had been a common price. Cab drivers and service station operators, those savvy cynics whose economic prognostications typically outperform the documented predictions of professional economists, were saying the whole thing was a hoax; that as soon as the price of gas leveled off between $1.20 and $1.30 so that the oil companies, or the government, or whoever ran the conspiracy, got what they wanted, the shortages would vanish and there'd be gas aplenty.

". . . In the current situation," Tulane University psychologist Dr. Frederick Koenig said, "there's no explanation. So the natural and normal thing to do is to look for a conspiracy to explain the shortage."[4] Like a flashback from 1974, the unsinkable story of loaded oil tankers anchored off New York harbor awaiting word of the price hike surfaced again. Secretary of Transportation Brock Adams ordered the Coast Guard to report any such "loitering oil tankers." Democratic Congressman Peter Peyser of Westchester, New York, charged that Gulf Oil had 30 million gallons of gasoline stored between New York and Philadelphia while the corridor sputtered for lack of fuel. Fear and distrust ricocheted from coast to coast, culminating in a gasoline riot in Levittown, Pennsylvania, a prototypical American suburb built on the foundation of an automobile-powered society. Jimmy Carter was in Tokyo at the time, scrapping for a sense of control over the Western alliance, and OPEC set the price of crude at $23.50 a barrel—ten times its cost before the 1973 embargo.

"There is an easy chance," UCLA econometric forecaster Larry Kimball had said, "that this could delay the purchase of durable goods."[5] Kimball had only to look closely at sales patterns in the biggest durable goods industry of them all to see that the delay had already begun. In early May, Chrysler's Hal Sperlich had been in Los Angeles on business and was leaving his hotel for the airport when he noticed some of the lines building at service stations. "Eight in the morning," he thought, glancing at his watch. "Nothing too unusual about that. Business day just getting underway." Then he realized he'd left his watch set on Detroit time. In fact, it was only 5 A.M. "We are in big trouble," he thought to himself.

Even in the Midwest, where no serious shortages ever occurred, station closings became commonplace. Resorts dried up. As each summer weekend approached, Americans tuned in their radios to get the latest on service station openings the way winter weekenders listen for ski conditions. It mattered little psychologically that back in California, where it had all started, gasoline prices had settled into a stable range somewhat over $1.10 a gallon and the long lines of May miraculously had disappeared.

Springtime in Detroit is marked by a burst in sales more than by a blossoming of flowers. In anticipation of the vacation season to come, devotees of the outdoors—users of motor homes and recreational vehicles (RVs)—begin buying even in the dead of winter. Chrysler sales executives knew the pattern well; the company had become the leader in the RV and motor home business, supplying cabs and engines to the RV assemblers, who are clustered in northern Indiana as well as in Wisconsin.

Frightened by talk of oil cutoffs in the Middle East, traditional buyers began hanging back as early as December 1978. By March, RV sales were off 26 percent. In May, Winnebago, one of the best-known names in the RV industry, shut down for six weeks, and by June, Chrysler's once-booming business with the trade had been literally decimated, falling to less than a tenth of its normal levels.

In April, Jeeps, the darlings of the off-road, four-wheel-drive set, showed a sales decline for the first time since 1976. In May, vans, Chrysler's other claim to U.S. industry leadership, plunged 42 percent. "The van market," reported Iacocca, "has dropped like a rock."

A renaissance in public transportation appeared to be taking place. Amtrak reservations soared 128 percent that spring. The California coastal resorts, normally scenic links in a chain of campers and motor homes gliding along the Pacific shore on Highway 101, felt a 50 percent drop in tourism. L.A. simply didn't have the buses to handle the sudden surge of commuters. The bicycle business began a boom that would continue for years.

Diesel-powered vehicles picked up new support as customers reasoned that the government wouldn't allow truckers and farmers to run dry. The VW diesel Rabbit, with a city EPA rating of 40 mpg, quickly became the most sought-after car on the market. Even big Oldsmobiles, Cadillacs and Mercedes offering diesel options were scarfed up off the lots. Chrysler, however, had no diesels.

Subcompact sales exploded—anything with decent mileage sold out. Among the biggest sellers early on, along with the Chevette, Mustang and even Pinto, was the Plymouth Horizon. Waiting lists for the Horizon and its Dodge twin, the Omni, extended to twelve weeks. At the beginning of April, the combined days-of-supply of the two cars was the lowest of any small car on the market. Iacocca desperately sought additional engines to free production from VW's 300,000 annual limit, but to no avail (see Chapter One). The one car Chrysler had to meet the market of the moment was locked out.

Japanese imports, which at the end of January were sitting on the docks in California waiting for a 129-day backlog to clear up, were simply swept up in the gas scare. By the end of May, the Japanese had led all imports to a record 24.3 percent of the U.S. car market and inventories were at a third the levels they had been in January.

There was no bigger winner that spring, however, than General Motors. The April introduction of the new, fuel-efficient, compact X-cars from four of GM's five automotive divisions had been planned for years. The cars were eight hundred pounds lighter and twenty inches shorter than the Chevy Nova class cars they replaced, but interior dimensions and the capacity to seat up to six passengers had been preserved. The weight and space savings were achieved largely through the use of front-wheel drive, and GM advertising was geared to dramatize the benefits. Most of all, the new, smaller cars, available by the thousands in four body styles ranging in price from $3,983 to $5,327, were rated at 24 miles per gallon in city driving by the EPA. Three months after the Shah left town and almost precisely at the moment when the first gas shortages were appearing on the West Coast, the GM X-car net was lowered into Jouppi's river at mid-channel (see Chapter One). It was, said a forlorn Lee Iacocca, "as if God had touched them on the shoulder."

The divine intervention was not total—even for GM. Increasingly concerned during the latter part of 1978 and into early 1979 that they were bringing out a small car at the wrong time, GM skewed engine options in favor of the more powerful six-cylinder. Sixes, GM reasoned, would be the choice of 60 percent of the buyers; 40 percent would favor fours. By summer, company president Pete Estes was admitting that the demand was reversed, and part of the reason for waiting lists of up to nine months on X-cars during their first year on the market was the shortage of four-cylinder engines.

The disappearance of the RV and van markets and the near-total shift to scarce small cars had a devastating effect on Chrysler's balance sheet. Working capital—the difference between current assets and current liabilities, and a measure of a company's ability to pay its bills—had been just under $1.1 billion at the end of 1978—an adequate but not comfortable level for a company Chrysler's size in an unusually volatile industry. By the end of June, working capital was down to $800 million and fast approaching the $600 million floor established by Chrysler's leading lenders in a revolving credit system arranged by John Riccardo and Bill McGagh in April of 1977. If Chrysler were to maintain access to the $567.5 million provided by the revolver—and it was clear cash was not coming in from the sale of cars—they would have to cut costs and sell assets at an accelerated pace, or face a confrontation with their banks.

The sudden market drop also raised the specter of a bloated sales bank for the first time since 1975. Iacocca had seen R. K. Brown's sales team get away with it in March, but he knew the job was getting rougher by the day. During his first six months, he threw $50 million in dealer incentives at Chrysler's stock of cars and trucks and cut production by 90,000 to clear the pipeline. In May, he found out why it had been so tough for earlier chief operating officers to purge the system. Iacocca and Laux informed dealers in mid-month that the party was over; they were cutting off the sales bank and ending the traditional 5-percent rebate for model-year inventory clearance. "This is a real cancer that we must get rid of," said Laux.

The dealers responded angrily. "This is the first time Iacocca has stubbed his toe," said a New York dealer. "We really got the shaft."[6] Raphael Cohen, leader of a New York area "Independent Dealers Committee Dedicated to Action" and a former Chrysler-Plymouth dealer, threatened to sue the company. The sales bank by then had reached 44,000 units—an idle inventory worth some $250 million while it sat in the spring mud around Detroit.

John Riccardo, "Mr. Outside" under the new executive arrangement, and Bill McGagh completed a grueling tour of some eighty individual banks in the spring of 1979. Riccardo personally visited every major bank in Europe in an effort to secure new credit and solidify the old. He barnstormed Washington, visiting every agency and department in town where some form of relief might be forthcoming: Doug Costle of EPA for relief from '80 and '81 emissions standards that would have saved Chrysler $500 million; Mike Pertchuk of the Federal Trade Commission and Justice Department antitrust lawyers for exclusion from a longstanding investigation of GM's potential for monopoly in the industry. Riccardo consulted with Charles Schultze of the Council of Economic Advisers for general advice and spoke with Joan Claybrook of NHTSA about exemption from air-bag and bumper requirements. His greatest hope, however, was for a major piece of tax relief, based on a scheme submitted by a company Tax Department official, whereby Chrysler would ask the Treasury Department for tax credits they presumed they would be eligible for in future years. Riccardo was less than subtle in letting Washington know things were getting rough in Highland Park, where Iacocca, for the time being, was fully occupied playing Mr. Inside. Straightening out the marketing and quality-control mess were time-consuming operations by themselves.

To soften the blow of the X-car launch, Iacocca resurrected Lynn Townsend's old 5/50 warranty and ordered the new Kenyon & Eckhardt crew to rustle up an appropriate campaign. In June, the company extended the warranty on their Class A and C motor homes to cover the use of liquid propane as a fuel—a shoring-up measure against the growing gasoline shortages. The sudden cash shortage called for emergency measures, though. Assembly shutdowns in the face of rising inventory had idled 13,500 Chrysler hourly workers by late May and the figure would reach 20,000 by early June. Payments of Supplemental Unemployment Benefits to laid-off UAW members kept the cash outflow up while the inflow stopped—one of the fundamental reasons why the sales bank had been created in the first place. The only way to cure the disease permanently was to amputate. There were plenty of candidates. Iacocca simply had to choose.

The first to go was an aging trim plant in Lyons, Michigan, a tiny town northwest of Lansing with a population of eight hundred. The factory employed seven hundred people and had been in operation for thirty-two years when notice was posted in May that the doors would close for the last time in June. Workers openly wept.

The next was the fading flagship of the Chrysler plants: Dodge Main, an eight-story colossus that predated Chrysler itself. Once the workplace of as many as 35,000 and still the very essence of the Polish enclave of Hamtramck, the plant embodied the history of the automobile business in the United States. Although the plant had grown undeniably inefficient, it was still the centerpiece of an inner-city community and the provider of thousands of jobs—many of them held by blacks. The early June announcement of its closing gave one year's notice, but protests erupted almost immediately. The "Save Dodge Main" movement was met only by an acceleration of the closing schedule from June of 1980 back to January, hastened by poor sales of Aspens and Volares and the desperate need to cut losses.

By September, Iacocca had chopped $360 million in fixed costs from Chrysler's operations. By the end of 1979, white-collar layoffs and early retirements had reached 8,500. Left virtually untouched in the cutbacks were Hal Sperlich's $13.6 billion future-products program,

Irving Minett, former Chrysler vice-president, International. *Credit: Chrysler Corporation*

Charles M. Heinen, former Chrysler vice-president, Engineering (Director, Research and Materials). *Credit: Chrysler Corporation*

Chrysler president J. Paul Bergmoser. *Credit: Junebug Clark*

Chrysler's chief financial officer, Jerry Greenwald. *Credit: Junebug Clark*

(Left to right) Senator Donald Riegle, Congressman James Blanchard and chairman Lee Iacocca. *Credit: Chrysler Corporation*

During a House Banking Committee hearing in 1979, Wendell W. Larsen (left), a Chrysler vice-president, confers with Howard G. Paster of the UAW on their lobbying efforts. *Credit: George Tames/NYT Pictures*

Douglas Fraser (facing camera, second from right) with the UAW lobbying team. *Credit: George Tames/NYT Pictures*

Senator William Proxmire in December of 1979. *Credit: Chas. Geer*

bert S. (Steve) Miller, Chrysler's treasurer
l the chief architect of the restructuring
Chrysler's debt. *Credit: Chrysler Cor-
ration*

John F. McGillicuddy, president and chairman
of the board, Manufacturers Hanover Trust
Company. *Credit: Dick Winburn*

G. William Miller, Secretary of the Treasury (July 1979-January 1981).
Credit: U.S. Treasury

Tearing down the old Dodge Main plant, February 1981. *Credit: Peter Yates*

Unimate robot welders building Chrysler K-cars at the Jefferson Avenue plant, August 1980. *Credit: David Franklin*

Lee Iacocca drives the first K-car off the line at Jefferson Avenue, August 8, 1980. *Credit: Chrysler Corporation*

ranging from the down-sized Dodge Mirada and Chrysler Cordoba due out in September to a front-wheel-drive mini-van scheduled for 1985. The centerpiece of the program—what became the rallying point for Chrysler throughout 1979 and 1980—was the K-car. That summer, amid the debacle in the market, the K-cars were going into the crucial phase of prototype testing and preliminary tooling. Although it was as old and decrepit as Dodge Main, the Jefferson Avenue assembly plant had been chosen to build the Ks, using $100 million worth of the most modern automation available—an Italian-designed, French-made "robogate" that put the car bodies together with computer precision, using Unimate robot welding arms that cost $45,000 apiece.

Iacocca argued that any cutback in product for the sake of short-term savings would only postpone death in the marketplace, as well as delay Chrysler's ability to meet the requirements of the law. Despite all the layoffs and plant closings, Chrysler continued to shell out $100 million a month on new products, a figure that increased to $160 million by year's end.

Amid all this trauma, Chrysler stockholders gathered for the 1979 annual meeting, held in mid-May near Syracuse, New York. Critics accused the company's management of fleeing Detroit's woes, but the real reason was to take some comfort from the New Process gear plant nearby, where Chrysler manufactured four-wheel-drive transfer cases not only for its own vehicles, but for the entire industry. New Process, even with the drought in the off-road market, remained a highly profitable plant—by that time, one of the few in Chrysler's stable.

Among stockholders, the mood was unusually calm, given the circumstances and the raucous debate that had occurred the year before when John Riccardo was hard pressed to win approval for his preferred-stock offering. Although the first quarter had yielded a $53.8 million loss and yet another domestic market share drop, from 11.3 percent to 10.9 percent, shareholders felt secure with the company now in the hands of Lee Iacocca. Encomiums trumpeted from the audience for the new president, though Iacocca himself was appropriately downbeat. "No one can promise any easy answers or any quick turnaround," he warned the gathering. "The problems are too complicated for that, the lead times too long and the competition too intense." He referred to his massive reorganization program only in general terms, talking about "restoring a sense of discipline" to the company. He drew a picture of "turmoil" created by the energy crisis —a picture that could not do justice to the dire predicament of the company.

Behind the scenes in Syracuse, however, was turmoil of a different nature. Felix Rohatyn, senior partner in the New York investment house of Lazard Frères, had come with a plan. Rohatyn, the architect of New York City's loan guarantees, the chairman of Big MAC—the oversight board that monitored the city's subsequent fiscal well-being —and a recognized expert in corporate mergers and acquisitions, had served as a consultant to Chrysler for the past six months. Rohatyn was a useful sounding board on a variety of matters. He explored the market for potential partners for Chrysler's expensive ancillary operations in real estate and even the New Process gear plant. Riccardo was eager to find another finance company to buy into Chrysler Financial Corporation, because of what he thought was an imprudently large amount of Chrysler equity devoted to the company's credit arm. Because of Lazard Frères' international connections, Rohatyn was an appropriate counsel on possible joint ventures with foreign car companies to replace Chrysler's own foreign network as Riccardo dismantled it.

If it was possible, Felix Rohatyn was more pessimistic about Chrysler's prospects than even John Riccardo, who was throwing ballast out of the gondola as fast as he could. Rohatyn, according to Chrysler officials, saw an immediate need to take life-saving action. Quite naturally, since he had just come off the New York City bailout and was a continuing influence on the city's affairs, Rohatyn modeled a similar, albeit private, bailout plan for Chrysler. It even had its own version of Big MAC, an oversight board that would bring together dealers, suppliers, banks and all other interested parties to sort out the various sacrifices that needed to be made in order to save the company. (With the notable exception of federally guaranteed loans and the requisite involvement of Congress and the executive branch, the plan was remarkably similar in concept to the Chrysler loan guarantee package passed by Congress seven months later—not surprising, since it was partially modeled on the New York plan, which had been the Treasury Department's maiden voyage into major institutional restructuring.)

The catch in Rohatyn's plan, however, was his proposal to serve as chairman of the oversight board, just as he headed up Big MAC. Moreover, suggested Rohatyn in Syracuse, if Chrysler wasn't interested in his plan, then there was no further need for him to remain involved with the company.

It was, in effect, an ultimatum—and to make matters harder for John Riccardo, Rohatyn waited until only a few minutes before the evening session of the board was to convene before laying it out on the table. There had been conversations about bits and pieces of the concept, but the full details, including Rohatyn's proposed chairmanship of the oversight committee, were a complete surprise. Even outside board members were taken aback by the abruptness of the presentation. "It wasn't good salesmanship," recalled one board member. "There were others there who thought of themselves as fairly competent people. What he [Rohatyn] wanted in effect was to take over the strategy of how this company was run."

Besides being somewhat affronted, a number of board members and executives, Iacocca included, thought the plan was overly severe and ran a real danger of destroying the company's already tenuous image in the market. The only way to convince the world of the necessity of such sweeping measures, argued opponents, would have been to lay out in gory detail an exact and wholly dismal picture of the company's ills and prospects. While such tactics might convince bankers, suppliers and the UAW that they had better pitch in and sacrifice, they were equally likely to drive customers away from Chrysler showrooms for good. It was a dilemma Chrysler faced on even poorer terms later in 1979.

Riccardo was incensed. A pair of Chrysler colleagues walked him around the hotel three or four times to settle him down. "It was like cooling off a horse," recalled one. The next day, at the full board meeting, Rohatyn and Chrysler parted ways for good.

Hindsight suggests that the Rohatyn plan had merit and that only tender egos prevented an early and comfortably private rescue attempt from getting off the ground, but there still appeared to be a number of options open to Chrysler at the time—not the least of which was some kind of joint venture or consortium with another company.

Ever since selling the New Stanton assembly plant to the German company in the mid-Seventies, John Riccardo had nursed thoughts of closer ties with Volkswagen. He had pushed the idea of doing business with VW tenaciously, using Gene Cafiero as a point man. On and off for four years, Chrysler had pursued a wide range of deals, but it had been a slow-building process. First had come the four-cylinder-engine contract for the Omni/Horizon—Chrysler agreed to purchase 300,000 of them a year until they could afford to build their own. Then Chrysler wanted to talk about transmissions and axles. VW might be interested in buying the automatic transmissions and trans-axles Chrysler was experienced in building in exchange for manual boxes, in which the Germans had expertise. Beyond parts, the conversations had remained general—talk of perhaps sharing dealers in a few cities, maybe using some excess Chrysler capacity to assemble Volkswagen or Audi models in the United States, and maybe some exchange of equity. It never got very specific. There were no hard numbers—just casual conversations, a testing of the waters, on the prospect of putting Volkswagen and Chrysler together in one form or another.

By the time Iacocca became involved in early 1979, hopes were raised rather high in Highland Park that a consortium of real import could be worked out. Toni Schmuecker had known Iacocca since the early Sixties, when Schmuecker was still with Ford of Europe. Schmuecker also knew Paul Bergmoser, who by that time had signed on full-time as Executive Vice-President for Purchasing at Chrysler. The formula discussed by Schmuecker and Iacocca wasn't any more elaborate than Riccardo's plans had been. The difference was in pizzazz, in enthusiasm, in imagination and grandeur. "We called it 'The Grand Design,'" said Iacocca.

Initially limited to the U.S. market, the scheme offered considerable advantages of size. Three dealer networks—Dodge, VW and Chrysler-Plymouth—would equal 6o percent of GM's distribution network instead of 40 percent; purchasing power would be improved, with the ability to combine orders to companies like Dana, Budd or Kelsey-Hayes and reap the benefits of a price break; and the fixed costs of Chrysler's Trenton engine plant, for example, could be spread over a dramatically improved production run. "It was so clear-cut a baby could have figured it out," recalled Iacocca a year and a half later. "It was the holding company concept of Alfred Sloan's."

Volkswagen and Chrysler were moving along the same product-development lines. Indeed, the Rabbit and the Omni/Horizon were not only the same cars in concept, but VW had taken a good, hard look at the engineering specs of the Simca 1301, the Omni's sire, before putting the Rabbit together. "It was a marriage made in heaven," said Iacocca. "Their cars and our cars, all about the same size, and they fitted . . . power trains. . . . Well, who knows what might have evolved."

Hundreds of hours were spent talking out the Volkswagen plan. According to Iacocca, Schmuecker "got very excited about the concept," although the exact structure of the venture never took shape. There was talk of building Audis in St. Louis or Warren, where Chrysler's truck capacity was vastly underutilized. How much of the talk on the German side was serious remains difficult to assess, since Volkswagen executives remained stonily silent on their relations with Chrysler long after the plans died. Certainly, the scheme was alive with detail on the yellow notepads of Lee Iacocca and Hal Sperlich, whose weekend dreams of "Global Motors" inched delectably toward reality. "The Grand Design" was the foundation of just the kind of international consortium both men knew would be the salvation of the small automakers in the years ahead. "Ford is over there [in Dearborn and England] doing 600,000 Omni/Horizons [Ford's "World Car" Escort/Lynx]. They're late, but they're working like hell. GM is starting with eight [hundred thousand] and going to a million-two," posed Iacocca to Schmuecker, "and we're doing three [hundred thousand] and you're doing three [hundred thousand Rabbits in Pennsylvania], and they're all the same! We're going to have two designs, and they're going to have just one. GM's going to have double that with one. Just think of it that way. They're going to beat our brains in with that—long term—and we're dead in the market. Long term may be ten years. But you can't go it alone."

It was an analysis that was shared by many in the auto industry. The underlying motive of Peugeot's purchase of Chrysler's shaky European operations was to get big as quickly as possible so as to be ready when General Motors and Ford blended American production capacity with European design. For years, Fiat has sought interlocking relationships with other auto and truck producers to share expenses and build with the advantage of the economies of scale. American Motors chairman Gerald Meyers and Renault's Bernard Hanon saw the mutual benefits of shared technology, dealer networks and financing when they pieced together their own arrangement in 1978. Meyers saw the world's thirty-odd car companies winnowing down to a dozen or so over the decade of the Eighties. Iacocca saw an even smaller group—"six biggies." The numbers and the names of the survivors differed; the dynamics and the causes did not.

"In the next five years," predicted Iacocca, "there will be consortiums, mergers, amalgamations of the remaining auto companies to take on General Motors and Japan, Inc. I count Japan as one big automobile complex. There's not much in England anymore. What we'll have will be GM, Ford-plus-somebody-else, Chrysler-plus-somebody. . . . (If we'd had 35 percent of Mitsubishi plus more of Peugeot, we'd be there already.) You'd have a German group, and that'll be a powerful one. The French group . . ."

Nationalism, Iacocca thought, was the biggest block to natural intercontinental alignments. The Common Market's slow development clearly demonstrated the emotional impediments involved. Most countries worked to prevent any advantage from falling into the hands of another country. The French feared a Volkswagen-Chrysler marriage while Chrysler was still big in France. Only the American government used different criteria: consortiums with foreign manufacturers were watched most closely by the Justice Department in case they gave an American company an undue advantage against its U.S. competitors. It was an attitude that always amused, if also puzzled, the Japanese and the Europeans.

In any case, Volkswagen and Chrysler as a partnership, beyond the 300,000 four-cylinder-engine contract, was not to be. The Germans very understandably developed a case of cold feet as the American market collapse pulled Chrysler deeper into the hole. The size of Chrysler's debt, combined with ever-worsening market projections, made it too risky a venture.

Late in June 1979, *Automotive News*, the industry's trade journal, announced that it had uncovered a next-to-complete plan for Volkswagen to buy a controlling interest in Chrysler. The plan was very specific, including an actual tender offering price of $15 a share. The plan, said *Automotive News*, was to be presented to VW's supervisory board for approval that very week.

Everyone involved quickly and categorically denied the story. "I don't know what they're talking about," said Iacocca flatly. Besides, noted the Chrysler president, $15 was too low; Chrysler's book value at the time was over $40 a share. Kurt Markert of the German Cartel Office fueled speculation by admitting he had heard talk of Volkswagen using a Chrysler plant in the United States, but Schmuecker denied it outright. Even Wall Street's risk-happy arbitragers would have none of it, though less sophisticated traders pushed Chrysler's stock up nearly three points on the news that Friday.

Automotive News publisher and editorial director Keith Crain, whose story it was, stood fast. His sources were German, and one of them, at least, had access to Volkswagen's top-management thinking. The real reason the story survived so long, despite denials, was that everybody thought it was such a good idea. John Riccardo, meeting with Stuart Eizenstat of the White House and Treasury Secretary Michael Blumenthal the day the story broke, found the federal officials urging him to take the offer. However, there was no longer an offer to take.

The VW merger story would be one of the very few bits of optimism to settle on Chrysler for some time to come. The following week, the sages of Dow-Jones dropped Chrysler from the benchmark list of thirty industrials. Rumors out of Washington—leaks from Riccardo's frank talks with federal officials—began making the rounds that Chrysler was in deep, deep trouble, with second-quarter losses as high as $350 million coming up. When second-quarter results were announced on July 31, the numbers weren't that bad—$207 million—but the message was clear. Chrysler was sitting on an inventory of 80,000 cars and trucks as of June 30—an inventory worth more than $700 million at market prices, with interest due daily—and John Riccardo was going to go to Congress for $1 billion in tax relief.

CHAPTER TWELVE

Going for Broke

Five days before Christmas 1979, representatives of the House and the Senate met beneath the cold gray walls of the hearing room for the House Committee on Banking, Finance and Urban Affairs. They met to resolve the differences between two bills that promised federal aid to Chrysler. What John Riccardo had started in August 1979 had consumed an entire congressional session and provoked a fierce national debate, but the Joint Conference Committee meeting on December 20, 1979, marked the final opportunity for legislators to influence the terms of what had grown from a plea for tax relief into the Chrysler Loan Guarantee Act.

The Joint Conference sessions are far more informal affairs than the full sessions of either house. Until the government in the Sunshine Act took effect in 1977, they remained closed to outsiders and took place in tiny rooms more suited to dining than debate. Even since lobbyists and the press have been allowed to attend the meetings, legislators have continued to speak freely. Since no minutes are taken, they know that their remarks will not be included in the morning's Congressional Record or splashed into headlines. Masks are dropped and extreme positions abandoned as discussion focuses on the critical words and numbers in the bill to be sent to the White House.

The twelve senators and congressmen still had time to influence the fate of Chrysler. Although the Senate and the House had provided two bills that were similar in thrust, they differed in detail. It was the detail that mattered. The House had approved a $3.43 billion aid package; the Senate had opted for $3.6 billion. While both bills called for $1.5 billion in loan guarantees, they demanded different contributions from the United Auto Workers, which accounted for much of the difference in the totals. The Senate wanted the union to cough up $525 million, while the milder House version demanded $500 million; meanwhile, the company's non-unionized workers were asked to contribute $150 million by the Senate and $100 million by the House. In addition, both bills demanded that Chrysler dispose of $300 million of assets, squeeze $500 million from its domestic lenders and $150 million from its foreign bankers, line up $250 million from state and local governments and extract $180 million from suppliers and dealers. The Senate bill also required that Chrysler launch a $175 million employee stock-option scheme, while the House was content with a $150 million plan. Finally, the Senate insisted that Chrysler issue new stock, 1.04 shares for every outstanding share, and use part of the proceeds to repay the loans.

Even the choice of the committee room was largely an accident, indicative of the haphazard workings of the United States Congress. The afternoon of December 20 had begun on the first floor of the Capitol, with a crowd milling around the entrance to the Speaker's dining room. The venue was a miserable choice, directly opposite a restaurant and a candy counter, and too small to accommodate more than a few of the interested observers. Outside the room, Capitol police hurriedly rigged up a rope to keep the television and newspaper reporters at bay. Inside, the twelve conferees, officials from the Treasury Department, aides and a couple of lobbyists sat around a dining table or leaned against the walls. Tempers were rising, both inside and outside the room. Wisconsin Senator William Proxmire, the chairman of the Senate Banking Committee and Chrysler's sternest foe, had arrived late, bearing a surprise proposal which covered several major points, including the size of the United Auto Workers' contribution. Breaching a basic rule of the Congress, he had failed to inform his fellow senators of the plan and hurriedly pushed it across the table to the half-dozen congressmen. Don Riegle, Michigan's Senior Democratic Senator and Chrysler's closest friend in Washington, was close to apoplexy. "It's bullshit," he yelled. "It's not bullshit," countered Proxmire.

While the mood soured inside the room, it became heated in the hallway, where journalists and Chrysler lobbyists were forced to monitor the conference via a pool of three reporters. Judith Miller, a correspondent for the New York *Times* who had covered the debate with scrupulous attention, was incensed. Furious at her exclusion, she called her editor in Washington and received permission to type a letter of protest on New York *Times* stationery, which she gave a guard to hand to Congressman Henry Reuss. When the senators emerged to attend a roll-call vote, Miller buttonholed Proxmire and handed him a royal drubbing for his insistence on privacy. For about the first time in six months, Proxmire, one of the most skillful propagandists on Capitol Hill, was left speechless. The prospect of the morning's papers was sufficient to make Proxmire, Reuss and their colleagues adjourn to a larger room so a motley caravan, numbering well over a hundred, trooped through the basement corridors, up a couple of elevators and along the underground railway to the spacious House Banking Committee Room. "Without Judith Miller," said Chrysler group Vice-President for Public Affairs Wendell Larsen, "we wouldn't have had a workable bill."

Coming at the end of a decade that had spawned hundreds of special-interest groups, the battle over Chrysler managed to unite the oldest and strongest blocs—big business, government and organized labor—but behind the imposing facade (which was riddled with sufficient fractures of its own) many of the encrusted political allegiances and alliances had crumbled. UAW president Douglas Fraser, who had been traipsing to Washington for the best part of three decades, knew full well how easy things used to be. "In Sam Rayburn's day, if you had a tax proposal and you got Wilbur Mills to agree, that was it. Now you cannot get anyone even to second a motion. It's chaos." Jim Blanchard, a Michigan congressman at the center of the Chrysler debate and of a generation less inclined to kowtow to authority, concurs: "Ten years ago, if you talked to ten right people you'd have had a bill. Today everybody gets a crack at bat."

In the House committee room there was plenty of room for everyone to fight their private battles: the conferees and their aides; the lobbyists; officials from the Treasury Department, Chrysler and the UAW; a couple of Chrysler creditors and the press. One way or another, all the major participants in the debate were either in attendance or represented by lobbyists. The twelve conferees, who pulled their chairs up to the witness table in the center of the room, might have been expected to vote along party lines on an issue as clear-cut as the first bill to directly provide federal loan guarantees to a company primarily engaged in commercial business, but the Chrysler debate straddled party lines and made nonsense of preconceived ideas and old-fashioned ties. There was no better example of the changing spirit than the couple of Democrats, both in their sixties, who faced each other across the center of the table. Both represented Wisconsin, both were chairmen of their respective committees and both were opposed to federal aid for Chrysler. Congressman Henry Reuss, chairman of the House Banking Committee, had stated his opposition several months before, but had then willingly let William Moorhead, a Democrat from Pittsburgh, Jim Blanchard, a thirty-seven-year-old Democrat from the outskirts of Detroit, and Stewart McKinney, a Republican from Connecticut, conduct hearings in the Subcommittee on Economic Stabilization and steer the bill through the full House. Proxmire, however, had taken on the fight rather than hand it off to Riegle, Chrysler's chief supporter in the Senate.

"There's no way we can win this," Proxmire had told his aides the previous August; he had assured Chrysler that he would not block floor action on the bill. For the succeeding four months the Wisconsin senator had characteristically battled Chrysler every inch of the way. Although he had looked the other way when American Motors, the largest private employer in Wisconsin, won a $22 million tax write-off in 1968, his opposition to federal aid to business had, thereafter, continued. In 1971, during the debate over federal loan guarantees to Lockheed, he had resisted a boycott of Wisconsin beer and cheese organized by aerospace workers, and voted against the bill. Proxmire established in 1975 the "Golden Fleece," an award to be given to federally funded projects which were "smooth legalized theft from the taxpayer." In 1975, he had championed short-term aid to New York City, but he had firmly opposed long-term aid in 1978. Frugality has always been a way of life for this Democrat who runs five miles to his office every day and who, despite spending a mere $177.50 during his last election campaign, still managed to run away with 75 percent of the vote. "The less I work, the worse I feel," he's fond of saying—and during the debate over Chrysler, the largest fleece to come his way, he barely let up.

Seated at Proxmire's right was Don Riegle, who wore a white turtleneck sweater to coddle a sore throat. Like Proxmire, Riegle had voted against aid to Lockheed, but that had been during a different incarnation. In 1971, Riegle was a young Republican congressman, aged thirty-three, from Flint, Michigan, who had irritated a lot of his colleagues in 1972 by publishing a book titled *O Congress*, which made his final goal, 1600 Pennsylvania Avenue, abundantly clear. Ever since a remarkably filthy Democratic campaign in 1976 for a Senate seat in Michigan, when most attention was focused on some leaked tape recordings containing the intimate moments of a love affair, Riegle had been a friend of the auto industry. He had dropped by Chrysler headquarters the day the Detroit *News* first published transcripts of the tapes. "He looked lower than a snake's belly," one Chrysler official remembers, but Riegle stayed true to his pledge and in 1977 he led the Senate fight to relax the Clean Air Act. During 1979 he virtually became "the senator from Highland Park."

William Proxmire and Don Riegle were joined by four Senate colleagues. Paul Tsongas, a liberal Democrat from Massachusetts who had served in the Peace Corps, was distinctly uncomfortable with the notion of offering aid to a large company. Although he had received contributions from the UAW as a congressman, the ties had been weakened after the union made contributions to his opponent, black incumbent Ed Brooke, in the 1978 senatorial race. During the closing six weeks of the Chrysler debate, Tsongas had worked closely with Republican Richard Lugar, a former mayor of Indianapolis who represented Indiana Chrysler workers and railed quietly against the burden of regulation. Alongside Proxmire sat Jake Garn. An impeccably conservative Republican from Utah and a Mormon who neither smokes nor drinks, he finally voted against aid, while Nancy Kassebaum, the only woman in the Senate in 1979, did the same. Facing the senators were six congressmen. Beside Reuss, Moorhead and Blanchard sat Stewart McKinney, a Republican from Connecticut. Former president of a family-owned Firestone store, McKinney had immersed himself in the details of Chrysler's business and, unlike most of his colleagues, displayed a thorough grasp of the automobile industry. He had been critically important in persuading fellow Republicans to vote for federal aid. New York Congressman Stanley Lundine, who had consistently argued in favor of employee stock options, sat close by.

At the foot of the table, trying to make sense of the bickering, were the legal counsel for both committees: young men with their shirt sleeves rolled up and the two bills spread out before them. They busily compared the language in the documents, patiently read back passages to the congressmen and with quiet strokes of their pens added, deleted or amended sentences. Surrounding the table was the itinerant gallery, which had followed the discussions with increasing earnestness and was, for the most part, an intimate part of the proceedings. The most detached were a couple of television reporters who lolled in the leather chairs behind the committee members' desks, wondering whether the conferees would have the decency to reach a decision before their evening news programs. The various officials, lobbyists and reporters sat in chairs that crept closer and closer to the conference table as the afternoon lengthened. They ended the day leaning over the congressional participants like spectators in an arm-wrestling match.

Directly behind the senators were their aides. (Few congressmen can afford the retinue of aides who habitually trail senators like so many articulate caddies.) Despite the public debate—and no issue was more fully aired at the end of the Seventies—much of the shape of the federal aid package was worked out by young congressional aides, with little knowledge of the auto industry, who were intent on gaining headlines for their masters or prestige for themselves. Apart from the few senators closely involved with the legislation, most relied on their aides to guide them on the finer details of the bills. It was the aides, working out of cramped quarters noisy enough to make a machine shop sound quiet, who were the main contacts for lobbyists, for these mandarins held sway over the lines, clauses, words and punctuation so crucial to the lobbyists. If the Chrysler bill was debated publicly, it was most certainly fashioned privately. By far the most zealous staffers worked for Senator Proxmire. Ken McLean, the staff director of the Senate Banking Committee and Elinor Bachrach, a member of the committee's staff, were more than a notch above the rest of the aides. With far less overt political ambition, they nevertheless exerted greater influence over the debate, if only because of their greater experience. Early in the proceedings, McLean had delegated the bulk of the work to Bachrach, who was one of the sharper staffers in the Senate—bright, perky, armed with a sense of humor and stern self-confidence. "The federal government," she observed, "was asked not to save Chrysler, but to build a monument for Lee Iacocca." A cloistered New Englander, educated at Brown and the University of Chicago, she had worked for Maine Congressman (and later Senator) William Hathaway before joining the Senate Banking Committee. Forever at Proxmire's side, she supplied her boss with detailed information while more junior staffers, wearing yellow floor passes, lounged in the deep chairs against the wall. Bachrach sat beside Proxmire (aides have to sit, as a matter of courtesy, on lower seats than the senators) plucking documents from piles of files, whispering advice in his ear, coaching him, arranging and scheduling hearings and engaging in horsetrading sessions with counterparts on other Senate staffs. Loan guarantees were not new to her. She had battled through the debate over New York City, for which she had greater sympathy than her senator, and for her efforts had been nicknamed by friends "Billion-Dollar-Bailout Bachrach." On Chrysler, she was in total agreement with Proxmire. Despite the public outbursts of other politicians and businessmen, it was Bachrach, pumping the phones until midnight, drawing up lists of witnesses for the Senate hearings, drafting documents in the early hours of the morning and working weekends, who became Chrysler's most implacable foe. "She'd knife you in a back alley without a second thought," said a Chrysler executive with more than a tinge of admiration. Days before the final mark-up of the Senate bill, Banking Committee staff director Ken McLean and Bachrach had sat down with aides from the offices of senators Lugar and Tsongas and bargained on the shape and substance of the document to be presented to the Senate committee. McLean and Bachrach insisted that any bill had to contain a "wish list" of the amounts to be contributed by non-federal parties. In the discussions during the joint conference, as Bachrach bobbed up and down in her seat whenever Proxmire scored a point, the strong influence of the staff was publicly recognized. At one point, when Proxmire leaned over the back of his chair to confer with McLean and Bachrach, an exasperated Tsongas curtly pointed out, "The Senate staff is not going to run the Chrysler Board." Congressman McKinney added that he "would prefer not to negotiate with the Senate staff."

Roaming around the back of the committee room, joshing patiently with the press and huddling with lobbyists, was Chrysler's Wendell Larsen. Almost bald, with a skinny crescent of gray hair, Larsen had been intimately involved with the appeals to the government from the beginning—and had inherited the full responsibility for priming and firing Chrysler's legislative fusillades. (Unlike Riccardo, who had retired three months before the Joint Conference session, Lee Iacocca made only five trips to Washington in the fall of 1979, and two of those were to testify. While Riccardo used the shotgun approach, Iacocca was like a rifle marksman. Though he totally delegated the work in Washington to Larsen, his mere presence in Detroit cast a persuasive shadow over Capitol Hill.) Inside Chrysler, Larsen was the man most closely identified with John Riccardo. The two were close. Larsen was one of the few officials who would dare yell back at the chairman when he threw a tantrum, and he had proved his value to Riccardo as an adviser and consultant. Always a stubborn man, Larsen had joined Chrysler in 1962 as a speech writer, had once been fired (and quickly rehired) by Virgil Boyd for a customary burst of candor, and later became a prominent participant in the operation and policy discussions of the company's senior circle. By the end, Larsen was as much a part of the Washington debate as Chrysler's chief opponent, Elinor Bachrach. For every position paper she prepared, Larsen matched it with late-night work on testimony, white papers, "Dear Colleague" letters and lengthy analyses of a Chrysler failure.

Throughout the Conference Committee meeting, as during the previous five months, Larsen conferred almost constantly with Chrysler's full-time Washington representative, Bob Conner, and with Tommy Boggs, Bill Timmons and Tom Korologos, three of the best-connected lobbyists in Washington. The son of former House Majority Leader Hale Boggs, whose wife Lindy inherited his Congressional seat, Tommy Boggs had impeccable political ties. After graduating from the Georgetown University Law School and working in campaigns for his father and for Democratic presidential candidates, he had unsuccessfully run for the House and finally settled down to practice Washington's own peculiar brand of persuasion. (Boggs' wife, Barbara,

weaves a different path through Washington life. In 1969, along with
Mrs. Ellen Proxmire and other partners, she founded Washington
Whirl-Around, a business that provides entertainment for spouses ac-
companying political and business visitors to the capital.) Boggs' political links are buttressed by his fund-raising activities. In 1978, he
reported personal contributions of nearly $25,000 to thirty-five
Democratic candidates and had helped to raise considerably more.
With a staff of fifty, Patton, Boggs and Blow has an imposing list of
clients, including the states of Louisiana and Alaska, General Motors,
and Ralston Purina. Boggs had accepted the Chrysler work early in
the summer of 1979 and, along with his colleague, Dave Todd, had
devoted the rest of the year almost entirely to Chrysler.

By the end of December, the footwork had all been done, and
Boggs, with his snow-white capped teeth, broad shoulders and ever-
present cigar, confidently conferred with Tom Korologos, a partner in
the far smaller firm of Timmons and Company, Inc. Korologos, who
looks and acts more like a senator than most senators, had worked on
Nixon's White House staff and now had taken on the task of pressuring Senate Republicans. Timmons, the quieter partner of the firm,
worked the House. Meanwhile, Garry Brown, a former Michigan congressman who had been a member of the House Banking Committee,
had been specially hired to handle his former colleagues. Former
Maine Senator Bill Hathaway and another former Michigan Congressman, Jim O'Hara, had been retained to do the same. Two of the
most badgered men milling around the committee-room floor were
Howard Paster and Howard Young of the UAW. Like Proxmire and
Riegle, the UAW had performed a neat flip-flop on government aid
and, like the two senators, had opposed aid to Lockheed with then-
president Leonard Woodcock testifying, "We will face dangers in the
future if government gets itself into the business of bailing out big
corporations whenever they find themselves in serious trouble." Paster
and Young's particular trouble was the size of the UAW contribution,
which was being discussed by the conferees. Paster, the Legislative
Director of the auto workers, was, like many of the other white-collar
staff, not a union member, which displeased some of the gritty old-
timers. Fond of a fine Monte Cristo cigar (the brand also puffed by
Iacocca and Jim Blanchard) the curly-haired Paster was a bouncy
gremlin. "There is," he chortled, "only one thing better than politics
and that's talking about it," which he did with relish. Young, a stolid,
dour-faced man, resorts to none of the emotional outbursts of the
younger Paster. As the union's resident actuary, Young's specialty is
the costing of contract provisions. "Howard," winked Paster, "can cal-
culate the hourly cost of a trip to the bathroom."

By the winter of 1979, the corridors of Washington were as familiar to Chrysler executives as the faded green carpet of the Highland Park executive suite. Like all the automobile companies, Chrysler was no newcomer to Capitol Hill, but the bargaining that took place during 1979 was not planned in any detail and the course chosen by Chrysler at the beginning of the year proved less predictable and more treacherous than insiders had expected. During all its appeals to the government, Chrysler displayed feline agility. What started as an appeal for a delay in the fuel, safety and emissions standards stammered and stuttered its way through the year until there was an appeal for tax relief and, finally, for what Chrysler had never wanted at all: the loan guarantees.

It had been, from the start, a numbing time. Mornings, as often as not, began with John Riccardo heading from his home straight to the executive air terminal at Pontiac Airport and the blue-and-white corporate Gulfstream II which would carry him to Washington for a day of lobbying. The first objective was plain: an outright assault on the federal regulations that gave Riccardo bilious attacks. For Chrysler, government regulations were an obvious place to begin. The company had been in the vanguard of complaints against what was perceived in Detroit as a vicious blight, and most of the arguments against regulation had been the subject of inevitable speeches at Chamber of Commerce lunches or dinners with groups of certified public accountants, and were matters of record.

Chrysler had not been slow in making its case known to the Carter administration. Within weeks of the 1977 Inauguration, Treasury Secretary Michael Blumenthal and President Carter's newly appointed domestic policy adviser, Stuart Eizenstat, had been briefed by Riccardo about the problems Chrysler foresaw in raising money. Toward the end of 1978, the Chrysler chairman had repeated his plea in another series of visits to Washington. The pleading had been pretty successful. At the beginning of 1979, the Secretary of Transportation, Brock Adams, wrote a letter—the result of pressure exerted by the White House—which stated that Chrysler would not be fined if it failed to meet the corporate average-fuel-economy standards. In an effort to win even more relief, Riccardo and Iacocca summoned the leaders of the UAW to an unusual council of war at Highland Park. The Chrysler bosses were blunt with the group, which included president Douglas Fraser, Marc Stepp, the head of the union's Chrysler Department, and legislative director Paster. Riccardo, stating that he had been winning favorable hearings from some legislators, appealed for the UAW's help in gaining special relief for Chrysler from all the federal standards. The union, which had aided the entire industry in a partially successful attempt in 1977 to reform some of the regulations, weighed the proposal, made some soundings of their own and refused the plea. The labor leaders were skeptical of helping a single company and, with far more sophisticated political instincts than the corporate chieftains, questioned Riccardo's judgment. Union president Fraser observed, "John Riccardo heard what he wanted to hear. Silence in Washington doesn't necessarily mean acquiescence." There was never much hope, for example, that Edmund Muskie, the principal architect of the 1970 Clean Air Act, would agree to reopen discussions. Chrysler also had to contend with environmentally conscious senators like Colorado's Gary Hart, who insisted (August 6, 1979) that emissions standards were "neither an excessive burden on industry nor a luxury we can dispense with to help a company through financial trouble." Before Riccardo could find out that he was not an automotive Metternich, the trouble in Iran and rising gas prices forced Chrysler to abandon all talk of regulatory relief. With the enormous switch in demand to small cars, the immediate benefits of regulatory relief became questionable. Any regulatory relief would have failed to provide Chrysler with what it needed most: hard cash. The quest for a solution to the structural problem of how to tide an industry over an awkward few years suddenly turned into a debate on how to bandage Chrysler's hemorrhaging. The need for a quick and clean remedy took on fresh urgency.

It was then that Chrysler eyed the bottom of the balance sheet with increasing attention and began a long, twisting pitch for some tax relief. Congressman Jim Blanchard reckoned that the task was doomed from the start. "It didn't take a Philadelphia lawyer," Blanchard said, "to recognize tax relief was impossible. It was the politics of 1955." Yet tradition offered some comfort, precedent even more, and familiarity with the arguments and procedure made Chrysler take the gamble. Chrysler knew all the ins and outs of tax shortcuts. Since investment tax credits and tax deferrals are part and parcel of government policy toward business, Chrysler, in the politicking leading up to the request for $1 billion of tax credits, argued that they were hardly setting a precedent. They had a point since, in 1967, American Motors had received a special tax credit which allowed a cash rebate of $22 million.[1] Chrysler, like the rest of the industry, had come to expect that tax breaks were an indication of federal, local and state governments' willingness to accommodate business. The State of Pennsylvania had wooed Volkswagen with a promise of a $40 million tax break. Lee Iacocca was fond of explaining how areas or countries competing for new business would toss bait at a company. He told of "bidding wars" between Michigan and Illinois and between Canada and the United States, and pointed out, "We get outright grants and subsidies in

Spain and Brazil. General Motors and Ford get several hundred millions annually from state and local tax breaks."[2]

In the mid-Seventies, the City of Detroit had quickly buckled to similar pressure. Faced with the ugly prospect of more automobile plants fleeing toward the Sunbelt, where both the climate and the lack of unions made life more agreeable, the city had looked to its own coffers to bribe an industry to stand fast. Chrysler, the city's largest taxpayer, had received tax breaks since 1974 and had certainly not been loath to resort to more than gentle persuasion during its 1974 appeal for tax relief. Thanks to a Michigan state law designed to encourage large industries to renovate dilapidated plants in urban areas rather than depart, Chrysler had been granted relief for twelve years from additional taxes on additions and improvements. Just at the Mack stamping plant in east Detroit, Chrysler had realized savings of between $7 million and $8 million a year. During the debate at City Hall, Councilwoman Maryann Mahaffey[3] pithily observed, "They've got us over a barrel. They say lower the taxes or we'll move." In 1979, Chrysler enjoyed city, school and county tax abatements of $3.1 million. More than anything, an appeal for relief from taxes was one with which fellow businessmen, constantly grumbling about taxation, could sympathize.[4] It was not the affront to dearly held beliefs that the loan guarantees later became.

There were also a couple of purely practical reasons for the ploy. The company had tried a similar maneuver in 1975, when Michigan Senator Philip Hart had led a futile bid. By tacking an amendment onto a major tax cut aimed at ending the recession, Hart's measure would have provided Chrysler with an estimated $250 million, Lockheed with $85 million and Pan American with $40 million.[5] The measure was ultimately boiled down into language designed specifically for Chrysler and would have permitted the company to carry back losses incurred after 1970 and write them off against profitable years stretching back to 1962. Senator Robert Dole (who voted to help Chrysler five years later) vehemently opposed Hart's bill, which quickly had been tagged "the Michigan Employment Protection Act." Moreover, Al Ullman, who later became chairman of the House Ways and Means Committee, said it was "just not proper" to pass legislation for one company's benefit. Four years later, the presence of a friendly Al Ullman was one of the most important reasons behind Chrysler's decision to seek tax relief.

All requests for a tax break come up before the House Ways and Means Committee and the Senate Finance Committee. During the 96th Congress, both houses had large Democratic majorities and it was the imposing, and friendly, presence of Russell Long, chairman of the Senate Finance Committee, that offered a political buttress to

Chrysler's business decision to plump for tax breaks. Indeed, lobbyist Tommy Boggs' close friendship with Long (both hail from Louisiana) was one of the primary motives behind Chrysler's selection of Patton, Boggs and Blow as their chief Washington trumpeters. Similarly, in the House, Al Ullman, chairman of the House Ways and Means Committee, was prepared to listen to Chrysler. On the other hand, any bill granting loan guarantees comes up before two different committees: the House Banking, Finance and Urban Affairs Committee and its counterpart in the Senate. The latter was chaired by William Proxmire and composed of nine Democrats and six Republicans. The likely opposition stance of three Democrats—Proxmire, North Carolina's Robert Morgan and Illinois's Adlai Stevenson—made the Senate committee the stiffest possible test and an obstacle to be avoided at all costs. With the political strategy mapped out and with all their tax carry-back credits exhausted, Chrysler, in an elaborate press conference at the end of July 1979, went public with a plea for $1 billion of tax relief, to be repaid from profits projected for 1981 and 1982. "It was," as Senate aide Elinor Bachrach remarked, "an appeal for a thinly veiled grant."

July 1979 wasn't the most propitious month to go running to Washington. It was one of the darker months of the Carter administration, and the President had retired to Camp David to ponder his political future and rearrange his Cabinet. While the resignation of Transportation Secretary Brock Adams brought muted hoots of delight in Detroit, the change at the Treasury Department was to have profound consequences for Chrysler.

Secretary of the Treasury W. Michael Blumenthal had been at odds with the Carter White House almost from Inauguration Day. The White House felt that Blumenthal, like Health, Education and Welfare Secretary Joseph Califano, was more intent on establishing his own reputation than that of the Administration. He gave wide-ranging press interviews, even allowing *Fortune* to record his frustrations as a Cabinet officer. However, Blumenthal possessed a deep understanding of the auto industry. From his days as chairman of Bendix Corporation, a prime supplier of the auto companies, with headquarters just three miles from Highland Park, Blumenthal was well aware of Chrysler's frailty. Blumenthal also had close ties with the United Auto Workers. Indeed in 1976, when he had contemplated running for a Senate seat in Michigan, he had taken pains to make preliminary soundings with Doug Fraser. It was Blumenthal, at a New York dinner for West German Chancellor Helmut Schmidt held in June, who had tipped off Fraser to the severity of Chrysler's problems.

When Riccardo approached the Treasury Department in the spring of 1979, Blumenthal, though Chrysler took him to be an ally, remained unmoved. "None of us had the impression that he'd done his home-work and understood the seriousness of the cash flow problem," Blu-menthal recalled. The Chrysler chairman was told that he would need to provide Treasury officials with the same kind of information he would marshal for a due-diligence application to underwriters—a process, as every corporate executive knows, that requires consid-erable research. "All of this was kind of news to John," Blumenthal said.

About the only thing that Blumenthal had in common with his successor, G. William Miller, the chairman of the Federal Reserve Board, was experience at the top of a major corporation. Unlike Blu-menthal, Miller was not acquainted with the intricacies of the automo-bile industry, was unfamiliar with anything more than the general problems confronting Chrysler and was contemptuous of both the company and its management. An imperious man, the former chief ex-ecutive of Textron had clear ideas about how a company should be run and had precious little time for John Riccardo. While still head of the Federal Reserve Board, Miller had called Riccardo and told him in no uncertain terms that Chrysler had no business seeking federal aid, should strive to arrange funds from its bankers and, if that failed, contemplate reorganization under Chapter 11 of the bankruptcy code. Above all, Miller was determined that Chrysler should not embarrass the President. "Miller," scoffed UAW president Douglas Fraser, "is the ultimate team-player. If they put a gas tank on the rear bumper of a Pinto, he'd try to defend it." The tone deteriorated after Miller moved his papers into Blumenthal's desk. The news of Miller's opposi-tion to tax relief was conveyed to Riccardo and his financial and legal colleagues at a lunch in Highland Park on July 24. Accompanied by representatives of the New York Federal Reserve Bank, Brian Free-man, later the executive director of the Loan Guarantee Board (and an acknowledged master of the Big Lemon, having worked on Penn Central, Lockheed and New York City), told Riccardo that tax relief was out of the question and Chrysler would have to put together a proposal for loan guarantees. Riccardo erupted. On July 31, after re-ceiving hints from another Treasury official that all was not lost on the issue of tax relief, Chrysler publicly appealed once again for $1 billion of tax credits. After conferring with officials at the Environmental Pro-tection Agency, the Federal Trade Commission, the Justice Depart-ment, the Office of Management and Budget and the White House, Miller flatly rejected Chrysler's request. Instead, on August 9, the Treasury Department, in a terse one-page statement, held out the prospect of loan guarantees up to $750 million, provided that satis-factory contributions were extracted from other parties.

Loan guarantees were the last thing Chrysler wanted. With interest

rates over 10 percent, the federal money would add to already bur-
densome interest charges. It quickly became obvious that the government was intent on insisting that Chrysler put its house in order and
come forth with sacrifices from all quarters—but at least loan guarantees were familiar to congressmen. Lockheed and New York had
traipsed a similar path before and, in Lockheed's case, at any rate, the
government's confidence had been justified.[6]

While Chrysler had not contemplated, even in its darkest months,
appealing for loan guarantees, the arguments that had to be mustered
were not entirely foreign. A year earlier, in May 1978, there had been
inquiries about the possibility of $300 million worth of federally guar-
anteed loans to help renovate the Trenton engine plant; a few months
later, there were murmurings about $250 million of guaranteed aid to
finance construction of a transaxle plant in Richmond, Indiana. In
early 1979, Chrysler renewed efforts to obtain guarantees—this time
$50 million from the Farmers Home Loan Administration to provide
funds for the expansion of the Kokomo transmission plant.

Loan guarantees had long played a part in U.S. economic policy. As
early as the First World War, Congress had established the War Finance Corporation to keep companies afloat and to enable them to
transform themselves when the war was over. A decade and a half
later, in the midst of the Great Depression, the Reconstruction Finance Corporation was formed to bolster banks and businesses against
bankruptcy and, until its collapse at the end of the Korean War, it
doled out nearly $40.6 billion. These two agencies spawned others, in-
cluding the Small Business Administration, the Farmers Home Loan
Administration, the Export-Import Bank and the Commodity Credit
Corporation. By 1980, more than $400 billion in federal loans was out-
standing and it was difficult to find a government department that did
not have its hand in the till. During 1979, almost $50 billion of new
guarantees were extended. The Farmers Home Loan Administration,
the Department of Health and Human Services and the Small Business Administration all doled out guarantees. Other loans went to the
rural electrification program, to the development of geothermal energy and to the support of Native American programs. Even the construction of the Washington, D.C., Metro and the long-term leases of
NASA satellites depended on federal guarantees. Nevertheless, it was
the corporate precedents that were quoted more frequently. In 1970,
the Penn Central Railroad requested a $200 million loan under the
auspices of the Defense Production Act of 1950, a measure that authorized private borrowing from the Treasury for defense purposes.
Congress refused, and only after the railroad filed for bankruptcy was
it granted $125 million in loan guarantees to keep the trains running.[7]

A year after the collapse of the Penn Central, Lockheed Aircraft

Corporation narrowly squeaked through a bill (it passed by only 1 vote in the Senate) giving $250 million in guaranteed loans. Lockheed appealed for help after the British Rolls-Royce Company, supplier of engines for the Lockheed 250-passenger Tristar, went bankrupt. Troubled not only by the $900 million bill for developing the Tristar, but also by cost overruns on its military contract for the gigantic C-5A military transport, Lockheed was refused further help by its banks without federal guarantees. The close congressional debate was to be echoed a decade later in the haggling over Chrysler. New York Senator James Buckley sonorously warned, "If the inefficient or mismanaged firm is insulated from the free-market pressures that other businesses must face, the result will be that scarce economic and human resources will be squandered on enterprises whose activities do not meet the standards imposed by the marketplace." In the end it was the prospect of unemployment for Lockheed's 17,000 workers and the 43,000 employees of supplier companies scattered around thirty-five states that won the day. Montana Senator Lee Metcalf remarked at the time, "I would not take upon myself the responsibility of closing out all those jobs." Before passing the final version, both houses had reported bills authorizing $2 billion of loan guarantees for major businesses on the verge of failure, but these bills were whittled down to no more than an answer to Lockheed's troubles. The act that emerged was a prototype for Chrysler. Among other things, it established a two-year emergency loan-guarantee board (composed of the Treasury Secretary, the chairman of the Federal Reserve and the head of the S.E.C.) to administer the aid. Well before Chrysler went crawling to Washington, Lockheed had managed to put its balance sheet back in order, repay all the guaranteed loans (albeit three years late) and handsomely reward the Treasury Department with $31.2 million in fees.

Three years after Lockheed's narrow escape, President Nixon, in January 1974, signed a bill that provided $2.1 billion to establish the Consolidated Rail Corporation (Conrail) from seven bankrupt railroads. Congress had already dallied with the rail network by setting up Amtrak in 1971, through legislation which authorized annual appropriations of $40 million and a total grant, in subsequent years, of $225 million. In 1980, Amtrak, despite the infusion of what was supposed to have been temporary federal assistance, sucked $800 million out of the budget, over three times the total aid originally contemplated.

If the plight of the railroads was scarcely mentioned during Chrysler's agony, Lockheed and New York City were on the tip of almost every lawmaker's tongue. In 1975, when the nation's largest city threatened bankruptcy and provoked fears about an international economic crisis, President Ford refused to forward funds until New York brushed its own doorstep. Battered by an eroding tax base, the recession of 1974–75 and the $12.3 billion yearly cost of services, New York ran up $6 billion in short-term debt and saw the financial markets close as fears grew about its ability to repay the debt. New York was unable to borrow to meet its service bills.[8] After New York City raised city taxes, lopped its payroll and slapped a wage freeze on municipal employees, Ford approved a bill giving $2.3 billion a year to help meet seasonal cash needs. (The short-term loans were designed to be repaid every June, when municipal tax revenues had been collected.) In 1975, House Minority Leader John Rhodes noted, "This is certainly not a bail-out bill. It is a stretch-out plan aimed at giving the City and New York State time to make necessary adjustments in spending and revenue-raising and to balance its budget." By 1978, despite the City's efforts to better its situation, the bond market remained closed to New York and Congress voted long-term guarantees for New York City bonds.

Despite Chrysler's inability to make headway on tax relief, company officials ignored Jim Blanchard, the representative from Michigan's Oakland County. Blanchard had earned an MBA from Michigan State and a law degree from the University of Minnesota before running for Congress in the Watergate election year. Challenging a millionaire incumbent in the primary, he conspicuously failed to attract UAW support. Before the general election, he plastered billboards with his telephone number and the message "If I can help you let me know." The tactic proved successful. During the summer of 1979, Blanchard practically implored Chrysler to let him help. As the only member of the Michigan delegation on the House Banking Committee, Blanchard knew he would be the linchpin if aid came in the form of loan guarantees. Chrysler's Wendell Larsen later admitted, "We didn't even know Jim Blanchard," but within hours of Treasury Secretary Miller's rejection of the request for $1 billion tax relief, John Riccardo, who had only met Blanchard once, in 1975, was on the phone. "Hello, Jim," said the Chrysler chairman. "I understand you've made a generous offer to help . . . I appreciate it."

One of the sprightlier members of the new breed of Democrats, Blanchard was quick to admit that he was not particularly sure of his political philosophy. Blanchard reveled in the water-cooler bargaining he had learned as president of the Ferndale High School student council in 1959 and later as an Assistant Attorney General in Michigan. He had concentrated on legislation like the "Sunset" bill, which sought to provide frequent reviews of federal programs. Blanchard also had strongly supported the fuel-economy standards, had served on the Gasohol Commission and favored funneling money toward solar research. He had never taken any particular interest in the automobile industry.

Shortly after taking Riccardo's call, Blanchard took off for a two-week vacation on the Canadian shore of Lake Huron, where he found time to plow through a two-inch briefing file on Chrysler. He made good use of the telephone in the country cabin, calling Banking Committee colleagues across the country and urging them to stay neutral rather than make public commitments against aid to Chrysler. As Democratic Whip of the Michigan delegation, Blanchard attended the weekly briefings on scheduling from Speaker Tip O'Neill. He had worked closely with Thomas Ashley, who had drafted the House's version of the energy bill and had traveled with House Majority Leader Jim Wright to witness President Sadat's first visit to Israel. As a whip, for the Democratic leader John Brademas, as a pal of House Rules Committee chairman Richard Bolling and as a faithful five-year member of the House Banking Committee, Blanchard had little difficulty persuading influential Democratic leaders of the House to do as he asked. While Henry Reuss, the chairman of the House Banking Committee, had publicly denounced the idea of federal aid for Chrysler, he readily agreed to let the Economic Stabilization Subcommittee, headed by Pittsburgh Congressman William Moorhead, less vehement in his opposition, to hold hearings. Stewart McKinney, a moderate Republican, was the senior minority member of the subcommittee; thus, there was no rallying point for disenchanted Democrats and no convincing leader for a Republican opposition. "It all fitted together very nicely," said Blanchard. "I was playing with a full deck."

After Labor Day, the course was determined. Chrysler publicly set a deadline for aid: Christmas. "Those who were unalterably opposed knew that all they had to do was fight the clock," said Paul Nelson, staff director for the House Banking Committee. "Even some of the neutral ones said, 'You mean this used-car salesman by the name of Iacocca is looking for a handout and the son of a bitch is gonna tell us what to do and when?' "[9]

One of those who remained undecided was the new Treasury Secretary, G. William Miller. Chrysler was dead without his support, because, as Treasury Secretary, Miller was the main link to the White House. Since early in August, when Miller had flatly rejected the request for $1 billion of tax relief, Chrysler had been scrambling to draw up a definitive operating plan and a revised request. Miller demanded that Chrysler limit its request to $500 million in loan guarantees. At a Saturday-morning meeting in the Treasury's fourth-floor conference room, Riccardo and Iacocca, along with thirteen Chrysler directors, presented a detailed 101-page plan to Miller. Near the front was the dismal news that Chrysler needed to raise $2.1 billion before

1982 and had "some confidence" that it could raise $900 million, but, to make up the difference, would need $500 million in immediate loan guarantees and $700 million in contingency guarantees. Miller was not amused. Ten minutes into the meeting, after hearing that Chrysler wanted more than $1 billion, Miller hit the roof. "Why are we still talking about this? What are you guys doing?" he asked. "I told you' this was unacceptable." After two hours of further wrangling, Iacocca and Riccardo, their fingers severely rapped by Miller, were sent packing back to Detroit to draw up yet another request.

The Treasury Department did not like Chrysler's operating plan. Throughout the year they had been receiving accelerating graphs of misery. With little experience of the penalties of falling sales in the industry, they did not trust what they were receiving. In March, Riccardo had told Treasury officials that Chrysler would lose $400 million in 1979. By June the figure was up to $600 million, in July it was $800 million and by September it was over $1 billion. In one of his early presentations, Riccardo had produced a matrix with one axis describing U.S. auto-market volume and the other Chrysler's market share. The worst case called for Chrysler to lose $870 million. By September, Riccardo was telling Miller that the company had fallen off the chart. Miller's predecessor, Michael Blumenthal, believed that Chrysler had fallen prey to a beguiling corporate optimism, which he liked to characterize as "the hockey-stick approach": a steep declining line of losses followed by a sharp upward turn at the end. If the Treasury was skeptical about Chrysler's proposal, so was Proxmire aide Elinor Bachrach. The plan looked as if it had been drawn up quickly and seemed optimistic. Worst of all to the Washington critics of Chrysler's image as a builder of gas-guzzlers, the plan assumed that the company would continue to produce a full line of cars. After perusing the contents of the folder, Bachrach called her counterpart at the Treasury. "Where's the plan?" she asked. "We're wondering the same," replied the Treasury official.

Despite the sneers in Washington, Chrysler's plan, if necessarily vague on the manner and price of possible dispositions, gave an unprecedented biopsy of an automobile company. It had taken Chrysler, along with outside consultants from Booz Allen & Hamilton and Salomon Brothers, more than a month to put together what was to serve as the sales brochure for members of Congress. Indeed, the day it was released, Chrysler's Washington representatives humped suitcases full of copies of the plan through the hallways to every congressman's office. The plan and exhibits gave away Detroit's most sacred secrets: future-product plans, profit margins on particular models and planned capital expenditures were spelled out for all to see. Chrysler, quite simply, spilled its guts on the foot of Capitol Hill.

Chrysler forecast that 1979 losses might climb as high as $1.073 billion, followed by $482 million in 1980 and a profit of $383 in 1981. The plan repeated some of the savings which had already been made: the $1 billion purportedly lopped off fixed costs, the sale of the bulk of the overseas operations and the recruitment of a new managerial team. Chrysler also revealed that the banks refused to extend any more credit and that its existence would depend largely on the goodwill of suppliers, the UAW and, of course, the federal government.

Meanwhile a series of studies conducted by Data Resources (for the Congressional Budget Office), the Transportation Systems Center (for the Department of Transportation) and Chase Econometrics (for Chrysler) each painted a similarly doleful picture of a nation without Chrysler. A Chrysler bankruptcy, they all agreed, would be the largest ever in the United States. It would mean a decline of about 0.5 percent in the Gross National Product, a rise in the national unemployment rate of between 0.5 and 1.09 percent, a negative impact of about $1.5 billion on the balance of trade. The nation might face a bill of $1.5 billion in welfare payments and an annual tax loss of $500 million. In addition, the federally chartered Pension Benefit Guarantee Corporation, which had not been designed to handle major failures, would be swamped by the $800 million of unfunded liabilities washing around in Chrysler's enormous pension funds. Although most concluded that the U.S. financial markets were broad and deep enough to withstand a Chrysler collapse, the vast macro-economic statistics hid the sharper, regional considerations. A straightforward corporate fire sale threatened 113,000 production workers. More than half of those punched time clocks in Detroit, where 25,000 of the company's 38,000 minority workers were employed. The Michigan unemployment rate would be jolted by another 4 percent while Detroit's would rise by 10 percent. Detroit's budget was already in such sorry shape that four hundred police officers had already been laid off in 1979. In the Wilmington-Newark area of Delaware, Chrysler affected 14,000 jobs, and in St. Louis, Missouri, more than 25,000. There were predictions that the unemployment rate in Syracuse, New York, would double after a bankruptcy, while two out of every five employed persons in Kokomo, Indiana, would be out of a job.

Although reorganization under Chapter 11 of the revised bankruptcy code was intuitively attractive as an alternative and quickly galvanized a flock of excited sympathizers, it did not bear close scrutiny. Most legal experts agreed that Chrysler would have been submerged in courtrooms for between five and ten years, rearranging its complicated debt and coming to terms with thousands of creditors. Advocates fondly recited the manner in which Penn Central and the department store chain of W. T. Grant had survived reorganization proceedings, but neither of those companies relied on consumer confidence to the same extent as an automobile manufacturer. It was expecting a lot of consumers to buy an $8,000 car from a company that might not be around to meet warranty claims or provide parts and service. Under reorganization proceedings, it's quite likely that Chrysler would have watched orders evaporate at the very time it needed ready cash.

Some of the more doctrinaire theorists ignored almost entirely the likely fates of the suppliers, dealers and future-product programs. Even the econometric models could not predict the effect of the cancellation of orders for about $2 billion worth of machine tools, since no company had ever canceled of that magnitude. Neither the suppliers nor the dealers could have been expected to drum their fingers while Chrysler tried to satisfy bills, warranty claims and inventory financing. Furthermore the provisions of Chapter 11 forbid a company from making capital expenditures for future products without the approval of the presiding bankruptcy judge. Although the provision sounds innocuous, the effect of having a frozen product program in an industry where the progress of cars is measured in days would have had catastrophic effects.

Although it was blithely assumed that production workers would have floated into new jobs, the rehiring of laid-off workers would (as time showed) have been severely hampered by the distribution of the Chrysler plants and the capacity of the other auto manufacturers to accommodate the maelstrom. General Motors and Ford either had excess capacity (where there would be no call for extra workers) or no slack (where the addition of extra capacity would take several years). In any case, both companies had eagerly pursued their "Sunbelt strategies"—building plants far from heavily unionized Detroit. Apart from the relatively few Chrysler workers employed by the marine and defense operations, and the senior corporate officials, who would have little difficulty hopping into the back seat of another corporate limousine, the prospects were bleak.

Even the foreign manufacturers were not likely to snap up Chrysler plants at a corporate auction and quickly transform them into a new automobile company. Only five of the Chrysler facilities were vaguely presentable: the Belvidere, Illinois, home of the Omni/Horizon; the New Process gear plant in Syracuse, New York, which made transaxles; the renovated Kokomo, Indiana, transmission plant; the small Introl Division in Ann Arbor, which made instruments; and the Huntsville, Alabama, electronics factory. Congress clearly had a choice—loan guarantees or liquidation. There would be no Chapter 11 reorganization.

Chrysler's congressional allies were keeping a wary eye on the clock. From the beginning of July, 1979 Don Riegle and Jim Blanchard had been clutching bills; they were ready to introduce them at the drop of a hat. The pair waited through August for the Administration to make its position clear. Then they waited through September while Chrysler and the Treasury Department played musical chairs. By the second week in October, House Speaker Tip O'Neill was murmuring that he hoped to wrap up the session by Thanksgiving. If O'Neill stuck to his word, time would run out. There were barely enough weeks left in the session to hold hearings, push the bills through both banking committees, ram them through the House and the Senate and whip them out of the Joint Conference Committee.

By October 12, Blanchard and Riegle had decided to snatch the bill away from the Administration's sedentary quarterback, William Miller, and make their own dash. Blanchard decided to announce the start of hearings in the Economic Stabilization Subcommittee and summon his most important witness, Lee Iacocca. No sooner did word of this crass display of independence reach the Treasury Department than Treasury officials, via intermediaries at Lehman Brothers in New York, conveyed a message to Highland Park: If Iacocca dared to testify, the Department would publicly ridicule Chrysler's plan for survival.

The Treasury Department, meanwhile, was feeling the heat of a Proxmire inquisition. The Wisconsin senator, along with Utah's Jake Garn, fired off an eighteen-page letter to Miller, plainly stating that in order for the Senate even to consider legislation, there were a lot of questions about Chrysler's plans, its projections for market share and its hopes for full-line production that needed satisfactory answers. Miller can scarcely have found the answer in Chrysler's renewed request for aid. In response to the Treasury Secretary's September scolding, Chrysler produced a new plan. None of the details or projections had changed, but in what was purely a political ploy to appease Miller, the government was now asked to approve $750 million in loan guarantees. Oddly enough, Undersecretary of the Treasury Robert Carswell seemed mollified. Carswell wrote to Blanchard that the new plan ". . . appears to meet one of the key standards set by the Secretary . . . namely that federal aid be limited to loan guarantees in amounts substantially less than $1 billion." Chrysler was certainly complying with Treasury Department wishes by presenting a recovery scheme costing far under $1 billion, but Chrysler officials were also telling anyone who cared to listen that the numbers made no sense. They still needed $1.2 billion.

Undeterred by the Treasury Department's attempts at intimidation, Iacocca, along with Doug Fraser and Detroit Mayor Coleman Young, began a spirited defense of Chrysler. The same day that Blanchard re-

ceived the hint from Carswell that Miller would not sandbag his legislation, Iacocca appeared to testify in Washington. Unlike the list for
the hearings held later by Proxmire, the House witness list was
specifically designed to give Chrysler's case the hard sell. Ever since
Riccardo's resignation on September 18, Chrysler's critics had been
deprived of a major source of ammunition: a quick-tempered automobile executive willing to heap blame for most of the company's troubles on federal regulations. (His departure had been hastened by a
blunt warning from doctors that the fight for Chrysler, coupled with
his heart condition, would almost certainly kill him.) Riccardo himself
had recognized that he might be Chrysler's largest outstanding liability. Iacocca was another matter—most of the congressmen treated him
like a demigod. Stewart McKinney greeted the new Chrysler chairman
and remarked, "If you do what you did for Ford with Chrysler, you
are going to be a man that needs a big bronze statue put somewhere."
Iacocca replied, "I hope it's a live statue."

Laughter that might have been canned for the Johnny Carson Show
filled the hearing room. It returned periodically, more often than not
to punctuate the exchanges between Chrysler's friends and Florida
Congressman Richard Kelly, whom the TV networks quickly made a
star. A former circuit judge from the Zephyr Hills District, a staunch
anti-communist and a fervent advocate of free enterprise, Richard
Kelly cut a lonely swath. A tall, stooping figure with flat feet, he wandered the corridors like some mildly suntanned Scrooge, lambasting
Iacocca for trying to "put a con on the American people." All the
while, his colleagues snickered about "the hanging judge from Disney
World."[10] Hidden in Kelly's taunts was the clear reflection of a widespread belief that Chrysler was tinkering with the nation's economic
chromosomes. His lone vocal ally, Ron Paul of Texas, wanted to know
why Congress didn't concentrate on the heart of the issue, regulation.

The hearings were for show and Kelly played court jester. He
pricked the UAW's Fraser on the second day of testimony with exaggerated nastiness. Although the silvery-haired Scotsman was occasionally acidic in his responses, he held his temper in check. "Shit,"
whispered a Republican staffer to a colleague, "he didn't fall for it."
In five days of hearings, the congressmen listened to thirty witnesses,
who provided more of an education than a debate on matters of substance. It was clear from the first round of questions to Iacocca that
the committee members, with the exception of McKinney, knew next
to nothing about the automobile industry—and in most instances what
they thought they knew was wrong. The testimony, which was eventually recorded in more than thirteen hundred pages bound in three
volumes, probably did not change a single vote.

To outside observers, Congress, Chrysler, the UAW and the Carter administration looked like one big happy family starting on its Christmas shopping. Within, the voices of dissent were cacophonous, with the men in Detroit struggling to win the Administration's support. In early October, Vice-President Mondale attended a fund-raising lunch in Detroit and the hometown Democrats made sure that he was seated next to a high-ranking Chrysler official. Wendell Larsen used the occasion to explain the severity of the problem and urged Mondale to prod Miller. Doug Fraser then journeyed to the capital to badger his old ally, Mondale, to obtain a proposal from the Treasury Department with the utmost haste. Blanchard pestered White House domestic policy adviser Stuart Eizenstat for the same. Eizenstat buckled on October 23 and informed Blanchard that the Treasury officials would indeed have something ready by the end of the month. The very next day, he was back on the phone, with Bill Miller tied into a conference call, repudiating his promise. Miller added that it would be completely impossible for him to give his support by November 1 because of the pressure of other business. Eizenstat's reneging telephone call came hours before a dinner arranged to endorse the President for renomination. Blanchard, none too hot for Carter, arrived at the dinner hopping mad. "I charged through the doors of the Hyatt Regency," he later recalled, "like a bull at Pamplona and told everyone I knew that the Administration was flushing Detroit down the toilet and Carter didn't even know what was going on. I told everyone what a bastard Miller was and pointed so he could see me." However, on the dais, seated at the President's elbow, was Coleman Young, the mayor of Detroit, whose standing with the Carter administration was impeccable. He had been one of the first Democrats, and one of the first blacks, to support the Georgia governor in his bid for the White House and in the succeeding years he had remained loyal. Young, a one-time street fighter and a former UAW organizer, now cashed in his impressive stack of chips, hectoring and exhorting the President to announce a rescue deal for Chrysler. The President absorbed Young's expletives and took the hint. At the end of the dinner he immediately called a meeting with Eizenstat and Miller. By the end of October, the Administration was ready. Even William Miller was ready, and interested congressmen and senators were summoned to the White House to hear details of the plan. UAW president Fraser and the head of the union's Chrysler Department, Marc Stepp, had hired a jet to fly from Kansas City, where they had been outlining details of their recently concluded contract to the 256-member Chrysler Council, for a private briefing from the Vice-President. Distrust of the intentions of the Administration and of the goodwill of the Treasury Secretary ran so high that, on the eve of Halloween, riding in from the Washington airport,

Fraser wondered aloud whether he was going to meet Mondale "for trick or treat."

It was a treat. They were told by the Vice-President that the Treasury Secretary, who, just days before, had been voicing doubts about whether he would even support loan guarantees, was set to announce a plan far larger than the one he had hurled back at Chrysler six weeks before. Prodded by an estimate from consultants Booz Allen & Hamilton that Chrysler needed $2.8 billion to weather the storm and estimates from Ernst and Whinney, accountants hired specially by the Treasury Department, that the automaker would need $3 billion, Miller backed a plan calling for $1.5 billion in loan guarantees, to be matched by an equal amount raised by Chrysler from sales of assets and from concessions by various parties. Miller's lavish presentation when he finally testified in November left Chrysler's supporters smirking and provoked many a fatuous message of gratitude. With Miller finally aboard, the discussions centered on the size of the contributions to be exacted from the banks, state and local governments, suppliers and dealers, and the UAW.

Shortly after Miller journeyed to Capitol Hill, Alfred Kahn, President Carter's ebullient adviser on inflation, leaped into the fray and irretrievably colored the final two months of debate. His remarks, which were offered at a Saturday-morning press conference in Washington, had a devious origin and, like so many of the public statements about Chrysler, sprang from a political source. A few days before making his statement, when he labeled the settlement recently negotiated between Chrysler and the UAW as "outrageous," Kahn had attended a meeting with the President and the Treasury Secretary. (Stuart Eizenstat and Vice-President Mondale were attending a steel workers' conference.) The three men fretted about Ted Kennedy's increasingly harsh attacks on the Administration's attempts to fight inflationary wage settlements. Looking for a way to dull Kennedy's jabs, the White House authorized Kahn to attack the UAW's settlement with Chrysler—which, if inflationary, was far less so than the contracts the union had concluded with General Motors and Ford. (The union's agreement with Chrysler shaved $203 million off the total cost of the three-year contract and also permitted deferred payment of $200 million into the company pension fund.) When Kahn's remarks were disseminated, they aroused a vitriolic outburst in Detroit, with the UAW president labeling them as "absolutely shocking and incomprehensible." Viewing the reception, the White House and the Treasury Secretary adroitly disassociated themselves from Kahn's statements and left the anti-inflation adviser twisting in the wind.

One result of Kahn's outbursts was that interest was ignited regarding the size of the UAW contribution to the Chrysler loan-guarantee package. Indiana's Richard Lugar, on one side of the Senate aisle, and Massachusetts' Paul Tsongas, on the other, both interested themselves in this aspect of the debate. Lugar, one of the more thoughtful conservative Republicans, was torn between the interests of the Chrysler workers he represented and his opposition to loan guarantees. A few weeks earlier, he had written to Chrysler, offering his support in a campaign to temper federal regulations, but the company replied that it was too little, too late. Lugar's call for the UAW to agree to a three-year wage freeze excited his aides. They were tickled pink at the public reception. Aide David Gogel recalled, "We wanted to go it alone, given the press reaction. We had headlines every day." Eventually, reason got the better of enthusiasm and Lugar lined up alongside Paul Tsongas, whose ties with labor and high ratings by bodies such as the Americans for Democratic Action gave the call for a wage freeze added respectability. Tsongas, a liberal Democrat, was as repulsed as Lugar by Chrysler's heavy breathing. Privately he confided to friends, "I think federal aid is a bad idea, but nobody's going to vote against me if I vote for it." The pair—an unlikely combination if ever there was one—jointly presented a proposal for a loan guarantee with the provision that the UAW make a $1.2 billion concession—the equivalent of a three-year wage freeze. (The previous August, at the start of contract negotiations, Lee Iacocca had asked the union to agree to a two-year wage freeze.) At the end of November, the Senate Banking Committee embraced the Lugar-Tsongas proposal and voted for a bill that included a three-year wage freeze for union and non-union employees and a total of $1.43 billion in contributions from dealers, banks, suppliers, and state and local governments.

Congressmen and senators could hurl brickbats at Chrysler with few pangs, and they did. The company was too large to elicit sympathy. As a member of the *Fortune* Top Twenty, its influence was mysterious and its shape defied comprehension. Chrysler's problems were not, on the whole, local problems, unless a plant happened to be plopped in the middle of a congressional district. The aches and pains were national concerns, matters of policy to be solved either by the marketplace or by federal intervention.

The corporation's 4,500 dealers and 19,000 suppliers were another matter. Unlike the company's, their presence was tangible and their plight immediate. There was a Chrysler dealer or supplier in every congressional district in the country. These were the merchants of the nation, men who had inherited businesses from their fathers and had, in some cases, passed them on to their sons. Family commitments stretched back to the days of Walter Chrysler, and the businesses were located in the small communities of Middle America, like Great Bend in Kansas. These weren't garish swashbucklers from Detroit,

bouncing billions and tweaking communities with the flash of a calcu-
lator. The dealers and suppliers could make the numbers understandable and explain—as Wendell Miller, a Binghampton, New York,
dealer did—that a Chrysler bankruptcy would force "independent
businessmen in every congressional district . . . out of business." The
boondoggles and sales junkets to sun-soaked islands were forgotten.
Chrysler officials made sure that each congressman knew about the
local dealers and suppliers. The company drew up computerized lists
outlining contributions in every district and showing congressmen
how much local, state and federal tax was contributed by Chrysler
showrooms. Working through the Dealer Councils (the officials
elected by the dealers themselves), an average of two hundred dealers
a day came to Washington to lobby their representatives. Coached for
an hour in the early morning about what they should and should not
say, the dealers spent their days roaming corridors, rapping on doors
and buttonholing congressmen as well as their administrative and legislative aides. The sight of these independent small businessmen, some
of whom returned two or three times, was mighty effective.[11] The
dealers quickly ridiculed the notion of Chrysler filing for bankruptcy.
Charles Swift, a Sacramento dealer for more than thirty years, told
senators, "When you don't have a live body come through the dealership it becomes an automatic morgue and mausoleum."[12] Others explained that the closure of just one dealership could result in unemployment for five hundred people. While Iacocca's arguments for the
need to maintain production of a full line had largely been interpreted
as vanity, a Utah dealer could effectively point out that Chrysler still
needed to manufacture large cars because "the big families of the
Mormon communities of Utah [have] to pile their kids in the car to
get to grandmother's house on Christmas Day."[13]

Similarly, the suppliers had demonstrated their faith. As a group,
they provided everything from wing mirrors to carburetors and, because of the nature of the payment terms, they usually had around
$800 million in accounts receivable from Chrysler. In many cases they
were on familiar terms with their congressional representatives. Peter
Scott, for example, a group Vice-President of United Technologies and
president of the Essex Group, which made harnesses and magnet wir-
ing for Chrysler, was a friend of Connecticut's Stewart McKinney.
Reginald Lenna, president of Blackstone Corporation, which churned
out radiators and heater cores, was on nodding terms with New York's
Stanley Lundine and Jim Blanchard belonged to the same college fraternity as the brother of Norman Peslar, the president of a Michigan
welding company.

It was indeed the quiet touches of home that emphasized the consequences of a Chrysler failure. David Bonior, a young congressman

from Michigan's blue-collar Macomb County, recalled a childhood spent in the shadow of the Dodge plant in Hamtramck. "I remember walking to the corner of Joseph Campau and Leeman," he told his colleagues, "to meet my father and grandfather as they returned from work on the streetcar." Even Paul Tsongas appreciated the devastating results of the flight of the textile companies from Massachusetts and observed that he didn't "want to do to Detroit what others had done to my city" of Lowell. But no one summed it up better than the Chrysler dealer who observed, "The very survival of a lot of good people in this country and a lot of small businesses depends upon the whims . . . of the political system."[14]

While Chrysler and its supporters oiled eight cylinders to power the bill through Congress, the opposition ran with all the zest of a one-horsepower lawnmower. The forces opposed to the bail-out were certainly powerful, but, unlike Chrysler's allies, they were not united by fear. Almost the entire business community was opposed to helping Chrysler. General Motors chairman Thomas Murphy, an incorrigible ideologue who has said in virtually every interview he has given that "a society without risk is a society without reward" was quick to announce his distaste. The rest of the nation's boardrooms were quick to echo Murphy and, although Ford chairman Philip Caldwell hedged the inevitable question by saying, "Chrysler is not helped by kibbitzing from the sidelines," there was no mistaking his true belief. Of the automobile company heads, only Gerald Meyers, AMC's chairman, who knew something of the pain of asking for help, made a public statement in support of Chrysler. The prominent and vociferous Business Roundtable, along with the National Association of Manufacturers, expressed dissatisfaction. Former American Motors president George Romney observed that a decade earlier it was clear that if "American Motors couldn't make it on its own we were going out of business." Almost every economist from Milton Friedman to Alan Greenspan and former head of the Federal Reserve Board Arthur Burns chipped in to voice their apprehension. Even Ralph Nader found himself on the same side of the table as General Motors, denouncing "corporate welfarism" and quietly hoping that a Chrysler bankruptcy would speed the day when General Motors would be fodder for the trustbusters. Behind the stream of witnesses in Washington, editors and journalists almost unanimously condemned federal help. *Fortune,* the glossy voice of the boardroom, ridiculed Chrysler's timetable for recovery as "a pie-in-the-sky plan for survival" while the *Wall Street Journal* rattled off a series of editorials culminating in one headed "Laetrile for Chrysler." Cartoonists had a field day. Herblock depicted a Chrysler official standing at the back of a line in a welfare office; one of his brethren showed two people standing outside the

Capitol with one asking, "What do they call that place anyway?" and the other answering, "The Chrysler Building."

The journalistic cannons were better loaded than the political ordnance. In the House, Richard Kelly lost serious points in his bumbling answers. Although William Proxmire demonstrated a detailed grasp of Chrysler's plight, he was unable to rally the forces of either the new or the old right. Although Barry Goldwater denounced the loan guarantees on the last day of debate as "the biggest mistake Congress has ever made in its history," he and others of his ilk remained docile during the early wrangling. Connecticut Senator Lowell Weicker was one of a few Republicans who showed much consistency for several months, but though he had distinguished himself as the first candidate to withdraw from the 1980 Presidential race, his unpopularity with fellow Republicans made him an unlikely opposition leader.

The austere mood that settled on the country after California's tax revolt in 1978 continued to buffet Capitol Hill, and it was congressmen like Michigan's David Stockman, eventually the only member of his state's delegation to oppose aid, who gathered plaudits for their fluent attacks on federal intervention. (Lost in the compliments surrounding Stockman's apparent display of objectivity was the memory of some previous statements which reflected the same brand of confident dispassion. Had some of his earlier predictions been borne out, Stockman might possibly never have had to oppose loan guarantees. In 1977, in an article for *Public Interest,* Stockman hooted that a pessimistic CIA analysis of future oil prices was "ludicrous" and continued with utter assurance that "the global economic conditions necessary for another major unilateral price action by OPEC are not likely to re-emerge for more than a decade—if ever.")

Once in the open, Chrysler was fair bait for all and there was no shortage of opinions about what Congress should do. Tom Wicker, the New York *Times'* columnist, suggested that Chrysler concentrate on building mass transportation (the company had never built a single bus or railcar). The Reverend Jesse Jackson scurried to Detroit and demanded that blacks be treated fairly, while Angela Davis of the Communist Workers Party advocated complete revolutionary worker control.

In Congress, there were even more ideas about what should be in the bill. John Conyers, a liberal Detroit congressman, wanted one condition for aid to be the continued operation of the dilapidated Dodge Main plant, while Rep. Henry Reuss wanted Chrysler to build energy-efficient cars. Most important of all, Russell Long knew what he wanted. The chairman of the Senate Finance Committee tags a provision for an employee stock-option program (ESOP) onto almost every bill he is associated with. Believing that an ESOP encourages worker loyalty and boosts productivity, Long was not about to back aid for Chrysler without his pet plan. The deal was made in a breakfast meeting at the Hay-Adams in the middle of October between Long, Wisconsin Senator Gaylord Nelson and Doug Fraser. Although Fraser and Long had never before met for a sit-down conversation, Fraser emerged from the hotel with his neck in the firm but friendly grasp of Long, and from that moment it was clear that Chrysler was going to provide a comprehensive employee stock-option plan.

By Tuesday, December 11, the cool heads in the House believed that they had lined up sufficient votes to pass a bill and the UAW leadership was quick to tell Tip O'Neill of their preference for a vote within a couple of days. The Speaker, largely out of deference to Henry Reuss, the chairman of the House Banking Committee, who had remained amenable despite his opposition to the bill, postponed the vote for a few more days. Meanwhile, Bill Moorhead quietly discussed with Senator Tsongas the idea that the House bill should provide for a heftier union contribution, equivalent to the sum proposed by the Senate. The UAW wasn't slow to act on the new threat to its interests, flying in a regional director from Milwaukee to badger Reuss and prodding the House Democratic leadership to scold Moorhead.

The lobbyists' next ploy was largely procedural: the more favorable measure, the House bill, was passed before the Senate had a chance to vote on its stiffer terms. The House leadership, for its part, was anxious to ensure that the senators actually voted. In previous years, some House members had been stuck with embarrassing votes on a couple of labor-law reform bills only to discover that the Senate dropped consideration of the measure. The final maneuvering, however, was actually begun in the Senate, largely to quell the threats of a possible filibuster from Connecticut's Lowell Weicker, who during the previous ten days had become increasingly angry about helping Chrysler and was loudly threatening to postpone a vote until well after Christmas. Majority Leader Robert Byrd sensed the danger and, in a crafty move, late in the evening of Saturday, December 15, introduced the bill and persuaded Weicker to relinquish a procedural obstacle he could have used to postpone a vote. Byrd, delighted with his exploits and dressed in a red vest and a star-studded tie, left the floor to attend a Christmas party, where he entertained guests by playing the fiddle.

On Tuesday morning, December 18, Jim Blanchard and Bill Moorhead were poring over blueprints of corridors and doors leading to the House floor. Members of the Michigan caucuses buttonholed congressmen as they arrived, while union representatives, including

Doug Fraser, and a team of black ministers added their pleas. The
Chrysler men shook every hand they could reach.

It was against a background of Christmas jollity that the Speaker
rose, "as Tip O'Neill the Congressman," to make a rare and impas-
sioned plea for Chrysler. Before a House containing many members
with no memories of the Depression, O'Neill repeated the picture he
had drawn in a private meeting the night before. He recalled the chill
times in Boston, when unemployed workers would stand in the morning dark and beg for work shoveling snow. The congressmen were
duly moved, pressed magnetic cards into the voting slots behind their
seats and watched the vote tally flash up on the expansive board
above the Speaker. By 7:20 P.M., a bill to help Chrysler had been
passed by 271 votes to 136 and the House, which had been as hushed
as a church yard ten minutes earlier, broke into a deep, contented
hubbub. O'Neill puffed on his cigar, Don Riegle suddenly appeared to
pump hands and Detroit Congressman Lucien Nedzi even planted a
kiss on his surprised Wisconsin colleague, David Obey.

While the House irresistibly rolled to its conclusion, Chrysler had
blurted out yet another worry. On the advice of its financial advisers,
Salomon Brothers, the Chrysler financiers, had included a note of caution in a prospectus drawn up for the Securities and Exchange Commission describing the proposed sale of preferred stock to dealers. In
this gloomy document, the company admitted that it might run plumb
out of money as soon as January 15, 1980. The revelation provoked a
fit at the Treasury Department, where officials wanted to make sure
that Iacocca gave a public disclosure. Knowing the consequences of
revealing something as precise as the day Chrysler would run out of
money, Iacocca refused. There then began a series of telephone calls—
telling evidence of the web of alliances that had been built in the previous weeks—between the chief players. The Treasury Department
called the Vice-President to pressure Chrysler. Mondale, in turn,
called Doug Fraser, asking him to persuade Iacocca to offer a public
announcement. Fraser did as he was asked and placed a call across
Detroit. Miller, Mondale and White House aide David Rubenstein
then placed a conference call to the Chrysler chief. Rubenstein
asserted that Iacocca had a fiduciary responsibility to report the imminent shortage while Miller chipped in to say that the Treasury Department and the Administration might be better off letting Chrysler go
bankrupt. Finally, despairing of Iacocca, who continued to insist that
talk of a bridge loan would merely confuse the issue, the Treasury Department leaked the story to the New York *Times*. Minutes later, Vice-
President Mondale held a news conference announcing Chrysler's
need for financing to cover the gap between passage of a loan guarantee act and completion of all the necessary qualifications.

So, as the Senate convened for its final day of debate on Chrysler, the company's officials and their lobbyists were scrambling to word an amendment that would allow $500 million to be whisked immediately to Detroit. They were also busily mustering support for an amendment, sponsored by senators Eagleton, Roth and Biden, to limit the UAW contribution to $400 million. Almost from the moment Tsongas and Lugar had agreed to a joint proposal for the three-year, $1.2 billion wage freeze, the Massachusetts senator seemed to have realized his mistake. Prodded by Jim Blanchard, a friend from his days as a congressman, and faced with the prospect of running against the UAW for the rest of his political career, Tsongas tried to beat a hasty retreat.

From Detroit, Iacocca made it perfectly clear to Wendell Larsen and Tommy Boggs that the one thing he didn't want to see in a federal bill was a wage freeze. Frozen salaries, argued Iacocca, would make it practically impossible to recruit experienced executives and tricky to keep skilled craftsmen. Tsongas kept pressuring Lugar to soften his terms and Jim Blanchard made an appeal for compromise during an appearance on the MacNeil-Lehrer television program, but Lugar had special reasons for believing that the union would agree to concessions well above $400 million. Shortly after the union had informed the White House that they would agree to $400 million, the Treasury Department had slyly informed Lugar's office that the union might squeeze as much as $600 million from the recently concluded pact with Chrysler. Early in December, Doug Fraser had caught an early flight from Detroit to have a frank heart-to-heart talk with Lugar. In the quiet of the senator's office, Fraser explained the difficulties he would have persuading the Canadian union members to ratify a new contract that imposed lower wages as a result of an action by the U. S. Congress. Fraser trod gingerly, for Lugar was crucial to the outcome in the Senate. Without the Indiana senator's approval, five or six Republicans (including Senate Minority Leader Ted Stevens) would desert the cause.

It took until the day before the Senate vote for Lugar to relinquish his stand. Dropping his insistence on a total $1.2 billion wage freeze, Lugar suggested that the union contribute $800 million. Along with Lowell Weicker (who was now looking for another way to sabotage Chrysler), he tried to bring the Senate to a quick vote before the House finished its deliberations. The effort was blocked by Don Riegle, who held the floor for three hours, pacing with bowed head around his desk, repeating the old arguments and displaying the same charts that were almost as familiar as the chamber's furnishings. Riegle managed to postpone a vote until the following day (December 19) which allowed the Chrysler forces to regroup and mount a final charge. At 8 A.M., a group of senators convened in Riegle's office to plot strategy. From the White House, President Carter placed calls to a couple of wavering senators. Earlier in December, Carter had approved a bill calling for a hike in the military budget, an action which had pleased his fellow Georgian Sam Nunn. The President now telephoned for a return favor and Nunn obliged. Connecticut's Abraham Ribicoff proved more immune to the presidential pressure. Across Washington, Tommy Boggs had roused Lee Iacocca and asked the Chrysler chief, from his home in Bloomfield Hills, to call Illinois's Charles Percy and Kansas's Robert Dole. The neatest stroking was performed on a couple of telephones inside the Vice-President's office, just off the floor of the Senate Chamber. There, Doug Fraser was working the phone with all the skill of an old-time politician. While his colleague Howard Paster readied senators on one line, Fraser sweet-talked on the other. Louisiana Senator Bennett Johnston (who had provided Chrysler with a hideaway office) even called Tommy Boggs to say he was willing to vote for the package provided that Fraser called. The UAW had neatly lassoed every conceivable ally. The Vice-President was summoned from his sickbed, where he had been suffering from a severe bout of the flu, to preside over the Senate, while feminist Gloria Steinem, a friend of the UAW and of the Progressive Alliance (a liberal coalition founded by Fraser in 1974) called Oregon Republican Robert Packwood, who had sided with feminists on abortion. As senators strolled through the ornate Senate Reception Room, they almost tripped over lobbyists. Mitch Daniels, Senator Lugar's administrative aide, later observed that "it was like an American labor hall of fame. I would have believed it if Walter Reuther had been there." Fraser, dapper in a set of fresh brown pinstripes, buttonholed more senators while officials from the Urban League, the Black Caucus, the NAACP, the Urban Coalition, Coretta King's Full Employment Council, the Industrial Union Department of the AFL-CIO, the textile workers, teamsters and building trades persuaded others. Even Senator Russell Long blocked a doorway, exerting his considerable grip over the southern cabal: Stennis, Boren and Talmadge.

Only 43 senators were able to withstand the pressure, while the lobbyists rattled up 53 votes in favor of the $400 million amendment. Any celebration was quickly halted when Lugar, Tsongas and Weicker threatened to kill any loan bill carrying the provision. Lugar termed the $400 million figure (half the size of his compromise proposal) "a killer," while Weicker loudly complained that the bill was being railroaded through Congress and that he "saw no possibility of a vote on a Chrysler bill until January 3." Proxmire, hunched earnestly over his desk, snapped that the amendment was "an open invitation to raid the Treasury by unions everywhere." The mood in the Senate, which had bubbled an hour previously, quickly turned grim.

Majority Leader Robert Byrd, standing with his hands on his hips in the middle of the Senate floor, immediately detected the change and summoned senators Tsongas, Lugar, Riegle, Levin, Bayh, Cranston, Garn and Stevens to the Lyndon B. Johnson Room to negotiate a reversal of the victory. In the room aptly named after the quintessential horsetrader, the final details of the bill that the Senate was to send to the Conference Committee were hammered out. Everything had come down to a few figures and slices of small print; the lobbyists pressed advice on the senators before they disappeared into the Majority Leader's sanctum. Inside, Lugar—in exchange for a UAW concession of $525 million—agreed to reducing the management contribution from $175 million to $150 million, softening the ESOP from $250 million to $175 million and hoisting the federal guarantees from $1.25 billion to $1.5 billion. Lugar also agreed to include a couple of extra clauses: the first to cover a $500 million bridge loan, the second to permit the payment of dividends on preferred stock.

The group emerged from the hour-long meeting with Senator Biden clasping the shoulders of the UAW's Paster and Chrysler's Larsen and telling them that he would make sure that Weicker went along with the freshly struck deal. A group of senators promptly gathered around Weicker's desk, and Biden was as good as his word. He crossed himself and briefly knelt before Weicker while Lugar prepared to list the new terms. Rattling off the list of numbers, Lugar failed to mention either the bridge loan or the dividends on the preferred stock. "What the hell happened?" Larsen angrily asked Lugar a bit later. "I thought we had a deal." Lugar replied with an embarrassed grin, "It was only a partial deal." Sternly rebuffed on one front, Chrysler, through Senator Carl Levin, introduced an amendment requesting a bridge loan, but when it came to Senate maneuvering the skills Levin had learned as a Detroit City Councilman were no match for the wily Proxmire. Largely out of courtesy, Levin offered Proxmire a copy of his amendment before discussion began. Proxmire studied the paper carefully and immediately tore it to shreds.

With the Senate plainly unwilling to entertain another plea from Chrysler, Riegle called the Treasury Secretary and extracted a promise that Miller would lean on the banking community and line up interim financing. Late in the evening, as the Senate prepared to vote, Majority Leader Byrd, along with Riegle and Eagleton, placed an insurance call to the Treasury Secretary, who was attending a Christmas party in the Department's offices. Byrd reported to the Senate that Miller "was confident that with the help of the Administration, Chrysler could obtain interim financing" while Riegle added that the

Treasury Secretary would "begin tonight contacting critical parties."

After the Senate passed the bill by 53 votes to 44, there was one minor matter to settle before the Joint Conference Committee meeting. A small group gathered in Senator Eagleton's office, where Eagleton himself tried to call Riccardo, but no one had the telephone number of the former Chrysler chairman's Mexico vacation home. Then Riegle was tickled by an idea. Running to his office, he returned with a defective Dodge clutch housing mailed by a constituent. With his hands covered in grease, Riegle started giving out awards. He placed part of the housing over Larsen's head and gave Eagleton a clutch plate, which now stands among the senator's china collection. Paul Tsongas was not present, but had backed the $525 million union concession after proposing the $1.2 billion wallop. He was presented, in absentia, with a flipper which swung madly from side to side.

Although Tsongas had been outgunned on the union concession, he had his sights dead-level when it came to the conference meeting. "Let's add up the House offer and the Senate offer," he kept advising the other conferees, "and divide by two." That is more or less what happened. One amendment, proffered by Senator Heinz, would have prevented a windfall for existing Chrysler shareholders by forcing the company to raise money by issuing 1.04 shares for every one outstanding. Henry Reuss fliply dismissed it as "a welfare plan for investment bankers" and the amendment disappeared forever. There was, however, a last-ditch fight. Elinor Bachrach—who, by the time of the conference meeting, had perhaps the best command of the details contained within the House and Senate bills—also had a blueprint for battle. Determined to maintain the Senate requirements and egged on by Bachrach, Proxmire suggested that Chrysler should not receive any money until $750 million of contributions were legally committed. The figure did not mean much to Reuss, who was unfamiliar with the small print, so he simply bade the Treasury officials lounging behind him to add the stipulation, but to Chrysler's supporters, the possible result of Proxmire's cunningly worded suggestion was plain enough. To obtain firm commitments of contributions amounting to $750 million would take several months, while the company was promising to be down to its last penny within weeks of the conference meeting. Carswell duly whispered with his advisers and, in a voice barely audible above the insistent murmur, told the meeting that "once we have $750 million legally committed and the rest on assurances the money could roll." Carswell seemed to be in a deep slumber and was quickly woken by Riegle, who, red in the face, leaped to his feet and insisted that Chrysler's future could not be pinned to "a figure taken out of the air." He railed, "All success or failure rides on an off-the-cuff judgment." Cooler heads—like Lugar's—finally prevailed and the extemporaneous number vanished into the smoky haze, but Bachrach had another dart to hurl. While the House bill read that Chrysler need only receive "adequate assurances" before the money could roll, she had been careful to see that the Senate version defined a financial commitment as "a legally binding commitment," and the two contradictory phrases remained in the final act. Once again, Chrysler resorted to its surrogates. When the senators and congressmen adjourned to discuss the proposed settlement, Jack Nugent, a lobbyist in Bill Timmons' firm, sidled up to Nancy Kassebaum and asked her to tell the Conference Committee that, despite the conflicting definitions, it was clearly the intent of Congress that Chrysler merely obtain reasonable assurances. The senator, although she had voted against the bill, quietly told her colleagues that if they wished to help Chrysler, they should not hamstring the company with impossible restrictions. Once the final terms of the UAW contribution, $462.5 million, had been passed on for approval to Doug Fraser, the Conference Committee quickly wrapped up business and the tortuous debate was at an end. All that remained were the final votes in the Senate and the House, and the President's signature.

John Riccardo, the man who had started it all, heard the news in Mexico. Douglas Fraser was heading back to Detroit by plane and Lee Iacocca was in New York, having spent the day trying to pacify the company's bankers. Outside the committee hearing room, the UAW's Paster was complaining to anybody who would listen that the final package was unfair. He stated, "The working man has taken a disproportionate amount of the burden." Wendell Larsen, having dashed to Senator Kassebaum to express his thanks for her crucial intervention, was quickly surrounded by reporters. His hands trembling, he read from a tatty piece of paper a statement of thanks dictated minutes before by Iacocca. In the foyer of the Rayburn Building, the TV cameras' red buttons were winking, and a crumpled crowd, the creases in their clothes caught by the klieg lights, watched the politicians perform for their constituents. Riegle, looking older and more doleful than his forty-one years, remembered that "several months ago there was little chance that the bill would pass" while Blanchard smoothly expressed the hope that the package would be assembled quickly. Meanwhile, David Gogel, Lugar's assistant, earnestly assured his counterpart on Weicker's staff that no bridge loan was insidiously hidden in the final bill, "despite what will be in tomorrow's New York *Times*."

After the TV cameras were turned off and icy rushes of air started to blow through the lobby doors, groups of stragglers wandered through the Rayburn Building, which was deserted, apart from a rock band blaring away at a basement party. It was, after all, nearly Christmas.

CHAPTER THIRTEEN

Patience and Prudence

Bankers function by reference to prudence. It's imprudent for them to do anything until they have to.

— Brian Freeman, Executive Director,
Chrysler Loan Guarantee Board

Unlike the cars that littered Detroit's parking lots, Chrysler's bankers were invisible. They did not rust in winter, sink to their ankles in mud or have weeds growing in their pockets—but the bankers were as deeply mired in Chrysler's rot as any sales bank auto that ever spent a week shivering in the Michigan state fairgrounds. Headquartered in twenty different countries and in almost every major city—banks or insurance companies held $4.75 billion worth of debt issued by Chrysler or Chrysler Financial. The loan agreements were written in English and French, Spanish and German, Italian and Japanese—even Persian.

In New York, bankers muttered about Chrysler around the locker rooms of the University Club and the Racquet and Tennis Club. Others fretted in the nation's regional money centers: inside Chicago's Loop, along Chestnut Street in Philadelphia, on Montgomery Street in San Francisco and in downtown Los Angeles. There were frowns in Atlanta and Houston and St. Louis and Denver. There were fervent debates about the virtues of free enterprise at monthly board meetings held in small towns across America: in Shreveport, Louisiana; in Gulfport, Mississippi; in Darlington, South Carolina; and in Sheboygan, Wisconsin. Abroad, bankers in Toronto and Ottawa, London and Frankfurt, Paris and Tokyo watched the tapping of their Telex machines. Almost everywhere people congregated to talk about money, Chrysler's name was mud.

Yet the key to the loan guarantees lying in the government vault was clasped by the banks. To be sure, other parties had to grant concessions before Chrysler could draw down on its loans, but no group proved as obdurate as the financial community. Within weeks of President Carter signing Public Law 96-185, the United Auto Workers had pared $462.5 million from its contract. Chrysler representatives fanned out to badger officials from state and local governments, trooping into offices in Lansing, Michigan; Springfield, Illinois; Dover, Delaware; Indianapolis, Indiana; Albany, New York; Jefferson City, Missouri; and Columbus, Ohio. Others traveled to Ottawa, the Canadian capital, to win aid from the government of Prime Minister Joe Clark. In Highland Park, the legal staff drew up yet another prospectus—this time for a private stock offering among the company's dealers and suppliers. Purchasing agents tried to shave more dollars off contracts with suppliers, while other negotiators drove down Woodward Avenue to bargain with Detroit Mayor Coleman Young. While all this was going on, it was the bankers who, for close to six months, seemed nearly as impassable, immovable and insurmountable a competitor as General Motors itself.

The initial restructuring of Chrysler's debt was, according to Treasury Secretary William Miller, the most complicated financial restructuring ever undertaken in the United States. It took Chrysler longer to obtain $655 million in concessions from its four hundred lenders than it did to win the $1.5 billion in loan guarantees from the 535-member United States Congress. Compared to Lockheed, which had dealt with only twenty-four banks, Chrysler's task was a nightmare. The banks were the one remaining vestige of the company's worldwide empire. The parent company dealt with 160 banks and had $1.18 billion worth of debt outstanding, while Chrysler Financial had dealings with 282 banks holding $2.5 billion. The parent company alone had lenders involved in twelve different agreements, and the total involvement of the banks ranged from the $163,000 lent by a combination of three small banks to the $211,895,000 extended by Manufacturers Hanover Trust. Some of the banks were only involved with Chrysler, others just with Chrysler Financial, and some with both. Chrysler had to grapple with the whims and wishes of two thousand lenders and negotiators. "We were proposing the preposterous," said Chrysler's senior financial officer, Jerry Greenwald, "to assume that all our lenders would stick together." After six months of intrigue, with negotiating sessions and parlous accords given names that sounded like those of battles and peace agreements from some nineteenth-century European war, Chrysler managed to persuade its lenders to sign on four hundred dotted lines. On occasion the company skirted bankruptcy by no more than a couple of hours, but finally, together with the banks and the Treasury Department, Chrysler sorted out terms far removed from the instructions of Congress: terms equally uncomfortable for all.

The Chrysler restructuring raised questions about the way in which some of the country's most prestigious banks monitor their substantial customers and about the propriety of a bank's involvement with a client. The negotiations forced to the surface many of the jealousies and rivalries that existed between the banks and finally caused all to ponder whether there might not be a more efficient way to deal with a large, sickly customer—or, indeed to deal with enterprise as a whole.

For the most part, the banks had not been all that interested in Chrysler while it continued to pay its interest and principal on time. Over the years the company had assiduously courted the financial community at home and abroad, and had turned to the banks to finance Lynn Townsend's global dreams. In 1971, when a dozen of Chrysler's twenty-three directors were also directors or trustees of major banks or financial institutions, the *Wall Street Journal,* in a masterpiece of understatement, noted that "Chrysler has strong bank ties." In 1979, of the thirteen outside directors on Chrysler's sixteen-member board, ten had affiliations with banks and other financial companies.[1]

Chrysler's senior financial staff had made a point of attending bank clan gatherings like the annual American Bankers Association Convention. John Riccardo and Chrysler treasurer Bill McGagh had embarked on two around-the-world trips during the mid-Seventies to visit prominent foreign banks and keep them abreast of Chrysler's activities. For their part, most of the banks had eagerly solicited business from Chrysler and Chrysler Financial. Barely a day went by without some bankers calling on the company, trying to sell cash-management systems or lock boxes or any of the other profitable sidelines that, to banks, are like stereos and air conditioners are to automakers. Foreign banks had been especially willing to offer Chrysler tempting deals, partly to win business, partly to establish a stronger presence in the United States and partly for prestige. "We were a better customer to the banks than Ford or General Motors," Bill McGagh admitted ruefully. "They made money off us." A loan officer for a large midwestern bank noted, "Chrysler was good business for the

banks. Nobody bothered to question a good thing, especially when it
was such a big good thing."

As Chrysler began its tussle with the banks, one senior Treasury
official remarked, "The real question is how the banks ever let
Chrysler get into the position it reached." As Chrysler's debilitating
losses slopped from one quarter to the next, it became startlingly clear
that there was something strangely lacking in the bankers' credit analysis. "None of the bankers seriously thought that this major corporation was going to flop on its belly," said Ed Lord, an assistant vice-
president at Barclay's Bank International. Like the Penn Central
shortly before its collapse, Chrysler had been able to negotiate new
loans only months before its appeal to Congress. In November 1978, it
successfully persuaded the Prudential Insurance Company to increase
its loans from $106 million to $175 million, and the Aetna Insurance
Company lent $24 million on top of its existing loan. In April 1977,
Chrysler had renegotiated the terms of a revolving credit arrangement
with its U.S. banks, pushing the upper limit from $463 million to
$567.5 million. Most spectacularly of all, John Riccardo had, in June
1978, managed to sell $250 million of preferred stock. Although the
stock was aimed at individual investors who were prepared to place
their faith in the good name of Chrysler Corporation, the launch and
sale had been underwritten by many of the nation's blue-chip investment banking houses. Indeed, the offering had been so successful—
thanks partly to some elaborate wining and dining at Detroit's Renaissance Center—that Chrysler could quite easily have sold even more.
There was nothing new about optimistic buys. Indeed, William Langley, a Manufacturers Hanover senior vice-president, had seen it many
times before. "Hope," Langley diagnosed, "springs eternal."

The bankers treated Chrysler much like any other major company.
Although they gossiped among themselves that Chrysler had what
they politely called "a distinct personality," they were content
enough with the quarterly statements, annual reports and the SEC's
more detailed 1 O-K forms issued by the company. The documents
that the bankers used to maintain their watch over Chrysler were all
readily available to the general public. Every few months, the loan
officers in charge of the banks' Chrysler accounts would journey to Detroit to attend briefings from Chrysler's top management. At the small
briefings, the loan officers were not shown (and did not ask to see)
clay models or prototypes of future cars, and none ever bothered to
tour the plants. "We deal in figures, not models," observed Richard
Cummings, the affable vice-chairman of the National Bank of Detroit.
When Riccardo and McGagh jetted about the world, they found that
most of the questions they answered during their hour or ninety-
minute sessions with foreign bankers dealt with macro-economic ques-

tions—interest and inflation rates, wage and price controls, and the like —rather than the details of Chrysler's plans and operations. Diligent loan officers flicked through the automotive trade journals and analysts' reports, but they were bankers, not automobile men. Almost none of the banks, including Manufacturers Hanover, the lead bank, had a loan officer with a wide experience in the auto industry. Even some of the most respected and most widely quoted Wall Street analysts were scoffing, as late as May 1979, at suggestions that Chrysler might topple into bankruptcy. For the smaller banks, which generally relied on the word of analysts and, more particularly, the research of the major lenders, Chrysler's fall provided a severe test of faith. All around, there had been precious little attempt at independent analysis, with the bankers content to remain, as Manufacturers Hanover chairman John McGillicuddy told Congress, "the lubricant."[2] "No one person in any bank knew enough to suggest that they do certain things. Chrysler was just too big for that," remarked one loan officer.

Relying on Chrysler's own financial projections was, as the Treasury Department discovered in the fall of 1979, a dangerous habit. Jerry Greenwald admitted, "There wasn't the depth of the understanding in Chrysler of the depth of the problem." When the roof caved in, Greenwald observed, "The banks didn't even know what questions to ask." By the morning of December 21, 1979, just hours after the House and Senate Joint Conference Committee had sorted out the final terms of the aid package, the banks were beginning to shape some tough questions. Most had been holding their breath, waiting to see what would roll down Capitol Hill. Few had followed the congressional debate closely and scarcely any were intimately familiar with the role that they were being asked to play.

Congress had stated its case plainly enough. Indeed, the provisions of the Loan Guarantee Act that applied to the financial community were beguilingly simple, thanks largely to officials from the Treasury Department, who were determined to retain the maximum amount of flexibility. The U.S. banks and financial institutions were asked to make concessions of $500 million—$400 million in "new loans" and $100 million in "concessions" with respect to outstanding debt. The foreign banks were asked to provide $150 million in "new loans or credits." Both the domestic and foreign financiers were informed by Congress that the $650 million they were to provide was to come on top of all loans committed to Chrysler and Chrysler Financial before October 17, 1979, the date Chrysler's final operating plan had been sent to the Treasury Department.

To bankers and lawyers long used to poring over the fine print of loan agreements, the terms of the act were comfortingly vague. The thirteen lines that applied directly to the banks did not define "concessions" and made no reference to how the burden should be split. The bankers did not know whether concessions referred to deferrals of interest payments or outright gifts. They didn't know whether the Loan Guarantee Board could modify the act or what sort of conditions they could make before granting any aid. "Congress doesn't understand finance," said Steve Miller, then Chrysler's assistant treasurer, who headed the banking negotiations. "Congress understands politics." Chrysler's lenders were faced with a choice: they could either force a bankruptcy and let their lawyers salvage some of the loans in the musty confines of a bankruptcy court, or they could make concessions.

It was Greenwald who spelled out what concessions the company wanted in "the pit," a second-floor conference room at Manufacturers Hanover's New York headquarters. Greenwald had bad news for the representatives of the U.S. banks sitting around the conference table. He briefly explained the terms of the Loan Guarantee Act, barely concealing his impatience when some of the bankers asked questions about clauses which had formed part of the House and Senate bills from the start of the congressional debate. Noting that Congress had refused to provide a loan to bridge the period before the federal guarantees started to flow, Greenwald asked for an immediate $500 million loan to tide the company over. He had $800 million of bills to pay within the month and $100 million left in the till. He stuck by his projections that Chrysler would soon be plumb out of cash, and offered the Trenton engine plant, the New Process gear plant in Syracuse, 1.8 million shares of Peugeot stock and an inventory of unsold cars as security. The bankers scoffed at the notion of security. A secured credit, they argued, was only as good as the claim on the assets, and the government had established a senior claim on all but $400 million of Chrysler's assets. A last-minute clause in the bill, the result of an explosive burst of lobbying, allowed the Loan Guarantee Board to give equal claims on up to $400 million of the company's assets. In addition, the banks wanted to know what an engine plant would be worth without a company that produced cars.

The bankers were not feeling charitable. Most hooted at the act, calling it "The Suppliers Loan Guarantee Act." The future of Chrysler, the bankers were convinced, was for the benefit of suppliers and workers. The banks, they quietly murmured, were innocent victims. Chrysler had, after all, made mincemeat of all its loan agreements. All the cleverly devised ratios, interest coverages and working-capital balances had been shredded. Chrysler not only had stopped paying debts that were coming due, it was also expected to violate what was supposedly a sacred undertaking in the world of international finance: a credit agreement with a group of Japanese banks who financed the import of Mitsubishi cars. (In the middle of January 1980, Chrysler actually stopped payments to the Japanese.)

Greenwald dropped his final bomb when he asked Steve Miller and a Los Angeles bankruptcy expert, Ron Trost, to explain the details of a ten-page "Memo for Liquidation" which had been frantically prepared in a suite at the Carlyle Hotel during the previous few days. The tersely worded memo was Chrysler's own doomsday pamphlet, and it dealt a blow to what for some banks had become a part of the company folklore: that the assets of Chrysler Corporation and Chrysler Financial were separable in a bankruptcy. The bankers were told that the situation was so complex that both the parent company and the subsidiary would tumble into the same barrel. Even more disconcerting was Chrysler's opinion that the banks, all unsecured creditors to Chrysler Financial, would, during the course of lengthy bankruptcy proceedings, only be entitled to the low "legal" rate of 6 percent interest. To top things off, Chrysler told the bankers that the Pension Benefit Guarantee Corporation would probably have a senior claim to the company's assets. For the bankers, who had three times as much tied up in the finance company as in the parent corporation, the news was something they had privately feared but had never before heard directly from the company. Furthermore, they disagreed with Chrysler's analysis. Instead of salvaging all their loans to the finance arm, they stood to win as little as seventy-five cents on the dollar if the court battles lasted for five years. That, together with the expectation of a payoff as low as ten cents on the dollar for loans extended to Chrysler Corporation, shattered the bankers' decorum. They started to interrupt Greenwald, snorting with derision at some of the arguments and insinuating that Chrysler had purposely concealed the news. The banks desperately wanted to separate Chrysler from CFC so that the former could be pushed into bankruptcy without jeopardizing loans to the latter. When Chrysler announced that both the parent and CFC would fall together, it was not just an analysis but a threat. Altogether, it was an unpleasant and inauspicious start.

The bankers already knew enough about Chrysler Financial, which had felt tremors from Chrysler's chronic condition long before Washington started to quake. Pleased with the experience of joint ventures in Europe with France's largest finance company, Sobac (controlled by the investment banking firm of Lazard Frères), and in Britain with the Mercantile Credit Company, Gordon Areen, the cherubic president of the financial subsidiary, had, in the spring of 1978, started tentative discussions about the possibility of joint ventures in other countries, including the United States. The talks had formed one part of

John Riccardo's efforts to raise money (see Chapter One) to finance
Chrysler's spending program. Although the finance company helped
Chrysler sell cars both to dealers and to retail customers, it was an expensive operation. Chrysler had twice the amount (in relative terms)
plowed into Chrysler Financial that GM had invested in General
Motors Acceptance Corporation and Ford in Ford Motor Credit. Toward the end of 1978, Areen had made a further attempt to slice off
part of his company, but negotiations stalled with the turmoil following the arrival of Lee Iacocca and the devastating events of the spring
of 1979. The irony did not escape Areen: with $48.5 million in profits,
1978 was the best year ever for the company he had headed since
1964.

Easter week of 1979 brought disaster. Confronted with reports of
the parent company's losses, the two credit-rating agencies, Moody's
and Standard and Poors, lowered Chrysler Financial's debt ratings
and commercial paper ratings. (Like all similar companies, Chrysler
Financial depended on good credit ratings to borrow money at rates
that allowed it to make profits from its loans.) Chrysler Financial
could not, despite its impeccable record, be given ratings higher than
those awarded Chrysler, on whom it depended for future business.
For the first time ever, both agencies had lowered all their ratings for
both Chrysler and the finance company. "Once the ratings were lowered," Areen recalled, "the banks knew it was raining." Two bankers
knew that it was pouring cats and dogs. Chemical Bank's Benjamin
McCleary and Morgan Guaranty's Richard Flinthoft dashed to Washington to brief the Treasury Department while an official at the Federal Reserve Board in New York monitored Chrysler Financial's every
move.

Deprived of access to the short-term debt market and the commercial paper market, the finance company was thrown back on the more
expensive credit lines it had painstakingly negotiated with each of its
282 lenders over the previous few years. The credit lines were designed as a form of insurance to cover temporary instability in the
short-term paper market or a disruption within Chrysler or the auto
industry.[3] The loss of the ratings marked the start of what was a perpetual theme throughout the restructuring of Chrysler. Some of the
smaller banks had seen enough and were so terrified by the sight of
Chrysler Financial borrowing $50 million-a-day that they abruptly
canceled their credit lines and fled. The First National Bank of
Atlanta, for one, used a deposit of Chrysler Financial to reduce the
size of its loan to the company—an action that provoked an angry response from bankers whose obligations to Chrysler were too large to
seize without provoking an immediate bankruptcy. Indeed, Areen and
his staff couldn't even draw down on all their credit lines lest they vio-

late conditions of some of the loan covenants which, in turn, would accelerate the maturity of debt repayments and threaten the stability of the entire company. It was largely to quell the fears of the small lenders and shore up his company's rapidly crumbling buttresses that Areen turned to other alternatives.

One of the first stops was with other finance companies, and here the ties of the trade were more than helpful. One morning Bob Baker, a Chrysler Financial vice-president as well as president of the National Consumer Finance Association, took a telephone call from Gilbert Ellis, chairman of the Executive Committee of the association. Thinking that the call concerned the association's affairs, Baker was delighted to discover that Ellis, who doubled as the chairman of Household Finance, the third-largest financial company in the United States, was offering help. Areen and Baker grabbed at the offer and within days teams of officials from Household Finance were scouring records at Chrysler Financial's headquarters and its branch offices. After Ellis and the president of Household Finance, Donald Clark, had lunched with John Riccardo and Lee Iacocca, the sale of $500 million of accounts receivable (the payments owed by dealers and car buyers) was set. In a separate agreement, Areen sold another $230 million to General Motors Acceptance Corporation. The sales shrank Chrysler Financial by one-third, reduced its borrowing needs and allowed Areen and his colleagues to start mollifying the bankers.

The banks were more difficult to please than some finance companies eager to expand their business by snapping up some high-quality loans. At the end of July 1979, while John Riccardo was gearing up for his $1 billion pitch for tax relief, Areen was preparing an appeal of his own. He outlined his plan at a meeting with representatives of twenty-six of the nation's leading banks, held in Manufacturers Hanover's Park Avenue office. It was here that the tensions and anxieties within the banking community and many of the arguments used repeatedly during the restructuring of Chrysler were voiced for the first time. Areen asked the bankers to substitute a revolving credit agreement for the lines of credit they had extended to Chrysler Financial.[4] The choice of Manufacturers Hanover as a venue was natural enough. Manny Hanny, as it is familiarly called, was the largest correspondent bank in the United States and had long had ties with Chrysler. It had been the automaker's agent bank for years, acting as a financial shepherd to the ever-expanding flock of banks. In 1970 and 1974, when Chrysler had previously encountered stormy weather (see Chapter Five) Manny Hanny had launched the lifeboats. In the first crisis, which occurred after the collapse of the Penn Central, the bank's vice-chairman, John McGillicuddy, had flown all over the country with Gordon Areen and Lynn Townsend, pacifying nervous bankers. Four years later, McGillicuddy and Manny Hanny had played a prominent role in establishing a $455 million revolving credit agreement. In 1979, McGillicuddy, invited to appear before both House and Senate Committees, testified strongly in favor of federal aid. "We are not a bank that wants to close down plants and run for the hills," said senior vice-president William Langley.

Some of the other U.S. banks were suspicious about Manny Hanny's relationship with Chrysler. "There was a perception that the bank was soft on Chrysler," said one lawyer involved in the restructuring. "They had rescued Chrysler originally and were heroes. They had a vested interest in seeing that the rescue didn't collapse into failure." Some other bankers were less charitable. Noted Barclay's Ed Lord, "They were asleep at the switch. They should have been sounding the red alert earlier." The fact that McGillicuddy's predecessor as chairman, Gabriel Hauge, was a Chrysler director and that Hauge's predecessor, Robert McNeill, had also sat on Chrysler's board did not go unnoticed. Indeed, Lynn Townsend had been a director of Manufacturers Hanover for nine years.

While McGillicuddy testified in support of Chrysler, other bankers, especially Citibank's Walter Wriston and A. W. "Tom" Clausen, president of the Bank of America, voiced their opposition to a federal bailout and thereby underlined Manny Hanny's isolation. Manufacturers Hanover, the other banks felt, had far more riding on its relationship with Chrysler than the $246.3 million it had committed. At the August meeting, Manufacturers Hanover proposed to the other banks that they all extend their lending commitments to Chrysler Financial for one year as a show of support and a rallying point for the banks that had canceled their credit lines. The other New York banks—especially Citibank, Morgan Guaranty and Chemical—would have no part of any such deal. If Chrysler hoped to get a revolving credit agreement, all the banks that had fled would have to participate. The New Yorkers were contemptuous of the smaller banks, many of whom had scuttled away to the corners during previous credit crunches. Said one banker, "It's as if you put four hundred people in a skyscraper office with just one window and the whole place catches fire. If you tell them that only four can get out the window, it just won't work." By October 17 the debt had been restructured. Chrysler Financial Corporation had agreed to a 35-percent reduction in the banks participating in its revolving credit agreement and CFC also agreed to maintain $94 million in lines of credit with some of the banks that had refused to join the revolving credit system. In exchange for these concessions, the banks had to settle for a revolving credit arrangement that included only 200 of the company's 282 banks and that had shrunk from $1.8 billion to $919 million. The banks had also cannily changed some of the terms of the agreement, to prevent the siphoning off of money from Chrysler Financial into the gulping parent company—a ploy designed to help isolate Chrysler Financial in the event of a bankruptcy.

Though some of the terms of the renegotiated credit for Chrysler Financial had been specially worded to insulate it from the problems of the parent company, the Memo for Liquidation that was read to the bankers on the Friday before Christmas 1979 set the tone for the following weeks. The bankers assumed that Chrysler would try to sell part, or all, of the financial subsidiary and for the succeeding weeks they concentrated on the parent company. In early January 1980, the banks suffered another set of shocks when Chrysler outlined the form it would like the financial community's concessions to take.

Steve Miller asked the banks to lower the rate of interest on all the loans outstanding to one percent, extending this relief to the parent company for four years and to the financial company for one year. The savings, Chrysler reckoned, would amount to more than $400 million during the first year alone. The banks, not surprisingly, refused the proposal and added that they certainly would not consider making new loans to the company as required in the Loan Guarantee Act. Nothing had changed since Manny Hanny's John McGillicuddy had noted in his congressional testimony, "We don't lend money in circumstances in which we don't expect to be repaid, and that's where Chrysler Corporation is."

Chrysler also asked the banks to restore $159 million of the $567.5 million U.S. revolving credit agreements, which had been frozen when the losses started to heap up in the summer of 1979. During the Washington debate, senators and congressmen had used the $159 million of frozen credit to illustrate (depending on their inclinations) either the obduracy of the banks or the futility of Chrysler's cause. The majority of the U.S. banks had been in favor of canceling the entire $567.5 million credit agreement (though there was little hope of getting the money back) but heavy lobbying by Manny Hanny in the fall of 1979 had ensured that the credit agreement (including the frozen $159 million) remained. The other lenders, the foreign banks and the insurance companies, had squinted at the haggling of the U.S. banks. Cancellation of the agreement would have been interpreted as a signal that the banks were reconciled to bankruptcy proceedings, but the nature of the final equivocal verdict meant that the U.S. banks had given their tacit, if grudging, approval for a restructuring.

However, the American banks formed just one part of Chrysler's panoply of lenders. With the start of the restructuring, the financial community had to decide how to distribute the burden. In circles where it was notoriously tricky to convince ten people that the sun rises in the east, it became a hideous task. The sharing of the burden became a test of strength, fragile alliances and organization. The U.S. banks, however, did manage to gain one early advantage over other lenders. They had already organized a committee of representatives to deal with the rejuggling of Chrysler Financial's debt. In the middle of January 1980, a recast committee, chaired by Garry Scheuring, a vice-president of Continental Illinois, was separated into working groups to investigate Chrysler's remaining sources of funds, the shape of a possible restructuring and the prospects for bankruptcy. Though the smaller and larger banks disagreed vehemently about the depth of their commitments to Chrysler, they all were united on one issue: Congress, they felt, had dealt them a raw hand. The contributions required from U.S. financiers represented a doubling of their outstanding loans to the company and saddled them with two-thirds of the aid being sought from the world financial community, even though they held only about one-third of the credit commitments made by Chrysler. Foreign banks, which had eagerly fought to provide two-thirds of the total lines, were only asked to contribute a small part of the package.

The European lenders, on the other hand, came from countries that spoke different languages, had diverse financial customs and private economic worries. Meanwhile, six Canadian banks had illustrated the ease of unified action when only a few institutions were involved. At the beginning of December 1979, they had refused to release $60 million that Chrysler had deposited. Within several weeks—much to the fury of the American banks when they discovered the action—they had applied it against Chrysler's Canadian debts. The Japanese banks were yet another matter. Seven Japanese banks that looked to the Mitsubishi Bank for advice and guidance provided letters of credit to help finance the cars and trucks imported by Chrysler from Mitsubishi Motors. The group considered themselves as supplying trade financing rather than as general lenders to Chrysler or Chrysler Financial. They merely guaranteed payment to Mitsubishi Motors for their exported cars and trucks within 180 days of shipment from Japanese docksides.[5] Finally, two American insurance companies, the Prudential and Aetna, which had long provided loans to Chrysler, cooperated closely with each other and presented a united front against the arguments of the other lenders.

Some of the overseas lenders had private reasons for doubting the grit of the U.S. banks. Both the European and the Japanese lenders believed that the Americans were playing a waiting game and would eventually settle Chrysler's problems among themselves. Bankers from both East and West had dealt with similar, if less serious, problems by themselves and had, on occasion, bought out the foreign banks. The

Europeans followed the turmoil at the West German electronic company AEG Telefunken with more than passing interest, while the Japanese reminded the American bankers of the fall and rise of the automaker Toyo Kogyo. Both companies had faced bankruptcy; the respective governments had refused to intervene, and in both cases the domestic banks had designed the rescue.

AEG Telefunken had lost $160 million in the first half of 1979, on top of a $173 million loss in 1978, and was buried beneath $3.8 billion of debt. From the outset, the West German government had made it plain that there would be no federal help. A prominent West German newspaper called Telefunken "A test case of private enterprise."[6] It was left to the AEG management, unions and banks to devise a salvage operation. The banks, led by the giant Dresdener Bank, agreed to restructure the company's debts (deferring most of the interest payments and extending more operating capital) in return for a more effective voice in daily management. Although thousands of jobs were lost and the executive suite was swept clean, the banks, thanks largely to the strong equity positions they maintained, had played the major role. Some other Europeans, particularly the British, were used to the Bank of England (roughly the equivalent of the Federal Reserve) corraling commercial banks to help companies. On occasion, the British banks had even been appointed receivers of troubled companies.

In Toyo Kogyo's case, the Japanese had been faced with the sort of choice confronting Chrysler's banks: provoke bankruptcy or extend aid.[7] In 1973, Mazda had been flush with the success of a rotary engine that gave a devilish zip to a sports car but only offered 11 mpg in city driving. After the oil shock that followed the Yom Kippur War, Mazda's market suddenly collapsed by almost half in Japan and by more than a third in the United States, despite a round of discounts. By 1975 Mazda was spluttering toward a bankruptcy that threatened 100,000 jobs. What allowed Mazda to regroup, manufacture the massively successful rotary-powered RX-7 sports car (built around an improved engine giving 17 mpg city and 28 highway), produce the sprightly GLC compact and turn a $30 million profit in 1979, was not the outstretched hand of the Japanese government, but the first aid coolly administered by Japanese banks.

Although Mazda wasn't in the same sort of straits as Chrysler (it had only $2 billion of sales in 1974, a profitable light truck business and a model line based on one platform) the similarities were close enough to provoke eerie comparisons. Mazda, like other Japanese companies, carried nearly ten times more long-term debt than equity, and the banks, which held much of the stock, also had access to detailed proprietary information. At the first hint of trouble, Sumitomo, Toyo Kogyo's lead bank, leaped in, gently eased the company chairman upstairs, slashed the dividend by three-quarters, encouraged early retirement all around and syndicated a new $1 billion loan. In return, Mazda obliged by sliding off its sickbed and doubling productivity within the five years following 1974. The firm received an ironic certificate of good health when Ford purchased a 25-percent interest in 1978.

In the light of both Toyo Kogyo and Telefunken, the U.S. banks and Chrysler had a particularly difficult time persuading the international banks that the Americans weren't going to treat Chrysler as a family affair and buy out the stakes held abroad. Indeed, the Americans resorted to blunt and unmistakable threats to banks eager to increase their business in the United States. The foreigners were warned in the diplomatic (and sometimes none-too-diplomatic) language of international banking that if they dared to pull their loan from Chrysler, every boardroom in the United States would hear that a particular bank "cuts and runs." Moaned one European lender, "They had us by the short hairs."

Looming over the bickering and squabbling between the lenders was the indubitable presence of the U.S. government. Both the American and the foreign lenders conducted their business at the mercy of Congress, the Federal Reserve Board and other federal agencies. Every facet of banking—from electronic cash dispensers to new bank branches—was monitored, directly or indirectly, by the same politicians who had granted aid to Chrysler. The European banks, aggressively acquiring U.S. banks, were particularly anxious not to irritate the Federal Reserve Board (which was designing new rules for foreign banks operating in the United States) or Senator Proxmire, who had watched their emergence with increasing apprehension.

All the banks had another worry that served to highlight the ambiguous nature of the federal aid. In September 1979, examiners from the Federal Reserve Board, the Federal Deposit Insurance Corporation and the office of the Comptroller of the Currency had downgraded loans to Chrysler from "substandard" to "doubtful," a credit rating a notch above a total loss.[8] Philip Lowman, a vice-president with the National Bank of Detroit and a prominent member of the U.S. bank committee, noted, "One arm of the government was telling us to lend Chrysler money while the other was telling us not to lend any money." Meanwhile, the banks had groups of regulators poring over their books. Doubtful loans were more than just a blemish on a balance sheet, they provoked questions from directors and shareholders and certainly provided a fine argument against any new loans.

For Chrysler, already choking on debt and struggling to cope with interest rates around 20 percent, the banks' refusal to furnish fresh loans was an oblique act of charity. For close to three months the

company and its lenders batted about alternative suggestions center-
ing on the interest Chrysler owed on its debts. The committees representing U.S. and European lenders struggled to design a package that
would reduce the rate of interest and allow some deferral of interest
payments. Each time one party made a suggestion, the other lenders
immediately wanted to know the overall effect. To help speed negotiations, Scott Taylor, a Chase Manhattan vice-president, programmed
his own Radio Shack computer to spit out various plans. Meanwhile,
Chrysler's Steve Miller was engaged in the same pursuit with his
Apple II computer in the den of his Michigan home.

The arduous talks with the banks developed their own characteristic pattern. Every morning a facsimile of Chrysler's daily cash
statement was electronically transmitted to the company's New York
lawyers. Each day Miller and his associates pored over the five-page
statement, which became a measure of the fading corporate pulse, to
see if there was enough money left to pay the Friday wage bills.
Twice a month, on the tenth and the twenty-fifth, Miller had to gear
up for the average $400 million in payments owed to suppliers. For
Miller, who had joined Chrysler in October 1979 at the invitation of
his former boss at Ford Venezuela, Jerry Greenwald, it was baptism
by the numbers. Known to the bankers as "Little Miller" (to distinguish him from Treasury Secretary G. William Miller), the 220 pound,
6-foot-4-inch Harvard and Stanford graduate had been hired as an assistant treasurer. Within weeks, he was Chrysler's direct and tenacious
mouthpiece to the international financial community.

Every Friday, Miller would wing back to Detroit for brutal all-day
meetings with Greenwald. Starting at 7:30 in the morning, the pair,
along with colleagues, would listen to fifteen-minute reviews from
each of the twenty-two task forces appointed to nail down one piece
of the package Chrysler needed to qualify for the loan guarantees.
Each task force would give a terse progress report on its negotiations
with state and local governments, the suppliers, Mitsubishi and all
the other parties. On Tuesdays, Brian Freeman, the executive director
of the Chrysler Loan Board, would fly to Detroit to monitor Chrysler's
progress.

Miller, Greenwald and the banks all had dates ringed on their cal-
endars, which later became known as "D-D Days" (Drop-Dead
Days). On several occasions the company picked a date on which, it
told its lenders, there would be no cash left in the till. The first D-D
Day occurred in the middle of January and was avoided by a delay of
payments to suppliers. The second was avoided when Chrysler suspended its payments to the Japanese banks that financed the import of
Mitsubishi vehicles. Chrysler's third D-D Day was its most important.
Having secured a $100 million loan from Peugeot by pledging its 1.8

million shares of the French automaker, Chrysler needed the banks to
agree to waive their rights to the stock. The banks' subsequent compli-
ance provided the first sign of unanimity.

Toward the end of March, as the self-imposed April 1 deadline for
qualifying for federal aid loomed and rumors of stinging inquisitions
from the Senate and House banking committees began to circulate,
the bankers began to feel the pressure. For their part, the banks, in a
glittering convention of twenty-five chief executive officers, had explained to Robert Carswell, the Assistant Secretary of the Treasury,
and to Elmer Staats, the Comptroller of the Currency, that they would
not be able to comply with the letter of the Loan Guarantee Act. As
March drew to a close, representatives of the four major groups of
lenders—the U.S. banks, the Europeans, the Canadians and the insurance companies—were summoned to thrash out a compromise that
could be presented to the Loan Guarantee Board. It had taken three
months for representatives of all the lenders to meet around the same
table. While the silver market crashed and the Hunt Brothers lost a
fortune, the lenders met in the Chrysler boardroom on the 54th floor
of the Pan Am Building. Even a take-out order to a local delicatessen
underlined the fragility of the talks. On learning that the order came
from Chrysler's lenders, the deli demanded payment before it agreed
to deliver the sandwiches. Finally, after two inconclusive days of bargaining, a group of eight American and European bankers adjourned
for dinner at the Waldorf-Astoria to hammer out what was later
known as "The Waldorf Agreement."

The financial concordat, reached over rounds of English stout and
Heinecken, modified the concessions to be given by the European
banks, allowing them to save face in return for having been squeezed
by the Americans into providing a greater share of the overall financial contribution. Satisfied that a deal was at hand, Michael Rayfield, a
flamboyant senior vice-president from Britain's Barclay's International,
bade the maître d' open a $200 magnum of Dom Perignon '54—"the
kind that James Bond drinks." Although the Americans nervously
protested that the unofficial gathering hadn't agreed to anything, they
sipped champagne, wondering all the while whether the other lenders
would agree to the latest deal.

Hours after Rayfield and his colleagues had downed the last drop of
champagne, Steve Miller had a nasty shock for the bankers as they
filed into the Chrysler boardroom for a meeting where contributions
from the various parties were to be settled once and for all. An unusually subdued Miller started with an announcement. The management of Chrysler, he told the financiers, had pored over projections for
the economy, the automobile industry and the company in hours of
meetings the day before. After a detailed review, the senior manage-

ment had decided that Chrysler stood no chance of survival, and a small group of directors had concurred. As a result, Miller continued, in a room that was quieter than a vault, Chrysler had filed for bankruptcy earlier that morning. Pencils and pens crashed to the oak boardroom table as Miller politely thanked the bankers for all their efforts over the previous months.

Jerry Greenwald, sitting in on the meeting, was as astonished as the bankers. Gauging the impact of his remarks, Miller began to bluster. "It's April Fool's Day. It's a joke," he said. The room filled with nervous mirth as the glum group erupted into cheers. "It wasn't very damn funny," said one banker. "We believed him." Miller's idea of humor served a purpose: it convinced the bankers of the need to complete as quickly as possible the restructuring of the parent company. However, two days after a compromise had been reached, the lenders were hit with another piece of bad news. Negotiations for the sale of Chrysler Financial had capsized in the turbulent wake of the Federal Reserve Board's credit crunch of mid-March. Prior to the hike in interest rates, Chrysler Financial president Gordon Areen had conducted further talks with his counterparts at Household Finance. The finance company had stated its willingness to purchase 31 percent of Chrysler Financial, provided that the banks purchase another 20 percent. Leery of dealing with a bevy of partners, Household Finance wanted to limit the partnership to one or two banks. For their part, the banks were skeptical about the legal implications of holding stock in a company to which they had loans outstanding. It was largely on the hazy relationship between stockholder and creditor that the talks snagged. For the rest of the lenders, it meant yet another bout of bone-wearying days and nights restructuring the debt of Chrysler Financial before Steve Miller could announce to a meeting of four hundred bankers in Detroit on April 17 that Chrysler had finally reached agreement with its banks.

The Treasury Department, however, was not under the impression that an agreement had been reached. Ever since the start of the negotiations, members of the Treasury's office of Chrysler Finance had stayed on the sidelines, watching while the lenders tussled, but after Chrysler presented its restructuring plan, the Treasury Department minutely examined the precisely worded language of the loan covenants, peering at phrases and clauses that would determine whether the fate of Chrysler and Chrysler Financial was in the hands of the government or the banks.

As Treasury officials explained their misgivings to the bankers convened in the echoing Treasury cash room, it became clear that there was plenty of tough bargaining left. For a start, the men at the Treasury were unhappy that the banks had failed to take an equity stake in the company. A bank purchase of stock, the government officials believed, offered the only manageable way for Chrysler to reduce its crippling load of debt and offered a slim chance that the company might eventually be able to sell new debt. The Treasury, in short, wanted the banks to buy $750 million of Chrysler stock and wanted an increase or extension of the credit available to Chrysler Financial.

For yet another eight days, teams of bankers and lawyers camped out in the plush surroundings of Washington's Madison Hotel, negotiating separately and ponderously on Chrysler and Chrysler Financial. Messages were shuttled between the banks and the Treasury Department, were Roger Altman, an assistant secretary, held arrogant court. Finally the banks agreed to purchase Chrysler equity by exchanging delayed interest payments for stock. The loans to the financial arm were extended and the Treasury Department successfully enforced clauses that prevented the banks from draining money from Chrysler to the finance company. After the agreement was hammered out, another three weeks were consumed as the Canadian, Japanese and European banks sought to make deals of their own. The Canadians especially, negotiating with Chrysler's Canadian subsidiary, proved defiant. For close to two weeks, it looked as if the Canadians would steal a march by collecting interest from Chrysler almost three years before the other lenders. For their part, the Europeans disliked the prospect of being forced to take an equity stock in a fading American automaker. After Chrysler and Treasury negotiators played shuttle diplomacy in Toronto and around the major cities of Europe, the most complicated part of the concessions needed to qualify for the loan guarantees was completed.

As for the rest of the package, many of its features bore barely any resemblance to the terms laid down by Congress. The banks, after all, had not come forward with any new loans. Besides, though the UAW had conceded $462.5 million and Chrysler's non-union employees had forgone the appropriate $125 million, Chrysler had not completed the necessary sale of assets, had been unable to sell additional equity and had not been able to stimulate the level of support stipulated for suppliers and dealers. Any resemblance between the Chrysler plan and the requirements of Congress was difficult to detect.

With the Canadian bankers finally pacified, Chrysler started work on the final agreement. Lawyers representing more than fifty law firms helped the investment bankers draft the documents to be signed by every bank. The legal and financial help did not come at cut-price rates. Chrysler eventually paid financial and legal fees of more than $20 million. To get the agreements printed as quickly as possible, the work was split between Sorg Printing Company and Bowne and Company, the two largest financial printing firms in the country, who were more used to dealing with evening drop-offs and morning pick-ups of corporate stock issues. The printing bill: $2 million. Before the banks could be asked to sign the legal documents, Steve Miller had to sign on behalf of Chrysler. He spent an entire day at the printers', signing each of the four thousand documents. One assistant opened each document to the proper page, another stamped in Miller's title, while a third counted and stored the signed papers. Stacked on top of each other, the boxes of documents would have topped seventy feet. As each box was filled, it was trundled off to the three New York metropolitan area airports for shipment to the banks.

By June 10, Chrysler had run out of a $150 million loan from the State of Michigan furnished six weeks before and could not pay the $50 million of supplier bills that were coming due. Every hackneyed automotive cliché could not describe Chrysler's condition. The road had never been rockier, nor the lanes narrower. The gas gauge pointed to empty and even the fumes had dried up. Chrysler had stopped.[9] Some banks were now threatening to let the air out of the corporate tires.

Twenty banks—some foreign, some domestic, most small and all with relatively minor loans to Chrysler outstanding—were refusing to sign the loan agreements. All wanted their money and all hoped that some of the major banks would pay them off on the courthouse steps, but the reasons for their reluctance varied. For some, it was a matter of national pride. For others, shaky financial conditions or belligerent shareholders and directors handcuffed executives. In other cases, there had been a change in management since the loans had been made. Although the "recalcitrants," as Chrysler immediately called them, only held $33 million of the total $4.75 billion debt, they threatened the aid package to such an extent that the meeting of the Loan Guarantee Board where all was to be finalized had to be postponed three times.

Chrysler had no time for niceties and needed four hundred pinstriped ducks lined up in an unwavering row. On June 13, Steve Miller met with senators and members of the House in Washington, clutching a list of twenty banks. The list included the West German Deutsche Genossenschaftsbank, which had seized an $8 million payment heading from Volkswagen to Chrysler.[10] Meanwhile, Banque Bruxelles Lambert of Belgium had filed suit for a $10 million loan Chrysler had failed to repay. In the United States, the Bank of the Southwest in Houston, York Bank and Trust in York, Pennsylvania, the Whitney National Bank of New Orleans and the Peoples Trust of Fort Wayne, Indiana, felt slighted by the major banks.

Once more Chrysler marshaled its battalions of lobbyists. With the aid of its top banks, yet another computerized list was assembled. This time it contained the business connections and names of every officer and director of the banks encircling the financial stockade. Calls were made by John McGillicuddy from Manufacturers Hanover and by William Miller from the Treasury Department. Richard Cummings, the vice-chairman of one of Chrysler's staunchest allies, the National Bank of Detroit, took to the road to persuade some of his nervous colleagues. As Gordon Areen left Chrysler Financial's headquarters to lend his muscle, subordinates joked that they were sending the gorilla out again. Steve Miller, who had made 116 flights during the restructuring, took to the air.

Standing almost in the shadow of Chrysler's truck-assembly plant in St. Louis, the Crestwood Metro Bank felt the heat. Citing, like many of the other dissidents, prudent banking management, Crestwood stood fast, but finally the resistance crumpled. "We realize we're nowhere without Chrysler in business," said a Crestwood official. "We're somewhere with them still in business." By far the toughest nut to crack was David W. Knapp, the bespectacled president of the American National Bank and Trust Company of Rockford, Illinois. Steve Miller, Gordon Areen and Wendell Larsen all flew to Rockford to try to persuade Knapp to join the club. Circling the town on June 18 they finally found the city hall, where the meeting with Knapp had been convened in the mayor's office, parked their Dodge Omni at the foot of the steps and were promptly met by a gaggle of reporters, TV cameras and photographers. Knapp remained unmoved by the arguments. "If you take a loan, you pay it back," he told the Chrysler men. Even a barrage of telephone calls from the mighty of the financial world left him undaunted. "Their crystal ball tells them this solves the problem," Knapp countered. "Mine doesn't." Knapp, who seemed to revel in the attention, told reporters that his bank was "just not interested" in saving Chrysler.

Following their unsuccessful meeting, Miller held a press conference, snippets of which played on that night's network newscasts. Miller predicted that Chrysler would be bankrupt in a matter of days if Knapp refused to sign. Within hours, the people of Rockford, many of whom worked at the nearby Chrysler Belvidere plant, started to picket the bank and withdraw deposits. It was the withdrawals, which could have turned into a run on the bank, and what Knapp, in a masterful understatement, called "a certain divisiveness in the community," that helped him change his mind. Threatening phone calls and a bomb scare finally convinced the president of the American National Bank and Trust Company of Rockford to let Chrysler live to fight another day.

On June 20, the final domestic holdout, the Twin City Bank of North Little Rock, Arkansas, was treated to a Chrysler double act. Steve Miller arrived after flying through the night and Gordon Areen ducked in beneath a heavy bank of fog in a propeller-driven Queen-Air. The bank, which had $78,000 loaned to Chrysler, buckled and was followed shortly afterward by West Germany's DG Bank.

All that remained was the final act of any loan agreement: the closing. Even that nearly failed. Chrysler's first problem was to locate documents stuck in an airport strike in Beirut. With a $15,000 chartered plane standing by in Paris to whisk the documents to an airport for an international flight to New York, they were finally taken to a local American consulate, from where their authenticity was conveyed to the Loan Guarantee Board. The night before the closing, though, the documents, the loan agreement, the federal aid package and Chrysler all nearly went up in smoke.

On June 23, as dusk settled over Manhattan, Chrysler's lawyers were putting the finishing touches on the loan agreement, thirty-three floors above Park Avenue in the office of Debevoise, Plimpton, Lyons and Gates, when wisps of black smoke started to curl past the windows. The lawyers and bankers trooped down an emergency staircase with some joking that the fire was "Rockford's Revenge," but what started in the Bank of America's computer center quickly caught hold, melted the aluminum stair railings and sent buckling sheets of glass cascading to the street below. Jerry Greenwald was strolling toward the law office when he bumped into Steve Miller, heading for a local restaurant. "Can you imagine if that was our building?" Greenwald asked Miller as he looked at the fire trucks pulling up to the Westvaco Building. It was.

The fire, fought by 125 firemen, was the worst skyscraper blaze in New York for twenty years. At 2 A.M., a small group of diehard bankers and lawyers argued their way past police barricades, struggled through the smoke that obscured the ends of hallways and stuffed the soot-covered documents into fifty cardboard boxes and twelve metal mail carts. At 2:30 A.M., hours before the deal was due to close, a straggling caravan wheeled Chrysler's future up Park Avenue and over to the Citicorp Center law offices of Shearman and Sterling.

Ten hours later, a hundred people jammed the conference room where the documents had been hastily reassembled. Speaker phones lined the walls and Debevoise lawyer Richard Kahn began to call the roll. Other law offices in New York said they were ready; from Washington, the three members of the Loan Guarantee Board said they were ready. From Paris and Toronto, there were similar responses. Finally, Steve Miller was asked whether Chrysler was ready. At 12:26 P.M. on June 24, eleven months after John Riccardo had asked for tax relief and six months after President Carter had signed the Loan Guarantee Act, Chrysler had permission to draw down its first $500 million of guaranteed loans.

CHAPTER FOURTEEN

Global Motors

The auto industry has played a central role in the definition and accomplishment of our broadest national goals: work for Americans, energy security; and, perhaps most important, national security. In the future direction of this industry will lie critical answers about America at home and in the world: about the numbers and kinds of jobs for our people; about our ability to supply our own energy needs; about our competitive position in an evolving international economy.
—Secretary of Transportation Neil Goldschmidt in a
letter to President Carter, January 1981

Far from the financial pressure chambers of Wall Street, the marbled corridors of Washington and even Bloomfield Hills' neo-colonial castles, the urban enclave of Hamtramck, Michigan, breathes its own history of the American automobile industry. No sooner had the 1980s begun than Hamtramck lost the soul of its existence—an eight-story, 4.8-million-square-foot factory known as "Dodge Main." From 1910, the Hamtramck plant lived the cycle of Detroit's industrial booms and busts, sheltering the Dodge Brothers' first efforts to supply Henry Ford I with axles, transmissions and steering gears, churning out the sturdy Dodge cars and enduring the violent birth of the UAW.

Dodge Main made Hamtramck. In the Twenties and Thirties, thousands of Polish families, following a trail of promises, booked passage to Montreal and continued by train or boat to Detroit to fill the assembly lines and hammer the sleepy German farm community into a bustling workmen's city. During World War II, 40,000 women and men built military vehicles in Dodge Main, doing their part to earn Detroit its title as "The Arsenal of Democracy."

At Dodge Main's peak in the Fifties, 35,000 workers packed the streetcars, stepped down into the pits armed with welding guns and helped to satisfy the nation's pent-up demand. The city's 55,000 citizens, mainly Polish-Americans, crammed pin-neat homes pinched together along residential streets like McDougall, Yemens and Poland. It was a clean, Democratic, working-class town, which drew Harry Truman, Adlai Stevenson and John Kennedy to campaign alongside proud mayors like Albert Zak, Joseph Grzecki and Raymond Wojtowicz. It was the very model of American success—a melting pot of immigrant families forging a new life for themselves as part of an industrial machine unmatched in history.

Sometime in the Sixties, Dodge Main began to lose its competitive edge. The eight floors that made sense when the factory housed its own foundry, sewing room, stamping plant and test track proved increasingly inefficient as Chrysler and the industry turned to less integrated facilities that specialized in the various stages of production. Dodge Main was reduced to an assembly plant. The lines started way up on the sixth floor, then bumped and creaked their way down an inclined conveyor belt toward the second-floor inspection deck. The vast, low-ceilinged rooms required inordinately expensive equipment, especially designed to fit them.

In the good years, like 1973, it didn't matter. Volume—half a million cars—poured onto the inspection deck and simply buried the inefficiencies, but in the bad years, which most were thereafter for Chrysler, waste rose up like cankers. Thirty-two freight elevators carried parts and people from one floor to the next, at a cost that was forgotten when energy and workers were cheap. Jim Caton, a Chrysler manufacturing veteran called in late in 1979 to ease Dodge Main into retirement, could look at the layers of anachronism and point out where Dodge Main went wrong, or rather, where life had simply passed it by. "The plant itself didn't become obsolete," said Caton, "so much as things caused it to become obsolete." When flaws were found in the cars along the line, they were sent back upstairs at enormous cost. The hundreds upon hundreds of 12- by 18-inch windows, caulked and painted over a dozen times each, were no longer a match for Michigan winters—and coal was now at $40 a ton, instead of $2.50.

Time and again, Chrysler executives talked about upgrading or abandoning Dodge Main. In the Sixties, workers heard that the company was going to spruce it up with $500 million. Then, in the Seventies, the rumor was that they were going to shut it down and build the new Aspens and Volares in New Stanton, Pennsylvania. They ended up doing neither, and the Aspens and Volares were the last cars to roll out of Dodge Main.

Just as Chrysler captured the history of the greatest industry the United States had ever known, so Dodge Main was a portrait of Chrysler at its worst. In the heyday of proliferation, it spewed out Barracudas, Darts, Valiants and full-size Dodges and Plymouths off two assembly lines, but warranty costs ran twice as high as at newer plants like Newark or Belvidere. Distrust between workers and managers was a way of life. The men and women on the line who were constantly berated—first for not building enough cars and then for building them badly—new management had no monopoly on morality. Theft of parts from Dodge Main was rampant, but only subtler, on the part of management. Welds were intentionally missed; the men in sub-assembly often set their own quotas and went home when they were finished. At one point, plant clerks calculated that they were paying out $375,000 to workers who failed to punch in and out for lunch hour. When management cracked down, the workers broke the time clocks by pouring sealant down the slots. When management countered by turning the clocks upside down, the workers got spray cans of sealant. "Too bad," sighed one plant official, "you couldn't channel that ingenuity into productivity."

As Dodge Main declined, so did Hamtramck. Higher wages allowed many of the original families to afford larger houses in the suburbs and cars to commute to the plant. The fulfillment of the American dream ironically whittled away at the community's sense of community—thanks partly to the success of Henry Ford I's notion that the auto worker might one day be able to afford the product of his labor. The second and third generations of Polish immigrants moved to places like Warren and Royal Oak, leaving Hamtramck with a dwindling, aging population. Each year, fewer heads bowed in the pews at St. Florian's Church. The Old World bakeries and sausage shops along Joseph Campau Avenue began closing, as did the bars and beer gardens that huddled around the giant factory to wet a thousand throats at shift change.

In the summer of 1979, when Chrysler announced it would close Dodge Main for good, the future of Hamtramck was thrown into question. On top of the gradual decline in population and subsequent tax revenues, the city suddenly faced a loss of $2.3 million in annual tax income from the plant—almost half the annual city budget. Mayor Robert Kozeran was forced to slash the municipal payroll from around five hundred to two hundred, leaving just forty-three policemen and forty firemen. "They used to take up a whole block on Joseph Campau marching in parades," Kozeran reminisced.

With crisis impending, outside experts were asked to find a future for both Dodge Main and Hamtramck. At a symposium of academics in late August of '79, some suggested turning the plant into a bus factory to fill the nation's need for mass transportation. Others thought solar panels would correct energy inefficiencies. Others said to forget about the plant and transform Hamtramck into a free-trade zone or a tourist attraction like a Polish theme park. "What Hamtramck does," suggested the Librarian of Congress, Dr. Daniel Boorstin, "will be an example for the rest of the nation." But University of Pittsburgh history professor Samuel Hays was more pessimistic. "It's almost as if you're seeing the death of the manufacturing city right here," he noted. "Don't resurrect it. Why try to build something that is gone?"

For those still living and working in Hamtramck, there was plenty of reason, although as Dick Lada, a Dodge Main employment supervisor, admitted, "It's more emotional than rational." Too many children of immigrant parents owed their college educations to Chrysler and Dodge Main. Too many judges and attorneys had worked on the assembly line to pay their way through law school. "I was born here," said Lada. "I've worked at this plant fifteen years in the employment office and hired thousands of people, many of whose fathers and grandfathers worked here. It's been good to a lot of people."

There was that dull sense of loss on Friday, January 4, 1980, the day the last blue Dodge Aspen rolled down the line, leaving behind groups of instrument fitters, engine installers and wheel mounters to clean up quietly and go home. By then, there were only 2,300 workers on the one remaining line. No one working at Dodge Main had less than ten years seniority and each had a healthy cushion of unemployment benefits to tide him or her through the idle times ahead. The huge factory went silent and the burghers of Hamtramck began their struggle for survival.

Following passage of the Loan Guarantee Act—just a week before Dodge Main closed—Iacocca and corporate advertising began touting "the New Chrysler Corporation." To many, it was a hollow claim, a desperate ploy to shed the image of ineptitude and obsolescence.

Nothing symbolized the ambiguity of "the New Chrysler Corporation" better than the old Jefferson Avenue plant on Detroit's east side. Even older than Dodge Main and indeed older than the company itself, the factory had survived a number of closure threats during the Sixties and Seventies to emerge as one of two assembly plants for the K-car. Most of the first $500 million in federally guaranteed loans was pumped into Jefferson and the K-car plant in Newark, Delaware. One hundred million dollars was spent equipping Jefferson with the most modern machinery available, including Unimate robot welders and Robogate body assemblers to pinch the pieces of the frame together accurately and consistently. Shabby and dirty on the outside, the plant was a paragon of efficiency within. Not only did robots jab and nibble at car bodies; there was also a perceptible change in the attitudes of the people who worked there.

In June, the UAW and Chrysler established joint management-worker quality committees and began the first tentative steps toward worker participation in quality control—not the vague pronouncements of total responsibility offered by previous management, but a structured system, a variation on the Japanese theme. Among the workers at Jefferson Avenue, a new militancy emerged. "Ain't nobody going to get away with nothin'," growled Herb Anderson, a seventeen-year machinery repairman at the plant, "and that includes the bosses."

No one at Jefferson Avenue worked under the delusion that anything short of fear prompted the new diligence. On the day in August when Iacocca came with a gaggle of politicians to launch the first K-car from the plant's assembly line, the mood at Chrysler and its prospects for survival never seemed better. Workers lined the bay entrance to the brightly lit plant and cheered lustily as the chairman, stogie clenched between his teeth, strode inside to take a seat behind the wheel of K-car Number One, a yellow Plymouth Reliant. Behind him, union president Doug Fraser, by then a company board member, pointed a friendly finger at one of his constituents. "Build 'em good," charged Fraser. "We will," assured the man. "We have to."

After the June photo finish with the banks and the first $500 million loan, the summer months had been kind to Chrysler. Attention had shifted gradually from Washington and Wall Street back to Detroit and Jefferson Avenue in particular. "Reindustrialization" had become the reigning buzzword as the nation came to realize that the problem was bigger than Chrysler. Ford by then was bleeding heavily and was on its way to a 1980 net loss of more than $1.5 billion and an operating loss of $2.35 billion that was nearly double Chrysler's operating loss that year. Even mighty General Motors stumbled to its first full-year deficit since Durant's folly in 1921—$763 million.

"This is the beginning of the reindustrialization of the American automobile industry," declared Lee Iacocca (never one to let a clarion go unsounded) at the August K-car launch ceremony. He was greeted by thunderous applause from workers and politicians. Don Riegle told a delighted partisan audience that he was looking forward to offering Bill Proxmire a ride in his newly ordered K-car. It was a moment of triumph. A parade of diminutive, shiny sedans followed Iacocca's through the crowd—one driven by Fraser, another by Mayor Coleman Young, still others by Michigan Governor Bill Milliken, senators Carl Levin and Don Riegle, Congressman Jim Blanchard and others. Beneath the big blue-and-yellow sign plastered on the wall of the plant, inscribed "We Can Do It," hung another that read, simply and smugly, "Consider It Done."

It wasn't that easy. At the time of the launch, the prime rate stood at about 11 percent, the lowest it had been since Iacocca joined Chrysler back in the fall of 1978. After a dizzying ride on the back of the national banking system, the American consumer was just beginning to regain some balance. In the economic glow of a presidential campaign, Washington was doling out federal funds and holding austerity in the wings while Jimmy Carter tried to fend off Ronald Reagan's conservative attacks. With the new model year approaching, Detroit had its usual hopes of recovery. The K-car and Ford's front-wheel-drive subcompacts, the Escort and its twin, the Mercury Lynx, were, after all, hard evidence that the U.S. carmakers were capable of responding, albeit belatedly, to new demands. No one was bold enough to suggest, as Henry Ford II had in the early Seventies, that Detroit would push the imports into the sea. Foreign cars had won nearly 30 percent of the U.S. market in July, with the Japanese alone taking 23.7 percent. There was a sense of confidence, nonetheless, that the long siege was turning in Detroit's favor. "I really do think we've bottomed out," Iacocca allowed hours after he had driven the first Reliant out of Jefferson Avenue.

It had been an unusual year. Entering 1980, having just signed the Chrysler Loan Guarantee Act into law, Jimmy Carter had become possessed by a concern for inflation. It had been running in double digits for a full year, and the "inflationary psychology" that led people to make financial decisions on the assumption that prices would only continue to rise and the value of money sink lower had settled into the collective logic. Carter was swayed by the argument that the American way of credit, whether a source or a by-product of inflation, was contributing to its continuation. So he sought, through credit restrictions imposed in midwinter, to break the cycle that led consumers to charge today what would inevitably be more expensive tomorrow.

The program appeared to recognize that two industries had to be cast as exceptions. Housing and autos—and, to a lesser extent, all consumer durables, like washers, driers and refrigerators—were separated, theoretically, from the villainous frivolities perceived as drains on America's savings. In a sad display of administrative ineptitude, however, the Carter program failed to provide an effective method of separating durable goods from the rest. Even after they were told by the Federal Reserve Board that they should not restrict auto loans, banks across the country continued to do so anyway, dropping them off the bottom of their loan portfolios in favor of more lucrative loans and investments. In some of the forty-seven states where usury laws capped interest rates on auto loans at up to 10 percentage points below the going rate, it would have been outright foolhardy to lend money toward the purchase of a new car.

With the high price of fuel, the continued demand for small cars that, in the 1980 model year, could not be met by domestic producers, and a general economic decline afflicting the nation, it was not entirely clear that the Carter credit crunch was solely responsible for the precipitous decline in auto sales. However, two-thirds of the new cars bought by Americans each year are paid for at least in part by credit, and the monthly car payment is as common in most households as the monthly rent or mortgage payment. It was more than coincidental that when the prime rate hit 20 percent in April 1980, the U.S. auto market went into a nosedive that left sales in May at the lowest annual level since 1958—fully a third lower than a year earlier, when the Iranian crisis was buffeting the market. Even the imports were off by 10 percent.

Early in May, at Neil Goldschmidt's urging, Jimmy Carter called the top executives of the five U.S. auto manufacturers (Volkswagen of America's Jim McClernon was included) to the White House for the first of a series of exchanges on the state of the industry. Doug Fraser and Marc Stepp of the UAW were asked as well.[1] As the beleaguered executives waited for the President, Anne Wexler of the White House staff offered sardonically, "We've been thinking that maybe Charlie Wilson was right after all."[2]

Jimmy Carter prided himself on his personal command of detail and was diligent in preparing himself for such meetings. Thus it was all the more disturbing for Carter to learn for the first time, directly from the auto executives, how badly his credit program was hurting the industry. For AMC and VW, which had no captive credit arm, the crunch was the most damaging factor in their declining sales. Not only was the policy discouraging buyers, it was also deterring dealers from ordering cars, since their carrying costs for inventory were typically a point and a half above the prime rate.[3]

Hearing the news, Carter icily ordered his staff to find ways of relieving the credit burden. Eventually, they came up with a package of special low-interest guaranteed loans for dealers in trouble, but such targeted relief had only minimal effect as long as the underlying cost of money was as high as the Volcker Federal Reserve forced it that spring. In 1980 alone, more than sixteen hundred car dealers closed their doors.

Car prices were clearly part of the problem too. Although American automobiles had trailed the Consumer Price Index (CPI), the standard measure of inflation, for twenty years, the impact of double-digit inflation, led by energy costs, *plus* the $80 billion transformation bill that had to be paid whatever the market conditions, was correcting for that lag rather rapidly. General Motors, in all segments of the market except subcompact, set industry prices and usually did so at regular intervals. Once semi-annual, these "price adjustments" (as they are euphemistically labeled) had in recent years become quarterly and, by early 1980, almost monthly. In their first eighteen months, some GM X-cars climbed more than 30 percent in price. In six weeks in early 1980, Ford cars rose an average of $250 apiece.

It was hardly a matter of gouging. Like all businesses, the auto industry had to pay higher prices for raw materials and labor. Since 1975, steel had gone up 64 percent; some plastics had increased 45 percent and aluminum had shot up 77 percent. Regulations for safety and emissions (fuel-economy expenditures excluded) had added $666 to the cost of each new car by 1979. With the 1981 models, they were about to add $300 to $400 per car more for the electronic fuel-monitoring gadgetry needed to comply with the '81 emissions standards—what Iacocca called "the unholy climax" of the original Muskie Clean Air Standards.

Such explanations were of little comfort, however, to the potential car buyer who'd been out of the market for three years and had last paid less than $5,000 for a gleaming, 4,800-pound, eight-cylinder highway cruiser. With a trade-in value reflecting its old gas mileage, his used cruiser was likely to leave him paying more money on top of the trade than the car had cost him altogether three years earlier. In a consumer climate which the University of Michigan's Survey of Consumer Attitudes found, in the first quarter of 1980, to be more pessimistic than at any time since the survey had first been taken in 1946, it was indeed a wonder that anyone bought *any* car—let alone a car from a company that might not be in business long enough to make the first oil change.

The interest rates plummeted even more rapidly than they had risen, though, and car sales were recovering slightly as Detroit readied for the fall new-model introduction. Iacocca decided that the new-model press preview should be held in the shadow of the Capitol so that he could spread before the legislators—both friend and foe alike—the fruits of their guaranteed loans. The Washington preview was also an acknowledgment that the federal government was indeed a partner in Chrysler's operations.

At least once a month, usually on the Friday following the regular monthly board meeting in New York, Iacocca headed the corporate Gulfstream southward into National Airport for a session with Messrs.

Miller, Volcker, Staats and Freeman—the three voting members of the Loan Guarantee Board and its executive director. These were progress report sessions, following a preordained system that allowed the government oversight group to see how Chrysler was doing. Following the June bank rush and the first two loan drawdowns (the second $300 million loan, approved July 31, was almost routine and received very little attention in the press), the sessions had none of the frenetic feeling that had marked the pre-closing meetings. They were dominated by staff questions about market share and model mix. No one presumed Chrysler was out of the woods, but there was hope that, if economic conditions continued to improve and Chrysler's new cars caught the market, there would be at least a prolonged period in which the company could test its survivability.

The Loan Board meetings were private affairs, but Iacocca's strong performance September 23 on the lower level of the Shoreham Hotel, surrounded by reporters and a fleet of '81 models, signaled that the Master Merchandiser was back in the car business again. With the K-car as its centerpiece, Chrysler's '81 fleet offered a Corporate Average Fuel Economy of 25.5 mpg. The federal requirement for the year 1981 was only 22, and GM was projecting its own CAFE at just 23. Chrysler, said Iacocca, had more models with fuel economy better than 25 mpg than any of the imports, including Toyota, Honda and VW. It was good old hard-sell, with numbers to back it up. Iacocca breezed through the pitch, rattling off specs and technical data in the industry shorthand he knew so well.

Only one question, and his answer to it, stuck in the maw of the meeting. What was the one thing, asked a Washington reporter, that could jeopardize the company's recovery prospects? Interest rates, replied Iacocca with only a slight pause. "The thing that worries me now, that could upset everything in our business, is interest rates going back to fifteen and then to twenty percent. It would destroy everything."

Indeed, the prime had already begun to climb again. By dealer introduction day, October 2, it had already passed 13.5 percent on its way back toward 20 percent. Dealers, who had already ordered healthy batches of K-cars and even supplies of Chrysler's older rear-wheel-drive models (largely because of Iacocca's hard-nosed arm-twisting during summer dealer meetings), began hanging back as orders for November came due. The timing could not have been worse. Once again, outside forces utterly beyond Chrysler's control went to work, undoing the company's schemes for survival—but, this time, Chrysler contributed to its own undoing. In one of the few decisions left entirely to managerial whim, the men on the fifth floor of the K. T. Keller Building guessed wrong, and it cost them dearly.

Few automotive watchers disputed the timing of the K-car introduction. As Jim Dunne, automotive editor of *Popular Science*, said of
the launch, "If Chrysler could have designed a car that was right for
today's market just three weeks ago instead of three and a half years
ago, they still would have designed this car." With 25 mpg city and 41
mpg on the highway, front-wheel drive, intelligent lines and capacity
for five or six passengers, it was well positioned to catch the traditional big American car owners on their way down to fuel efficiency.
It was not meant to take on the imports in the newly brutal subcompact market, but rather to ease customers into a more modest version of the family car.

It was exactly this strategy, miraculously bolstered by the Iranian
crisis, that had launched GM's X-car eighteen months earlier. To be
sure, GM now owned that segment, selling half the compacts bought
in the United States, but most marketing analysts saw these smaller
compacts as the new center of an American car market that was continuing to skew toward smaller vehicles. In a sense, Chrysler's offer of
a car so similar to GM's seemed an illustration of the company's
chronic inability to strike out from the pack. But on the other hand,
the K-car, with a distinct fuel-economy advantage over the X-car (25
to GM's 23 mpg) and visibly distinguishable styling, was an admission
that the car market of the future would be far narrower and more dependent upon technical distinctions than on chrome and glamour.

Even with the concessions by the banks and the union, inherent
manufacturing cost disadvantages made it impossible for Chrysler to
achieve the same variable profit margins enjoyed by GM, but Chrysler
marketing people were determined to stay as close as possible to GM.
In the months preceding introduction, the jockeying became ferocious,
with GM starting out under Chrysler's tentative prices and gradually
boosting them upward to more than $6,000 for a base model. When
the final bell sounded, GM's stripped two-door Citation Hatchback
listed at $6,270 and the lowest-priced K-coupe was marked at $5,880.
Higher-priced versions for both ranged upward toward $7,000.
Chrysler undercut GM, hoping fervently that a buoyant market would
load up their cars with more lucrative options.

The decision didn't end with pricing and a prayer for option-hungry
buyers. Crucial to the introduction was the mix of cars to be shipped
to dealers for opening-day showroom perusal. Base sticker prices drew
customers into showrooms, but customers were more likely to buy cars
decorated with stereos, air conditioners and Landau roofs that could
easily jack up the price by $2,000 or more.

The original strategy called for 36,000 K-cars in the showrooms October 2. Some—not many—would be base-price models, there for bait
more than sale. Some would be moderately adorned, with sticker

prices in the $7,000 range. Many would be veritable gems, with velvety cushions, electric windows and all manner of discretionary comfort, and would set the customers back by $8,000 or $9,000.

How to spread the mix was a subject of earnest debate. Jerry Greenwald, the chief financial officer, whose natural instinct was with maximizing cash flow and getting Chrysler back into the black as swiftly as possible, pushed for higher margins and more options. Dick Vining, the chief manufacturing officer, argued for modest options, which would allow his assemblers to keep on top of quality control and minimize inventory costs. It was the decision of Gar Laux's marketing staff, and ultimately Lee Iacocca, that the cars shipped for introduction were weighted in favor of the loaded variety. The need for penetration—usually achieved through lower prices—was clear. Chrysler's share of the compact market had dropped from 18.2 percent in 1979 to 11.5 percent in 1980, and its overall market share had dropped a full point below that of a year that itself had been an unmitigated disaster. Nevertheless, the pressure to be in the black by the fourth quarter, something he had repeatedly promised that summer, and the conviction that the market was prepared to swallow the sky-high prices drove Iacocca toward loading the cars with options.

It was then that things began to go wrong. The K-car development, which up until then had gone as smoothly as axle grease, enabling Iacocca to order a two-week advance in the production schedule, hit a snag in late August and early September. Vining's manufacturing men had trouble with some of the new automated equipment, and the number of cars promised for introduction day kept growing smaller. More damaging by far, however, was that the cars that were shipped —only 10,000—were almost all loaded to the roofline with options. Hardly any base- and moderate-priced cars went out, and on opening day in October, customers drowned in a sea of $8,000 and $9,000 window stickers. Many who were primed to give Chrysler a fair shake for their new cars fled back to their old gas guzzlers in despair.[4]

Even the luxury Imperial, a re-skinned Cordoba with plush appointments and a workbench-full of electronic controls, was not meeting its sales goals. Chrysler had planned to sell between 20,000 and 25,000 of them in the '81 model year—a modest figure indeed. With margins of $5,000 apiece, the cars offered more than $100 million in badly needed profits for a relatively minimal investment ($75 million). Iacocca had won the free services of "Ole Blue Eyes," Frank Sinatra, who in turn recruited a host of Hollywood stars—from Gregory Peck and Angie Dickinson to Ernest Borgnine, Bill Cosby and Sally Struthers—to donate their valuable time and faces to a series of advertisements pitching the Imperial and other Chrysler cars. It was a car and a strategy based on reasonably good times, and the Carter double-dip recession blew away the assumptions.

Chrysler moved quickly to reverse the deadly pattern. The second round of K-cars pouring out of the Jefferson Avenue plant and Newark, Delaware, where the wagon version was assembled, had considerably fewer options, and after a shaky production start-up, the lines accelerated toward an eventual output of eighty cars an hour. By then, however, the prime was passing through the 16 percent level. By early December, the rate banks offered their best customers had reached 18.5 percent. Whether they could get auto loans for less didn't matter. Most Americans had taken to watching the prime as if it were the baseball standings in August—making key decisions, like whether or not to buy a car, based on what had become almost daily rate changes.

Prospects for a fourth-quarter 1980 profit faded quickly. With K-car sales falling markedly short of target, renewed questions about Chrysler's survivability rose up once more from the stark numbers on the ten-day sales reports. In Washington, the summer's calm was shaken, and a new team of Loan Board staffers, many new to the intricacies of the market, scrambled to make sense of the market-share tables and cash-flow projections.

This time, Iacocca went for the dramatic: a variation on the old rebate theme, but keyed to the infamous prime. Figuring that if the interest rate had stayed at 13 percent Chrysler would indeed have turned a profit in the fourth quarter, Iacocca personally developed a floating rebate that would pay back every Chrysler buyer who purchased on credit the difference between what he or she would have paid at 13 percent and whatever the going rate was. Whenever the prime moved, the rebate moved with it—up or down.

It moved up—to 21 percent at its 1980 peak—but the program, combined with Chrysler's emphasis on base-line models, succeeded in reversing the trend. Well into the first quarter of 1981, Chrysler's market share was still climbing upward from the trough of 7.8 percent in July of 1980. In January, it was back over 10 percent, and in February GM and Ford moved to rebates as well. The launch had come late, but it appeared that the cars were beginning to catch on, unencumbered by any of the flaws that had marred most of Chrysler's new cars throughout the Seventies.

Unfortunately, the delayed acceptance of the '81 models and the cost of overcoming federal monetary policy sapped every penny of the $800 million Chrysler had drawn down in the summer. After a brief respite in October, the cash flow turned red again, and by the second week in December, it was beyond debate that Chrysler would have to go back for more. The drain of capital expenditures and the wholesale disposition of any asset that hadn't proved its worth had reduced Chrysler's net worth to less than $200 million. As dealers pulled back into caution and some of the fleet buyers who had ordered 45,000 K-cars before introduction day hedged on accepting deliveries, Chrysler was forced to halt production of the K-car and even the durable Omni/Horizon, shutting down its most promising plants for most of December. The 15,000 cars Chrysler didn't dare build that month meant a drop of $100 million in projected cash flow. Chrysler had no choice but to tap at least several hundred million more of the remaining $700 million authorized by Congress if it was to avoid, for the second time in six months, bankruptcy and very likely liquidation.

"The Lord helps those who help themselves," Iacocca said the day he launched the interest-pegged rebate plan. It was a maxim that might well have been offered by the Chrysler Loan Guarantee Board in Washington. Crucial to the board's approval of any new loan application was a determination that Chrysler was likely to be what the law termed an "ongoing concern"—in short, able to pay back the money. With net worth evaporating and debt accumulating in the face of a continually deteriorating car market, that determination would be a marginal call at best. Board chairman G. William Miller knew it; Iacocca knew it; everyone privy to the company's books knew it. Meeting the arithmetic requirements for a new drawdown that meant Chrysler would have to come up with an equal amount of financing on its own was nowhere near as important as proving that the continued existence of the corporation was possible. The package of concessions completed in June 1980 was simply inadequate—at least in part because Treasury Secretary Miller had remained detached from the crucial negotiations and had left the burden of pressuring constituents on relatively powerless staff members. Now Miller was convinced that what the banks and the union had contributed had to be supplemented with more debt forgiveness and deeper wage cuts. The corporate debt in particular, at nearly $1.2 billion, not only drowned the company's remaining assets but served as a powerful talisman to ward off potential candidates for merger or joint venture.

Bill Miller changed after the 1980 election. The Carter loss had made him a lame duck in Washington, placing him in the unusual position during those last few months of being able to act with minimal consideration of the political implications—something with which he had never really been at ease. He seemed to take particular interest in Chrysler, since it had become a hallmark of his tenure at Treasury and because, perhaps, a successful restructuring might at least reestablish his reputation as a hard-nosed businessman.

Iacocca pieced together the blunt mosaic of what was in effect a whole new round of private contributions from Chrysler's constituents

—the banks, the union and the suppliers. Many of the bankers had already given up on the company and written off most of their loans as bad debt. The union members, on the other hand, still had everything to lose—their jobs. The suppliers—all 19,000 of them—had borne the beleaguered company along, patiently accepting late payments and shipping parts with no real assurance of continuity. Iacocca made a calculated decision that all of them had simple choices: either go along with his appeal for further sacrifice or face what would come close to a total loss. He concluded that his only alternative was to call in the last few chips, ask for another $1 billion in concessions and go for broke.

He asked the banks for some $600 million through the conversion of debt to preferred stock, part of which was an acceleration of a scheme outlined in the original bank deal. He asked for a freeze on cost-of-living adjustments (COLA) from UAW members that would save the company some $570 million in projected wage increases. Suppliers were asked to accept delayed payments and then give an across-the-board 5-percent price break for the first quarter of 1981. The company itself, proposed Iacocca, would cut its own operating budget by 10 percent, chopping yet another few thousand white-collar jobs.

The reaction on Wall Street, in Solidarity House and at supplier headquarters throughout the country was one of shock. The bankers, after all the haggling of the spring and summer, were, in the words of one of them, "just plain tired." The workers had mixed reactions—some blurting out that enough was enough, but most resigning themselves to any pay sacrifice that would keep them on the job. Most of the suppliers were willing to wait for payment, but many claimed they simply didn't have 5 percent profit left in their business with Chrysler.

If they were shocked by Iacocca's flat proposition, the three groups would be stunned by the hard-nosed attitude of Bill Miller. Although somewhat vague (and eventually pliant) on the concessions from suppliers, Miller gradually made it clear to the banks and the union that he not only concurred with Iacocca's conditions, he wanted more. He wanted not only half the bank debt converted to preferred stock, thus shifting a large piece of liability onto the asset column of Chrysler's balance sheet, but he also wanted outright forgiveness of the remaining debt. As for the UAW, Miller wanted an even bigger bite from the average future paycheck, and he wanted some assurance that the union would not come back at the 1982 contract and demand a quantum leap upward along the pay scale toward parity with workers at GM and Ford. It was "take it or leave it," and Bill Miller allowed that he was perfectly willing to leave it to the Reagan administration and almost certain rejection.

Outrage gradually turned to resignation. The alternative this time was quick liquidation and maybe ten cents on the dollar for the bankers, after four to seven years litigating what would surely be the most complex bankruptcy settlement in history. Steve Miller began anew the grueling round of airplane rides and negotiating sessions with bankers. This time, at least, they numbered only 159, since the sacrifices did not involve lenders to Chrysler Financial Corporation, but only to the parent corporation itself. After two prior rounds of contract talks, the UAW was able to streamline bargaining and indeed win a number of significant non-wage concessions from Chrysler, including a profit-sharing plan for hourly workers, a say in future plant closings and access to Chrysler's books, including both operating and productivity data.

On the day before he left office, Bill Miller presided over a last meeting of the Carter administration Chrysler Loan Guarantee Board that gave preliminary approval to $400 million in new loans, thus raising Chrysler's total obligation to the federal government to $1.2 billion. In return, Chrysler gave the board a package that included:

—the conversion of $560 million in long-term debt to equity in the form of preferred stock, and the forgiveness, at Chrysler's option, of the remaining debt at thirty cents on the dollar;

—a corporation-wide pay freeze consisting of $622 million in further concessions from UAW members and another $161 million from salaried workers;

—$36 million in price concessions from suppliers, plus the company's "best efforts" to secure another $36 million in concessions;

—$200 million in loan guarantees from the Canadian government;

—Chrysler's own commitment to almost $3 billion in internal cost reductions from further layoffs, payment deferrals and the postponement of several product programs.

The UAW's third concession left Chrysler with an aggregate advantage over General Motors and Ford of nearly $1 billion over three years and, more significantly, established a precedent that Walter Reuther's description of the wage contract as a "living document" could work both ways. For the first time in the history of the auto industry, the union sustained monetary losses and proved that wages as well as profits can shrink as well as expand.

The bank concessions set no such precedent, but may have been equally significant for Chrysler's future. The essentials were worked out on a paper placemat in the dining room of the Washington Hotel across the street from the Treasury Building on Saturday, January 10. Bill Miller sketched out for Chrysler's Steve Miller how he envisioned the banks breaking down their capitulation. It was for the Treasury

Secretary the most important piece of the plan, since it virtually relieved Chrysler Corporation of non-federal debt and thus made it at least a plausible candidate for partnership.

None of the constituents was happy with the settlement, but the union was resigned to do as much as it dared to save Chrysler without inviting GM and Ford to demand similar concessions. The banks got at least a chance to salvage money through the ownership of preferred stock and, in the short run, the equivalent of fifteen cents on the dollar for the total loan amount, probably a better deal than they could have gotten from a protracted liquidation proceeding.

Not all the banks agreed, and before the package went to the new Reagan administration Loan Board for final approval in late February, a group of about a dozen banks, led by New York's Citibank and Irving Trust, wrested one last ounce of principal from the restructuring plan by demanding and getting payment of $68 million in cash up front because they didn't believe Chrysler would be alive long enough to pay them off according to the original plan.

For Chrysler, the program called for the unhappy prospect of further layoffs and the precarious prospect of delaying introduction of three new cars for the early Eighties—underlining even more dramatically Chrysler's need to find partners to bolster its product line and help it achieve economies wherever possible. Miller extracted from Iacocca a commitment to establish a board-level committee to explore merger and joint-venture possibilities and to report the fruits of its work periodically to the Loan Guarantee Board. Finally, and to Iacocca's extreme annoyance, Miller demanded that he sell Chrysler's last remaining jet, the blue-and-white Gulfstream II that had become the Chrysler chairman's second home during 1980.

The financial and operating plans for Chrysler that grew out of the new round of concessions envisioned the company returning to profitability in 1982, a full year later than Chrysler had projected in the fall of 1979. Gone were the predictions that Americans would be buying at least 11 million cars in 1981 and 12.1 million in 1982, of which Chrysler would sell 11 percent and 11.5 percent respectively. The new plan, after the scorching Chrysler and the entire industry had taken in 1980, called for Chrysler to capture an unpresumptuous 9.1 percent of a 9.6-million-unit market in 1981 and 9.8 percent of a 10.6-million-unit market in 1982. Truck sales were projected 157,000 units less for 1981 than Chrysler had predicted in its December 1979 operating plan. With cost reductions approaching $3 billion over the coming five years, Chrysler could recalculate its break-even point down to 1.1 million cars and trucks annually—half the vehicles it would have to have sold in 1979 to make a profit. There was no guarantee that Chrysler would make it, but an automobile company had been fashioned that had reasonable prospects in all but the worst of circumstances, at least for a few more months.

There was, not only on Wall Street and in Washington but at the highest levels of Chrysler's new management, serious thought given to an alliance between Chrysler and the Ford Motor Company, which was itself in serious trouble in the spring of 1981. While some dismissed a Ford/Chrysler merger as nothing more than an amalgamation of losers, a doubling of disaster inviting not only personality clashes between Lee Iacocca and Henry Ford's management team in Dearborn but almost certain antitrust action from Washington, others saw beyond such difficulties. They envisioned an American car company with the size, the distribution system, the product line and, thanks to UAW concessions to Chrysler, a forced lower wage scale covering Ford that would represent the only clear competition to General Motors and the Japanese. Chrysler, through Salomon Brothers' Jim Wolfensohn, actually approached Ford through its own investment banking representative, Goldman Sachs. The detailed white paper outlining the proposed merger plan was dismissed not only curtly but publicly by Ford, thus nipping in the bud one of the more intriguing ideas in American business history. "We don't go to parties we're not invited to," said Iacocca of the Ford rejection.

By the spring of 1981, Chrysler was a far different company from the one whose management had nervously contemplated spending $72 million on a new car for its French subsidiary in 1977. Lynn Townsend and John Riccardo's ungainly multinational had been trimmed into Lee Iacocca's lean domestic manufacturer: a company without the wherewithal to survive independently in the new world automobile business, but an increasingly clean prospect for an equally new form of partnership. Gone were all the European, South American, Australian and South African operations. The only foreign ties remaining were to the highly profitable Mexican subsidiary and the Canadian operations, which were inseparable from the U.S. parent. Chrysler held 15 percent each of Japan's Mitsubishi, which continued to supply subcompact cars and trucks despite increasing product conflicts, and Peugeot, whose stock served as collateral for a $100 million loan. Both Mitsubishi and Peugeot also supplied Chrysler with engines and other components, and the prospects were good that further exchanges—perhaps even a joint venture—could be arranged.

Gone was the realty company, the resort at Big Sky, the shopping centers and the boat companies. Although the express purpose of the Democrats in Congress in passing the Loan Guarantee Act had been to preserve jobs, Chrysler employed less than 60 percent of the people it had in 1978, only a third of the 250,000 who had worked there in 1977, and its continued survival depended on even more plant closings and consolidations. Although it had been argued before Congress that Chrysler's collapse would have a national impact, more than half the jobs lost through the consolidation process were in Michigan, Ohio and Indiana, and roughly half the jobs that remained were still in Michigan.

The isolation of the impact did not lessen the potential pain for the midwestern region that stood to suffer the most from a Chrysler failure. Indeed, one of the blessings of the widespread distribution of jobs in the last major liquidation—that of the W. T. Grant department stores—had been that the 50,000 who lost their jobs in 1976–77 were sprinkled throughout communities that were able to absorb them with relative ease. The heavy reliance of the midwestern states on the auto industry and its suppliers left them struggling desperately during the 1979–80 downturn because they were unable to absorb the massive unemployment. Even without the collapse of Chrysler, the City of Detroit and the State of Michigan faced budget deficits and service cutbacks that threatened their own financial stability at a time when a strong social "safety net" was needed most.

In Detroit, two stamping plants had been closed, putting 6,500 people out of work. Another 4,100 went when the Missouri truck-assembly plant closed in St. Louis. Only 2,260, compared to 8,000 in the early Seventies, still worked at Chrysler's transmission plant in Kokomo, Indiana. The town of 47,000 still clung to the hope that Chrysler's corporate heart would continue to tick. All around Kokomo, smaller companies were moving away, leaving more than 10-percent unemployment in the strip of northern Indiana that was still a satellite of Detroit. State welfare payments and Trade Readjustment Assistance payments (compensation to those who lost their jobs because of imports) kept poverty at bay, but in January 1981, when the third round of wage concessions came up for a vote at Kokomo's UAW Local 685, 64 percent cast a gloomy "aye" vote.

By April 1981, the wreckers' balls had reduced the dark walls of Dodge Main to rubble, and the city of Hamtramck struggled to ready itself for a new Cadillac body and assembly plant that would employ six thousand. The new Cadillac plant, a replacement for the old Clark Street factory on Detroit's west side, provided Hamtramck with its greatest hope and offered some solace to the entire frostbelt region that it would not be deserted entirely. (At the same time, the brand-new facility was one more piece of evidence of GM's increasing domination of the domestic industry.)

The dire consequences of bankruptcy, so luridly spelled out in Washington, were no longer quite so dire—largely because the restructuring under the Loan Guarantee Act had allowed much of the shrinkage to take place in an orderly manner over a span of several years.

Many suffered, to be sure, but there had been little of the jarring social disruption that would indeed have resulted from a precipitous failure of Chrysler in 1979, and the chances of wholesale disruption in the future had been distinctly lessened.

A bankruptcy reorganization, the pipe dream of academics and die-hard free enterprisers, could not have worked for Chrysler. Car companies depend too much on public confidence, thousands of suppliers and sprawling dealer networks. Consumers deprived of service, suppliers deprived of payment and dealers deprived of cars to sell would have kept Chrysler in court for years. The $160 million Chrysler had to spend on the development of new cars would have been frozen immediately in court under the provisions of the bankruptcy code. By the end of the Seventies, the company was too closely intertwined for factories like Belvidere, which made the Omni/Horizon, to be sliced cleanly away.

Instead, it was the Loan Guarantee Act, though it was certainly never designed to do so, that provoked a total reorganization in public, allowing the company to do everything a bankruptcy judge would have taken years to organize while it spent money at the same time. The act provided breathing space—not only for displaced workers and disrupted communities, but for suppliers in search of other business, dealers in need of other franchises and banks that had to sort out their balance sheets. Also, those unnerved by the precedent set by the Chrysler bailout might examine the company's wrenching public agony. The biting jibes and public humiliation surely served as a deterrent to prospective supplicants waiting for the arrival of a state consecrated to subsidizing the inefficient, propping up the weak, rewarding poor management and puffing up the featherbeds of indolent workers. Indeed, if anything, the act went too far in insisting on pillory. Inevitably, Chrysler's returns to the Loan Board invited not only renewed speculation of imminent collapse, but use of the very short-term criteria for reward that had so often perverted the acumen of past management.

Although Chrysler never had been, as sadly uninformed critics right up to Jimmy Carter had charged, a maker of nothing but gas guzzlers, by 1981 the company had managed to transform its model line dramatically. Eighty percent of the scheduled 1981 production was for front-wheel-drive cars powered by four-cylinder engines. Even with 10 percent of the U.S. car market, Chrysler had, with one million engines in six different sizes, more four-cylinder engines available than any other company building in America.

As for the future, Chrysler planned to build cars from three platforms—really two and a half, considering that the largest body would be built on a "stretched" version of the K-platform. Thanks partly to pressure from the Loan Guarantee Board, which had tempered some of Chrysler's earlier optimism and forced them to be leaner and simpler, Chrysler's product program grew from an optimal use of common parts. The subcompact L and the compact K, supplemented by the "stretch K," were to be divided into basic, sporty and luxury categories. There were plans for a mini-pickup truck built on the L-platform, as well as a truck based on the K-platform. A special van/wagon vehicle, built on a compact platform and powered by front-wheel drive, was scheduled for the mid-Eighties. All passenger cars would come in two-door, four-door and wagon versions, and there was even a program for a K-convertible.

By 1983, Chrysler planned to offer nothing but front-wheel-drive cars and trucks, a considerable achievement considering that in the winter of 1980, more than 80 percent of its capacity was for rear-wheel drive. As Iacocca explained, "The biggest car we will build will weigh less and get better fuel economy than the smallest car we built in 1975."

Analysts who projected Chrysler's inability to compete usually argued that Chrysler was certain to drown in a sea of competitive variety in which GM would be offering an entirely new model every six months through the mid-Eighties, with Ford not far behind. Chrysler was doing what American society had demanded of it, though—compressing its products and its aspirations and relying more on imagination than market inundation, and doing so despite extraordinary and often implausible odds. Some criticized the Omni/Horizon as "aging," but the most fuel-efficient versions, the "Misers," got 50 mpg on the highway and 30 mpg in city driving, better than the Datsun 200SX and the Honda Accord. The Omni/Horizons were, in fact, the first domestically built cars to reach the 50 mpg mark.

Perhaps Chrysler's most dramatic change during the years of crisis was in the quality of its cars. Independent surveys taken throughout 1980 showed a marked improvement in buyer satisfaction from the dog days of the mid-Seventies. One confidential GM marketing report showed Chrysler in 1980 with a 78 percent satisfaction rating, the highest of all the U.S. manufacturers.[5] GM trailed with 73 percent, followed by Ford with 72 percent and AMC with 71 percent. Most of the improvement could be traced to a new relationship between management and workers and tighter control over manufacturing. Prompted by fear and a healthy dose of Hans Matthias' aphorisms, the workers had begun to concentrate on quality. Although the launch of the K-car was marred by frequent stoppages, the cars that rolled out of Jefferson Avenue and Newark were good ones. Even the New Yorkers at the Lynch Road plant showed none of the gruesome defects that had ruined their introduction in 1978.[6]

The old adversary relationship had begun to peel away from the rusty hinge that linked management and labor. The first moves were made in the summer of 1979 when Iacocca made an unprecedented appearance at the bargaining table and asked for a two-year wage freeze. The union refused, but ratified the milder $203 million round of cuts. Thereafter, confronted with unemployment, Chrysler workers voted away some of the gains made over thirty years of bargaining, winning in return what was at the outset a sixth of the company's outstanding common stock and something that had previously been regarded as pure heresy: a seat on the board of directors.

"Conflict of interest," the critics cried. GM chairman Thomas Murphy argued that the duty of a corporate director was to represent the interests of *all* the shareholders of a company—not, as union president Douglas Fraser said he would, just the interests of the workers. Many UAW members were equally upset. "It's a sellout," said Maye Lean Amos, a sewing machine operator at Chrysler's Detroit trim plant. "How can he see the best interests of the union while he's sitting on a board that, by its very nature, is dedicated to the best interests of management?" Other American labor unionists feared Fraser's membership would amount to nothing more than tokenism: one ineffectual voice among seventeen—a partner in failure, ignored in success.

Fraser himself envisaged a time when the union was represented on the boards of all the companies—a notion that churned stomachs in Detroit and raised antitrust questions in Washington. He sought a form of the West German "mitbestimmung" which gave labor unions the legal right to be represented on the supervisory boards of all large corporations. Critics argued that the West German practice posed as many problems as it solved and threatened to compromise the auto industry's competitive secrets.

Few competitive details remain secret all that long in Detroit anyway. More important, the composition of the typical American corporate board does not permit the "conflict of interest" argument to be sustained. For decades, bankers, lawyers and suppliers have sat on the boards of companies with which they conduct business. Following the civil rights and consumer movements of the early Seventies, a number of defenders of special interests were ostentatiously appointed to a number of boards. Their principal value has been to provide insight into different elements of society with which a company must interact. Certainly that was the primary reason why the Reverend Leon Sullivan, the black pastor of Philadelphia's Zion Baptist Church and author of the "Sullivan Principles" governing investment in South Africa, was nominated to the board of General Motors. A union representative has no more of a conflict of interest than any banker with loans outstanding, and no less of a pedagogical function than the Reverend Sullivan.

Following his election to the Chrysler board, Doug Fraser added a firm grasp of the mechanics of the automobile business and valuable political instincts. He refrained, as he had promised, from participating in any discussion of wage contracts that would have compromised his position with either shareholders or union members (though an increasing number of union members were becoming shareholders). Nevertheless, he helped both parties by carrying back to his members a clearer understanding of the need for painful decisions. Above all, he successfully undermined the abiding hostility between labor and management that has colored American industry for the better part of a century. "Maybe," Fraser mused in the midst of the controversy surrounding his board membership, "the adversary relationship is precisely what's wrong with the American labor movement."

At Chrysler, the struggle for survival very quickly forced management and labor to stand on common ground. In the face of imminent unemployment, the need for cars of impeccable quality brought a degree of cooperation that five decades of expansion and profitability had failed to produce. Although U.S. automakers still lagged behind the Japanese, partly because of habit and partly because of cultural differences, Detroit began listening to the quiet wisdom of men like Soichiro Honda. "Division of labor," offered Honda, "must not deprive people of their right to think. An industry prospers only when everybody involved in it thinks about how it can be improved. An industry cannot last long where human beings are equated with automatic machines. Their collective wisdom in the end will hold the key for the future of their industry."[7]

Chrysler was not alone in accepting advice from the East. General Motors had actually been nursing a Quality of Work Life (QWL) program at many of its plants since the early Seventies. In 1972, after years of strife, GM's Tarrytown, New York, assembly plant was the site of an unusual truce between plant management and UAW Local 664. "For many years," observed local president Ray Calore, "General Motors' attitude toward hourly rated employees was to hire a faceless robot, a pair of hands, a pair of feet, one strong back, and no head and no face." Before the truce, no effort was made to explain the reasons for changes and no effort was made to elicit ideas from workers. Once the veil of hostility was pierced, however, GM found that workers not only understood why certain actions were necessary, they also contributed ideas of their own. The most telling example at Tarrytown involved a chronic problem of loose and leaky windshields. Once plant managers started to talk to windshield fitters, they discovered that while one worker would start a line of sealant at the top corner and work his way around, another would start in the middle and spread the glue in either direction. Finally, one worker demonstrated how he started his line ten inches from the corner—just at the point where the embedded aerial protruded—and came full circle so that a little extra dab formed a puddle to seal the gap left by the aerial outlet. No one had ever thought of that—but once the workers were informed, the nagging problem was solved.

At Chrysler, such revelations were contributing increasingly to efficiencies seldom before realized at the company. Behind the aging walls and hokey slogans, a quiet revolution was taking place, though it was largely ignored by critics who were obsessed with Chrysler's dependence on government aid. There was, among many who railed against the loan guarantees, a touching ability to see the world not as it was but as they thought it should be. In the decade of the Seventies, the world changed more than most Americans were prepared to admit. Like Dodge Main in the Sixties, America in the Seventies was passed by. In 1980, the U.S. standard of living was the fifth highest in the world; it had been the highest in 1972. Overall economic growth slid to 2.9 percent a year, compared to 4.1 percent during the Sixties. The American share of world exports slipped from more than 40 percent in 1962 to less than 25 percent by 1980. Around Akron, erstwhile "tire capital of the world," executives clung to the safety of high-volume production while France's Michelin, which didn't even build a plant in the United States until 1975, grabbed a huge chunk of the market. Between the beginning of 1979 and the middle of 1980, more than a sixth of all rubber workers in the United States were laid off permanently. Around Pittsburgh and other American steel towns, iron ore was still melted in open-hearth furnaces while Japanese mills turned out half of their steel using American-designed continuous-slab casting. Not a single wholly owned American company made radios on American soil; only a couple manufactured black-and-white television sets, while most U.S. color receivers were assembled from foreign components. Even the videotape recorder, another product of American ingenuity, was left to the Japanese to produce and exploit. In more modern industries—in aerospace, chemicals, plastics and drugs— the United States lost ground to other nations.

It was a far cry from the previous generation, when America, and especially the American automobile industry, had promised a larger tomorrow. In California, one Los Angeles radio station used as its slogan "The Freeway Is Forever," and so it seemed. When Soichiro Honda first visited America, he was struck by a reflection of the pioneering stagecoach in the contemporary touring cars. "The cars had to be that big," he mused, "in order to span great distances."

It was not just Detroit that taught Americans that everything large was adorable. There were few limits to the use and display of national wealth. The government built the freeways, towering dams and sprawling military bases. Houses grew larger and suburban yards stretched out to accommodate swings and pools and greenhouses. In restaurants, Americans ate food off plates larger than those seen in Europe; in theaters, they gorged themselves on buckets of popcorn; in supermarkets, their groceries were double-bagged. Along with the managers and diplomats who flew around the world spreading tales of American prowess went billions of dollars in foreign aid and cargo holds filled with charity. Jack Kennedy shot for the moon and Chrysler went after Ford and General Motors. The pie was only getting bigger. Lyndon Johnson asked for guns and butter while the UAW demanded higher wages and better supplemental unemployment benefits. Society asked for clean air and big stock dividends; and government and industry assured the nation that it could have both.

Overseas, meanwhile, economies like Japan's and West Germany's took full advantage of brand-new factories and grew faster after the Second World War than the United States had ever grown. They accepted the American helping hand and used it to pull themselves into a running position, but their economic surge was tempered by a presumption of limits and the importance of quality rather than quantity. In a terse rejection of Lynn Townsend's formula for success, Volkswagen's chairman from the mid-Seventies, Toni Schmuecker, once said "To hell with volume" as he guided his company through its most troublesome period of transition from the ubiquitous Beetle to the refined Rabbit and its up-market, fuel-efficient cousins.[8]

Not all Americans in those years were swept up by the promises of expansion. Somewhere amid the social upheaval of the late Sixties and early Seventies, a plaintive note of caution was sounded, but the economic complex could not react quickly. A corporate system geared to quick returns on its investments, managers who made commitments on the assumption that bonuses and stock options would pay quick and handsome rewards and a government that assumed social programs would always be financed by the success of private enterprise could not turn on a dime. A complex systemic inertia, spawned in part by complacency, in part by an addiction to the fast buck, in part by an adversarial relationship that governed the financing, the taxing, the regulation and the employment of American industry, slowed the wheels of the nation to three-quarter speed while others accelerated.

Caught between the two colliding worlds was the U.S. automobile industry, and buried deep in the habits and attitudes of Detroit was Chrysler. More than any other industry, the American Big Three had committed themselves to size and conspicuously demonstrated the two-tiered nature of the world economy. As the volume of their production had increased, the incentive for innovation had declined. Wage contracts were negotiated by managers and workers who could divide the spoils of 90 percent of the world's largest auto market. Prices were based on the costs of those few companies; engineers and product planners worked in a world of limited horizons and little technological pressure. There was competition, but it was limited. The smaller companies were at the mercy of General Motors. True competition, the sort free enterprisers speak of, was long gone. When the federal government could no longer keep expensive oil from pouring through the floodgates that had isolated America, the other world arrived, washing away the delusion of oligopolistic comfort.

The inefficiencies and constraints showed up in bold relief, just as they had for Dodge Main: the tax system that suppressed capital formation, the bureaucracy that clumsily redistributed income, the banking and investment community that channeled resources into minimum-risk enterprises and the legal system that encouraged litigation. Product liability and a penchant for suing companies for even the most unforeseeable misuses of their products had frightened the creativity out of many businessmen. The auto industry was a swamp of such constraints by the end of the Seventies. "Sometimes when I wake up in the morning," Iacocca sighed once during the fall of 1979, "I think of what I'm doing. Yeah, I'm trying to save a company. But I never invent anything anymore. I never create a job. I need a law—everything I do needs a law. It worries me—for all of industry."

Meanwhile, the Japanese industrial machine continued to roll. Companies using lasers to cut silicon chips grew up alongside factories in which giant presses stamped out car fenders, while Americans debated over which industry to choose. Although Japanese auto executives and trade officials were fond of saying that their day in the sun had passed and that their U.S. market share would fall once Detroit geared up for small-car production, a study released by Neil Goldschmidt's Department of Transportation was far more pessimistic.[9] While Ford and the UAW, with the assent of GM and Chrysler, sought to block the Japanese from further successes in the United States, the study observed that these same Japanese were increasing their domestic capacity by two million units. It seemed unlikely, given the trade restrictions in virtually every other market, that the Japanese executives believed their own word. Goldschmidt certainly didn't, and suggested that they really thought they would have only GM as a manufacturing competitor in the United States by 1990.

The Japanese may be right. At current rates and with American consumers strengthening their loyalties to Japanese cars, these imports will penetrate even deeper into an American market that will probably grow by only 2 percent a year. With increasing automation, employment in the industry is unlikely ever again to reach its peak of 1.6 million in 1973. With the disappearance of the two tiers of the world automobile market, thanks to the muscle of OPEC, the needs of American car owners could easily be met by a single, efficient domestic producer and a handful of competitors headquartered overseas. In such a world, the 1979–80 recessionary cycle would be remembered as the economic purge of automotive deadwood that bankrupted Chrysler, forced Ford to abandon its U.S. manufacturing facilities to become an offshore supplier, and turned AMC into a French subsidiary.

Those who accept such a future must also be prepared to watch a handful of major steel companies, rubber manufacturers and appliance makers follow Chrysler into oblivion, and they should be prepared to live with the consequences of a society essentially deprived of the control of some basic industrial capacity. The dynamics that brought Chrysler to its knees were, in 1981, still at work, and were as unlikely to forgive on some obscure moral grounds as they were for Chrysler.

The new world industrial battleground is ruthless and is certain to force changes in the competitive structure of the international automobile industry. The embryonic concept of the "world car," a single model designed and manufactured by one multinational from a variety of sources in many countries, may be obsolete before reaching puberty. Although Ford and GM were already making world cars by 1981, the shrinking and increasingly nationalistic markets of the world seemed loath to allow any single multinational—or cars made in any one country—to gain a dominant position. Meanwhile, the increasingly homogeneous nature of the world automotive market certainly promised to encourage a further reduction in the number of automobile companies. What's likely to emerge from the struggle are interlocking networks of companies that share components and compete around the world. It would be in America's interests to have a share in as many of these consortiums as possible in order to maintain a level of industrial capacity as well as jobs.

The framework for such networks already existed in 1981. AMC agreed to help design and assemble a new Renault model in its Kenosha, Wisconsin, plant. In the United Kingdom, British Leyland planned to assemble a car designed by Honda. Nissan and Volkswagen were progressing with a scheme to build VWs in Japan. Nissan also had acquired a major stake in Motor Iberica in Spain and agreed to a joint venture with Alfa Romeo in Italy. Renault, Peugeot and Volvo jointly operated the French company PRV, which supplied both its parent companies and outsiders like DeLorean Motor Company in Northern Ireland with engines produced in large volume.

American companies were catching on to the game as well. Ford was strengthening its parts exchanges with Japan's Toyo Kogyo, maker of Mazda cars, and was well on its way to an agreement with Toyota to build a Japanese car in a domestic Ford assembly plant. Even General Motors, the one multinational equipped for self-sufficiency, had agreed to allow its Japanese trading partner, Izuzu, to produce the subcompact J-car in Japan toward the end of 1981, making the J the first U.S. automobile to be built in Japan since before World War II.

These new liaisons allowed companies to take full advantage of economies of scale, spread the risks and accommodate fewer competing models while casting a haze over national identities. The labor movement was not blind to their implications, and there were tentative calls for an alliance between some Japanese unions and the UAW. In quiet testimony to the changing world, executives at General Motors dropped their references to GM's share of the U.S. market alone and started talking about world market shares.

It was in such a world, where changes were coming with increasing speed, that Chrysler had to survive. In the spring of 1981, Chrysler's health was as fragile as ever. Net losses of $2.8 billion over two years had left the company vulnerable to any further downturn in the market—bereft of the financial defenses needed to survive another blow and wholly dependent on the success of its cars in the market to generate the funds needed to keep up technologically with resource-rich competitors like Honda, Volkswagen and, of course, General Motors.

At Chrysler, hope of finding a partner before all the partners were taken was tempered by a realization that the company had to demonstrate a solid streak of profitability before anyone would step forward. Iacocca's "Global Motors" was no longer a pipe dream; it was a matter of sheer necessity.

While the industry looked forward to new configurations on a global scale, others looked for institutional devices to ward off the disruption promised by the coming changes. Interestingly, many harkened back to the Great Depression, when Franklin D. Roosevelt created quasi-governmental bodies to extract businesses from the economic mire. Lee Iacocca himself advocated a National Recovery Act to formulate long-term policy goals for American industry. Felix Rohatyn, who once had a hand in trying to salvage Chrysler, and who chaired New York City's Municipal Assistance Corporation, also known as "Big MAC," suggested forming a new Reconstruction Finance Corporation, free from political and legal constraints, to channel money toward ailing companies and hard-pressed communities.[10] It would be, in effect, a national Big MAC and a permanent Chrysler Loan Guarantee Board for everyone.

Rohatyn's idea seemed to ignore the achievements of ad hoc restructuring demonstrated by the Chrysler Loan Guarantee Board, and his hope that a new RFC, financed by the Treasury Department, could somehow remain free from political pressure seemed vain. Under the most amicable conditions, boards and managers don't like outsiders breathing down their necks. Most of all, the creation of yet another source of planning in a nation already riddled with conflicting strategies seemed certain to create more problems than it could solve. Surely Chrysler had demonstrated the danger of being caught in the middle of an economy fraught with the perils of central regulation but bereft of the virtues of central planning.

The creation of such institutions also appeared to presume that Chrysler and other basic industries were only exhibiting early symptoms of "the British Disease" or "Lemon Socialism." Chrysler was constantly compared to British Leyland, but beyond the fact that both companies had been supported because the U.S. and U.K. governments had not been prepared to accept the effects of failure on employment, the contrasts were little short of astounding.

The U. S. Loan Guarantee Board did not impose a "British solution" on Chrysler. British Leyland was one of four automobile companies in a country barely large enough to support one. Even at its peak, BL made Chrysler, at its worst, look like a model of efficiency. In 1979, British Leyland produced less than half as many vehicles as Chrysler with almost 30,000 more workers. In 1975, when the first moves were made to bail out British Leyland, the British government provided a grant without insisting that the company, its workers, its suppliers or its dealers make unpleasant sacrifices. After the injection of government funds, there was little change in the shape of a wildly inefficient company and, if anything, there was a deterioration in the attitudes of workers. BL continued to be dogged by wildcats and demands for pay raises in the face of accumulating losses. Not until 1977, two years after the first government grant, when a new management adopted the toughest stance seen in postwar Britain, did even a faint sense of realism creep in. Still, stoppages and labor unrest plagued the launch of BL's "Mini Metro," the company's do-or-die equivalent of Chrysler's K-car, as late as the fall of 1980.

In the United States, there was at least emerging a recognition that the country faced a fundamental and rather stark choice: whether to move back toward a freer economy or toward more central planning. It was Chrysler's crisis that hastened an active reexamination of corporate tax rates, depreciation schedules, the double taxation of dividends, the effects of regulation and the efficacy of antitrust laws that prevented automakers, for example, from sharing safety and emission technology while the real competition was coming from overseas.

Detroit, it was always said, was a town that was ill-equipped for change. The two-story-high dies and presses could not be torn out in a day; the prejudices and preconceptions of decades could not be flushed away in a week. Yet Chrysler, between 1977 and 1981, demonstrated a remarkable capacity for change. The company at the very least succeeded in something that had hitherto been impossible: it had distributed large economic losses and won sacrifices from all. It had showed that the often-distrusted alliance of business, labor and government could, when pushed, work. Its transformation pointed to changing times, to a nation nudging its resources in a different direction, accommodating itself to a different role in the world economy and displaying a willingness to learn from countries it had once tutored. Far from being a symbol of failure, Chrysler was a testament to change—a cause for immense optimism rather than woeful despair.

In the midst of one of his laments over the state of American enterprise, Lee Iacocca plaintively asked, "Where are all the tigers?" Chrysler's metamorphosis, whether the company survives or not, was a stunning testament to the presence of tigers—both a reassurance and a warning regarding the power of the individual. The company smashed the popular belief that, somewhere between the rise of the entrepreneur and the growth of managerial capitalism, the authority of the individual had faded. The history of Chrysler, from Walter P. Chrysler through Lynn Townsend to Lee Iacocca—and indeed, the history of the American automobile industry—demonstrates that, far more than institutions and strategies, it is men and their ideas who succeed or fail.

NOTES

CHAPTER ONE

1. *Wall Street Journal,* July 7, 1976.
2. GM used front-wheel drive in larger Oldsmobiles and Cadillacs as early as 1967, but these larger cars took no advantage of the possible space and weight saving allowed by front-wheel drive. American engineers had been suckled on rear-wheel-drive cars that transferred the engine's power to the rear axle through a bulky transmission and drive shaft running through a tunnel down the center of the car. Front-wheel drive not only eliminated the need for the ungainly hump, it also allowed the engine to be slung sideways over the front axle, where it provided direct power through an attached transaxle.
3. The jealously guarded comparisons, which gave away Chrysler's darkest troubles, showed that GM gained $169 and Ford a $91 advantage thanks to a larger model line. In the manufacturing plants, Ford benefited by $35 over Chrysler; GM, by $140. The greater purchasing volumes gave Ford $52 and GM $72 extra, while their scattered plants gave Ford a $20 edge and GM a $26 edge in shipping costs.

CHAPTER TWO

1. Bernard A. Weisberger, *The Dream Maker: William C. Durant, Founder of General Motors,* p. 120.
2. Ibid., p. 122.
3. John Holmes, unpublished History of the Maxwell Corporation, Detroit Public Library Automotive History Collection.
4. Christy Borth, "The Chrysler Family Tree Has Many Roots," *Ward's Quarterly,* Winter 1963, p. 98.
5. John Holmes, op. cit.
6. Walter P. Chrysler in collaboration with Boyden Sparkes, *Life of an American Workman,* p. 171.
7. Ibid., p. 170.
8. Ibid., p. 105.
9. Ibid., p. 140.
10. Ibid., p. 158.

11. Quoted in William Serrin, *The Company and the Union*, p. 88.
12. Walter P. Chrysler, op. cit., p. 183.
13. *Automobile Topics*, December 29, 1923, p. 639.
14. Ibid., p. 639.
15. Ibid., April 18, 1925, p. 845.
16. Ibid., August 21, 1926, p. 678.
17. Ibid., December 10, 1927, p. 394.
18. Alfred P. Sloan, Jr., *My Years with General Motors*, p. 42.
19. Ibid., p. 153.
20. Alfred P. Sloan, Jr., *Adventures of a White-Collar Man.*
21. Walter P. Chrysler, op. cit., p. 191.
22. *Automobile Topics*, July 7, 1928, p. 752.
23. Ibid., June 9, 1928, p. 371.
24. Apart from a corps of some of Chrysler's most successful managers, Rockwell chairman Robert Anderson and John Z. DeLorean, chairman of DeLorean Motor Company, were graduates.
25. Walter P. Chrysler, op. cit., p. 200.
26. *Automobile Topics*, December 30, 1933, p. 641.
27. Ibid., p. 642.
28. Ibid., August 11, 1934, p. 72.
29. *Fortune*, November 1935.
30. *Automobile Topics*, January 26, 1935, p. 747.
31. Ibid.
32. William Serrin, op. cit., p. 106.
33. William Manchester, *The Glory and the Dream*, Bantam Books, 1975, p. 131.
34. Detroit *Free Press*, March 8, 1937.
35. Ibid.
36. Ibid., November 8, 1939.
37. *Fortune*, November 1935.

CHAPTER THREE

1. *Time*, May 15, 1950.
2. Quoted in Serrin, op. cit., p. 20.
3. Alfred P. Sloan, Jr., *My Years with General Motors*, p. 399.
4. K. T. Keller to the seventh Stanford Business Conference, July 22, 1948.
5. *Forbes*, December 15, 1954.
6. Serrin, op. cit., p. 172.
7. Ibid., p. 30.

CHAPTER FOUR

1. *Wall Street Journal*, February 1, 1973.

2. B. J. Widick, a UAW staff member and later a professor of industrial relations at Columbia University.
3. Serrin, op. cit., p. 18.
4. *Fortune*, January 1961.
5. Based on Mira Wilkins and Frank Ernest Hill, *American Business Abroad: Ford on Six Continents*, Wayne State University Press, Detroit, 1964.
6. Hansard No. 739, 1966–1967, p. 38, quoted by Stephen Young and Neil Hood, *Chrysler U.K.: A Corporation in Transition*, Praeger Publishers, 1977, pp. 38 and 43.
7. New York *Times*, August 9, 1968.
8. New York *Times*, April 19, 1968.

CHAPTER FIVE

1. *Fortune*, November 1968.
2. *Ward's Quarterly*, Winter 1965.
3. *Wall Street Journal*, April 19, 1967.
4. Alfred P. Sloan, Jr., *My Years with General Motors*, p. 125.
5. New York *Times*, May 1, 1966, quoted in Lawrence J. White, *The Automobile Industry Since 1945*, Harvard University Press, 1971, p. 189.
6. *Automotive News* 1980 Market Data Book.

Officer	*1961–1968*	*1970–1977*
GM Chairman	$5,199,208	$5,461,300
Ford Chairman	4,180,219	6,099,304
Chrysler Chairman	2,076,558	3,201,731
GM President	4,731,316	5,050,500
Ford President	3,962,021	5,999,191
Chrysler President	2,540,634	2,779,403

CHAPTER SIX

1. By contrast, in 1966 C-bodies had grown by 6 percent compared to 3.3 percent for the rest of the Chrysler fleet.
2. Both Ford and Pontiac were lured to the racetrack. Benson Ford told a crowd in Monte Carlo in 1963 (*Ward's Quarterly*, Winter 1965, p. 25), "We Americans are beginning once again to hearken to the deep, full-throated music of a fine-tuned engine pouring it on, the whine of the gearbox, the squeal of hot rubber on asphalt."
3. Ms. Austin, a walk-on at the casting sessions in Los Angeles, had almost no acting or modeling experience when Chrysler retained her. She blossomed into prominence as a result of the ad campaign and won a contract with Universal Studios. Her first and only film ironi-

cally was *The Perils of Pauline,* later to become a journalistic gold-mine for Chrysler analogies. The movie bombed.

4. Serrin, op. cit., p. 32.
5. *Wall Street Journal,* February 6, 1969.
6. *Fortune,* March 1969.
7. *Forbes,* December 1, 1973.
8. *Wall Street Journal,* April 14, 1971.
9. Chicago *Tribune,* April 14, 1971.
10. "Meet the Press," September 6, 1970.
11. In 1979, wages cost the company $2.9 billion or 22.1 percent of all U.S. costs. (Economic Report to the President, January 1980; U. S. Department of Labor, Bureau of Labor Statistics, 1979.)
12. Serrin, op. cit., p. 146.
13. New York *Times,* August 18, 1973.
14. Detroit *News,* April 30, 1974.
15. Serrin, op. cit., pp. 235–36.
16. Actual sales turned out to be 12.6 million.
17. New York *Times,* January 14, 1975.
18. New York *Times,* March 7, 1976.
19. New York *Times,* April 16, 1975.
20. Comparative salary and bonus payments for 1961–1968 and 1970–1977:

CHAPTER SEVEN

1. Henry Bliss, who was killed while climbing off a New York City streetcar.
2. This is the plausible contention of Donald MacDonald in *Detroit 1985,* Doubleday, 1980.
3. *Fortune,* April 1972.
4. *U.S. News & World Report,* December 18, 1972.
5. IIFHS Status Report, September 9, 1974.
6. *Time,* May 4, 1970, p. 16.
7. Ibid.
8. According to Dr. William Mason of the Los Angeles County Museum, the Spanish explorers, sailing with Juan Rodriguez Cabrillo, probably saw an Indian rabbit drive, wherein the first native Los Angelinos purposely set fires in the brush on the plains south of the Santa Monica hills to "smoke out" the rabbits and drive them into their nets. The columns of smoke seen from the sea were more likely the source of the name than any smog created by L.A.'s plenteous petroleum supply.
9. *Fortune,* June 1973, p. 120.
10. *Christian Science Monitor,* April 14, 1971.
11. Gary Witzenburg, *Ward's Auto World,* October 1976, p. 65.
12. Charles Burck's thoughtful analysis in *Fortune* June 1973, "Let's Take a Look at Automotive Pollution," and Jude Wanniski's series in the

Wall Street Journal around the same time bothered to delve into the data enough to show how weak the government's case actually was.

13. Dryden Press, 1972.
14. In a radio interview with WWJ automotive editor Joe Callaghan in 1979.
15. Lawrence J. White, *The Automobile Industry Since 1945*, Harvard University Press, 1971.
16. Charles Burck, "What's Good for the World Should Be Good for GM," *Fortune*.

CHAPTER EIGHT

1. "Potential for Motor Vehicle Fuel Economy Improvement," October 24, 1974, p. 18.
2. "The Wreck of the Auto Industry," November 1980, pp. 45–60.
3. "Detroit Turns Against the Gas Guzzlers," *Fortune*, January 1974.
4. Report No. DOT-TSC-NHTSA-78-49, November 1, 1978.
5. Harbridge House, Cambridge, September 1979.
6. "Innovation and the Regulatory Paradox: Toward a Theory of Thin Markets," William J. Abernathy, Harvard Business School, presented at the Symposium on Technology, Government and the Automotive Future, October 20, 1978.
7. Although Chrysler had failed to sell the public on the virtues of the turbine, the onset of the petroleum crisis underlined the need to develop *any* alternative to the gasoline internal combustion engine that might decrease reliance on petroleum. The turbine, while it was not very fuel-efficient at current weight and performance, continued to have the potential for reducing reliance on petroleum. First, it could burn almost any liquid fuel, from alcohol to French perfume; second, it had few moving parts and was therefore technically simple; and third, if it could be lightened, it could indeed achieve fuel economies competitive with the best gasoline engines. However, the necessary research and development programs required investments that Chrysler could not afford to make, so the program languished in the Engineering Library.
8. William H. Forbis, *Japan Today: People, Places and Power*, Charles E. Tuttle Co., 1975, p. 381.
9. General Motors Corporation fact sheet, April 7, 1980.
10. "Japan Gets Ready for Tougher Times," *Fortune*, November 30, 1980, p. 108.
11. *Time*, September 8, 1980, p. 53.
12. "Toyota Production System and Kanban System: Materialization of a Just-in-Time and Respect-for-Human System," Y. Sugimori et al., Toyota Motor Company Ltd., Japan, as cited in the Department of Transportation's study, "The U.S. Automobile Industry, 1980," Neil Goldschmidt et al.
13. Debra Whitefield, Los Angeles *Times*, April 20, 1980.

14. *Der Spiegel,* July 21, 1980.
15. Based on *Chrysler U.K.: A Corporation in Transition,* Steve Young and Neil Hood, Praeger, 1977.
16. *Wall Street Journal,* July 29, 1976.

CHAPTER NINE

1. In 1979, Ford Motor Company's profits dropped to $1.17 billion; in 1980, the company lost a record $1.54 billion, and it had only marginal prospects for profitability in 1981.
2. Iacocca made this remark to *Time's* Detroit bureau chief, Leon Jaroff, in 1964. Reminded of it in 1980, Iacocca smiled thinly and said, "Yeah, and I used to like Adolf Hitler before he invaded Czechoslovakia."
3. Ford was actually borrowing the maxim from Benjamin Disraeli.

CHAPTER TEN

1. "Quality Control Practices in the Auto Industry: U.S. and Japan Compared," Robert E. Cole, presented at the University of Michigan forum, "The Japanese Automobile Industry: Model and Challenge for the Future," January 14, 1981.

CHAPTER ELEVEN

1. *U.S. News & World Report,* February 26, 1979.
2. "Energy: An Emergency Telescoped," R. Stobaugh and D. Yergin, *Foreign Affairs,* 1979, Vol. 58, No. 3.
3. *Newsweek,* December 11, 1978, p. 89.
4. *U.S. News & World Report,* May 28, 1979.
5. *Business Week,* June 21, 1979.
6. *Wall Street Journal,* May 18, 1979.

CHAPTER TWELVE

1. *Hearings Before the Committee on Banking, Housing and Urban Affairs, United States Senate, October 10–12,* 1979, p. 625.
2. Interview with *Time,* September 27, 1979.
3. Detroit *Free Press,* August 15, 1974.
4. *Hearings Before the Subcommittee on Economic Stabilization of the Committee on Banking, Finance and Urban Affairs on HR 5805,* p. 356.
5. Detroit *Free Press,* February 7, 1975.

6. In 1976, Congressman James Hanley, the chairman of the Automobile Industry Task Force, had raised the very question of loan guarantees, arguing, "Serious consideration should be given to the provision of loans and loan guarantees to permit domestic automobile manufacturers without adequate access to the traditional sources of capital to produce energy-efficient vehicles and to forestall excessive industry concentration."

7. Paragraph based on *Congressional Quarterly*, August 18, 1979, p. 1698.

8. By comparison, Chrysler's expenses in 1975 ran to $11.7 billion.

9. Detroit *Free Press*, May 20, 1980.

10. The ultimate irony of Kelly's description of the debate as an "exercise of how Congress buys votes" was his conviction in January 1981 in the Abscam bribery scandal.

11. The night of the final Senate vote, a California dealer, eager to help, was steered toward Senator Hayakawa's office. The California senator listened to the dealer's arguments. Later, in the Senate Chamber, he made a short speech and reversed his earlier negative vote.

12. *Senate Hearings*, p. 763.

13. *House Hearings*, p. 594.

14. *House Hearings*, p. 628.

CHAPTER THIRTEEN

1. John Coleman had been deputy chairman and a director of the Royal Bank of Canada; Jean de Grandpré was a director of the Toronto-Dominion Bank; J. Richardson Dilworth was a director of Chase Manhattan; Martha Griffiths was a director of the National Bank of Detroit; Najeeb Halaby was a director of the BankAmerica Corporation; Gabriel Hauge was a former chairman and a director of Manufacturers Hanover; William Hewlett was a director of Chase Manhattan; Jerome Holland was a director of both the New York Stock Exchange and Manufacturers Hanover. Tom Killefer was chairman, president and chief executive officer of the United States Trust Company and Robert Semple was a director of the National Bank of Detroit. Chrysler or Chrysler Financial had loans with each of these banks.

2. *House Hearings*, op. cit., p. 853.

3. A line of credit usually takes the form of a letter from a bank. If a lender believes that the financial condition of the borrower has changed dramatically from the time the credit line was drawn up, it can be canceled without warning.

4. A "revolver" offers a firm contractual obligation between lender and borrower, rather than the easily canceled letter which accompanies a credit line. A revolver negotiated with a consortium of banks, though more expensive, is easier to administer than credit lines, which are specially tailored to suit individual banks.

5. What distinguished the agreement from other letters of credit commonly used to finance international trade was that the guarantees remained unsecured. If Chrysler ran plumb out of money, the Japanese banks (which did not hold the titles on the cars and trucks) had no alternative but to pay off Mitsubishi Motors.

6. *Wall Street Journal*, November 26, 1979.

7. *Fortune*, June 18, 1980.

8. Examiners recommend, though they don't insist, that banks write off 50 percent of all doubtful loans. Many banks, however, have house rules that require them to write off half of any such loans. Some banks had already written off their loans to Chrysler and were faced with providing new loans which would have to be written off immediately. The bank examiners, however, doled out tougher treatment to the smaller banks, ordering them to write off their entire loans.

9. Rather than irritate some suppliers, who quite easily could have provoked a bankruptcy, Chrysler halted payment on all bills, apart from payments needed to cover essential work on the retooling of the Jefferson Avenue plant. The company continued to meet its payroll.

10. The payment completed Volkswagen's purchase of Chrysler's Argentinian subsidiary.

CHAPTER FOURTEEN

1. Knowing that the network cameras would be there to record the arrival of the auto industry leaders, Iacocca, President Paul Bergmoser, and Public Affairs Vice-President Wendell Larsen selected a fuel-efficient maroon Dodge Omni subcompact to drive through the White House gates. Behind them, the UAW's Fraser and Stepp were in a Plymouth Horizon. To their great satisfaction, their counterparts from GM and Ford arrived in traditional full-size cars, which were parked right behind the little Chrysler cars in the White House driveway.

2. It was "Engine Charlie" Wilson, GM's president in 1953, who had been misquoted in testimony before a Senate committee. "What's good for General Motors," Wilson purportedly said, "is good for America." He was roundly criticized, though what he actually said was, "I have always thought that what was good for our country was good for GM and vice versa." In the auto crisis of 1980, however, even the misquote was not without merit.

3. Wendell Miller, a Binghamton, New York, Dodge, Honda and Lincoln-Mercury dealer who was, at the time, First Vice-President of the National Automobile Dealers Association (NADA), reported that his inventory in the spring of 1980 was costing him $50,000 a month, whereas a year earlier it had been only $20,000. George Irvin, a Denver Chevy, Subaru, BMW and Mercedes dealer, claimed he was losing half his business because customers could not obtain financing for cars they had decided to buy. As president of NADA that year,

Irvin, like Miller, had an ear to thousands of fellow car dealers who told him similar tales.

4. Within a month of the disastrous launch, Dick Vining was telling friends that he thought his days at Chrysler were numbered. He was taking much of the blame for the production problems that marred the introduction of the K-car. Sure enough, by January 1981, Dick Vining took "early retirement" from Chrysler and was replaced as Executive Vice-President for Manufacturing by Steven Sharf.

5. These confidential GM studies were obtained and reported by Joseph B. Espo of the Flint *Journal*, January 17, 1981.

6. Chrysler was actually anxious to close down the Lynch Road plant permanently, but orders for the full-size R-bodies continued to dribble in through 1980 and early 1981—just enough to justify keeping the production lines rolling.

7. From an interview with *Time* magazine Tokyo correspondent S. Chang, December 1980.

8. *Fortune*, August 13, 1979, "Volkswagen Hops a Rabbit Back to Prosperity," p. 180.

9. "The U.S. Automobile Industry, 1980: Report from the Secretary of Transportation," DOT-P-10-81-02, January 1981.

10. "A Better Way to Bail Out Chrysler," the New York *Times*, January 13, 1980, Op-Ed page.

BIBLIOGRAPHY

Abernathy, William J. *The Productivity Dilemma*. Baltimore: The Johns Hopkins University Press, 1978.

Ayres, Edward. *What's Good for G.M. . . .* Nashville: Aurora Publishers, 1970.

Chandler, Alfred D., Jr. *The Visible Hand*. Cambridge, Mass.: Harvard University Press, 1977.

Chase Automotive Division. *A Cost-Benefit Analysis of the 1979 to 1985 Fuel Economy Standards*. New York: Chase Manhattan Bank, 1978.

Chrysler, Walter P. *Life of an American Workman*. New York: Dodd, Mead, 1937.

Connolly, Charles H. *Air Pollution and Public Health*. New York: Dryden Press, 1972.

Donner, Frederic G. *The World-Wide Industrial Enterprise*. New York: McGraw-Hill, 1967.

Drucker, Peter F. *Concept of the Corporation*. New York: The New American Library, 1972.

Forbis, William H. *Japan Today*. Rutland, Vermont: Charles E. Tuttle, 1975.

Galbraith, John Kenneth. *The Affluent Society*. New York: The New American Library, 1976.

———. *The New Industrial State*. Boston: Houghton Mifflin, 1979.

———. *Annals of an Abiding Liberal*. New York: The New American Library, 1980.

Harbridge House. *Energy Conservation and the Passenger Car: An Assessment of Existing Public Policy*. Cambridge, Mass.: Harbridge House, Inc.

Kahn, Herman and Pepper, Thomas. *The Japanese Challenge*. New York: William Morrow, 1980.

MacDonald, Donald. *Detroit 1985*. New York: Doubleday, 1980.

Nader, Ralph. *Unsafe at Any Speed*. New York: Grossman, 1965.

Nevins, Allan. *Ford: The Times, The Man, The Company*. New York: Scribner's, 1954.

Rae, John B. *The American Automobile: A Brief History.* Chicago: University of Chicago Press, 1965.

Reuther, Victor G. *The Brothers Reuther.* Boston: Houghton Mifflin, 1979.

Royer, Carol. *An Unpublished History of Chrysler.*

Schnapp, John B. *Corporate Strategies of the Automotive Manufacturers.* Lexington, Mass.: D. C. Heath, 1979.

Serrin, William. *The Company and the Union.* New York: Alfred A. Knopf, 1973.

Servan-Schreiber, J.-J. *The American Challenge.* New York: Atheneum, 1968.

Sloan, Alfred P., Jr. *Adventures of a White-Collar Man.* New York: Doubleday, 1941.

——. *My Years with General Motors.* New York: Doubleday, 1963.

Smith, Philip Hillyer. *Wheels Within Wheels.* New York: Funk & Wagnalls, 1968.

Thurow, Lester C. *The Zero-Sum Society.* New York: Basic Books, 1980.

United States Department of Transportation. *Effects of Federal Regulation on the Financial Structure and Performance of the Domestic Motor Vehicle Manufacturers.* Cambridge, Mass.: Transportation Systems Center, 1978.

Vogel, Ezra F. *Japan As Number One.* New York: Harper and Row, 1979.

Wainright, H. C. & Co. *The Impact of Government Regulations on Competition in the U.S. Automobile Industry.* Boston, Mass.: 1979.

Weidenbaum, Murray L. *The Future of Business Regulation.* New York: AMACOM, 1979.

Weisberger, Bernard A. *The Dream Maker: William C. Durant, Founder of General Motors.* Boston: Little, Brown, 1979.

White, Lawrence J. *The Automobile Industry Since 1945.* Cambridge, Mass.: Harvard University Press, 1971.

Widick, B. J. and Howe, Irving. *The UAW and Walter Reuther.* New York: Random House, 1949.

Wilkins, Mira, and Hill, Frank Ernest. *American Business Abroad: Ford on Six Continents.* Detroit: Wayne State University Press, 1964.

Wright, J. Patrick. *On a Clear Day You Can See General Motors.* Grosse Pointe, Michigan: Wright, 1979.

Young, Stephen, and Hood, Neil. *Chrysler U.K.: A Corporation in Transition.* New York: Praeger, 1977.

INDEX